Prometheus Revisited

A volume in the series
CRITICAL PERSPECTIVES ON MODERN CULTURE

edited by David Gross

Prometheus Revisited

The Quest for Global Justice in the Twenty-first Century

§ ARTHUR MITZMAN

UNIVERSITY OF MASSACHUSETTS PRESS
AMHERST AND BOSTON

LC 2002014518
ISBN 1-55849-389-1 (library cloth ed.); 390-5 (paper)

Designed by Dean Bornstein
Set in Garamond No. 3 with Gill Sans display by Graphic Composition
Printed and bound by The Maple-Vail Book Manufacturing Group

Library of Congress Cataloging-in-Publication Data
Mitzman, Arthur, 1931–
    Prometheus revisited : the quest for global justice in the twenty-first
century / Arthur Mitzman.
       p. cm. — (Critical perspectives on modern culture)
Includes bibliographical references and index.
    ISBN 1-55849-389-1 (Library Cloth Ed. : alk. paper) — ISBN
1-55849-390-5 (Paper : alk. paper)
    1. Social justice. 2. Globalization. 3. Nationalism. I. Title. II. Series.
HM671 .M58 2003
303.3' 72–dc21

                                                                    2002014518

British Library Cataloguing in Publication data are available.

To the memory of David Gritz
(1978–2002)

On July 31, 2002, two weeks after his arrival in Jerusalem for a year of study, David and six others were killed by a bomb in the cafeteria of Hebrew University. David was raised in the tolerant, cosmopolitan atmosphere of Paris's rue Mouffetard by his father, Norman, a teacher born in the United States, and his mother, Nevenka, an artist of Croatian origin. Gentle, intelligent, and open to the world, he became a gifted musician and a thoughtful student of philosophy at the University of Paris. His goal in Jerusalem was to explore the cultural and intellectual traditions of Judaism conducive to the development of pluralistic societies. For the many who knew and loved David, his spirit will live on to remind us of the best humankind has to offer.

THEREFORE one must write for one's age, as great writers used to. But this does not mean that one should close oneself off within it. To write for one's age is not to reflect it passively, it is to wish to sustain it or to change it and thus to surpass it toward the future. This effort to change our age implants us most profoundly in it, for it can never be reduced to the dead totality of tools and customs, it is in movement, it surpasses itself, perpetually. In it coincide rigorously the concrete present and the living future of all human beings who make it up.

JEAN-PAUL SARTRE, "Écrire pour son époque"
Le Monde, April 16–17, 2000

Contents

User's Manual for *Prometheus Revisited:*
Enlarging the Globalization Debate

Prometheus Revisited was begun shortly after the simultaneous demise in the 1990s of Soviet Communism and welfare state Keynesianism, in the conviction that the victory of corporate capitalism over all alternatives to it— culmination of two centuries of triumphant industrial modernity—could bring history to a much less pleasant end than the one celebrated by Francis Fukuyama. By the summer of 2001, it was becoming clear that large numbers of concerned citizens everywhere on our planet shared this view, as evidenced by the protests that had, since the Seattle WTO meeting of 1999, greeted every international gathering of economic elites. Then came the terrorist attacks of September 11, 2001, on New York and Washington, the immolation of some three thousand human beings in the rubble of the World Trade Center, and the universal realization, in the light of the fanatical hatred of a handful of suicide commandos and the lashing out of a wounded giant at one of the poorest countries in the world, of how fragile the civilization created by liberal modernity really was.

My book, intended as a contribution to the ongoing discussion of corporate globalization and neoliberalism, now reaches readers who inhabit a world in danger of conflagration and a West in fear of renewed terrorist attack. Nonetheless, most of what I have written over the course of nearly a decade remains relevant to the new situation. In fact this book may be more necessary than ever. The disgust of the world at massacres of innocent civilians, European unwillingness to follow Pentagon hawks into an ever widening war, and the reluctance of Americans to send hundreds of thousands of young men to face death in distant deserts and mountains in pursuit of elusive terrorists are factors that make unlikely the decades of war promised by the Bush administration. The overwhelming support of ordinary Americans in the fall of 2001 for military exorcism of the demons of terrorist massacre is likely to dissipate before the end of 2002. This will return us to the increasingly hollow ideology of neoliberal globalization, whose planners, after fixing their 2001 WTO rendezvous for the remote emirate of Qatar to escape demonstrations, nearly moved it to Singapore because of a post– September 11 fear of Middle Eastern terrorism. Besieged by protesters, with their "new economy" moribund after the collapse of the information technology bubble and the longest recession since the thirties, and with the evident intention of the American government to rebuild the military-industrial complex denounced by President Dwight D. Eisenhower (a transparent, if unadmitted, Keynesian stimulus to the industrial economy), those planners are more susceptible to radical critique than ever. [1]

Even before September 11, however, while increasing numbers were recognizing the conjoined dangers of social malaise and ecological menace stemming from the hegemony of neoliberal capitalism, the intellectual debate had lagged behind events, particularly in North America. Although excellent books like Naomi Klein's *No Logo* and Thomas Frank's *One Market under God* attacked the ideological pretenses of the defenders of corporate domination, and a few brave forays such as David Harvey's *Spaces of Hope* and Immanuel Wallerstein's *Utopistics* had offered notions of a different kind of social order, several vital elements nonetheless appeared to be lacking in the discourse on the alternatives. The intent of this book is to supply them.

Central among these deficiencies has been a recognition of the historical complexity of our present situation. Partly this lack is a result of the tendency, in contemporary radical discourse, to dichotomize the world into the rich capitalist countries and the rest, a polar opposition influenced by Wallerstein's notion of a world system, in which the only relevant distinction appears to be between capitalist core (Europe, enlarged in the nineteenth century to include North America and, in the twentieth, Japan) and colonial (or third world) periphery. For decades, American and European scholars concerned with the nasty effects of modern capitalism on the poor and the powerless have been oriented almost exclusively to the "third world" and to the internal echo of third world misery in the situation of impoverished minorities in the Euro-Amercian "core." The seductiveness of Wallerstein's theory induced many intellectuals of leftist inclination to abandon any serious consideration of the complexities of the relationship between Europe and the United States, indeed of the countercurrents to this hegemonic impulse within Europe itself.

This tendency of radicals to dismiss Europe as an only occasionally unruly satrap of American power was a perhaps inevitable consequence of the decline since the Second World War of a Euro-centered political radicalism in America, and, particularly in Europe since the seventies, of the fossilization of the anti-Stalinist revolutionary Left. It was, however, accentuated by several major shifts in intellectual fashions. One was the flattening out of historical perspective generally, to the point where concern for the advantages and pleasures of the moment tended to undermine interest in the past as well as concern for the future. Justifying this shallowness intellectually, postmodernism dismissed historical "grand narratives" and postmodernist radicals focused on the separate and incommensurable problems of marginal identity groups. In the United States, the problem was compounded by the general abandonment of traditional academic concern for European history.

Persuaded as I am that our present miseries have deep roots in the history of Western culture, in the heady mixture of power worship and idealism that has invested our most basic values and that shapes the conventional understanding of the modern myth of Prometheus, I believe it is indispensable, if we are to transcend our present impasse, to understand the movements and ideologies which have laid claim to this Promethean inheritance in the last two centuries. Crucial, moreover, to such a transcendence is an educated awareness of those progressive counterforces within the modern world that have competed with the hegemonic forces for the mantle of Prometheus: no fundamental change like that now yearned for by millions can occur without historical foundation. In particular, I argue that the Promethean impulse in the arts and in social thought, particularly in French and English romanticism, provides us with an alternative notion of modernity to that of industrial capitalist development, dubbed "the unbound Prometheus" by the economic historian David Landes.

The Preface, in presenting the double wall of apparently insoluble social and ecological problems that humankind now faces, establishes the challenge this book addresses. The Introduction examines, as a counterpoint to the dominant significance of Prometheus as patron-saint of economic modernism, the very different understanding of Prometheus and modernity in Shelley's *Prometheus Unbound;* it then offers a summary of the theoretical and historical foundations of the rise of the Promethean spirit.

Part I discusses nationalism, socialism, and consumer capitalism. In it I analyze the background of today's consumer society in the light of ideological and social evolution since the French Revolution, showing how both nationalism and socialism originally constituted "Promethean" responses to the atomistic individualism propagated by liberal capitalism, how both were ultimately subordinated to it, and how the ideology of consumer capitalism purports to inherit, while transforming into pure egoism, the social idealism incarnated by its ideological predecessors. Woven through these texts is the perception of the main trends of the modern age outlined in the Introduction, in which countercurrents to atomistic individualism that were manifested both in the arts (most conspicuously in European romanticism) and in social movements (such as those generated both by European nationalism and by the socialist movement) are understood in the light of the contributions to historical understanding of Karl Marx, Max Weber, and Norbert Elias. Marx and Weber demonstrated the ineluctable triumph of capitalist rationalization and the modern bureaucratic state over feudalism and the varied forms of the ancien régime; Elias revealed, in the "civilizing process," the psychological dimension of that triumph. All three discussed the hostilities it aroused.

Following this analysis of the historical background of the present critical moment, *Prometheus Revisited* examines a second absence in the present debate: the failure to consider the sources of resistance to corporate ideology's celebration of individual selfishness. These sources are the subject of the first two chapters of Part II.

In the first of these (Chapter 4), I examine the suppositions regarding human nature inherent in the most advanced thinking on this subject in the twentieth century: psychoanalysis. Here I focus in particular on the fundamental revisions of Freudian assumptions by Ernest Schachtel in his theory of allocentric and autocentric modes of perception. Schachtel's work is helpful both in comprehending the psychological bases of commercial mentalities and in offering a basis for the aesthetic and social idealism of the "other Prometheus" discussed in the Introduction.

The second chapter of Part II (Chapter 5) looks at the new social movements active in opposing corporate globalization and war, focusing on France and the United States. Since the most effective resistance to the world hegemony of American capitalism may plausibly arise from a more socially oriented European Union, it is important to understand the European movements of resistance to neoliberal privatization, especially those in France that led to the socialist government of Lionel Jospin.

The last chapter in the second part (Chapter 6) is a sketch of what a utopian democratic project for the twenty-first century might look like, a project which would, on a global scale, combine a rational use of existing technology with principles of democratic governance, social control, individual as well as collective rights, local identities, and ecological sustainability. The argument is that this sketch is comprehensible both in terms of the history depicted in the first part of the book and the theories and movements presented in the second. It is, I repeat, a sketch, intended to stimulate debate, not a blueprint. It makes no pretense to creating a heaven on earth, but it may be a vision worth discussing for the medium-term future.

Preface: The Double Wall before the Future

We are dancing on a volcano.

NARCISSE ACHILLE, Comte de Salvandy (1830)

Visions of the future today are more likely to be dystopian than utopian, closer to the horrors of George Orwell's *1984* and of the films *Soylent Green* and *Clockwork Orange* than to the benign nineteenth-century optimism of Robert Owen's *New View of Society* or Charles Fourier's *Nouveau Monde Amoureux.*[1] Indeed, we live in dangerous times. Well before September 11, our world had become ecologically and socially so unpredictable that a book titled *Risk Society* had been written to describe it.[2] Since then, there has been increasing awareness at the highest levels of society of the dangers we live in. But it is doubtful that such awareness will improve matters without a powerful impulse for change from below.

The author of *Risk Society,* Ulrich Beck, has called the attack on the World Trade Center "the Chernobyl of globalization," exposing "the false promise of neoliberalism" just as the Ukrainian catastrophe of 1986 "undermined our faith in nuclear energy." Viewing the shoddy privatized airline security as partly responsible for the suicide bombings, Beck saw in the pictures of the World Trade Center inferno "an as yet undecoded message: a state can neoliberalise itself to death." He decried "the capitalist fundamentalists' unswerving faith in the redeeming power of the market" as "a dangerous illusion," and called for a reinvigoration of the state. "We need," he wrote, "to combine economic integration with cosmopolitan politics. Human dignity, cultural identity and otherness must be taken more seriously in the future. Since September 11, the gulf between the world of those who profit from globalization and the world of those who feel threatened by it has been closed. Helping those who have been excluded is no longer a humanitarian task. It is in the west's own interest: the key to its security."[3]

Note that Beck did not consider terrorism to be the world's principal problem. He realized, as did many other thinking people, that the dimensions of the danger were being inflated by a U.S. government eager, in September 2001, to rally an increasingly hostile public to its support and to distract its citizens from the ecological and social concerns underlying the growing protest movements of the previous two years. As Paul Krugman has written, "at least as far as domestic policy is concerned, the administration views terrorism as another useful crisis."[4] Beck understands that the enormous risks we face at the beginning of the twenty-first century have more to do with the ideological fundamentalism of neoliberal capitalism than with that of Islamic terror networks. In fact, there is a considerably greater danger to the world in general and to American formal democracy in particular of a prolonged and unnecessary state of war between the West and Islam than of renewed terrorism.

Nonetheless, despite the Bush administration's evident desire to parlay Americans' fear of new attacks into a decades-long "war on terrorism" and the wish of its more hawkish members to expand the war to Iraq, the chance is great that European doves and Washington realists will prevail, and that such expansion will not occur. In that case we return to the problems flowing from global capitalism itself. Indeed, just two months after the attacks on New York and Washington, bipartisan support for Bush's domestic program was vanishing, as congressional Democrats returned to the offensive against the administration's handling of the economic crisis.[5] These problems are perhaps more serious than even Beck believes them to be. For the ecological and social damage done to humankind by the savage globalization of recent decades has long been noticed, and had met with determined resistance well before the famous "battle of Seattle." A glance at the record, however, shows that this resistance has been of little avail.

In the autumn of 1998, "El Niño," a huge recurrent storm cycle whose violence, scientists said, was exacerbated by environmental pollution, tormented the earth's atmosphere, breeding storms and floods in Asia and Latin America, leaving thousands of dead and millions of homeless people in its wake.[6] Less than two years later, scientists were appalled to discover that global warming had melted a kilometer-wide gap in the ice cap at the North Pole.[7] Since this drastic worsening of our ecological condition was known much earlier, the United States had by then already agreed to the Kyoto protocol of 1997, which pledged each nation to reduce greenhouse gas emissions by 7 percent in relation to their 1990 level, an agreement which was revoked in 2001 by the accession to the U.S. presidency of the world's most celebrated denier of man-made climate change. Four months before that accession, however, on August 21, 2000, the conservative *Financial Times* pointed out that, halfway through the twenty-two-year period within which the nations of the world had agreed to such limitations, the pace of industrial growth had outstripped environmental measures to such a degree that "a 30 percent cut would now be needed to meet the commitment" in the United States, and a 14 percent reduction in Europe.[8] The *FT*'s editorialist described the prospects for cutting back greenhouse gases as "dismal," and warned that "if the danger of global warming is to be confronted seriously, sustained and probably painful measures will be needed over many decades." The same issue carried an article headlined "Chile Chokes on Its Economic Growth."

Twenty one months later, the United Nations World Food Program warned that torrential rain in Nicaragua, which left a thousand people homeless in Managua, heralded the return of El Niño to the Western hemisphere in the second half of 2002. At roughly the same time, meteorologists were establishing an increase in Alaska's average temperature of seven degrees over the previous three decades, and extreme heat, drought, and high winds in wooded areas of the West and Southwest of the United States were creating enormous wildfires. Excoriating George W. Bush's indifference to global warming, Bob Herbert, a *New York Times* columnist, exclaimed: "We're speeding toward a wall and the president is not only refusing to step on the brake, he's accelerating."[9]

Meanwhile, we have discovered another reason for choking. In the course of recent years, one food scandal after another has rocked the European continent, most of them the result of profit-oriented applications of industrial technologies to agriculture. Europeans discovered that Mad Cow Disease, transmittable to humans, resulted from feeding the carcasses of dead bovines to living ones, so as to increase their weight and profitability—a practice long widespread in the United States as well.[10] Genetically modified foods and beef with hormone additives, pushed by the agro-industry as a panacea for food shortages and blandly accepted in the United States, encountered import prohibitions in environmentally aware European nations, which consider genetically modified organisms an incalculable danger to all forms of life.

Outside Europe, from the summer of 1997 on, financial and equity markets crashed in distant places, creating new hordes of paupers and unemployed among those nations considered only a year earlier the "tigers" of the world economy; three years later, recovery was still distant in many Asian countries.[11] The effects of these crashes were echoed in Russia and South America, stimulating concern among Euro-American elites that, despite the windfall profits of recent decades, their belief in unregulated circulation of capital and commodities as the path to salubrious, unceasing growth might be at least partly responsible for the economic malaise.[12] In Europe itself, starkly contrasting with such profits, unemployment climbed above 10 percent, while real hourly wages in the United States and Europe continued a decline that had begun around 1975, creating an ever sharper division between rich and poor. At the moment I write (June 2002), the United States seems to be dragging much of the world into prolonged recession.

Whether or not the economic malaise deepens, the ecological problem is bound to worsen. And in either case, large numbers of wageworkers, small shopkeepers, farmers, and unemployed will continue to be trapped in a downward trajectory that engenders bitterness against the propertied minority receiving unprecedented salaries and dividends. In Europe, the struggle against this widening gulf between the wealth of the top and the insecurity and misery of the rest has been going on since the mid-nineties. From 1995 on, in key nations of the European Union, "downsized" employees, their income, status, and hopes diminished by corporations competing for investments and by governments privatizing to cut budget deficits, reacted angrily to being treated as industrial waste. Accused (by establishment spokesmen) of an archaic, corporatist mentality, they first demonstrated their militant opposition to privatizations and welfare cuts during the French strikes of December 1995. Innovative, radically democratic trade unions, supported by a revitalized Green movement and by movements of artists and intellectuals recently organized to help immigrants without papers and fellow citizens without jobs or homes, parlayed popular hostility to proposed "reforms" of pensions and social security into a month-long general strike of government workers, a strike that paralyzed the Gaullist regime and led to its downfall eighteen months later. That denouement paralleled the voting out of office of governments committed to supporting conservative capitalism in Germany, Italy, England, and Belgium. In the French-German heart of the European Union, red-green coalitions were empowered by the electorate to reduce unemployment by governmental stimulus of the economy, redistribute wealth, and end the worst abuses of the environment.[13]

Humankind thus, tardily, appeared to react against environmental and economic disasters triggered by the gospel of progress. Bringing them to an end, however, was to be no simple matter, as the incapacity of the new regimes to curb the fetishism of growth at any price, to lessen unemployment, and to curtail neoliberal greed demonstrated.[14] The fact that the social-democratic regimes which took over the reins of power in a large part of Europe have been unable to break with the neoliberal policies of their predecessors suggests that the swelling opposition to global capitalism needs to discuss radically new perspectives, ones that the Left—including the Left which since the sixties has called itself "new"—has been too timid or too trapped in traditional ideologies to formulate.

Coming after a century of unheard-of violence and social transformation, the incapacity to change free-market policies—even of governments born of popular disgust with neoliberalism—has profound roots in the ideologies and mentalities through which Western societies have conceptualized nature, progress, and themselves since the Renaissance. Closely tied to such self-conceptualizations, the problems of impending ecological catastrophe and social-economic malaise loom before us as a double wall blocking the future, noxious waste products of the unsustainable productivity created by instrumental reason in the last century and a half.[15]

Environmentally, our spoliation of the earth's resources and our poisoning of air, earth, and water may have led us to a point of no return. The results of a social order founded on technological hubris and on individual and collective avarice are already being felt: the steady destruction of the earth's rain forests by huge lumber and agricultural combines, the acid rain denuding woodlands throughout Europe, and the warming trend which, if unreversed, will probably lead to the inundation of the earth's coastal areas and the death or homelessness of hundreds of millions of people by the middle of the present century. In the enormous land mass of the former Soviet Union, nuclear and other varieties of pollution have diminished life expectancy by ten years in the last generation, proof that the state capitalist rape of nature can be as traumatic as the private capitalist variety.

A recent quantitative study of our biological environment—the 2002 Living Planet Report of the World Wildlife Fund[16]—underscores our perilous condition. The report argues that a continuation of humankind's current pillaging of the earth's natural resources will lead, by the year 2030, to an unavoidable decline in human welfare, as measured by average life expectancy, educational level, and world economic product. The report measures our "ecological footprint" by calculating the land area required to sustain consumption of the total human population at current levels. This averages about 2.3 hectares for each of the six billion people on the planet. The "biological capacity" of the earth, however—the level of exploitation consistent with replenishment of resources—is equal to just 1.9 hectares per person. Having passed the point of sustainable use of resources in the 1980s, we now consume annually about 20 percent more of the earth's biological capacity than we restore, and given current trends we will be consuming about 50 percent more by the year 2050. The report indicates that the ecological footprint is much deeper in North America and Europe— 9.6 and 5 hectares per person respectively—than in Asia and Africa, where the use of resources is estimated at 1.4 hectares per person.

Politically, the danger of fueling a world economy on unsustainable energy resources is perhaps more immediate than the ecological hazard. The more affluent societies have enjoyed a free lunch until now on the basis of fossil fuel supplies—oil, gas, and coal—which, apart from their destructive effects on air, land, and water, will be largely exhausted before the end of this century. In the case of oil, given the steady decline in the discovery of new reserves, educated predictions are that output will peak between 2004 and 2008, a peak that will be followed by declining production and a rapid rise in the price of oil-based fuel; the latter will drastically increase the cost of transporting persons and goods.[17] We have already seen the violent reactions from auto-addicted Europeans and Americans to sudden increases in gas pump prices.[18] The *Report of the National Energy Policy Development Group,* signed by the American vice-president and most of the cabinet in May 2001, blandly forecasted an increase in U.S. energy needs of 32 percent in the next two decades. While they indicated where they hoped to procure it (in part, the Caspian Sea), the authors mentioned neither the probable rapid increase in the price of oil nor the political turmoil this was likely to create toward the end of George W. Bush's present term of office. But it is not unreasonable to speculate that the military adventurism in central Asia and the Middle East of an American government headed by oil barons may be motivated by more than the hunt for an elusive gang of terrorists.

Socially and economically, the global expansion of capitalist markets has been fueled by the development of an information technology that makes most traditional production jobs as well as many third sector employments obsolete. In the 1990s neoliberal globalization combined with computerization led to two equally dangerous phenomena. One was a runaway speculation in financial capital and technology shares which, though slowing down for a presumed "soft landing" in 2000, dangerously destabilized the world economy. Starting with the summer of 1999, European commentators expressed repeated fears of a world crash equivalent to that of 1929. The other was a redistribution of world income in favor of the 20 percent of the world's population which possessed either capital or the high-level education in the manipulation of abstractions that is necessary for information technology. For the majority of ordinary mortals, particularly in those large parts of our planet where modernization and industrialization have replaced religious notions of a hereafter with the tangible prospect of ever-increasing material welfare, the recent downturn in expectations has had a serious impact on self-esteem and identity.[19] It has been hundreds of years since an adult generation in the Euro-American heartland of "progress" realistically expected a harder, instead of an easier, life for its children.[20]

These worsening, seemingly insoluble, ecological and social problems result from the persistence of institutions and ideologies that have become totally inadequate to our situation. I am convinced that if we cannot question, or at least consider modifying, these institutions and ideologies, we are going to vanish like sparrows flying into a jetliner. It is, in other words, imperative that we step back and take a longer perspective on the course of human history as well as on the resources for changing that course. More than the post–September 11 threats of war and terrorism, the crises of environmental decay and economic malaise that I shall discuss in this book cast a shadow on the future of humanity, leading many of us into an unreal kind of living for the moment, an almost psychotic egoism.[21] How we arrived at this dark passage and how we might get beyond it are the themes of this book.

While I am aware that we are in desperate straits and am apprehensive about the future, I nonetheless am convinced that the most powerful "realism" today is the utopian imagination. The forces we have created and that currently shape our thinking about the future have a contradictory character. When applied in appropriate dosage they can cure rather than kill. Think of the mix of social and individual forces at work in the creation of modern society. Historians, anthropologists, and sociologists understand the dependence of healthy individuality on strong social settings that encourage it, as evidenced in the first flowering of classical culture in the Greek polis, or in its later blooming in the Italian Renaissance. In the modern world, the hypertrophy of individualism unleashed by ideologies that have abandoned the social nexus has produced anomic criminality as well as the avarice and financial power of the superwealthy, but in a more humane social context, modern individualism could also find expression in the sonnets of Shakespeare, the operas of Mozart, the novels of Zola, and the art of Picasso. Similarly, the social impulse is maleficent only when it loses sight of individual needs. If it has led to the creation of totalitarian empires, bureaucratic tyrannies, the techno-corporate monstrosities of contemporary capitalism, and the opposed terrorisms of Western and Eastern fundamentalisms, it has also powered revolutions demanding social justice for oppressed masses. At a more local scale, social bonding may have created lynch mobs and pogroms, but it also nurtured neighborhood friendships, romantic love, idealistic brother bands in art and politics, and communal self-help.

The Western cultural tradition has for nearly three millennia evoked these opposed potentialities—the dark sides of human existence as well as the cures for present and future ills—in the figure of the Greek god Prometheus. The importance of the myth of Prometheus has increased rather than decreased in the modern era, epitomizing the innovative economic and social force of modernity expressed by most ideologies of the last two centuries. Other myths, sometimes competing with and sometimes supplementing the Promethean one, have of course also served as seedbeds of modern ideologies. Individuals and groups in contemporary society continue to believe in the salvationist myth of Christ. Others revere the devotion to aesthetic perfection associated with the myths of Orpheus and Apollo, or the demonic productivity of Faust or the intoxicated descent into instinctual life associated with Dionysos. Insofar as the Promethean ethos is a myth of heroic creation and sacrifice, however, I believe it has been the principal inspiration of the continual transformations of our world, the dominant myth of the modern age. In Freudian terms, it has defined the principal link between rational ego, moral will, and instinctual impulse in our world, for the better in the democratic revolutions to which we are the heirs, for the worse in the catastrophic scenarios to which uncontrolled nationalism and industrialism, by-products of those revolutions, led in the twentieth century. The complexities of the Promethean tradition are the complexities of the contemporary world; the faces of modern Prometheanism are as multiple and contradictory as those of modernity itself.

This book, in contrast to the prevailing interpretation of Prometheanism, has as its point of departure a vision of the Titan God that may nurture hope rather than terror of the future.

◈ ◈ ◈

Among those whose critical appreciation encouraged me to expand "Thoughts on the Second Millennium"—an essay which I wrote and rewrote between 1991 and 1994—into a book were Arno Mayer, Natalie Zemon Davis, Gabriel and Joyce Kolko, Michael Löwy, Russell Jacoby, Joep Leerssen, Roel van Duijn, Marleen Wessel, and Jean-Paul Deléage, who published the first half of it in Écologie Politique, no. 11/12 (1994–95). In 1996, drawing on perspectives common to "Thoughts on the Second Millennium" and the yet unwritten Prometheus Revisited, I organized, together with Marcel van der Linden and Michael Krätke, a conference titled "European Left Alternatives to Neoliberalism" (ELAN), held in Amsterdam in February 1997. Both Marcel and Michael contributed to shaping the ideas of Prometheus Revisited, as did several of those who supported ELAN at the time, most notably (apart from those already named) Pierre Bourdieu, Alain Lipietz, Claus Offe, Riccardo Petrella, Juliet Schor, Hilary Wainwright, Dominique Voynet, Alain Caillé, and Immanuel Wallerstein. Versions of the manuscript were given enthusiastic if sometimes critical commentary by Michael Löwy and Gary Price. David Gross, editor of the series in which this appears, helped considerably in improving the book's first complete draft. My wife, Marleen Wessel, applied her customary acuity and sensitivity to discussions about the book's main points, and her last-minute critique of Chapter 6 added importantly to the final version. Finally, three friends accompanied the entire project from beginning to end with a superb mixture of support, critical reading, and knowledgeable advice: Gabriel and Joyce Kolko and Joep Leerssen. For their wise counsel at several critical junctures I shall be eternally grateful.

Prometheus Revisited

The Other Prometheus

Shelley's Romantic Prometheanism

IN APRIL 1819 a young expatriate Englishman in Rome put the finishing touches to a long poetic drama, eloquent on the questions of freedom and resistance to tyranny but full of abstruse allegorical figures derived from the classical world. The poet was Percy Bysshe Shelley, friend of Lord Byron and a leading light, with Byron and John Keats, of the second generation of English romanticism. The drama, which seemed to be an adaptation of a 2,300-year-old tragedy by a Greek playwright, was *Prometheus Unbound,* a clear wink at Aeschylus's *Prometheus Bound.*

Shelley's poem illustrates the extreme complexity of the modern myth of Prometheus. In context, it offers a fascinating literary perspective on the potentialities of the modern world as it emerged from the age of the French Revolution and as it still stands before us. Shelley's generation of young idealists had already experienced the hardening of the revolutionary spirit into Napoleonic nationalism and the crushing of both by the victorious counterrevolution of the European old regime. Many were disillusioned, but some, like Shelley and his friends, retained a visionary hope for a rebirth, under more favorable conditions, of the revolution of 1789, a revolution that would transcend not only feudal monarchy and nationalism but also the crude middle-class utilitarianism which, in England and elsewhere in Europe, was rapidly substituting unbridled individual avarice for the collective restraints of traditional authority. Shelley, and the European romantics generally, wrote at the beginning of the triumph of the modern capitalism that embodied this avarice, a triumph whose latter-day epiphanies we observe around us today.

To understand the importance of Shelley's poem, for his age and for ours, we need to look at it in several contexts. The first is the prevailing meaning attributed in the twentieth century to Prometheanism, a meaning that links social, cultural, and philosophical progress, both of the individual and the collectivity, to technological prowess. On the one hand, idealistic collective ideologies—nationalism, socialism, and their rather disagreeable twentieth-century offspring—increasingly used the myth of Prometheus to justify cults of power. On the other, the contemporary manifestation of that myth, the individualist ideology of neoliberalism, pins its claim to the Titan by positing the dependence of wealth, power, and prosperity on the untrammeled expression of marketplace egoism. The significance attributed to Prometheus by Shelley and other romantics contrasts sharply with both the collectivist and the individualist uses of the myth to justify cults of power, and as I shall indicate, that romantic understanding of the myth has had fairly recent echoes. Secondly, there is the specific historical and intellectual context within which Shelley was writing and to which he was, in part, reacting. Thirdly, there is the larger cultural background of Shelley's understanding of the myth of Prometheus, both in his own work and in the currents of English and European thought that fed into his own. Only after examining these three contexts can we grapple with the meaning of the poem itself.

PROMETHEANISM AND MODERNITY

The Promethean ethos saw humankind as the genial architect of its own social, material, and intellectual order: "Man is his own Prometheus," wrote the French historian Jules Michelet. According to Greek mythology, Prometheus rebelled against Zeus to bring the gift of fire to suffering mortals; for this rebellion, Zeus had him chained to a mountain and daily tortured by a vulture feasting on his liver. Echoing the Christian legend of the God-man who sacrificed himself for humanity,[1] the myth of Prometheus resurfaced in post-Christian times as a metaphor both for heroic sacrifice and for humanity's first technological leap forward, the invention of fire. Prometheus, symbol of creative energy, of defiance of divine authority and endurance in the face of oppression, became the watchword of those who in the modern era hailed democratic revolutions against traditional despotism and industrial ones against scarcity. Against arbitrary privilege, the Promethean ethos celebrated *Homo faber,* man the worker. Through the linkage of the ideal of labor to those revolutions, Prometheus came to symbolize not only technological prowess but freedom, social justice, solidarity, and reason. In its varied versions, this progressive Prometheanism inspired the apparently beneficent modernity that was linked to intellectual independence, urbanization, and a market economy.

A fundamental question, however, in the modern interpretation of the myth of Prometheus is the relationship between its materialist values—the idealization of labor and increased productivity—and its ethical and social implications. Are productivity, the work ethic, and instrumental rationality to be viewed as ends in themselves from which material benefits for all are sure to derive, or are productivity and "growth" only to be valued where they serve the higher ends of social justice, freedom, and a notion of reason that transcends the utilitarian? A second related problem is the relationship between human productivity and nature.

The standard current interpretation of "Prometheanism," deriving from Plato's narration of the myth in his *Protagoras,* relates it to the Enlightenment project of "mastering" nature. This view is shared by those who celebrate the myth of Prometheus—ideologists of capitalism and, more broadly, of the instrumental rationality that has given birth to several industrial "revolutions" in the modern era—and those who view it with hostility, such as some ecological philosophers and feminists.[2] The early twentieth-century *Prometheus* of the Dutch novelist Carrie van Bruggen, who used the myth to capture the intellectual individualism that evolved from Enlightenment rationalism, is close to that celebration. David Landes's *The Unbound Prometheus: Technological Change and Industrial Development in Western Europe from 1750 to the Present* (1969) epitomizes it. According to the liberal Whig version of progress, Don Slater argues, "modernity unbinds the Prometheus of productive forces from the chains of superstition, authority and tradition: science and technology, the rational technical division of labour markets, the replacement of status by contract, demographic shifts to the city, all combine in a forcefield of initiative, ingenuity, invention and energy."[3] Similarly, a recent Marxist view of history emphasizes the Promethean character of humankind in arguing that "history [was] the ceaseless transformation wrought by a being who is essentially active, changing and productive. . . . one thing which never changes about humanity is its productivity, the source and matrix of everything which springs historically into being."[4]

Human productivity, of course—fetishized in the idea of industrial growth as universal panacea—is precisely what has led to the double wall of ecological and social disasters blocking the human future. It is, however, only one side of the Promethean ethos.

The myth of Prometheus is often misunderstood today, its polyvalence ignored. The interpretation of Prometheus simply as the inspiration of modern democracy and industrialism, the *demiourgos* of technology and capitalism, loses much of the meaning given to the Titan in nineteenth-century romanticism. Relying on Aeschylus's *Prometheus Bound* rather than the versions of the myth in Hesiod and Plato, the romantics emphasized the defiant hero in chains, the martyr for humanity. While this emphasis was also supported by revolutionary nationalists and socialists of the nineteenth century, who saw it as a tie between their movements and the powerful rise of modern industry, some romantic poets saw collectivist and naturalist implications sharply opposed to the cult of productivity. This other interpretation, hinted at by Aeschylus, is fully expressed in Shelley's *Prometheus Unbound,* where the union of the unchained Prometheus and his spouse, Asia, consecrating the end of Jupiter's despotism, signifies the amorous reconciliation of humankind, nature, and the fine arts.

SHELLEY AND REVOLUTION

Percy Bysshe Shelley (1792–1822), born into a branch of the Sussex squirearchy, came of age at the height of the Napoleonic wars, during which social dissent from the established order was repressed as treasonous. By temperament a rebel, he declared his atheism in a fiery pamphlet that earned him expulsion from Oxford and a simmering feud with his father for the rest of his short life. He was on the fringes of many of the oppositionist radical groups in his day, had a brief flirt with a utopian community, married very young, and earned the reputation of a libertine by eloping to France with the daughter and stepdaughter (together!) of his philosophical mentor, the anarchist William Godwin.

Shelley's long dramatic poem *Prometheus Unbound* epitomizes the romantic understanding, after the close of the revolutionary epoch, of Prometheus as a rebel in chains. Once liberated, however, Shelley's Titan signifies not just the victory of the revolutionary forces of the age, but the emergence of humankind from oppressive states and religions into an amorous union with nature.

Prometheus Unbound needs to be read today in two frameworks. Written as it was in 1818–19 by an expatriate English radical, it is embedded in a largely forgotten political situation, that of those who continued to believe in the secular and republican social ideals of the French Revolution during the restoration of autocratic and religiously orthodox rule between 1815 and 1848. Even in England, the only European country before the French revolution of 1830 to limit royal power by an elected parliament, the authoritarian reflex in the post-Napoleonic era was draconian. Shelley's response to the ferocious repression of political dissent and social protest in some of his shorter poems was unambiguous, as for example in his sonnet "England in 1819," where the poet stigmatized George III as "an old, mad, blind, despised, and dying king," flailed the royal family as "princes, the dregs of their dull race," condemned "rulers who neither see, nor feel, nor know," and memorialized the recently massacred demonstrators of Peterloo as "a people starved and stabbed in the untilled field."[5] In a longer (372-line) poem, "The Mask of Anarchy," Shelley devoted his talent exclusively to denouncing the Peterloo massacre, but, because of his friends' fears of legal action, this poem was not published until 1832.[6]

Such radicalism is less outspoken in Shelley's *Prometheus Unbound,* but the work nonetheless resonates to the rebellious romanticism of its author. As I have said, one of the salient meanings of Prometheus in the romantic era was his resistance to divine tyranny and his consequent martyrdom. Indeed, the young Karl Marx identified himself with the chained Titan (in the preface to his doctoral thesis of 1841) as "the holiest saint and martyr in the philosophical calendar."[7] It is noteworthy that Shelley's work was reprinted by the radical and chartist press in the 1820s, 1830s, and 1840s,[8] and that selections of his work were read out at meetings of German communist artisans in 1845.[9] While this aspect of Shelley's Prometheus—the revolutionary defending humankind against its oppressors—is compatible with progressive modernity, it can hardly be equated with the twentieth century's understanding of Prometheus as the "patron saint of technology."[10]

THE CULTURAL CONTEXT

The philosophical aesthetic of Shelley's verse drama reveals a lost, romantic underside of modernity: the reversion to esoteric, neo-Platonic myths of the natural circularity of all things, comparable to those used by Wordsworth in his *Prelude.* Combined with the apocalyptic fever of the age—a fusion of Christian and French revolutionary elements that permitted the notion of a radical break in time—these myths encouraged belief in an imminent end to oppression and in a reconciliation of humankind with nature based on love and wisdom.[11] Since Shelley, with an erudition not uncommon in the early nineteenth century, used ancient myths and literary references as codes, the task of penetrating the inner meaning of his poetry, particularly *Prometheus Unbound,* requires scrutiny of the poem's literary context, both in his own work and in the models that inspired him.

Prometheus Unbound is the last of three long dramatic poems which Shelley wrote during his short life, all of which depicted in more or less allegorical terms the misery of England in the first two decades of the nineteenth century and the sources of that misery in religious and political despotism, in the venality of the aristocracy, and in the greed of merchant princes. The three works in question also contain the prospect of a utopian future, in which personal, social, and political liberation are joined. The first of these poems, which is often seen as giving the themes and internal structure of the other two, was *Queen Mab,* written in 1812–13, when its author was barely twenty; the second, *The Revolt of Islam,* in 1817. Since *Prometheus Unbound* seems to be the most distant of the three from nineteenth-century concerns, it will be useful to look briefly at its prototypes.

Queen Mab had the advantage of being annotated by Shelley with long explanatory notes to specific verses, disquisitions embellished with long quotes (in Latin, Greek, and French, as well as English) from Homer, the Bible, Lucretius, d'Holbach, Spinoza, Newton, and Godwin. These notes are extraordinarily wide-ranging, running from astronomy to the defenses of atheism and vegetarianism,[12] questions of ethics, and, spectacularly for the time, a labor theory of value. The latter, a note to the line "And statesmen boast of wealth" (5.93, 94) is based on the ideas of the anarchist philosopher William Godwin, with whose daughter and step-daughter Shelley (already married to Harriet Westbrook) was to elope to France a few years later. Shelley's contempt for bourgeois moral standards was paralleled by his social radicalism, and it is easy to see why the precursors of English socialism, the Chartists, adopted *Queen Mab* as their "bible"[13] when we read in that note: "Wealth is a power usurped by the few, to compel the many to labour for their benefit. The laws which support this system derive their force from the ignorance and credulity of its victims: they are the result of a conspiracy of the few against the many." In fact, these pages reveal the kind of utopianism that today inspires much of the ecological Left. A citation from Godwin indicates the poet's awareness of the artificiality of human wants and the utopian possibilities that would result from reducing those wants to actual human needs:

> The commodities that substantially contribute to the subsistence of the human species form a very short catalogue: they demand from us but a slender portion of industry. If these only were produced, and sufficiently produced, the species of man would be continued. If the labour necessarily required to produce them were equitably divided among the poor, and, still more, if it were equitably divided among all, each man's share of labour would be light, and his portion of leisure would be ample. . . . Those hours which are not required for the production of the necessaries of life may be devoted to the cultivation of the understanding, the enlarging our stock of knowledge, the refining our taste, and opening to us new and more exquisite sources of enjoyment.

Shelley further cites Godwin as having calculated "that all the conveniences of civilized life might be produced, if society would divide the labour equally among its members, by each individual being employed in labour two hours during the day."[14]

A second major influence on *Queen Mab,* in both its attack on religion and its visionary form, was Volney's *Les Ruines, ou Méditations sur les révolutions des empires* of 1791, which had a considerable impact on French intellectuals during the Revolution, becoming, according to Kenneth Neill Cameron, "one of the revolutionary handbooks of the age."[15] Count Constantin-François Chasseboeuf de Volney (1757–1820) was before the Revolution close to the circles of the radical Enlightenment philosophers d'Holbach and Helvetius; as a Girondist, he was imprisoned during the Terror. Volney's influence on Shelley was considerable. Borrowed from Volney's *Les ruines* were not only the denunciation of Christianity and the journey through space in *Queen Mab* but also, according to Cameron, "the main political concept" as well as many particular passages of *The Revolt of Islam*.[16]

The message of all three poems is a mixture of personal, political, and philosophical idealism, rooted both in Shelley's life history and in the history of English culture, particularly where that culture was imbricated in the revolutionary currents of the early modern epoch. Shelley's inspiration was fed not just by contemporary radicals such as Volney and Godwin, but also by major poets of the Elizabethan and English revolutionary epochs. In this longer context, Shelley's poems reveal the complexity of the values and ideologies inspiring modernity as a whole. The predecessor that best bears comparison with *Queen Mab* as well as with the second of the three long topical poems, *The Revolt of Islam,* is Edmund Spenser's *The Faerie Queen,* which Shelley knew quite well and which, even longer than Shelley's work, was a book-length allegorical poem with clear religious and social undertones, a polemic for Spenser's time.[17]

Now Spenser's poem, dedicated to Elizabeth I as the poet's muse, was written from the standpoint of the militant Anglicanism of sixteenth-century England. If Spenser, as part of the Elizabethan establishment, castigated, in his allegory, the tyranny of Rome, he also detested mercenary greed: the sixty-six stanzas of book 2, canto 7 are devoted to the "cave of Mammon."[18] One scholar sees *The Faerie Queen* as reflecting "the apocalyptic light in which Spenser's countrymen saw the great conflict of their time between Protestant England and Catholic Spain," and compares Spenser's political moralism to that of John Milton,[19] the seventeenth-century poet of revolutionary Puritanism. The circle closes when we discover that Shelley viewed the Satan of Milton's *Paradise Lost* as an important model for *Prometheus Unbound.*[20]

Clearly, there are fundamental differences in social perspective between Spenser, the Elizabethan courtier, Milton, the plebeian bard, and Shelley, the rebel poet. I would suggest that the common denominator of the poets of these three revolutionary moments was that, coming from the traditional social elites but inspired by the values of the modern age, they shared a disdain for royal and religious absolutism (hence their enthusiasm for modernity's movements of revolt), while they despised the mercantile interests that came in its place: they detested the old regime but mistrusted the venality of the new classes struggling for power.

Spenser, Milton, and Shelley thus reveal the increasing individualism of artistic genius that was unleashed by successive waves of revolt against the established regime. Each of these poets was involved in the creation of a discourse for the revolutionary forces of his era that would reconcile personal liberty with the spirit of a new social order, an order free of the individualist greed and ambition that battened on the disintegration of the old order. With each succeeding century, of course, as mentalities and cultures became less feudal, traditional, and religiously impregnated, and more bourgeois, work-oriented and urban, the terms of this discourse changed. *The Faerie Queen,* though the work of a courtier-poet, represented the culture of the English Reformation during its phase of militant resistance to Spanish Catholicism. Religious revolt from above was merging with the beginnings of English nationalism, epitomized in Spenser's dedication of his poem to Elizabeth I.

In the middle of the following century, Milton's poetry was permeated with the heroic Puritanism of the English Revolution, in which a powerful element of specifically plebeian nationalism raised, in a still largely religious context, social and political demands for freedom and equality that were only to be addressed centuries later. Swept along by—and abetting—the revolutionary mood of mid-seventeenth-century England, Milton wrote tracts against episcopal control of the church, a defense of freedom of the press *(Areopagitica),* and pamphlets defending the idea of divorce and the execution of Charles I.[21]

Similarly, the English and German romantic poets in general, and Shelley in particular, were inspired by the transgressive power of the French Revolution, which, while combating traditional church and feudal monarchy, gave birth to the new collective religions of nationalism and socialism, comparable in their radical thrust both to the heroic Puritanism that had inspired Milton and his contemporaries in seventeenth-century England and to the national resistance to the Roman Church that characterized Spenser's poetry and the English Reformation of the sixteenth century. Both nationalism and socialism reflected the popular strata's needs for new belief systems in the rapidly developing urban commercial society. Also rooted in this society, however, and generally corrosive for its new secular religions, alternately exploiting and subverting them, was the capitalist individualism of the age. If the poets of the era were dazzled by the revolution and the collective beliefs it nurtured, they were usually skeptical, from a naturalist position, about its bourgeois, urban framework and were frankly hostile to capitalist individualism.[22]

Romantic poets nonetheless saw their world transformed by the events of 1789–93. Increasingly liberated from the sinecures and patronage of aristocratic salons by the new middle-class public and the literary marketplace, able to create their own aesthetic and social space (in cafés, periodicals, literary circles, and cénacles), writers gave more weight than ever before to libertarian ideals of personal emancipation, ideals that had been implicit centuries earlier in Rabelais and Villon and had been vigorously advanced a couple of decades before the Revolution by the poets of the German Sturm und Drang. If, appalled by revolutionary terror and Napoleonic despotism, they came to mistrust violent revolt, many of the English and German romantics—Wordsworth, Hölderlin, the Schlegels, Byron, Shelley—supported communal experimentation and held to esoteric beliefs celebrating nature and mutual love. These tendencies were sustained by what they saw as the exalted sentiments of the triumphant people and by the intense friendships of the new literary and artistic circles. The philosophical systems the romantic poets invoked were often pagan and neo-Platonic, anti-utilitarian, based on ideas of circular time, and they opposed the Christian or neo-Christian and utilitarian notions of linear progress common to the new bourgeois cultures.[23]

Whatever their reservations about the French Revolution (and regardless of the subsequent conservatism of a number of romantic poets), the importance of the Revolution as a beacon of hope against the perpetuation of ancient tyrannies is unmistakable, and nowhere more explicitly than in Shelley's *The Revolt of Islam,* written only two years before *Prometheus Unbound.* Shelley's readings on the French Revolution led him, in the central part of his *Revolt of Islam* that depicts the Revolution triumphant, to the portrayal of a revolutionary festival which combines details of the *fête de fédération* of 1790 and the *fête de l'Être Suprême* of 1793.[24] The unleashing of fantasies of transgression in the private as well as the public realm is apparent in the fact that Shelley, atheist and apostle of free love that he was, originally depicted as the central love relationship of his long poem—a counterweight to the scenes of terrifying oppression, revolution, and renewed terror—an incestuous love of brother and sister.[25]

PROMETHEUS UNBOUND

Shelley's *Prometheus Unbound* was a dramatic poem in four "Acts," of which the first followed fairly closely the structure of Aeschylus's *Prometheus Bound.* The Greek play was the basis of the interpretation of Prometheus as rebelling against tyrannical authority, but it was not lost on Shelley that in having Prometheus claim Themis and Gaia as his mother, Aeschylus made the rebellious Prometheus, child of the pre-Olympian chthonic deities of

ancient Hellas, the loyal offspring of Justice and Earth. Both divine arche-
types are shaping forces of the character of Shelley's Prometheus.

The thirst for justice, particularly social justice, is evident in Prometheus's denunciation of the human misery caused by Zeus in depriving man
of fire. In fact, for the educated readers of 1819, aware that Shelley was the
enfant terrible of English radicalism, the terrorization of the champion of humankind by Jupiter could not help but evoke the repression of European
revolutions at the hands of the restored ancien régimes, already depicted
graphically in Shelley's *Revolt of Islam.* For many, the chaining of Prometheus to a rock also brought to mind the imprisonment of Napoleon on
the rock of Saint Helena, but Shelley disliked Napoleon as a despot who
had usurped the revolution: there is little doubt that his main point of reference was the crushed revolution in France and the triumph, everywhere
in Europe, of its worst enemies.

The significance of Gaia is evident in Prometheus's (and Shelley's) vision
of a harmony between man and nature, represented by the wedding of Prometheus to a goddess who symbolized natural abundance. Relying on a version of the Prometheus legend recounted only by Herodotus,[26] Shelley gave
Prometheus for his spouse not Hesione—as in Aeschylus—but Asia, one of
the daughters of Ocean. Of all the earth's continents, Asia was most identified in the culture of Shelley's time with mystical nature religions, particularly in India, whose language and culture were being explicated
around the time of Shelley's birth by the orientalist and poet Sir William
Jones. (Jones seems to have had a personal tie with Shelley's college at
Oxford, and his *Palace of Fortune* had provided a model for *The Revolt of
Islam.*)[27] Indeed, Shelley's wife, Mary, the daughter of William Godwin
and Mary Wollstonecraft, wrote after the poet's death that "Asia . . . was,
according to other mythological interpretations, the same as Venus and
Nature. When the benefactor of mankind is liberated, Nature resumes the
beauty of her prime, and is united to her husband, the emblem of the human race, in perfect and happy union."[28]

Accordingly, acts 3 and 4 of *Prometheus Unbound* elaborate an earthly
utopia that would follow on the dethroning of Jupiter by Demo[s]gorgon,
the liberation of Prometheus by Hercules, and the marriage of Prometheus
and Asia. In a dialogue with Apollo, Ocean, father of Prometheus's spouse,
signals the nature of the transformed world that will result from the Titan's
liberation by promising an end to "blood and groans, / And desolation, and
the mingled voice / Of slavery and command" (3.2.29–31). In the new era
of reconciliation between man and nature, humankind will be guided over
the seas

> by the light
> Of wave-reflected flowers, and floating odours,
> And music soft, and mild, free, gentle voices,
> And sweetest music, such as spirits love.
>
> (3.2.31–34)

Prometheus himself exits from Shelley's poetic drama in some seventy lines of act 3, largely addressed to his beloved Asia. He proposes that she and her sisters Ione and Panthea (who consoled him during his long martyrdom) retire with him to

> a cave,
> All overgrown with trailing odorous plants,
> Which curtain out the day with leaves and flowers,
> And paved with veinèd emerald, and a fountain
> Leaps in the midst with an awakening sound. . . .
> A simple dwelling, which shall be our own;
> Where we will sit and talk of time and change,
> As the world ebbs and flows, ourselves unchanged.
>
> (3.3.10–14, 22–24)

In this womblike paradise, Ione will "chant fragments of sea-music, / Until I weep, when ye [Asia] shall smile away / The tears she brought." To this cave will come

> echoes of the human world, which tell
> Of the low voice of love, almost unheard,
> And dove-eyed pity's murmured pain, and music,
> Itself the echo of the heart, and all
> That tempers or improves man's life, now free;
>
> (3.3.44–48)

The Titan also anticipates a heightened human awareness of aesthetics, a sensitivity to: "lovely apparitions,"

> the progeny immortal
> Of Painting, Sculpture, and rapt Poesy,
> And arts, though unimagined, yet to be.
>
> (3.3.54–56)

In this new world, "man grows wise and kind, / And, veil by veil, evil and error fall." Prometheus's last lines are addressed to "the spirit of the hour," which he instructs to take a mystic shell whose "sound must be both sweet and strange" and to bear it "over the cities of mankind . . . loosening its mighty music," which M. H. Abrams interprets as the apocalyptic last trump.[29]

Thus, for all Shelley's Enlightenment-inspired materialism, he clearly yearns for a psychological and ethical revolution that he felt must accompany the political one, a precondition for cultural as well as material progress. According to Abrams, the close of *Prometheus Unbound* signifies that "man's moral conversion from self-concern and hate to imaginative fellow-feeling and love will liberate his full powers of scientific, technological, and artistic creativity, by means of which he will in the course of time remake his physical and social environment into a form adequate to human needs."[30]

If, however, there are a number of references in *Prometheus Unbound* to the unleashing of reason, science, and technology, the dominant note is the mystical transformation of nature into a beneficent force and the flourishing in this new cosmos of art, friendship, and love. Act 4 presents the liberation of human powers in a fantastic landscape of articulate cosmic forces, a poetic vision comparable to the apocalyptic poetry of William Blake or to the magnificent paintings of natural forces and mythical landscapes by J. M. W. Turner and John Martin, Shelley's contemporaries. The earth and the moon converse anthropomorphically, and a chorus of hours and spirits joyously evokes a world transformed by the release of Prometheus and the elimination of his Olympian oppressors. At one point, the chorus of spirits and hours chants:

> Then weave the web of the mystic measure;
> From the depths of the sky and the ends of the earth,
> Come, swift Spirits of might and of pleasure,
> Fill the dance and the music of mirth,
> As the waves of a thousand streams rush by
> To an ocean of splendour and harmony!
>
> (4.129–34)

To this, the chorus of spirits replies in four six-line stanzas, of which the last shows the combining of all human capacities in the name of the Titan:

> And our singing shall build
> In the void's loose field
> A world for the Spirit of Wisdom to wield;
> We will take our plan
> From the new world of man
> And our work shall be called the Promethean.
>
> (4.153–58)

While succeeding "Semichoruses" tell of "the spirits which build a new earth and sea," the dominant note is the merging of nature and art in "the enchantments of earth," as in

> We whirl, singing loud, round the gathering sphere,
> Till the trees, and the beasts, and clouds appear
> From its chaos made calm by love, not fear.
>
> (4.169–71)

and the answering

> We encircle the ocean and mountains of earth,
> And the happy forms of its death and birth
> Change to the music of our sweet mirth.
>
> (4.172–74)

The final lines of *Prometheus Unbound* are given to Demogorgon, the voice of revolutionary destiny, summing up the significance of the Titan hero in terms of defiance of the gods, defiance made heroic by suffering, hope, love, and forgiveness of the fallen tyrant:

> This, like thy glory, Titan, is to be
> Good, great and joyous, beautiful and free;
> This is alone Life, Joy, Empire, and Victory.
>
> (4.576–78)

THE PARADOX

This denouement of Prometheus's liberation in the reconciliation of culture and nature is very far from "the technocratic Prometheanism of the Enlightenment project" decried by Green theorists, or "Promethean assumptions of human separation from and superiority over 'Nature,'" or the "Promethean aspiration to transcend all natural limits on human self-realization."[31] Kate Soper, however, from whose *What Is Nature?* I have taken these contemporary notions, introduces an intriguing "paradox of Prometheanism" which suggests the complexity of the subject. She sees this paradox in Mikhail Bakhtin's way of looking at the relationship between the early modern "return to nature"—exemplified for him in Rabelais's emphasis on the grotesque body—and the modern "celebration of human powers to master it."[32]

In the Bakhtinian interpretation, Rabelais, writes Soper, "was seeking . . . to place carnivalesque inversion at the service of a revolutionary cosmology that would topple the Mediaeval conception of the universe, and thus release man from those cosmic fears which religion had always used to oppress him." Against traditional Christianity, which had exploited human fears of natural forces to subordinate man and nature hierarchically to an all-powerful deity, Rabelais, according to Bakhtin, invoked traditional folklore. In "the struggle against cosmic terror," the Russian theorist wrote, Rabelais rejected spiritual abstractions, relying "on the material principle in man himself . . . in his own body. He became aware of the cosmos within himself."[33] This self-awareness of human materiality thus recentered the heaven/hell dichotomy of Christianity into an upper body/lower body opposition, for which, analogously, the material "underworld/underground . . . was also the source of all true wealth and abundance." Bakhtin, who related the Rabelaisian inversion to older traditions in which the underworld was a source of humor, saw grotesque realism as a means of defeating fear by laughter. Rabelais, by creating a humanized cosmos, pointed to humankind's joyous future.

In this inversion of the traditional Christian cosmology, which had rejected the body from its notion of humanity, Rabelais, says Soper, joined other Renaissance thinkers—Pico della Mirandola, Giordano Bruno, Tommaso Campanella, and Marsilio Ficino—in the creation of "a new Promethean humanism." As opposed to the fixed Great Chain of Being, with its immutable hierarchy, this Promethean humanism viewed man "as unfinished and incomplete [which] is to allow him to become capable of anything." In the gods' fear of Pantagruel—whose children, according to Rabelais, might, by the discovery of some power-giving herb "visit the source of hell, the springs of the rain, the forge where lightning is produced . . . invade the regions of the moon, intrude within the territories of the celestial signs," and end up becoming divine themselves—Soper identifies traditional society's fear of "Prometheanism . . . symbol of human technical capacity."[34]

Thus the paradox: whereas earlier the animal body had been identified with base nature against spirituality and mind, in Rabelais the material body, reunited with humankind's mental powers,

> exposes adulation of the spirit as the product of superstition, religious bigotry and cosmic fear [and] their energy symbolizes the human technological capacity for mastery over that "nature" to which the "gods," as false idols of our own thinking, had previously held us in thrall. . . . The reversion to human nature in all its carnality and affinity with animality provides the support for an Enlightenment type of confidence in technical mastery and human dominion over nature.[35]

To Soper's "paradox of Prometheanism," the romantic Shelleyan version of the myth adds a second layer: the notion of a human nature which can find ultimate satisfaction only in reconciliation with, rather than "technical mastery and human dominion over," the rest of nature. In these terms, technology is valid only if it furthers such reconciliation. If, until now, every ideological consolidation of the political revolutions of modernity—the English, the French, the Russian, and the Chinese—has ended by distorting their original impulse of liberation into cults of power, that betrayal cannot extinguish the impulse of Promethean creativity, both individual and collective, which was their source. Perhaps, as Shelley intuited in his poetry, particularly in *The Revolt of Islam,* humankind as a whole was too brutalized at the onset of those revolutions not to fall prey to such cults. Betrayal it nonetheless has been, not only of the revolutions but of the Promethean spark that inspired them. This need not be so today, at the outer end of the long social, economic, and political development of modernity.

The Dual Character of Promethean Modernity

Shelley's transfigured, romantic version of the modern myth of Prometheus, which ties the notion of social justice to a transcendent creativity, is the point of departure for this book. Though largely forgotten today, romantic Prometheanism, I argue, is dormant rather than dead and may be due for a reawakening. To buttress that perspective, in this second part of this introduction I will outline the historical origins of Promethean modernity, its internal contradictions, and the main lines of the critiques of it by the Promethean intellectuals of the modern era. Later, in Part I, "The Rise and Decline of the Modern Prometheus," I present detailed interpretations of the ideologies and institutions of nationalism, socialism, and consumer capitalism. All these versions of Prometheanism, insofar as they have aimed to inspire and justify technological prowess and productivity through a humanistic ideal, have been fraudulent, self-contradictory, and self-destructive.

THE REBIRTH OF PROMETHEUS IN PREMODERN EUROPE

The Promethean ethos emerged gradually in Europe between the sixteenth and the nineteenth centuries.[36] Its rise was dependent on the revolutions in social organization, thought, and mentality we call modernity, revolutions which in turn were contingent on the gradual disintegration of older systems of social, political, economic, and cultural organization: feudal absolutism and Christian corporatism. Those who presently manage the world's dominant economic and political organizations assume that the version of the Promethean ethos that mandates ever-expanding productivity and individual energy is the only alternative to decadence and barbarism, but in fact it is a relatively new mentality, riven with internal contradictions.

To comprehend the unstable character of the new ideal, we should recall how it rose from within the social-political structures and ideologies of the feudal, absolutist ancien régime, in their day considered eternal by those in power. Indeed, the main ideologies that took the place of the theocratic basis of the old regime—nationalism, socialism, and capitalist individualism—all were latent within it, unleashed by its internal divisions and collapse in the period between the Protestant Reformation of the sixteenth century and the democratic nationalist revolutions of 1848. In this section I shall first summarize the principal phases of the foundation period of the modern system, before the dominance of Promethean ideologies. Then I shall discuss the intractable internal divisions that form the characteristic feature of European history, divisions that explain why the various manifestations of the Promethean spirit were able to flourish first there and not, say, in China. In the light of these divisions, I shall then return to the ideology of political and religious absolutism and to the national democratic revolutions that destroyed absolutism in England and France and put it on the defensive everywhere else.

The Emergence of the Promethean Spirit   The Promethean ethos, increasingly explicit in the writings of philosophers, defines man in terms of his capacity to transform the world by work (*Homo faber*). The predominant notion of this ethos posits the necessary triumph of rational will over nature and instinct, both in our understanding of the way we view the world (epistemology) and in our shaping of that world by our categorizations of it (ontology). The intellectual operations characterizing this triumph were, historians of ideas agree, first defined by Francis Bacon and René Descartes in the seventeenth century. However, the principal phases of development of the notion that humankind could transform its worldly existence precede seventeenth-century rationalism and extend to the nineteenth century. Schematically the main historical phases and aspects of this evolution look roughly like this:

   1. The successful sixteenth- and seventeenth-century challenge to the authoritarian church of the Middle Ages by the Protestant Reformation, representing the force of individual conscience. Powerfully assisted by the invention of the printing press as well as by social and political turmoil attendant on divisions in the church, this triumph of the indi-

vidual's right to study and interpret the word of God laid the basis for subsequent intellectual breakthroughs made by Galileo, Copernicus, Kepler, and Newton in interpreting the divinely ordered natural cosmos. In other words, the Reformation paved the way for:

2. The scientific revolution in the way European elites came to look at nature, accompanied by the rational view of man and society of the Enlightenment. Stimulating, as well as accompanied by, the rise of philosophical skepticism with regard to traditional beliefs and moral precepts, these new notions of a universe unified by rational laws of physics and logic served as a rational foundation for:

3. The state absolutism that came to dominate the chaos of feudal relations and independent cities in the early modern period. When, however, this absolutism appeared to have become corrupted morally, socially, and politically by the feudal and religious structures it had inherited and subjugated, the Enlightenment philosophy that had initially supported rational absolutism attacked it and became the seedbed of:

4. The Western European and North American national revolutions in the period up to the revolutions of 1848, and the Asian and eastern European ones in the twentieth century, revolutions that were preconditions for that political and economic modernization which we can otherwise define as the joint rise of the bureaucratic nation-state and modern capitalism.

On the one hand, all four of these historical forces—Reformation, scientific revolution/Enlightenment, absolutism, and national revolutions—can be viewed as expressing the creative power of the modern mentality, the Promethean ethos. On the other, they have created, through the modern institutional frameworks for the realization of *Homo faber* and for the separation of reason from a despised nature, the reifications of Prometheus. They have also nurtured secondary mentalities and ideologies of the modern age which represented and justified that separation and with which those forces interacted symbiotically. The secondary mentalities can be summarized in terms of:

5. The instrumental rationalization and centralization of all spheres of thought and activity: economic, political, religious, scientific, military—discussed by Max Weber as aspects of formal rationality—which vastly strengthened both the bureaucratic state and commercial capitalism, and:

6. The closely related "civilizing process" discerned by the sociologist

Norbert Elias and subsequently by the historian Robert Muchembled and others.[37] In this "process," the new social order created by rationalization and centralization redefined private morality in terms of cultivated self-restraint, and superego controls taught civilized men to view instinctually based, "irrational," or "superstitious" thought and behavior as an atavistic barbarism.

For purposes of simplicity, one can group modern ideologies under the dominant political-economic systems mentioned above: nationalism, liberal capitalism, social democracy, communism, and fascism. These and all their variants—democratic and conservative nationalism, Stalinism, Maoism, nazism, Christian democracy, third world nationalism, neoliberalism, etc.—are dependent in one way or another on the secondary mentalities permeating modern institutions: the instrumental rationalization of everything and the civilizing process. Religious fundamentalisms of the Muslim, Christian, Jewish, and Hindu varieties are, somewhat like fascism, versions of "reactionary modernism" in which techniques and codes of conduct derived from these mentalities are entwined with a profoundly conservative set of beliefs to prevent, by exclusion and terror, any further flights of the free Promethean spirit.[38]

In so doing, religious fundamentalism returns to the obscured roots of modernity in the feudal theocratic realms of the Middle Ages, from which only the inherent divisiveness of those realms permitted the Promethean spirit to evolve.

Mentalities in Medieval and Premodern Europe   Medieval Europe emerged from the breakup of the Roman empire and the Muslim and Norse invasions as a chaos of warring units, within which three spheres of social action gradually emerged in an unstable balance: a decentralized political economy based on agriculture, a centralizing politico-religious administrative force, and a somewhat marginal, trade-centered nexus of towns and markets. From roughly the eleventh century on, conflict was latent, and often manifest, within as well as between each of these spheres.

Within the decentralized agrarian realm, peasant communities were gradually subjugated and enserfed by feudal overlords.

Within the centralizing sphere, hereditary princes of the new monarchies and prelates organized by the Roman ecclesia engaged in a shadowy struggle for power over what both of them recognized as a divinely created order of society.

At a lesser level of importance, within the urban economy, artisan corporations struggled with merchant and banking guilds, oriented to international trade, for control over the governments of city-states and "free" cities in many parts of Europe.

Moreover, between the decentralized feudal nobility and the centralizing princes, between the Christian faith as defined by Rome and the local beliefs and rituals of an agrarian village life, conflicts were always latent, frequently bloody, and usually won by the princes of the realm and the church. An implicit antagonism between urban centers of trade and industry and the agrarian-based feudal-monarchic system only rarely erupted into violence; such antagonism was long overshadowed by the symbiotic relationship between the financial power of the cities and the needs of the feudality and princes (including the princes of the church) for money to fuel their wars and satisfy their need for conspicuous consumption. When this conflict between merchants and princes became manifest, however, as in seventeenth-century England and eighteenth-century France, it destroyed the entire system: out of the debris arose the ideologies of modernity mentioned above.

Religion, politics, social organization, and economics were inextricably intertwined in these conflicts. But crucial to their outcome was the struggle for the body and soul of the peasantry, disciplined by the church, exploited by the aristocracy. For at the local level of experience, most people lived in isolated rural villages where traditional beliefs about the supernatural were incompatible with the monotheistic Christianity of God-the-Father and with the idea of linear historical development to a Last Judgment. Just under a surface acceptance of Christianity, bishops and inquisitors were appalled to find archaic mentalities akin to those of antique pantheism, in which dependence on the nurturant productivity of the soil corresponded to a matriarchal element, and the implicit historical notion was cyclical, assuming the eternal return of the seasons and of the forces of nature rather than the linear movement to a last trump proclaimed in 1 Cor. 15.[39] Such mentalities were of course compatible, in a way Christianity could not be, with the decentralized agrarian social existence established in the Neolithic age and within which, mutatis mutandis, the majority of Europeans were born and bred until the late nineteenth century, and most Asians until the second half of the twentieth.[40]

In most parts of Europe, autarchic agricultural communities fell under the formal control of another decentralized structure: the feudal system of personal dependency created by military overlords during the chaotic tribal invasions that followed the disintegration of Roman military and administrative power. The price of feudal "protection" was the surrender of many traditional village freedoms, replaced by serfdom, tithes, and labor services to the overlord and his vassals. Often inarticulate but long-standing resentment of that loss was the basis of peasant uprisings in many parts of Europe in the late Middle Ages and the early modern period. Such uprisings were the breeding grounds of premodern movements of messianic or millenarian communism, like that of Thomas Münzer's followers during the German Reformation, Gerard Winstanley's "Diggers" in the English Revolution, or "Agrarian Law" adherents of Gracchus Baboeuf in the French one; distant echoes of these movements haunted the socialist and communist ideologies of modern times, and can still be heard in third world peasant movements like the Mexican Zapatistas and the Brazilian Movement of Landless Peasants.

Between the decentralized agrarian sphere, with its uneasy local coexistence of peasant and overlord, and the centralizing powers of the territorial prince and of Christianity, tension was constant. The territorial prince strove to expand his domain by intermarriage, alliance, and war against the local aristocracy or against smaller and weaker princes, who, of course, resisted wherever possible. In England centralization was brought by the Norman knights, who conquered the less developed Anglo-Saxon realm in 1066 and imposed on it the excellent administrative system created under the dukes of Normandy. In Germany, feudal resistance, followed by the religious disunion of the sixteenth century, succeeded for close to a millennium, despite a token emperor, in preventing unification: repeated concessions to German princes for military cooperation in enforcing the Holy Roman Empire's claims on Italy undermined imperial power. In the early nineteenth century, Napoleon found Germany divided into more than three hundred sovereign principalities, which he reduced to about thirty. The reforms he initiated continued after the Napoleonic era, eventually leading to unification (minus Catholic Austria) under Bismarckian Prussia. In France, feudal resistance to central control broke down earlier than in Germany, but the unification of the realm nonetheless took the Capetian, Valois, and Bourbon monarchs over five hundred years, being marked by wars in most directions from the small territorial base of medieval French kings, the Île-de-France.[41]

In the midst of these conflicts, everywhere in Europe the centralized ecclesiastical organization of the Roman Church imposed its own definition of Christian conviction on illiterate peasant villagers. Its success in colonizing the minds and controlling the behavior of the peasantry was similar to that of the monarchy in imposing the king's peace on feudal lords and commercial cities.[42]

The relatively small cities and the incipient regional and continental trading networks—the third element of the medieval balance of power—

were overshadowed by the powerful feudal agrarian order that dominated most of the continent, but they were crucial to its dissolution. For it was to the wealth of the cities that the princes turned to finance their wars and their pomp,[43] and it was international trade that offered local feudal lords the luxuries they had discovered in the Orient during the crusades and which became the symbols of their power and status. To pay for these luxuries, they increasingly, in the latter part of the Middle Ages, had to exchange the servile status of their peasants for money, thus freeing them in many parts of Europe and undermining local structures of domination.[44]

The Religious Synthesis and the Civilizing Mission   By the sixteenth century, substituting for this traditional domination, the processes of rationalization and centralization discerned by Max Weber were transforming the medieval feudal chaos into absolutisms of state and church (in Germany, at the level of the numerous feudal principalities). A new authoritarian synthesis integrated all the decentralized forces of feudal lords, peasant villages, and free cities that had characterized the earlier period. This synthesis was sustained by two ideological constructions. One was a religious consecration and stabilization of social existence: with legislation imperfect and frequently unenforceable, the wolf in man was constrained by customary social bonds and rituals, backed up by the state. These were strengthened by the sanction of a universal church. Every tie of vassal to lord had its sacral aspect; every neighborhood, trade, and festivity, its patron saint and its religious confraternity.

The other ideological cement was the initial religiously based version of the "civilizing mission," a manipulation of the "civilizing process" referred to above. From Christianity's stark juxtaposition of a (high) omnipotent God to the (low) human world, theorists of absolutism extrapolated the moral superiority and mandated dominion of the king over his subjects, the bishop over his flock, men over women, fathers over sons, pedagogues over disciples, masters over servants, and feudal lords over their peasants.[45] Subsequently bourgeois elites were to found their authority over the lower orders on a modified version of the civilizing mission.

Psychologically and philosophically these polarities were buttressed by overlapping assumptions of the superiority of man over nature, of mind over matter, and of reason and moral will over emotion and desire (translated topographically as the upper body over the lower)—assumptions that have equally grounded the "civilizing missions" of church, state, and middle class in the modern era. Just as aristocrats living from feudal dues and rents defined themselves as "above" plebeians forced to work for a living, urban

commoners applied the high/low dichotomy socially to the relation between those who worked with their minds (jurists and doctors—the free
professions) and those who worked with their hands.[46] The assumptions
were that everything that was "high" had a relation both of authority and
tutelage to (or at least control over) everything that was "low," and—following Descartes—that the metaphysically "high" and "low" were distinct
and impermeable qualities. Bishop Bossuet and others who hailed this system believed, as does Mr. Fukuyama about triumphant neoliberalism, that
it was the "end of history."

Repressing local belief systems, spontaneous aggression, and all other
behavior that civilizers deemed deviant, the "civilizing mission" was rooted
in classical philosophy and early Christian theology, but it only became a
pervasive ideology of social improvement, supported by church, state, and
bourgeois elites, from the period of the Reformation and Counter Reformation onward. Initially, its objects were the feudal elites of the centralized
royal courts. Subsequently the peasantries and—particularly under bourgeois hegemony in the nineteenth and twentieth centuries—the urban
working classes of Western and Central Europe were "improved" by it. Such
new codes of thought and conduct were made obligatory from without by
laws and courts and from within by social pressure as well as by new religious orders and sects—Catholic, Protestant, and secular. They were a necessary replacement for traditional mentalities that were being undermined
by the rise of absolutism as well as by the new bourgeois strata: the mentalities of feudal society, of local peasant communities and of premodern belief systems everywhere. It is thus not surprising that the first major pur-
veyors of the civilizing mission were the religious and political authorities
of absolutism.

Nonetheless, the apparent power and solidity of the new absolutist order
celebrated in royal courts of the seventeenth century was hardly more stable
than the feudal chaos it replaced. Because Europe was internally fractured,
for reasons of geopolitics and on grounds of principle, into a multiplicity
of power centers, this order was unable and unwilling to create a stable
European empire under centralized control.[47] Internal divisions were compounded by external irritants: its cities, urban leagues, and states were divided, from the sixteenth century onward, by competition for mercantile
control over the non-European world. Even its agrarian feudal order, hostile to the commercial values of the marketplace but avid for the luxuries
that symbolized status and power, had been open since the crusades to the
disintegrative, money-oriented impact of trade with the East. Moreover
its religious establishment bore within it the corrosive chemistry of both

rationalism and heretical creeds of poverty.[48] Thus was the absolutist authoritarianism of the new order assaulted in the states of early modern Europe by religious, ideological, and mercantile winds of change that gradually accelerated to hurricane force.

Democratic Nationalist Revolutions   In one country after another, dissident elites, increasingly supported by the middle and lower classes, undermined and attacked the authority of the church, the absolute prince and the feudal landlord-aristocrat—successfully in sixteenth and seventeenth century England and Holland and (after a false start under the aegis of late-sixteenth-century French Calvinism) in eighteenth-century France.[49] Germany took longer to exit from the absolutist order, since, given the political and religious disunity of the German states and the power of Prussian conservatism, the old regime was actually strengthened by the spread of Lutheranism in the sixteenth century and the later participation of its elites in the Enlightenment. Only in the nineteenth century were both national unification and capitalist hegemony possible in Germany. But bourgeois liberals failed in 1848 to end or even curb the authoritarian and bureaucratic Prussian monarchy. This failure insured that German nationalism, which conservatives stimulated to keep both liberals and socialists from power, would reach a peacefully modern and mercantile framework only after taking Europe through the hell of two world wars and Nazi totalitarianism.

Among the modern utopias, nationalism has probably been discussed the most. Ernest Gellner described it as the "sentiment" appropriate to the modern industrial era, where high culture elites have used it as a way of legitimizing their authority.[50] Democratic nationalism, inspiration of most revolutionary movements in the first half of the nineteenth century, saw the merging of ethnic and political unity—one people, one state—as the criterion of political virtue and the path to this-worldly salvation. In its early stages, it encouraged freedom as well as solidarity, but its closure to those outside the nation has put it at odds with the universal humanism of the Promethean ethos.

Nationalist ideologies, trickling down from the middle to the lower classes in the course of the nineteenth century, replaced the complex tissue of allegiances and identities—local, feudal, hierarchical, and corporatist—that held together preindustrial agrarian civilizations. Initially progressive, legitimate incarnations of Promethean idealism, expressing powerful impulses to freedom and solidarity within newfound senses of national identity, they revealed their limitations and dangers in the large and small wars of the twentieth century. Even their less violent manifestations have encouraged exclusions, and nationalist participation with capitalism in the imperialist exploitation of the non-Western world destroyed any possibility of local self-determination. Indeed, wherever democracy and freedom were created within what Benedict Anderson calls "imagined communities," they came at the expense of the more palpable solidarities of innumerable real local communities, whose languages, identities, and mentalities had to be crushed to make way for the, at best, indirectly democratic power of new nation-states.

In fact, during the nineteenth and twentieth centuries, everywhere outside a thin band of states in Western Europe and North America, something similar happened. Through eclectic creeds that frequently combined nationalist, socialist, and capitalist ideals with an authoritarian or totalitarian political framework, new elites wrested control over state, economy, and social order from age-old regimes based on exploitation of the peasantry. Whether they replaced the moribund monarchies of Mediterranean Europe or decaying bureaucratic empires, as in Russia, China, and Turkey, or local satraps of European imperialism, as in much of the Middle East and India, the modernizing regimes they installed, precisely because they aimed to destroy not only the webs of beliefs but the village communities and local identities on which such old regimes were based, were dependent for legitimacy on some version of democratic nationalist ideology. To secure popular support, they sometimes tolerated for a brief period a variety of peasant-proprietor socialism, but they regularly reversed this phase to replace it by forced, state-sponsored industrialism, and they usually reverted at the end of the road to some form of market capitalism. Spain, Russia, China, and Vietnam are well known examples.

In leveling the complex religious and social structures of the old regime, democratic nationalist revolutions, whatever their aims, presented commercial and industrial capitalism with broad vistas of opportunity. Accompanying democratic nationalism as an ideological cement of industrial and commercial modernity—and celebrating more openly than nationalism the *Homo faber* aspect of the Promethean ethos—have been liberal individualism, the credo of the new economic and political elites, followed by socialism, the ideology of those exploited by capitalist industry or alienated from its atomistic individualism, and, subsequently in Europe and North America, the welfare state, a compromise between socialism and capitalism that promised the security and solidarity of the first with the market economy of the second. Today we endure the hegemonic (and much discussed) ideology of personal style, wealth, and power of consumer capitalism, triumphant after the demise of all its predecessors and competitors—a hedonistic and crassly materialist democratization of liberal individualism. Paradoxically, the ever expanding corporate industrialism which national revolutions stimulated by their demolition of ancien régime restrictions has now become, in the age of multinational global capitalism, a force that weakens, where it does not nullify, the power of nations to determine their own destinies.

Clearly the more benign version of this metamorphosis, occurring earlier in the capitalist and democratic-nationalist revolutions of England, France, Holland, and the United States, was exceptional. But whatever the path to economic, social, and political modernity, for many of those who hailed the demise of the ancien régime as the dawn of freedom, as the liberation of Prometheus, the modern world created by these revolutions was as deficient as the one it replaced.

PROMETHEUS REIFIED

The problem has been that in this modern world all the major ideologies and institutions—starting with those idealistic offspring of the modernist revolution, nationalism, and socialism—have ended in cults of power. The deformed offspring of nationalism, totalitarian Nazism and Fascism, pretended concern for nature while crushing liberty and humanity in the name of national power. Stalinist Communism, the bastard child of socialism and Czarist despotism, destroyed liberty in the name of working-class power and, while desperately mimicking Western industrialism, created the worst ecological disasters of modern times. The currently dominant neoliberal order of global capitalism, regulator of our economic, social, political, and cultural existence, was well on its way to making the world unlivable when it experienced, in the attack on the World Trade Center, what Ulrich Beck called its "Chernobyl."

This order, like other, competing ideological pretenders to the incarnation of Prometheus, and like the Puritan asceticism which in Max Weber's imagery became an "iron cage" for the worldly productivity of modern man, has suffocated the creative energy that produced it. Despite our enormous wealth and productivity, we are now facing a prolonged era of cultural and material impoverishment. Our property system appears capable of survival only on condition of growing inequalities between rich and poor, which entail massive suffering both within the northern industrialized countries and between them and the largely southern rest of the world. Our representative democracies will depend on the increasing marginalization or repression of dissent. Worst of all, our very productivity, given its present mismanagement, menaces the earth with biocide.

Behind these threats to our future lies a tangled skein of moral issues, material interests, obsolete institutions, and bankrupt utopias.

Ethically, as the central ideal of modernity and its institutions, the Promethean ethos was associated, during the great social revolutions that leveled the old regimes, with the modernist values I have mentioned: freedom, solidarity, social justice, rationality, and productivity. In the course of time however, this ethos was ideologically defined in terms of the ideologies I have mentioned, each a utopia in itself, but often interacting with one or more of the others. These ideological creeds were established either to justify or to contest the suffering inflicted by the institutions of modernity on the majority of the population. Although all such constructions have paid tribute to the ideals that were central to the Promethean ethos, that ethos has been broadly subverted by the institutional and ideological frameworks in which it has been embodied.

Within such frameworks, solidarity and freedom have been caricatured out of recognition, and rationality and social justice, where not ignored, have shrunk to the size of a pocket calculator. What remains of those Promethean values has been subjugated to the end of material increase, with which the means, the work ethic, has been conflated. Variously encouraging *Homo faber* through workhouses, factories, economic plans, gulags and concentration camps, and suburban shopping malls, the ideological progeny of Prometheus offered a veritable supermarket of political and social nostrums to render socially acceptable the mass misery that their quest for power had created: the panaceas of parliamentary democracy, the nation-state, the organized working class, the welfare state, the totalitarian state party, xenophobic national identity, and consumer society. Since the French Revolution, these nostrums have become competing bases for beliefs in the future, modern inheritors of the religions that sanctified power in the agrarian and feudal world.

In the course of time, however, the evolution of liberal capitalism, the uncontested victor in the century-long quarrel between the heirs of Prometheus, came to undermine all of the historical belief systems with which the Promethean ethos has historically been associated and which made the reigns of those heirs acceptable to the masses who suffered their hegemony. This undermining was especially clear in the quarter century preceding the terrorist attacks of September 11. Over the graves of its vanquished totalitarian antagonists, and in the twilight of its social-democratic precursor, neoliberal capitalism pursued a course of globalization which strove to eliminate all alternatives to its rule. In so doing it followed a path of self-destruction comparable to that of the absolutist ancien régimes which, in the course of centralization and bureaucratization, destroyed the feudal institutions and belief systems on whose ambivalent support they depended.

In this book I argue that recapturing the original force of the Promethean ethos, the condition of our moral (and perhaps physical) survival, requires the transcendence of the ideologies and institutions in which it is currently embedded. If the Promethean ideal has served for two centuries as the motor of modernity, the shape it has taken in the contemporary social order now menaces us with a chaotic future of despotism, insecurity, and poverty on an earth that may become uninhabitable. Since September 11, this menace has become sharper than ever.

Reconstructing our institutions to avert these dangers will require a radical reexamination of the relationship between individuals and the social nexus as well as a rethinking of the relation of the human species to the natural world. Without abandoning the Promethean ethos, we must transcend and recreate the forms in which it appears.

This is not the first time modernity has evoked such a critical response, as Shelley's radical aesthetic demonstrates. Indeed, the roots of the aesthetic avant-garde as well as of anarchism and socialism are to be found in the questioning of the modern age that accompanied the initial victories of Promethean liberalism.

EUROPEAN ROMANTICISM AND THE CRITIQUE OF LIBERALISM

The source of much of this questioning was the European romanticism of the first half of the nineteenth century. In a sense, the romantic movement was the aesthetic equivalent of the French Revolution. Just as the Revolution abolished the corporate restrictions on individual deployment in economics and politics, romanticism abolished the classical rules for writing poetry and drama. Socially, it replaced aristocratic patronage of intellectuals and artists by networks of cénacles and coteries, often tied to independent reviews or newspapers. More radically, romanticism replaced the old regime's integration of artists and writers into its corporate order as holders of royal (or aristocratic or church) sinecures with the ideal of the free creative genius. Yet the English and German romantics had only a temporary enthusiasm for the French Revolution, opposing it as the Terror suffocated the initial explosion of liberty, as the Revolution metamorphosed into the Empire and conquered, rather than liberated, the rest of Europe, and as the bourgeois, mercantile culture it unleashed proved hostile to artistic and intellectual imagination. In Germany, moreover, French civilization, as the culture of the cosmopolitan aristocracy and the enemy of the new national literature, was paradoxically identified both with the ancien régime, whose elites were French-speaking, and with its revolutionary gravedigger.[51]

Nonetheless, the reasons for the opposition of European romanticism as

a whole to the institutions of the modern world go further than the particular relationship of German or English romanticism to the Revolution or
to one of its phases. In fact, the roots of romantic protest precede the Revolution, and we must be careful not to exaggerate the artistic "freedom" the
Revolution created. Although this freedom was made possible on a large
scale by the disintegration of the old corporate structures of the ancien
régime, which liberated the artist from the confines of aristocratic patronage and led to a literary marketplace where he was "free" to say what he
liked, it was normally circumscribed by the material precariousness of the
writers and the political orientations of those who put their work into
print—editors and publishers.[52]

Moreover, the origins of social criticism in literature long predate the
Revolution. Molière could easily mock the philistinism of the bourgeoisie,
since that was a standpoint shared by the aristocracy. Criticism of the aristocracy itself may have had to wait for Voltaire and Diderot, and especially
for Beaumarchais, shortly before the shipwreck of the French monarchy in
1789, but the ridiculing of bourgeois banality by the German Sturm und
Drang, roughly contemporaneous with Beaumarchais, was of a different order than that of Molière, anticipating the demonic egoism of English and
French romantics in the nineteenth century.

The Sturm und Drang's aesthetic individualism was a reaction both to
the stifling conformity of the German princely cultures and to the half-
heartedness of the bourgeois individualism that was beginning to prevail in
urban life. Decades before the French Revolution, this small circle of poets
railed against the timidity and philistine conformity of bourgeois existence,
extending the doctrine of individual self-expression from the purely religious and economic spheres to the artist's search for emotional fulfillment
in his life experience as well as in the creations of his imagination.

The French Revolution itself unleashed a storm of social criticism among
German and English poets and intellectuals, both against the bureaucratic,
sclerotic old regime and against the new bourgeois society being created
by the revolution. In Schiller, Novalis, Hölderlin, and Schlegel in Germany
and in Wordsworth, Coleridge, and Blake in England, we see all the elements of a profound universalist critique of modern civilization, borrowing
from mystical versions of Christianity, from cyclical philosophies of history
like that of Vico, and from popular myth and religion. With the exception
of Schiller, all the critical voices I have named were subsequently considered
romantics, though not of the nationalist variety that emerged in Germany
after the French invasion. The dialectical philosophy of Hegel and the importance of nature in Schelling are more refined philosophical versions of

this critique. Byron, Keats, and Shelley, who were followed after 1830 by a large number of French romantic and post-romantic writers, continued the post-revolutionary quest for a critical aesthetic.

The contradictory character of the romantic complaint was noticed long ago by Arthur O. Lovejoy, who despaired of finding a common denominator to it. For alongside of their individualism, another major trait of the romantics was precisely their collectivism. Many romantics, who joined circles or cénacles bound by close friendships, lamented precisely the individualism of the new age, which tended to pit them against one another, and they sought to create a more humane version of the corporate sociability of the defunct regimes.

Some socially oriented romantics echoed defenders of the old regime like Edmund Burke or of a traditional Catholic social order like the Frenchmen Bonald and De Maistre. This was particularly so in Germany, where late romantics like Josef von Görres looked back nostalgically to the supposed corporate harmony of the Middle Ages; in England, Thomas Carlyle did so as well.[53] Many others, however, realized the myth-making character of this celebration of the Middle Ages and strove, on the basis of their own understanding of community, to conceptualize a completely new social order. The numerous variants of this new social vision had in common a linking of the Promethean productive energies released by the French Revolution to the ideals of solidarity and equality that had led common people to sacrifice their lives for the Revolution. At the same time, the new vision rejected both the Terror and the ensuing personal despotism as well as the asocial individualism of the bourgeois hegemony. During the July Monarchy in France this current was represented by the Saint-Simonians, the Fourierists, and the social romantics: George Sand, Pierre Leroux, Eugène Sue, Jules Michelet, and Félicité de Lamennais.[54]

What linked most of these critics of the post-revolutionary age, despite the contradictory character of their criticisms, was the sentiment that they had been had by "modernity," that they had not so much been liberated from the prison of authoritarian control as moved from one jail to another. At the less superficial—and less visible—levels of social reality, that was so. For the new ideologies of post-revolutionary society were uniformly fueled by the reifying mentalities that had characterized the latter phase of the ancien régime. Liberalism, nationalism, and republicanism merely provided a new vocabulary for many of the assumptions that had characterized the earlier dispensation. The metaphysical distinctness and superiority of "high" over "low" was maintained in the hypostatized abstractions of spirit versus matter, man versus nature, reason and will versus emotion, disincarnated mind versus sexualized body, male versus female, elite culture versus popular culture, bourgeois versus plebs. To the contrary, social romanticism challenged all of these dichotomies from a holist position that nonetheless retained the ideal of *Homo faber* central to the Promethean ethos.

Alexis De Tocqueville, a liberal aristocratic critic of the modern order, noted astutely that modern democracies continued and perfected the bureaucratic centralization and leveling of social differences that absolute monarchies had begun. Social romantics like Jules Michelet agreed with this but added a more radical charge: where church and state absolutisms had imposed servility and inhumanity, the laws of the marketplace forced on humankind an asocial servitude which negated the very possibility of fraternity. For those who had hailed the Revolution as the incarnation of liberty and fraternity, the change was largely cosmetic. When Michelet, anticipating the new revolution of 1848, desperately created his own myth of the French people, he traced the origins of the new regime's industrial "machinism" back to the religious, bureaucratic, and military structures of the old monarchy. Michelet indicted both historical Christianity and the "eclectic" philosophy of French liberalism for their reified categories of "high" versus "low": their separation of man from nature, of reason from affect, and of the "thinking" elite from the laboring common people.[55]

French liberal eclecticism, which presided over the transition to capitalist modernity under the July Monarchy, had indeed profound affinities with the Catholic philosophy it was replacing, affinities manifested in the fact that its éminence grise, Victor Cousin, accepted Catholic control over the education of the masses. Cousin reserved for the higher levels of the *"université"*[56] only the education of French elites, whose philosophical outlook was intended to complement, not undermine, church control over the masses. Since the regime's narrow electoral base required at least the tacit support of the church, Orleanist liberals could not confront the Catholics over private secondary education, with the result that when Michelet denounced the growing influence in French education of the outlawed Jesuit order (in *Des Jésuites,* 1843), he found himself fighting a two-front war, against both the Catholics and many of his former liberal friends. It is also highly significant that the Christian theologian Félicité de Lamennais, who, after a conservative start, began his radical phase in the early 1830s by defying the church hierarchy in the name of the new ideals of liberty, ended it as the most conspicuous opponent of Cousin's eclecticism. In his earlier, conservative phase as well as his later radical one, he attacked an essential philosophical position that was common to Catholicism, to *doctrinaire* liberalism, and to the civilizing mission they both espoused: the Cartesian dichotomy of mind and matter.[57]

In fact, throughout Western culture, the more profound attacks on the new dispensation have come from those who, without abandoning the ideals of individual self-deployment and human liberation, saw through the false metaphysics of liberalism. From Fourier to Nietzsche, from libertarian socialism to the contemporary ecological movement, these critics attacked liberalism's assumptions of an ontological opposition between man and nature, between mind and body, as well as its reification of Prometheus into a capitalist culture hero, symbol of the achievement of ever-growing productivity through an economic war of all against all.

It is true that most critics of the new order failed to realize its tenacity and its capacity for strengthening itself by absorbing the arguments of its opponents. Liberals learned to soft-pedal their elitist disdain for the masses and to make the same kinds of compromises with their new aesthetic and democratic oppositions as they had with the older Christian ones. This was less difficult than it seemed at the time.

Avant-garde aesthetics and the criticism of bourgeois philistinism were allowed increasing freedom of expression throughout the nineteenth century in most of Western and Central Europe, but the realm of freedom turned out to be a giant playpen, within which ironic assaults, nihilisms, and aggressions of all sorts could be published (Jarry's *Ubu roi,* for example, a savagely satirical attack on bourgeois authoritarianism, or the German expressionist attacks on authority before World War I) on condition that verbal violence did not affect the "adult" world of the marketplace by becoming physical. When that happened, as with anarchist terrorists and Blanquist or socialist organizers of violent revolutions and general strikes, or the extreme-left violence of the 1970s and 1980s, they underwent an even more violent suppression, and renewed censorships cut off even the verb of revolt.[58] But once the "terrorists" had been safely incarcerated, the playpens were cautiously opened to new forms of verbal truancy. Herbert Marcuse, referring to the license given to extremist criticism in the 1960s, called this repressive tolerance.

Nonetheless, the large arena of tolerated dissent may well turn out to be the birthplace of revolutionary change, just as the Enlightenment tolerated by eighteenth-century French absolutism ultimately turned against it and nurtured the ideas of 1789. In fact, the Promethean impulse of challenging authority, of inventing and creating for humanity by working with nature—expressed through the scientific thought of Galileo and Newton, the philosophy of Descartes, Spinoza, Hegel, and Kant, the literary genius of Rabelais, Milton, Voltaire, Shelley, Goethe, and Hugo—was the gravedigger of Europe's old regimes.

This positive face of Prometheus is more or less what the sociologist

David Riesman referred to as the "autonomous personality" in his classic *The Lonely Crowd.* Riesman placed this personality in the period of "inner-directed" humanity that he saw as beginning with the Renaissance and Reformation and ending in the mid-twentieth century. In positing a continual struggle between such personalities and "the barriers of property . . . of hierarchy . . . of religion," Riesman suggested the tension between the creative side of the Promethean spirit and the ossified ideologies that also claimed the mantle of the fire-bringer. In the realm of material existence, such ideologies—based on productivist, utilitarian moralities of growth and progress and on the various identity codes of nationalisms and classes that are intertwined with those moralities—have served to justify the political, economic, and social institutions of modernity. As belief systems, they are functionally comparable to the religious systems that sacralized the institutions of the premodern world. All of these modernist substitutes for religion are thus reified forms of the Promethean ethos, and as such, in a state of tension with its spontaneous expression as intellectual or aesthetic creativity.

The history of European high culture shows that this tension has been inherent in modernism itself. From the end of the eighteenth century on, modernist intellectuals and poets, sometimes inspired directly by the legend of Prometheus, built their achievements on fundamental criticisms of their world's reified economic, political, and ideological structures. Like Shelley, they did so in the name of nature, humanity, beauty, or the autonomous spirit, multiply violated, they argued, by the institutionalizations of the modernist paradigm.[59]

VIOLENCE AND THE EROSION OF IDENTITY IN THE TWENTIETH CENTURY

Never has such criticism been more necessary than it is today. Coming at the end of what many viewed as the triumph of the rational spirit, the turbulent twentieth century seems often to have involved humankind in a dangerous and bloody return of the violence that the protagonists of the civilizing process thought they had repressed, via Euro-American and Japanese imperialism, fascism, xenophobic nationalism, genocide, and increasingly destructive wars. The notion that these phenomena were ended by the allied victory in World War II is, of course, belied by numerous more or less ideologically inspired massacres since 1945: the near genocidal attack by French governments on the Algerian people in the fifties and by the United States on the Vietnamese in the sixties and seventies; the mass murders perpetrated by the Suharto regime on Indonesian communists in 1965 and on East Timorese in the eighties, by the Khmer Rouge on city dwellers in Cambodia in the seventies, and, in the nineties, by the Hutus on the Tutsis in Rwanda, by virtually all the ethnic components of what used to be Yugoslavia on one another and by many of the components of the disintegrated Soviet empire on their neighbors.

Nonetheless, in no case have these abominations of the last half century threatened a renewal of global warfare, and the postwar period has on the whole been one of generous increases in industrial productivity and affluence, so rapid in the three decades after 1945 that the French even speak of the *trente glorieuses:* the thirty years of economic glory. These were the years in which the Promethean ethos made its triumphant return. It was toward the end of them (1969) that David Landes published his celebratory history of the industrial revolution, *The Unbound Prometheus.* The twentieth century can thus be broadly divided into a first half dominated by nationalist and imperialist rivalries and hatreds, twice degenerating into global war and totalitarian violence, and a second half broadly characterized by the resumption, in a less authoritarian framework, of the civilizing process, characterized by the rapid spread of the ideal and ideology of consumer society.

During the *trente glorieuses* of this second half of the twentieth century, consumerist ideology, swept along by economic reconstruction and decolonization, was embodied in welfare states in Europe and North America, instruments of a broad redistribution of income and security favoring the working and middle classes. In the decades since the oil crisis of the mid-seventies, however, neoliberal globalization has come to replace the Keynesian welfare state as the motor force of consumerism and the accelerating pace of change has reversed this redistribution, bringing vertigo and a sense of imminent catastrophe.

Welfare states, the safety net of the not always dependable postwar prosperity, had been the joint invention of Christian democrats, socialists, and social liberals, designed to recompense the European masses for their loyal sacrifices during the Second World War and to convince them that recourse to revolution was unnecessary to procure material welfare and security.[60] At the end of the 1980s, amid ever louder neoliberal denunciations of the cost and inefficiency of welfare systems, the Soviet Union, the last of the world's great multinational empires, collapsed. As I have indicated, this imperium, which had incarnated the welfare state in a totalitarian and repressive form, was no less concerned with the accumulation of capital than its Western competitors; it merely aimed at that accumulation by state ownership and planning rather than individual investment. Its disappearance, together with that of its eastern European satellites, was the death warrant of the welfare systems established under Western capitalist hegemony to compete with the communist order's social program; at one stroke about half a billion people and one-sixth of the earth's land surface opened up to Euro-American and Japanese investment capital. Western welfare systems lost their raison d'être as capitalism's social insurance against the attractiveness of an unfree but socially secure Soviet system. At the same time the high level of internal demand stimulated by the welfare state became replaceable by new global markets in the formerly closed Eurasian empire and more generally in the new Asian middle classes.

The sudden disappearance of the Soviet bloc was widely heralded as the result of a democratic revolution for both market capitalism and national independence. That disappearance, however, coincided with a decisive weakening of even the possibility of national autonomy and national democracy. During two centuries, nationalist idealism had, in Europe at least, seemed to be the Siamese twin of liberal capitalism. It had been the source of impassioned rhetoric, democratic revolutions, and welfare states, as well as of global imperialism and two world wars. But the worldwide victory of neoliberal capitalism over "communist" (that is, state capitalist) collectivism actually guaranteed the impotence of the nation-state as well as of the democratic decision making of its citizens. In Russia a decade after the collapse of the Soviet system, only a weak, mafia-ridden market economy has survived it.

In the 1990s, it was becoming evident that the European national welfare states, overburdened by the costs of social protection in an age of high unemployment and early retirement, their job markets crippled both by high-tech industrial developments (the replacement of Fordism by "postindustrial" society)[61] and by the social dumping made possible by the global capital market, were confronting a withering-away of a different sort than that promised by Marxist-Leninist ideology. If the menace of capital flight did not force governments into the path of economic virtue—cutting taxes, social services, welfare safety nets, and government regulation of trade and production—the threat of condemnation by the International Monetary Fund and the World Bank obliged compliance to neoliberal doctrine.[62] Under neoliberal hegemony, "supply-side" economics (government policies to stimulate production) took the place of the Keynesian stimulation of "demand," a substitution which has come to undermine consumer confidence or, where advertising whips on mindless consumption, to create the "overspent American" signaled by Juliet Schor's book.[63]

During the 1990s, as news of imminent and immediate ecological catastrophes elbowed national political events off the front page, the environmental front brought a second revelation of national impotence. Nation-states were largely powerless to cope with phenomena endangering their physical integrity, such as global warming. Since these were international problems, and international reductions of the pollutants that damaged climate, earth, air, and water were against the short-term interests of investors, no international agreements could be reached to fend them off or even delay them. Here too the threat of international blackmail from unscrupulous investors has blocked indispensable reform at the level of the nation-state.

Finally, new technological revolutions made possible a global investment market (as it turns out, a highly dangerous one) for speculation in financial capital and promised (or threatened) the end of work, or at least of the kind of secure, lifetime work that supported stable personalities. The result has been a new phase in the uprooting of personal identity. The creation of the modern world depended on new collective self-images of class and nation to take the place of older identities of peasant, artisan, aristocrat, and cleric, identities rooted in villages, towns, and regions. The end of a stable work identity and a viable national identity, signifying the closing of the modern era, destabilizes the social ego and menaces the institutions it supported.[64]

﹩ ﹩ ﹩

Global neoliberalism, the author of these dubious accomplishments, is unlikely to persevere. Before the current malaise, it seemed to be dependent on a casino-like play of financial capital in eternal quest of a quick fix,[65] engineering one high-tech investment bubble after another, which only the expectation of rapid and unceasing capital gains kept from bursting. The resemblance to the pyramid game that destroyed the Albanian economy a few years ago is uncanny. But the partial return, under the whip of terrorism and an Afghan military adventure, to the war Keynesianism of the military-industrial state, or even a "Tobin Tax" regulation of the financial markets (the current "realistic" goal of what remains of the traditional Left) would not touch the underlying problem. The double wall of ecological unsustainability and increasing social inequality, impregnable as long as the basic rules of capitalist expansion remain in place, will continue to block the human future.

To unblock our future a planetary awareness that alternatives to the current order of things are both necessary and possible will have to develop. This new global consciousness may someday emerge—the mass protests against the 1999 World Trade Organization meeting in Seattle and against other gatherings of elite decision makers in Washington and Prague in 2000 and in Quebec, Gothenburg, and Genoa in 2001 are hopeful signs of that. If this embryonic consciousness was, toward the end of 2001, being undermined by the Afghan War, creation of new solidarities across linguistic and ethnic frontiers as well as across the poverty line dividing North and South is likely soon to resume and to be accelerated by the spreading knowledge that ecological catastrophes—massive floods caused by global warming, looming water shortages, wholesale destruction of rain forests, poisoning of the food supply by industrial agriculture, acid rain, the long-term menace of nuclear wastes, depletion of plant and animal species—threaten everyone on the planet and that a planetary response is indispensable.

Before such awareness can become politically effective, however, there will have to be widespread comprehension that such catastrophes are being generated by the fetishisms of growth, commodity acquisition, and power that are at the heart of the currently dominant capitalist system. And, pursuant to this comprehension, there will need to be far-reaching public debate on the feasible alternatives, alternatives that, while accepting the principles of ecological sustainability and social justice, retain the basic premises of Promethean modernity. There are three such premises. In politics, the participation of all in self-governing communities. In culture, the liberation of human creativity. And in economics, the human use of human reason: the application of science and technology to the transcendence of scarcity and insecurity, to putting an end to the hard and meaningless labor suffered by most of humanity out of fear of hunger and destitution.

Grasping these premises rests on an understanding of how we have come to where we are. In the first part of this book, I examine in historical perspective three central versions of the Promethean credo in the modern world, together with the social-political institutions they inspire: nationalism, the ideology of collective liberation based on ethnic identity; socialism, the ideology of working-class liberation in industrial society; and consumerism, the ideology of individual style, power, and wealth propagated by global capitalism today. In the second part, I first discuss the theoretical and social resources on the basis of which we can envisage a fundamentally different kind of society. I then broach, as my contribution to the indispensable coming debate, a model of a two-tiered future world society which I believe to be both feasible and desirable.

THE RISE AND DECLINE OF THE MODERN PROMETHEUS

Marx was certain that the proletariat as the collective Prometheus would, in the universal revolution, sweep away the age-long contradiction between the interest of the individual and that of the species.

LESZEK KOLAKOWSKI

This element of violation and violence is present in all fabrication, and *homo faber,* the creator of the human artifice, has always been a destroyer of nature. . . . *homo faber* conducts himself as lord and master of the whole earth. . . . human productivity was by definition bound to result in a Promethean revolt because it could erect a man-made world only after destroying part of God-created nature.

HANNAH ARENDT

The hope that inspired Marx and the best men of the various workers' movements—that free time eventually will emancipate men from necessity and make the *animal laborens* productive—rests on the illusion of a mechanistic philosophy which assumes that labor power, like any other energy, can never be lost, so that if it is not spent and exhausted in the drudgery of life it will automatically nourish other, "higher," activities. . . . A hundred years after Marx we know the fallacy of this reasoning; the spare time of the *animal laborens* is never spent in anything but consumption, and the more time left to him, the greedier and more craving his appetites. . . . One of the obvious danger signs that we may be on our way to bring into existence the ideal of the *animal laborens* is the extent to which our whole economy has become a waste economy, in which things must be almost as quickly devoured and discarded as they have appeared in the world, if the process itself is not to come to a sudden catastrophic end.

HANNAH ARENDT

chapter one

The Nationalist Face of Prometheus

A patriot is a fool in ev'ry age.

ALEXANDER POPE

Patriotism is the last refuge of a scoundrel.

SAMUEL JOHNSON

No man can be a patriot on an empty stomach.

WILLIAM COWPER BRANN, 1893

AFTER SEPTEMBER 11, American patriotism was so popular that the government could wrap up the most grievous assault on the Bill of Rights since Joseph McCarthy—an alleged antiterrorist measure—as the "Patriot Act." Only one senator opposed it, and a parallel presidential order to have noncitizen terrorism suspects tried by military courts had majority support in the polls.[1] National solidarity after the suicide attacks seemed to put an end to decades of unfettered acquisitiveness in the United States as well as to the unashamed internationalism of its economic and political elites. Many compared the newfound unity of purpose with that created by the bombing of Pearl Harbor. Indeed many decent people, recalling the civil rights movement in the sixties and the various campaigns against poverty of Democratic presidents in that decade, were estranged by the encouragement of an amoral egoism under most administrations of the seventies, eighties, and nineties. Suddenly the cynicism and estrangement gave way to a long forgotten pageant: Americans united around flag and country.

For several years, a growing chorus of skeptics had pilloried—in dissident weeklies, on campuses, in trade unions, and in large demonstrations—the extension of U.S. corporate power to the global scene, blaming it for polluting the planet with industrial wastes and for abandoning American workers to profit from cheap third-world labor power. The economic elites,

39

who rejected any restraint on the exploitation of third-world resources and labor markets as archaic and unproductive, likened this criticism to retrograde nationalism. Ecological concerns and humane labor standards alike were reduced to Neanderthal protectionism. The attack on the World Trade Center, however (allegedly masterminded by a scion of the billionaire Bin Laden family, which is to Saudi society what the Rockefellers are to the United States), was widely seen as an assault on both the American people and its economic system. Its effect: capitalism and popular nationalism, divorced since the collapse of the Soviet Union and the global hegemony of multinational corporations, were restored to holy matrimony.[2]

Nurtured by fears of random violence and corporate downsizing, the free-floating anxiety that had long haunted Americans found in Islamic fundamentalist suicide bombers a terror capable of uniting them in renewed national fervor with their political leaders. From the standpoint of the oil barons who controlled the White House, of course, this sudden affection between the nation and its leaders was less a question of romantic love than an occasion for a profitable *mariage de raison*. Thanks to their newfound respectability, the leaders were able to pursue an Afghan War that required, for the huge majority that supported them, slaying the monster Osama bin Laden, and, for their more sophisticated constituency, eliminating unpredictable fanatics whose protected status in Taliban Afghanistan was blocking the construction of oil pipelines from the Caspian Sea reserves.

This favorable political conjuncture, at variance with the deepening recession in which it occurred, was of doubtful longevity. The administration was certainly aware, along with Senate Democrats, that as the threat of Al Qaeda waned and the menace of recession-induced downsizing increased, the flag-waving hysteria of the fall of 2001 was unlikely to endure into the elections of 2002.[3] In fact, while the bombs rained down and America's proxy army of tribal warlords chased the Taliban out of Afghan cities, its delegation to the World Trade Organization meeting in Doha was forcing through yet another round of "trade liberalization," which meant, among other things, further replacement of U.S. labor by inexpensive surrogates elsewhere and accelerated lowering of trade barriers in third world countries, guaranteed to wreak havoc with the domestic industries of the poorest nations.[4] Nonetheless, on both the Islamic and the Western sides, the terrorism and the subsequent military response reawakened wellsprings of nationalist emotion completely at variance with the main thrust of capitalist globalization. The episode, then, justifies a close look at the sources of modern nationalism and its relation to capitalist modernity and to religion.

Curiously, in an earlier age, nationalism had been a principle medium of democracy and social liberation, a bearer of collective Promethean idealism.

Strategies of Liberal Capitalism:
Nationalism, Militarism, and the Welfare State

Nationalism is inseparable from the great national revolutions of modernity that toppled feudal absolutist regimes, often incipient nation-states. In every one of such revolutions before the twentieth century, liberal modernizers were helped into power by coalitions of dissident elites, angry merchants, and enraged artisans and peasants. The new elites, who stood for "clean" efficient government with uniform standards, dismantled systems of hereditary privilege and encouraged the development of commercial and industrial capitalism. If such people had in principle no more affection for democratic nationalism than their predecessors during the old regime, the absence of equity and solidarity within the post-revolutionary modern order aroused, in most countries, a militant national-democratic opposition. The opposition was initially formulated by spokesmen for radical artisans and shopkeepers, but it was subsequently broadened into modern socialism by representatives of the industrial proletariat.

The liberal hegemony devised four strategies for taming such opposition. It accepted—gradually and grudgingly—the basic demand of popular nationalism and republicanism: universal male suffrage. It shared some of its new wealth with the industrial working class and co-opted its leaders, a strategy which after World War II took the form of the welfare state. It created a consumer culture in which decaying religious ideals of spiritual perfectibility and salvation in an afterlife were supplemented by the unquenchable thirst for ever more material symbols of the good life in the here and now.[5] And throughout the twentieth century, it exploited international tensions, totalitarian menaces and threats of global wars to control dissent, to regiment potentially unruly populaces and to create an enormous military-industrial complex. Recently given a new lease on life by the terrorist threat of 2001, the latter came to serve as a welfare state for the owners and managers of corporate industry, protecting them, at lavish public expense, against the dangers of too free a market.[6]

Some acceptance of popular nationalism was forced on liberal thought—in principle elitist—in a multitude of ways. Although the premodern masses of artisans and peasants—who, in alliance with discontented elites, overthrew ancient despotisms—were more inspired by material interest or religious fervor than by nationalist conviction, they were rarely enthusiastic about their new liberal masters. The latter, identifying the nation with the rise of the bourgeoisie, abandoned their progressive impulses as soon as they took power, and maintained their hold by excluding all but the wealthy from voting. At this point, the lower orders turned to popular tribunes—

dissident priests, self-taught artisans, and intellectuals—whose appeals to national pride had already supplied the fuel for the subversion of old regimes. Such appeals were a constantly recurring motif in the ideological wars against old regimes, from Luther's pamphlets against the papacy to late-eighteenth-century French broadsheets against the crimes of Marie-Antoinette (an Austrian princess), nineteenth-century Jacobin Republicanism, and Slavic populism. Nonetheless, revolutionary movements succeeded only under the national leadership of discontented elites of the old regime, and the latent conflict of interest between those oligarchically inclined elites and the preindustrial masses who brought them to power was kept below the surface only by nationalist rhetoric.

Presumably based on sentiments of ethnic, linguistic, and cultural solidarity, "national consciousness" was thus originally invoked by dissident elites, who clothed their quest for political and economic power in patriotic phrases. Appealing to their compatriots during the collapse of old regimes, the elites called on them to liberate their "nation" from exploitation by foreign oppressors and hereditary despotisms. Only in the second half of the nineteenth century did conservative and right-populist leaders systematically manipulate such consciousness to further national expansion and colonial aggression. In both the earlier and the later nationalist dispensations, however, this consciousness fused elements of the Promethean drive for productivity and self-assertion with millennialist dreams of social harmony.

If those dreams and that ideal of self-assertion became particularly xenophobic and dangerous during the European competition for empire before World War I, it was because the domestic reality had proven to be intractable. On the one hand, the asocial individualism that dominated was incompatible with the solidarist fantasies of the lower orders. On the other, the tenants of those fantasies were bitterly divided between a premodern shopkeeper-artisan class and a growing industrial working class alienated from traditional morality. Under these circumstances, integral nationalism became a refuge for communitarian impulses that could have been realized only through an impossible alliance between the preindustrial popular strata and the feared and despised factory proletariat. In such a situation, and in the absence of any future for the preindustrial strata other than slow strangulation, nationalist sentiments were ripe for manipulation by xenophobic ideologues, often in tacit alliance with national liberal capitalist elites. Both groups were eager to reorient nationalist energies from the deadlocked domestic scene to real or imagined foreign enemies.[7]

Liberals had before 1850 everywhere preferred the rational governance of the wealthy to both popular nationalism and democracy. In the regimes they formed during the post-revolutionary restoration, suffrage was always dependent on property, and limited to a small minority. But after the popular revolutions against liberal-led constitutional monarchies in 1848, liberals who came to power in the French Third Republic and the German Second Empire did not dare refuse universal male suffrage at the national level. They followed the example of Louis Napoleon in paying lip service to the nationalist conservatism of the premodern classes, while doing their best to revolutionize the economy. Of course, the economic turmoil this produced undermined the economic and social existence of precisely the premodern masses that had helped them into the saddle. Factory production and department store distribution ruined the artisan and the small shopkeeper, while capitalist agriculture forced the independent peasantry off the land and into the factories. Such a program could be accomplished only behind a smoke screen of ideological hocus-pocus, involving the manipulation of all manner of popular national and religious symbols. Ultimately, it also required concessions in the area of social legislation.

The manipulation of national pride by colonial adventurism had occurred even in the absence of an industrial revolution and before the mid-century revolutions made universal male suffrage a reality (or at least put it on the immediate agenda). Some July Monarchy liberals, for example, used the victories of the French army in Algeria as a means of maintaining domestic popularity; they sought valiantly for a victory in the conflict with England over the succession to Turkish power in Egypt,[8] and they paid dearly for their failure to impose a "French" solution on Egypt by the rapid growth of a republican opposition in the years following 1840.

Subsequently, the appeasement of democratic nationalism by means that did not interfere with state power became indispensable to the maintenance of bourgeois hegemony in France, Germany, Italy, and England (jingoism!) in the period between 1870 and 1914. In Germany and France, it also took the form of concessions by liberals to the premodern popular classes of artisans and peasants: in addition to universal suffrage, in both countries tariffs and other legislation protected those premodern classes economically, and in Germany the conservative wings of National Liberalism and the Catholic parties accepted many of their economic demands and much of the xenophobic program of *völkisch* nationalism, including anti-Semitism, to keep the traditional groups from flocking to extreme nationalist and anti-Semitic parties.[9]

These concessions did not, of course, do more than slow down the enfeeblement and erosion of the artisan, shopkeeper, and peasant strata. Nor did they protect triumphant liberal capitalism from attack by the new industrial working class and the parties representing it. For some time, the strategy used against the industrial proletariat, on whose exploitation the rate of profit depended, was simple repression: outlawing of strikes, unions, and workers' parties. As the number of workers grew, it became necessary to distinguish between those whose demands were modest and those who wanted the whole cake immediately. If the latter continued to suffer the martyrdom incumbent on revolutionary hubris, one compromise after another was made with the former. Strikes were legalized and unions were tolerated: social peace was purchased with a minor degree of profit sharing. Socialist parties were legalized if they renounced violence and accepted the parliamentary game.

Between 1914 and 1990, the liberal imperium, faced with the multiple challenges of global war and totalitarianism, added two new legitimating strategies. One was the joint threat of hellfire, in the event of military defeat, and moral decadence, in the event of infringement of the dominant morality. The other was social compromise with the working classes.

Until 1945, fear of national defeat legitimated nationalist militarism, which presented the nation-state and its armed forces as the only protection against the enslavement of "free peoples," the only rampart of the otherwise helpless nation against subjugation to rapacious foreigners aiming at world domination. Such militarism, which began before 1914 in a period of intensified imperialist rivalries (1880–1914), was inseparable from the high tide of the bourgeois civilizing offensive. The latter took the form of an anxious and punitive attitude to everything believed to partake of the abhorred world of nature and thus foreign to the national bourgeois culture. Anxiety about decadent sexuality, particularly in the youth, was an expression of this attitude, a reason for the harsh treatment of Oscar Wilde. Such anxiety was also the reason for the orthopedic straitjackets that bourgeois fathers devised for their round-shouldered male progeny in various "posture" cures, a cruel fad that reached its high point in the late nineteenth and early twentieth century.[10]

Another expression of the civilizing offensive was the popular periodical press, which, as one study of French middle-class glossies around 1900 has shown, was stuffed with articles giving vent to the anxious fantasies of the middle class about the dangers of sexuality, loose women, the working class, misbehaving children, other European nationals, and African tribes.[11] Not only did appeals to rally around the flag, accompanied by considerable repression of dissidence, bring large masses of otherwise recalcitrant citizens into frightened acquiescence, it also justified huge public expenditures on military equipment, so as to make credible threats to annihilate the enemy if it made the wrong move. After the twentieth century's thirty-year war against German expansionism these massive expenditures, given spurious justification by cold war tensions, functioned as a socialism for the rich, a continual Keynesian pump-priming that kept the Euro-American economy in equilibrium throughout the postwar recovery and boom.

The other new strategy was to enlarge the space, created by the social concessions before 1914, around the trough of capitalist productivity. Welfare states were created after World War II, rooted in the Fordist production system that linked mass consumption to high wages. They functioned both as a riposte to the menace of Stalinist Communism and as a supplement to and partial replacement for chauvinistic nationalism. The welfare state was more effective in dampening proletarian radicalism than the earlier concessions to the workers had been. It not only bound the leaders of the working class to the liberal hegemony (a tie that had already dampened the revolutionary ardor of socialist politicians before World War I). It bound the workers themselves to a pattern of consumption—of houses and cars, toasters and refrigerators, radios and TVs—that integrated most of them thoroughly into the domain of bourgeois taste and aspiration.

Moreover, the disastrous consequences for Europe of two world wars, unleashed by a nationalism that had turned into a sorcerer's apprentice, strengthened the resolve of European liberal elites after 1945 to weaken the links to chauvinistic nationalism that had earlier characterized bourgeois hegemony. In the light of the commitment to the European Union by elites as well as electoral majorities in its fifteen member states, extreme-nationalist parties and coalitions such as the Front National in France and Belgium, the Republikaner Party in Germany, and even the Austrian liberal–far-right amalgam of Georg Haider (junior partner in the Austrian government in 2002), are today marginal phenomena. Although symptomatic of the breakdown of the welfare state, these parties represent only the most nostalgic and reactionary elements of those excluded from the welfare of the late twentieth century.

It is true that the terrorist attacks on the United States of September 11 and the worldwide increase in tension between Islam and the West stimulated fears of Islamic immigrants and of immigration-related criminality, particularly in Europe. The attacks were partly responsible for skewing the elections of 2002 away from social issues; conservative and far-right parties that exploited popular xenophobia encouraged and benefited from the racist law-and-order mood. Nonetheless, only a maverick far-right party that, like Georg Haider's Austrian Liberal Party, combined racism with an economic program that endorsed the prevailing neoliberalism—the Pim Fortuyn list in the Netherlands—was brought into a governing conservative coalition. Parties closer to the fascism of the first half of the last century, like Jean-Marie Le Pen's Front National, remained more or less quarantined by the entire political elite as well as by the majority of ordinary citizens. And most people, even among the growing number that suffer exclusion through downsizing and inadequate training in computer technology, were repelled by the way the extreme right blamed misfortune on immigrant workers, left-wingers, Jews, and foreigners. The terrifying echoes it evoked awakened antifascist vigilance, as was shown in the massive demonstrations against Le Pen's freak presence in the second round of the May 2002 French presidential elections.[12]

Nonetheless, the neoliberal hegemony of the late twentieth century, by rendering inoperative earlier liberal strategies for lessening social insecurity, severely injured individual as well as collective identity among the wage-earning majority. Bribing the working class with the welfare state depended on two things: the menace of a totalitarian alternative to liberal capitalism, which claimed to guarantee security and welfare to the toiling masses; and the existence of those masses. The Soviet "evil empire" having returned to its horned progenitor, the threat to public tranquillity posed by its agents in Western communist parties likewise disappeared, and with them a major reason for the welfare states that developed all over Europe.

A second disappearance has been the working class itself in Western Europe and America. Perhaps half the unionized factory workers of a generation ago have been downsized into temporary service jobs or put on the dole, their factories run by robots and computers or reestablished in eastern Europe, Latin America, and the Far East. In China, Indonesia, and the Philippines, tens of millions of impoverished Asians in Export Processing Zones work twelve- to sixteen-hour days under subcontractors to Western companies for as little as thirteen cents an hour in the new industrial reserve army of world capitalism.[13]

All this has left the formerly left-wing parties with neither constituency nor ideology, able to cling to power only if they adopted a liberal, middle-class face, interested more in maintaining ministerial posts and their benefits than in the ideals they mouth. In France and the Netherlands, socialist parties in (or sharing) power during the last two decades have behaved like the most hard-nosed liberals in eschewing budget deficits even if it meant the abandonment of the welfare state.[14] At the moment, even the Keynesian social-liberal idea of stimulating capitalist growth through state intervention in support of purchasing power is a controversial, minority position in, or to the left of, most social-democratic parties.[15]

Moreover, repressive tolerance seemed to become less necessary as the bite of radical criticism was replaced by the toothless bark of postmodernism. This turn to conformity by the briefly rebellious mandarins followed the elimination of most institutionalized sources of dissidence. Since the sixties, the rapid technological evolution and the globalization of the world economy, together with the disappearance of world communism, has so diminished the internal opposition to global neoliberalism, whether from the working class, the students, or the large strata of small property holders, that criticism long became marginalized beyond the most fervent hope of those who had suffered the attacks of the sixties. Alongside of the weakening and disappearance of petty entrepreneurial sectors we witnessed the demise of the "little magazines" of independent intellectuals.[16] Radical thought, where it continued to exist in minor sects, had largely become fossilized. The radicalism of youth in the sixties was in subsequent decades crushed by insecurity, where it was not, in the case of a talented minority, co-opted by yuppie lifestyles and lavish salaries.

All of these tendencies led to one French critic's conclusion a few years ago that the Promethean ethos was currently trapped in the "totalitarian drift of liberalism."[17] Indeed, until about 1995, the neoliberal hegemony had squeezed radical opposition and alternative visions into the invisible margins of society.

Illusions of Nationalism

We have seen that nationalism is a relatively recent phenomenon, associated, as is *Homo faber,* with the democratic and industrial revolutions of the modern era. In the previous section, I discussed a political and economic question: the evolution of nationalism from democratic revolutionary messianism to an aggressive, xenophobic ally of competing national capitalist states, and, in the age of multi- and transnational capitalism, to a quarantined minority ideology, viewed as incompatible with the smooth working of global markets. What I would like to explore here is a cultural and social matter: nationalism's historical trajectory as a belief system that gradually replaced, or became intertwined with, more traditional faiths, and the implications of its apparent resurrection. Obviously the possibility of basing claims to nationhood on ethnic identity was largely dependent on the existence and awareness of a common language and culture. Concomitantly, a crucial condition for the appearance and spread of nationalism, most theorists agree, has been the invention of printing and the possibility of mass literacy. For these two phenomena were preconditions of the linguistic unity usually presupposed by the concept of national identity.[18]

In the European preindustrial age of mass illiteracy, social identity was shaped not by ethnic or national sensibilities but by the molds of caste and class, of region and dialect, of religious conviction and village mentality. Rulers came and went, their realms grew or shrank or were gobbled up by more powerful neighbors, but the identity and consciousness of nobles, peasants, and city dwellers were only marginally affected, if at all. Local dialects, which might be incomprehensible to those living fifty kilometers away, were rarely tampered with, and only fanatics like Philip II in the Netherlands interfered much in matters of local religion. Administrators had, of course, to be able to read and write the language of the ruling dynasty (it was often Latin), but in an age in which only administrators and clergymen were literate, the language spoken by the common people was a matter of indifference to those who taxed and exploited them.

Nonetheless, well before *nation* meant what it has since the French Revolution, and long before *nationalism* or *national identity* had any meaning at all, nation-states were forged in early modern France, England, Spain, and Portugal on the basis of a dynastic territory and a bureaucratic monarchy capable of administering it, defending it, and (more or less) monopolizing the use of legitimate force within it. The significance of those nation-states for subsequent "nation forming" was threefold: They established an administrative model and a "national" territory that revolutionaries could subsequently use as a point of departure for their reforms. Increasingly, they imposed, through their administrators and sometimes, as in France, through academies of learned men, a national language, the one spoken in the governmental center, which gradually reduced all other languages of the realm to dialects or patois. And, particularly in the eighteenth century, when European nation-states, through mercantilism, were forming the core of what Immanuel Wallerstein calls the capitalist world-system, they established a model for linking territorial and economic power that each postrevolutionary European nation would try to improve on.

Nations and their concomitant nationalisms have, therefore, a largely opportunistic relationship to a common language or ethnic origin. Instead of nation-states arising from ethnolinguistic unity, they have imposed such unity on a pre-national diversity, and then celebrated what they have created as representing a metaphysical core of nationhood. In fact, only a few nations have grown out of existing states, such as the ones I have mentioned, and even within those states the linguistic variation was considerable and the "national" borders were shaped not by ethnic or linguistic unity but by centuries of dynastic warfare and intermarriage. Moreover, nations which have shown a powerful inclination to take over foreign territories inhabited by people close to them linguistically or ethnically have rarely ceded voluntarily their own areas inhabited by nonnational ethnolinguistic groupings.

Where no prior nation-state existed, a loose conglomeration of ethnically or linguistically related territories might come together, usually for economic or religious reasons, to form one. Sometimes they had simply been long divided, like Germany. In many cases, their point in common was that they had been administered as a territory of a once-powerful empire and had had to fight for their independence from this imperium, as the Dutch did against the Spanish in the sixteenth century, the Americans against the British in the eighteenth, the Italians against the Austrians, the Greeks against the Turks, and the various Latin American colonies against Spain and Portugal in the nineteenth. As we know, the process has continued in the twentieth century with decreasing correspondence between the ideology of integral nationalism and the actual ethnic or linguistic coherence of the new nations. In the case of most of the liberated colonies of the twentieth century—for example, India and Pakistan, Indochina, the Dutch East Indies, Algeria, Iraq, and most African territories—the territorial unity imposed by the imperial power had welded together a hodgepodge of linguistic, ethnic, and religious diversity, with the result that the only language usable by the new "national" elites for administrative purposes was that of the old colonizing power, and a number of such potential "nations"—Indochina, for example—dissolved immediately into ethnic components.

To transform an absolutist nation-state like the Bourbon monarchy into the French "nation," or to weave a German "nation" around the dynastic state of Hohenzollern Prussia, or to transform a colony like the Dutch East Indies, with hundreds of local languages and scores of ethnic divisions, into "Indonesia," a shock was needed that delegitimized the existing political authority, and opened the way to power (in alliance with large segments of the population) for hitherto subordinate elites. Whether that shock was military defeat or economic collapse,[19] the resultant alliance of elites and common people called itself a nation and, usually under the guidance of a considerably more powerful administration than had hitherto existed, developed a national system of schooling, a national military and national taxation, and defined a national identity. This new identity, highly useful to new states that had built their power on the allegiance of the common people, then had to compete with and, so far as possible, subordinate or eliminate the earlier social, ethnic, or religious identities of the preindustrial or pre-independence era.[20]

Nationalism is thus a school of illusions. Its European ideologists have variously based it on the historical tradition of a developing monarchical nation-state (France and England), on a common language and ethnic culture invoked to overcome territorial division and domination by non-nationals (liberal German and Italian nationalism), or on racial or ethnic purity, which permitted the expulsion or domination of inferior "others" (fascist German and Italian nationalism). Apart from the contradictory character of these criteria, it is noteworthy that even those in substantial agreement on them, discussing the same phenomena at the same time, could come up with wildly different political programs. On the basis of national tradition, Edmund Burke argued in 1789 for preservation of the French monarchy at the very moment that French patriots were castrating it in the name of *la nation.*[21] Late-nineteenth-century liberal nationalists in France appealed to the common culture and the tradition of justice embodied in the French Revolution to defend Dreyfus and attack the influence of the military, while racist nationalists joined with monarchists to denounce Dreyfus and celebrate the honor of the army as providing the only chance to revenge their humiliating defeat in the Franco-Prussian war of 1870.

With the exception of British control over Ireland, most of the empires arising from European nation-states were in what after 1945 came to be called the "third world." The powerful European, or Eurasian, dynastic states that had escaped national revolutions until the beginning of the twentieth century—Russia, Austria, and Turkey—all had contiguous empires, founded on geopolitical strategies, rather than overseas ones that were commercially motivated. This created large numbers of subjugated peoples in eastern Europe, Asia Minor, and central Asia, the more powerful of which have been carving out, and quarreling over, their own "national" territories and destinies ever since the breakups of those unwieldy imperial states. In all cases, nationalist enthusiasm has been stimulated by new ruling elites looking for popular support in their quarrels with neighboring states. Very often, the new territory of the nation included minority ethnic groups which sometimes demanded cultural autonomy, sometimes independence, and sometimes attachment to an existing nation (or a hypothesized one, in the case of the Kurds or the Palestinians) with which they identified.

Few of the contradictory sources of European nationalist fervor apply to non-European nationalism. Outside of Europe, nationalism has been founded on the Hindu, Shinto, or Muslim religions in, respectively, contemporary India, Imperial Japan, and large swathes of North Africa, the Middle East, and Pakistan. As Ernest Gellner, Benedict Anderson, and Eric Hobsbawm have pointed out, in formerly colonial territories "nationalist" resistance normally sprang from the interests of an indigenous elite that had been educated by the imperial power to participate in the administration of the colony, but whose status and mobility were severely limited under the various imperial dispensations.[22] It is characteristic of non-European nationalism that with few exceptions, the "national" boundaries were drawn initially for administrative purposes by the English, Turkish, French, Belgian, Portuguese, Spanish, German, or Dutch empires which had divided up the non-European world between the sixteenth and early twentieth centuries. In a great many cases, the only linguistic or cultural unity exhibited by the new nations was that imposed by the colonial powers. After independence, the ethnic, linguistic, and religious diversity of third world "nations" created enormous administrative problems, and imposition of "national" policy was often possible only through authoritarian and military solutions, as in Indonesia and many of the new African states. Interestingly, after the turmoil in Indonesia in 1999–2000, which led to the breakdown of the Suharto regime's tight military control, the Indonesian state under the reformist leadership began (with the independence of East Timor) to crumble into its ethnic components.

Nationalism, though its effective power is everywhere attenuated by the global reach of multinational corporations now has very different meanings in different parts of the world.

In Europe it takes three forms. One is the xenophobic old-style nationalism, arising from the decreasing lack of control of European nation-states over their own economic and political destinies. Rather than emanating from genuine national pride, this nationalism is more a matter of traditional middle-class fear of foreigners, quickened by the economic pain caused by globalization and Europeanization. Examples are France's Front National (now, happily, split in two), the Belgian Vlaams Blok, and the Austrian Freiheitliche Partei Österreichs (FPÖ), the party of Georg Haider, which in 2000, after receiving a quarter of the vote, came to rule Austria in coalition with the Christian Democrats. A second form is ethnic regionalism, whose more extreme representatives, as in the Basque and Scottish cases, seek independence, but which in many others—Wales, Catalonia, Galicia, Brittany, and Provence—mainly wants a degree of local autonomy combined with the use of a local language or dialect in schools and administration.[23] The rise of these local ethnic movements is also a sign of the decreasing force and psychological value of nation-states in the globalized economy. In a number of cases—Scotland, for example—ethnic separatism feeds on the popular awareness that national states faced with the global dictates of neoliberal capitalism are inclined to preserve as much wealth as possible for their core areas and traditional elites, with serious degradation of the social climate in peripheral areas: accordingly it takes rather left-wing forms.[24] Finally, for reasons comparable to those of the emergence of regional ethnic movements, Europe witnesses the breakup of the Yugoslav and Czechoslovak nation-states created after the disintegration of the Austrian empire in 1918: the Slovaks felt put upon by the Czechs, and all the non-Serb ethnic groups by the Serbs.

In the third world, nationalism tends to merge either with religious movements hostile to the influence of Western culture on traditional morality, as in many Muslim countries, or with local reactions against domination by European and American capitalism (variously viewed in terms of globalization or of old-fashioned imperialism). The latter is the case in many South American countries, where progressivism has always been anti-Yankee, and in some African ones, like Nigeria, exploited by Western oil interests. Nonetheless, in most nation-states the willingness of national elites to oppose the networks of global capitalism is nearing the vanishing point because of the economic advantages to them of participation in it and the sanctions imposed by organizations like the World Trade Organization and the World Bank on states that evade them. Thus even the nominally Communist regimes of China and Vietnam accept a domestic capitalism and foreign investment in it.

The recent Afghan crisis illuminates the overbearing influence of global economic power on both right-wing religious and left-wing Marxist nationalism. In its various branches, militant Islamic fundamentalism, irreconcilably hostile to Western modernity and Christianity, has profound sources of support in the Muslim world, a fanatical following in Pakistan, Iran, Saudi Arabia, Egypt, and Algeria. Like non-Western Communist Parties of an earlier era, Islamic fundamentalism organizes and expresses profoundly nationalist resentments in an internationalist ideology. The most extreme version of this religious nationalism was represented by the Saudi- and Egyptian-led Al Qaeda network and its Taliban protectors. Though supported politically only by the isolated Afghan regime, overwhelmed within a matter of weeks by American bombings and the ground troops of the Northern Alliance, Al Qaeda and Bin Laden had been funded for years by the Saudi oil and construction elites, whose charitable foundations also financed the Pakistani madrasas (Koran schools) where pupils were imbued with implacable hatred of Jews, Christians, Israel, and the West.[25] Yet Saudi Arabian capital was locked into such a symbiotic relationship to European and American oil companies and consumers that a Saudi foreign policy overtly hostile to the American military was unthinkable.

Thus on the one hand, armed guerrilla fighters financed by that capital—called terrorists by their Western victims and a liberation army by their

Islamic supporters—were pledging war to the bitter end to drive the Satanic Americans and their mercenaries out of Islamic countries; on the other, their paymasters were obtaining their funds by the sale of Saudi oil to the devil. And European and American car owners and airline travelers, purchasers and users of that oil, were indirectly supporting those who had vowed to exterminate them. Mohammed Atah and his companions, suicidal fanatics though they may have been, were not stupid, and must have realized the macabre paradox in using tons of aviation fuel, perhaps purchased by the airlines from the same billionaires who financed their operation, to immolate themselves and their victims in the World Trade Center.

The paradox deepens when we examine the motives of the other actors in the Afghan drama. In declaring war on terrorism, the Bush administration was driven not just by the fear and revulsion of ordinary Americans at what had happened (we need not dwell on the obvious political profit of a successful war) but at least as much—probably more—by the longer-term necessity of securing a constant supply of oil for the world economy. Afghanistan lies southeast of the vast oil fields of Turkmenistan, and just south of the natural gas reserves of Uzbekistan. Particularly in view of the extreme complexity of the Saudi situation and the total unreliability of the Iranian one, pacification of the hostile state of Afghanistan, through which oil pipelines from the Caspian Sea could be run into Pakistan and on to the Arabian Sea, was necessary for the long-term security and stability of the international economic order.

The principal putative beneficiary of Caspian Sea oil, however, was not the United States but the People's Republic of China. Communist China, briefly seen by the Bush administration as a worthy successor of the Evil Empire of the Soviets, has recently been developing a market capitalism designed to participate, through Chinese membership in the World Trade Organization, in the new global economy. Its oil needs in 2020 were expected to be two and a half times what they were in 1997,[26] and its most feasible access to the world's major oil fields was indeed through the Arabian Sea.[27] This may explain why the government of the People's Republic, which ideologically exemplified the marriage of Marxism and Chinese nationalism and was earlier seen as the rampart of smaller nationalisms against the United States, never spoke out against, much less used its Security Council veto to impede, UN support for the American-led "war on terrorism" in Afghanistan.

A final paradox: the United States may have discovered forgotten reservoirs of patriotic fervor after the terrorist attacks of September 11, but the global economy that runs on oil—the principal reason for the U.S. presence in Saudi Arabia that infuriated Bin Laden—works to the material detriment of a majority of the American people. One need only look at the effects of the North American Free Trade Agreement (Nafta) on the American working and middle classes. Thus, apart from exceptional moments like the aftermath of the September 11 attacks, nationalist patriotism tends to be a marginal phenomenon in the United States, celebrated on the Far Right but rightly disdained by corporate and political elites as harmful to the development of global commerce.

Yet nationalism has powerful anthropological roots. In the Western as well as the non-Western world, it has intersected both with the religious needs of humankind and the impulses of adolescent youth. And these roots have been watered differently during the various phases of the development of modern capitalism.

A glance at the elements in nationalist emotion as it emerged in Europe before the middle of the twentieth century will illuminate such issues, relativizing, perhaps, the sharp contrast made after September 11 between "them" and "us."

Components of the Nationalist Apocalypse

Whether nationalism was cultivated by new elites (as in revolutionary France, Communist Russia and China, and most third world nations) or by old ones (as in Prussian Germany, Poland, and Austria-Hungary), its rise always had powerful religious connotations. Where these were not traditionalist, because traditional religion appeared as a competing, international, point of allegiance, nationalism fused older religious beliefs with new secular ones. This tie is easy to understand. Belief systems joining past, present, and future are a constant presence in human societies, reflecting our mental capacities to envisage the uncertain future and answering the need for reassurance in the face of inevitable misfortune and death. French and German nationalisms of the nineteenth and twentieth centuries offer abundant evidence of this link to religious belief, sometimes as the competitor to traditional religious faith, and sometimes as its partner.

Thus on the one hand, European nationalism has had an anticlerical aspect, since the claims of religion to hegemony over human conduct—and, in the case of the Catholic Church, to universal dominion—clashed with demands for allegiance to the national cause. On the other, it could find a powerful ally in existing faiths, when a particular nationalism turned out to have the same enemies as a national church: simultaneous with one of the fiercest outbursts of anticlericalism in France—the pillaging of church property by the Paris mob just after the revolution of 1830, because of Catholic support for the deposed House of Bourbon—Polish nationalist revolutionaries on the other side of the Prussian border, jubilantly supported by French Republicans, were receiving the blessings of the local Roman clergy for their revolt against Czarist (Christian Orthodox) imperialism. Patriotic architects of the British empire, German liberal nationalists in the last third of the nineteenth century, and French republicans were all more or less hostile to organized religion. Yet many of their ideas put nationalism on the same level as religion as a transmitter of morality and identity. Traditional religious belief was also tied to national conviction. In Ireland the Catholic Church powerfully supported patriotic sentiment, because the dominating English power was inspired by Protestant beliefs, just as it had earlier supported Polish Catholic nationalists against Russian Orthodoxy. Even in France and Germany, reactionary nationalism often received powerful reinforcement from the Catholic Church, as it did in twentieth-century Spain.

A summary look at French and German nationalism may clarify both the complex relation to religion and the two phases of nationalist ideology following on the French Revolution: the first, visionary, open, and inclusive; the second, closed, anti-Semitic, and xenophobic. We may also discern the relationship, in the nationalism of these two countries, both to the civilizing mission and to the capitalist version of *Homo faber.*

Between 1792 and 1794, revolutionaries in France, largely inspired by the deism of the *philosophes,* consciously attempted to replace Christianity by a worship of Reason and the Supreme Being. To illustrate the new reign of reason, they rearranged the calendar, eliminating the Christian sabbath by replacing the seven-day week with a ten-day one, renaming and relocating the months, and declaring 1792 the year I of the new era. The popular nineteenth-century historian of the Revolution, Jules Michelet, saw it specifically in religious terms, as the tardy triumph of a religion of Justice over one of arbitrary divine grace, and he specifically appealed to a romantic "religious and social revolution" as the necessary follow-up to the liberal "classic" revolution undertaken by Jacobins and Girondins.[28] By the revolution of 1848 and the ensuing Second Republic, which many took to incarnate the "romantic" revolution par excellence, popular religiosity had been politicized to such a degree that democratic-social and romantic revolutionaries were circulating lithographs of a proletarian Christ, bearing the message of Liberty, Equality, and Fraternity.[29]

Less beneficently, another sign that European nationalism was influenced by the old regime's Christian conceptions of social cohesion was its dressing up of Christian anti-Semitism in the new clothes of national populism. This

was, of course, not as evident in the early phase of European nationalism between the French Revolution and 1848 as it was in the late nineteenth and
twentieth centuries. As I have suggested, the national imagery of the revolutionary era and its sequel depicted the tormenters of the nation largely in
terms of class, as the parasitic aristocracy. Where socially radical nationalists criticized the new bourgeois order, they attacked it as a parvenu financial aristocracy whose arrogance was modeled on that of the older feudality,
but only occasionally did the popular anti-Semitism of the time lead those
ideologists to portray the new lords of commerce as Jews.[30] In contrast to
the xenophobic and misogynous nationalism of the late nineteenth century,
the dominant note of nationalist idealists before 1848 was a romantic in-
clusion of all those Others excluded by the civilizing mission of the old
regime—women, children, the popular culture, peasants, manual laborers,
Jews, etc.

Thus, during that earlier period, characterized by the stubborn retention
of power by Christian aristocratic elites, French nationalism was antifeudal,
anticlerical, and democratic. That some ideologists, combining Catholicism and republicanism, represented the common people as a suffering
Christ may have encouraged anti-Semitism, but the presence among educated bourgeois elites of a universalist philosophical outlook, particularly
where there was a strong tie between such elites and the popular strata, precluded anti-Semitism as a matter of policy. If this characterized French (as
well as Italian and English) nationalism up to 1848, it was less true of German nationalism. For one thing, German romantic nationalists viewed the
cosmopolitan enlightenment idea of the bourgeois with hostility, as French,
unnational. For another, the Napoleonic reforms had created a sharp divide
in the German states between the preindustrial popular classes who suffered
those reforms—the reference point of romantic nationalist intellectuals—
and bourgeois liberals who profited from them. Thus visceral nationalism
was always antibourgeois in Germany, where popular and bourgeois strata
were at war with each other from the first moments of the progressive nationalist revolution of 1848. Nonetheless, in neither France nor Germany
was anti-Semitism, before the mid-century divide, an issue for nationalists
comparable to the dismantling of the old regime.

Contrariwise, during the second half of the nineteenth century, particularly in Germany but also in France and elsewhere, the identification of the
common people with the suffering Christ encouraged an amalgam between
the older Christian anti-Semitism and the new, post-1848, aggressive nationalism. Hostile to the inclusionary emphasis of revolutionary nationalism after 1789, the much tougher nationalism that characterized the latter

part of the century was exclusionist. The bourgeois elites, which after 1850 took greater power in Europe, identified all of those Others mentioned above with the world of nature, against which they, no less than the royal and ecclesiastic elites before them, assumed the moral mission of domination, chastisement, and separation from civil society. And so did the increasingly conservative European nationalism.

Accordingly, the ideas of Christianity became linked to bourgeois notions of order and to nationalist images of a suffering Christ-people. The vehemence of the older civilizing mission returned in the corrections inflicted on all such symbols of the dangerous and "irrational" world of nature by the newly dominant bourgeois. These parvenu elites were now, in both Germany and France, in uneasy alliance with the ecclesiastic and aristocratic elites which had earlier been attacked by republican nationalism. The churches, which had always identified their Jewish parent religion with the crucifixion and had for generations viewed both bourgeois enlightenment and the revolution of 1789 as the Antichrist, generally supported the more conservative nationalism after 1850, for the latter was eager to find other scapegoats responsible for the nation's misery than those pilloried by republican anticlericalism. Thus, both the new social Christianity and the tough new nationalism of the second half of the nineteenth century located the source of social ills in "international" Jewish bankers, department store owners, and speculators. In some of the nationalist dispensations, biological doctrines of race lent scientific authenticity to ancient prejudice. As a degenerate species, Jews (as well as gypsies and Slavic *Untermenschen*) were seen as an inferior race meriting annihilation in the name of eugenics.[31]

One can see the link between the aggressive nationalism that some liberal capitalist circles cultivated before World War I and the emergence of racist fascism in the economic theory of Werner Sombart, coeditor with Max Weber of Germany's most important sociology review.[32]

Sombart was a weathervane to the ideological winds of his age. In the 1890s, when he was an eloquent spokesman for social democracy, he was already integrating a racist fear of nonwhite peoples into his justification for the labor movement and socialism.[33] Having gone through various phases of antimodern disillusion with the contemporary world, Sombart began, around 1910, to celebrate capitalist enterprise. In *Der Bourgeois* (1913), he distinguished a heroic "spirit" of capitalism that he identified with Germany, with aggressive industrial enterprise, and with the aristocracy, from an abhorrent commercial "spirit," which he attributed to the Jews and the European middle classes. Only two years later, this proto-fascist position, decades in advance of German public opinion as a whole, was replaced (in

Händler und Helden) by one congruent with the national mood in World War I: the basic categories remained and the struggling German nation continued to be seen as the incarnation of the spirit of heroic enterprise, but the onus of responsibility for the trading mentality was shifted from the Jews to the English.

Sombart's substitution of Anglophobia for anti-Semitism suggests the interchangeability of these and other exclusionist stereotypes in the aggressive, closed nationalism of the pre–World War I period. Was this nationalism merely the idiot in the basement of enlightened, liberal capitalism, or was there a functional relationship between the two? I would argue that there is a symbiotic relationship between, on the one hand, the increasing mutual aggressiveness of national political and economic elites engaged in imperialist rivalries before 1914 and, on the other, the violent antipathy to the modern order in the preindustrial strata: peasants being slowly ground down by capitalist agriculture or by grain imports from America and eastern Europe, artisans unable to compete with factory production and shopkeepers driven to the wall by department stores. For the latter groups, social decline could be camouflaged, indeed a measure of identification with the new dispensation attained, by channeling their antimodernism into hatred of those other nations and religions held responsible for their miseries. Nationalist militarism in all international conflicts fed on the confluence of such hatreds, but so did anti-Semitism: the Jews, as a "rootless" pariah people, largely poor but with a few highly visible wealthy bankers, were in the nineteenth century identified with amoral international capitalism, and, in the twentieth, with an equally evil international communism—in fascist theory more or less the same thing.

In addition to the ferociously competitive national bourgeoisies and the channeled aggressiveness of the preindustrial strata, the intense emotions of a third group also found an outlet in the apocalyptic warfare and the fascist challenge of the first half of the twentieth century: the young men, particularly those of the steadily expanding middle class, who were subject to the increasingly repressive norms imposed by European liberal culture during the Victorian "civilizing offensive." In general, young males, except where broken systematically by rural patriarchy or religious repression or child labor in factories, have always tended to test the limits of adolescence in violent combine and real or symbolic aggression. This occurred in the medieval aristocracy through organized competitions of young knights. In Europe's agrarian villages, since time immemorial, bands of youth fought with the youth of neighboring villages,[34] upheld the village sexual morality by inflicting ritual degradation *(charivari)*[35] on adults who violated it, and organized the often violent and licentious village festivals.[36] In the early modern artisanry, the mutual violence of competing *compagnonnages*[37] and the kind of ritualized mayhem, common to apprentices, described by Robert Darnton in *The Great Cat Massacre* were the province of unmarried young men.[38] It is worth recalling that Leonard Bernstein's musical about adolescent love and ethnic gang warfare in a New York slum, *West Side Story,* was based on Shakespeare's portrayal of the aristocratic youth feuds of renaissance Verona in *Romeo and Juliet.*[39]

Middle-class youth had fewer outlets, but, as the letters of Flaubert and other nineteenth-century young men reveal, they often formed circles, normally more libidinous than violent, that were closed to their parents and teachers. Moreover, there is abundant documentation of the participation of middle-class youth in school revolts (particularly against confessional influence), in circles of estranged artists or would-be artists who cultivated romantic disparagement of bourgeois culture, and in revolutionary movements against the old regime.[40]

Importantly, as the European bourgeoisie returned, in the high Victorian age, to the civilizing mission of the old regime, its male offspring largely abandoned such more or less progressive expressions of adolescent aggression. A part of the youth simply retreated from bourgeois society, either into an extreme immersion in nature and their own physicality (the German norm) or into adolescent dream worlds.[41] In early-twentieth-century France, where such dream worlds were more prominent, good examples are the adolescent cults around Débussy's *Pelléas et Melisande,* Alain-Fournier's *Le Grand Meaulnes,* the first part of Roger Martin du Gard's *Les Thibaults,* and Proust's *À la recherche du temps perdu.* Hanno Buddenbrooks and the poet seers of the circle around Stefan George represent this dream world in the German upper middle class and aristocracy.

Where there was insufficient motive or mental space for such retreat, fin-de-siècle middle-class youths in both France and Germany turned to an exaggerated version of their parents' exclusionary mentality: violent anti-Semitism, such as that of the Jew-hating university students of Berlin, who in the eighties flocked to support the anti-Semitic court chaplain Stöcker, or of those secondary and university students of Paris during the Dreyfus Affair who gathered outside Edouard Drumont's residence to shout "A mort les juifs!"

That the key issue here was not simply anti-Semitism is evident in the enthusiasm with which all the youth of Europe could be marched into the trenches in 1914 for purposes of mutual annihilation. As Sombart's development showed, it was easy to change targets from dangerous Jews to dangerous English, French, Russians—and Germans. In fact independently of the grand geopolitical strategies and nationalist fatalities behind the outbreak of carnage in 1914, one might view World War I as a desperate effort by Europe's conservative and capitalist elites to organize the violence of young males toward traditional national enemies, while maintaining rigid control of the happening. The outcome of that war a generation later was what convinced Europe's conservative elites to forswear mutual collective violence for good.

After the lost war, many young Germans continued to be inspired by ideals of national military valor and of the *Volk*. Bitterly resentful of what their "imagined community" had lost in 1918 as a result of the presumed betrayals of cosmopolitans, Jews, and socialists, extreme nationalist youth in the early twenties formed death squads that murdered hundreds of democrats and leftists.[42] In much larger numbers, resentful German youth and elements of the embittered *Mittelstand,* their already weakened identities shattered by economic crisis after 1930, swelled the ranks of a party that was determined to reverse both the Versailles treaty and the balance of forces between bourgeois society and anti-Semitic nationalism. After winning a majority with the aid of reactionary parties, youth-worshipping Nazis, while nurturing the national capitalist interests that had helped them into power, abolished both the representative government and the civil society of the German bourgeois order; worse, it forced on Europe a repeat performance of the First World War—now, however, without any fig leaf for the new nationalism other than a racist Darwinism that justified contempt for all other peoples, an aggressive *Drang nach Osten,* and a visceral hatred of the Jews.

The ensuing devastation and genocide seems to have discredited for good the alliance of militaristic nationalism and industrial capitalism that had produced such carnage. Through two world wars, Europe's elites had come to understand that, given the tensions and repressions of bourgeois society and the technological means of mutual massacre, the religion of the nation could consecrate the suicide of Europe and perhaps of the human species. It was this evident potential for total catastrophe that led the ideologists of industrial society after World War II to encourage (for example, through the Bretton Woods agreement) an increasingly internationalist liberal capitalism rather than the earlier nationalist variety, to dissociate the celebration of *Homo faber* from nationalist zealotry and to quarantine every reappearance of the extreme nationalism the older elites had tolerated and even cultivated before 1914. This was true not only in Europe and North America but in that other major example of the marriage of industrial capitalism and militarist nationalism, Japan.

The result of the disastrous era of world wars was that after 1945 warfare tended to be limited either to developing states or to a conflict between a developing state and a major occidental power, usually the United States. In fact, there was a recurrent pattern of American governments using conflicts with much weaker third world nationalisms based on religion or social ideology to sustain the military-industrial state: Korea, Vietnam, Grenada, the Gulf War, Somalia, Serbia, and, in 2001, Afghanistan. The first three of these conflicts occurred in the framework of the long-simmering conflict with international communism, whose alleged goal of world conquest, equated with the fascist aggressiveness of World War II, was used with diminishing success as a scarecrow to intimidate domestic dissenters and justify a large arms budget. Subsequent wars were validated by various alternative moral pretenses, but not until the Afghan war of 2001 was the American government again able to justify the carpet bombing of a small country by invoking the demonizing it's-us-or-them mentality that had earlier countenanced the incineration of Vietnamese peasants.

The renewal of American nationalism in the wake of the September 11 attacks was broadly based on the perception of Islamic fundamentalism as so alien and evil that it could be rooted out only with fire and sword. But an analysis of the religious elements of nationalism in the modernist revolutions that shaped the West, particularly German nationalism in the half century before the Second World War, suggests that the peoples of the Middle East, rather than acting according to a "clash of civilizations" ideology, are going through traumas familiar to many European countries.

Just as English Protestant dissenters of the seventeenth century saw a conspiracy of papists to crush them, just as revolutionary French Republican believers in the religion of Reason saw Catholic Christianity as their enemy, just as German Protestant nationalists of the early nineteenth century viewed French Catholics and French *civilisation* as the enemy of their *Kultur,* many in the Middle East look to their traditional religion and values as a defense against Western intrusion in their lives. The "purity" and asceticism some of them uphold against "decadent" influences from the West should be easily comprehensible to Americans, whose Puritan forefathers founded the rule of righteousness on the burning of witches. And the revolt of well-heeled but idealistic Islamic sons against their fathers' compromises with a modernist culture of materialism and power will be familiar to anyone who has studied the revolt of youth in the twentieth century, either in its proto-fascist form before the Second World War or in its libertarian expression in the 1960s.

Which is not to "justify" *anything.* Not the kamikaze fanaticism of Mohammed Atah and his companions, nor the murderous fundamentalism of Bin Laden and his Al Qaeda network, nor the Taliban's humiliating, inhuman treatment of women and dissenters, nor the West's record of wanton destruction over the centuries. I mean only to suggest that in looking into the cruel face of Islamic terrorism, we are looking not at aliens from another planet, but at fellow human beings whose twisted motives are entirely recognizable from our own historical experience.[43]

In any case, as far as national enmities are concerned, they have in general been on the wane, despite the flare-up of hatred in the Middle East. In fact, there has been no military conflict between one major industrial power and another since 1945. In the cold war between the Soviet-Chinese Communist bloc and the Western powers that erupted soon after World War II, there seems to have been a tacit understanding, because of the terrifying potentiality of nuclear warfare, to limit actual hostilities to border areas such as Korea and Indochina.

If much of the demonology that had earlier characterized Europe's national enmities was dragged out of the closet during the four decades preceding the collapse of communism, it had little to do with nationalist presumptions, and, contrary to appearances, it does not now either. To understand how far the individualist societies of the West have evolved from the heyday of lethal national hatreds to the age of global markets, we have to examine their subsequent sources of social cohesion: the welfare state and, more recently, consumer society.

chapter two

Socialism, the Welfare State, and the Heritage of the Left: Solutions Swallowed Up by the Problem

THE COLLECTIVE PROMETHEUS born of modern revolutions had, like a better-known deity, a triple incarnation. The Titan appeared in nationalism, in socialism, and in capitalism, the last of which turns out to have been the real driving force of the modern age. Nationalism, the initial focus of public passion in the great political revolutions of the late eighteenth and nineteenth centuries, seemed for generations to be compatible with the ambitions of corporate elites. But at least in the core capitalist countries since World War II, it has proven so recalcitrant, so hostile to the further evolution of a secure capitalist system that, except for passing manipulations of popular anxieties like that following the September 11 terrorist attacks, it has been limited to the margins of permitted politics. While the same might be said of socialism, social-democratic parties in Europe have often been nominally in power since the Second World War, and as of the fall of 2001 were the dominant political force in most of the nations of the European Union. How they came to inherit the mantle of Prometheus from European nationalism and why their victory has been as hollow in the face of capitalist hegemony as that of their predecessor is the subject of this chapter.

Crucial to an understanding of the relation of Promethean socialism to both nationalism and capitalism is a long view of European history.

Promethean Modernity and Scientific Enlightenment

In Europe, during the centuries that spanned the Renaissance, the Reformation and the French Revolution, a renewal of Promethean energies transformed mentalities and created new ideologies and technological forces. In so doing, these energies prepared the unprecedented changes in the economic, political, and cultural conditions of humankind we call modernity. New ideas were nurtured by the very divisiveness of Europe. Given a continent whose internal geography precluded domination by any one power, the elites of competing old regime states were prepared to use and encourage every technical and ideological innovation—engineering, gunpowder, printing, rationalism and mercantilism—to improve their position over internal and external enemies.

In this period, the existing lines of fracture within European society widened as a result of interstate conflicts that plunged much of the continent into wars, and disputes within the dominant church that produced a permanent schism between Protestants and Catholics. Benefiting from religious and political disunity, Europe's increasingly daring thinkers created a secular philosophy devoted to liberating the rational faculties of humankind from the straitjacket of religious dogma and political authority, an enlightenment that went hand in hand with scientific speculation and research to transform humankind's relationship to nature. The new philosophies divided into, on the one hand, a holistic view of the natural and social world that emphasized the harmony of man and nature and collective historical evolution (Spinoza, Rousseau, Hegel) and, on the other, an individualist view that emphasized the faculties of mind (epistemology) and saw nature and other men as external objects to be manipulated by a knowing subject (Hobbes, Locke, Hume, Kant, and Bentham). Based broadly on the premises of philosophical individualism, accelerated scientific speculation and research created a veritable "scientific revolution." Newton, Galileo, Descartes, Bacon, and many others, demystifying natural processes, transformed humankind's relationship to its nonhuman environment and opened the way to the exploitation of nature by political and economic elites.

Meanwhile, the mental colonization of the premodern popular culture, which Christianity had begun, was continued by state powers and commercial interests. The "civilizing offensive" combined the repressive moral values of Christian dogma with those of the new philosophy to teach "moral" behavior to peasant communities: local patois, community structures and traditional ways of life were condemned as irrational, violent, and barbarous; rural mentalities and rituals—often pre-Christian—as "superstitious." Obedience to church and state, instrumental rationality, and peaceful labor were the values inculcated.

At the turn to the modern era—roughly around 1800—most of these ideals, variously emancipatory and constraining, were harnessed by two powers, inheritors of premodern states and religions, which together transmitted Promethean energy to the broad masses. On the one hand, nationalism and the nation-state incarnated the will to collective liberation; on the other, capitalism organized the will to produce. Both were crucial forces in European, American, and Asian revolutions against traditional feudal despotisms. While unleashed capitalism transformed material existence; nationalist ideology gave society and politics new meaning. Largely defined by bourgeois reformers, nationalist sentiment translated the plebeian enthusiasm for the destruction of absolutism into collective myths that celebrated and hypostatized the existing territories of nation-states, their peoples, their languages, and the cultural norms—of the "civilizing offensive"—established by their elites.

Nationalists were on the whole democratic and generous in the first half of the nineteenth century, cooperating with republicans in demanding the participation of ordinary people in national politics. This progressive character was a response to the reimposition of authoritarian rule in Europe after the revolutionary and Napoleonic epochs. During the period in which the restored aristocracy persecuted nationalists as bloodthirsty revolutionaries, they identified themselves nearly everywhere as defenders of the common people, whether bourgeois, artisan, or peasant. But after the revolutions of 1848, when their most powerful supporters in the capitalist and middle-class elites came to fear the laboring masses more than they did a restoration of authoritarian government, nationalists turned increasingly militaristic and reactionary.

While the driving economic force behind the "unbound Prometheus" of the modern age remained capitalist industry, the ideology representing the liberatory aspect of Prometheus shifted, in theory at least, from liberal nationalism to socialism, and its popular agent, from the middle class to the working class. If liberal nationalism and capitalism had often been allied against the vestiges of the old regime, socialism was, increasingly, internationalist and anticapitalist. In continuing the work of those older siblings, however, socialism broke only marginally with their presuppositions. While attempting to direct Promethean values away from individual acquisitiveness toward collective liberation and productivity, socialism continued to depend on the Enlightenment's largely exploitative view of nature and on the scientific revolution.

Origins of the Modern Left

The European Left, like nationalism, had its origins in the upheavals that ousted old regimes and introduced political, economic, and social modernity between the seventeenth and the nineteenth centuries. Essential to all such upheavals was an alliance between dissatisfied elites and outraged masses.

The social perspectives and mentalities of these allies were actually at loggerheads in ways that went far beyond the clichés of capitalists and workers to which vulgar Marxism subsequently reduced them. On the one hand, reformist elements of the ruling elites, while more or less conscious of potential links to the populace, were imbued with the modernist values of instrumental rationalization and the civilizing process. On the other, artisans, shopkeepers, and peasants, hostile to the constraints of the old regime but mistrustful of modernizing elites, nurtured premodern perspectives and interests. Inspired by customary beliefs rooted in their local social horizons, and with material interests that went no further than holding on to a small piece of land or a local enterprise, the popular classes looked askance at the centralizing and rationalizing tendencies of the elites. Such premodern strata could only be galvanized to act in support of the reformers when changes in social structure, accompanied by the shock of military or economic collapse, caused outrageous injury to their welfare and dignity, delegitimizing the traditional powers (church, monarchy, bureaucracy, nobility, etc.).

Once cooperation between reformers and masses had reached the point of undermining an old regime, however, a dynamic of radical transformation ensued which the reformers had usually not anticipated. The classic examples of such changes and delegitimation are to be found in the three political revolutions that have shaped the modern age—the English, the French, and the Russian. The various movements of the contemporary Left are inconceivable without these upheavals, whose echoes are still present to various degrees in the Labourite, Socialist, Communist, and Green movements of most European nations.

Such national revolutions have been of central importance to world history. A way of understanding their long-term effects is to consider that they were to social history what charismatic leaders were to political history: catastrophic interruptions of the normal social-political routine. Underlying structures may persist, but they are modified by such upheavals as well as by the charismatic political figures seen to inspire them, both of which cast a long shadow over subsequent history. After the epochal events and individuals pass, popular memory of them remains for decades a potential historical force. Particularly in the revolutions, as the anger and the demands of the populace increased, a legend-forming interaction occurred between outraged masses and reformist leaders from the lower echelons of the old elites. The classic example of this interaction is the way the Tennis Court Oath of the French third estate in 1789 (to refuse to disband until their demands for equal representation with the aristocracy and clergy had been accepted) led to the attack on the Bastille by the Paris artisans, which in turn produced a collapse of royal authority and, via the renewed self-assertiveness of the third estate and the surrender of noble privileges on August 4, brought about the end of the ancien régime.

In all the major revolutions, a point was reached where the more moderate reformist groups were purged by popularly supported radicals, pushed by the masses to support—or seem to support—a millennialist popular utopia of direct participation in the governing system. The offspring of this collective impulse for liberation and self-determination were the ideologies of political modernity that came to dominate the nineteenth and early twentieth centuries: democracy, nationalism, and socialism. The radicalization leading to such popular utopias had, of course, built-in limitations, limitations that were felt in the English Revolution via the increasing reaction against the Levellers and Diggers, in the French Revolution during the Terror and the exhaustion of the revolutionary movement in 1794, and in the Russian Revolution through the dwindling effectiveness of the Soviets and the crushing of the Kronstadt uprising. Thermidor and its restorationist equivalents were the next phase, purges of Levellers under Cromwell; of Jacobins, sans culottes, and "agrarian law" communists under the directory of 1794–95; of anarchists and Left Social Revolutionaries under the new Soviet bureaucracy. Ultimately, since the triumph of Bolshevism lacked the sorts of popular bases that inspired the English and French Revolutions, and since it coincided with the age of totalitarian techniques, the Stalinist establishment managed to behead not only the czarist, Liberal, and Menshevik opposition, but also both the Bolshevik leadership and the proletarian vanguard of the 1917 Revolution. This ensured almost three-quarters of a century of continuity to the regime of Lenin and his successors, far more than in England and France. It moreover permitted the authoritarian counterrevolution—a return to traditional Russian imperial perspectives—to occur without any overt change of regime, simply within the consolidation of power by Stalin and the Soviet bureaucracy after 1930 and with many of the trappings of the revolution intact.

In the English and French cases, despite the restoration, within a generation, of the ancien régime, there were very long epilogues to the revolutionary narrative. In England, the Protestant revolutionary impulse went underground into the Puritan Dissenter sects, which preserved the direct participation of believers, and resurfaced politically, as E. P. Thompson showed, in the English radical movements of the French Revolutionary era. In France, the artisan/shopkeeper utopia of direct democracy reemerged in the revolutions of 1830 and 1848, and especially in the Paris Commune, which reinstituted the revolutionary calendar and revived the ideologies and the revolutionary press of 1793–94.

In both England and France, this populist chiliasm of the masses was tied to local social structures and mentalities that were incompatible both with the long-term interests of the major holders of property and power and with the perspective of the new factory workers. The local social structures were those of the artisan/journeyman/shopkeeper, sometimes also of the peasant, that is, of the preindustrial popular strata normally subordinated to the old and new national elites: nobles, upper clergy, gentry, upper civil servants, and merchant entrepreneurs. In the millennialist popular utopias I have mentioned, the sudden disintegration of traditional legitimations, of attitudes of deference to established authority, unleashed the social imagination and fused it to spiritual need, just as had the dissolution of the medieval world in the sixteenth century, just as such disintegration would do, without a revolutionary denouement, in the wild 1960s. In short, the moral and social force of radical movements since the seventeenth century has been rooted in the democratic and solidarist utopianism of preindustrial popular strata, coupled with the legend-forming power of national revolutions.[1]

But the English and French revolutions elicited these preindustrial democratic utopias in contexts of evolving political and economic modernity. Old regime elites locked in mortal struggle with new bourgeois ones had temporarily succumbed to their own inadequacies, but neither the old nor the new dispensation would have any use for the revolutionary *enragés* of the lower orders as soon as the rewarding march toward centralization and domination could be resumed. From the standpoint of the elites, conflicting economic interests and perspectives then merged with social disdain for the patois and the crude, violent, and "superstitious" character of the popular culture. Only at a later stage of political evolution, when the "civilizing offensive" of the new elites, with the school system as its cutting edge, had tamed the unruly urban and rural populace, would modernizing elites allow the masses some highly modified form of *indirect* political influence: participation in parliamentary elections.

In England, Leveller demands for a broad popular suffrage were centuries in advance of any possible establishment of modern democratic institutions, since the latter were unsuited to a largely agrarian society with a powerful gentry and a low level of popular education. Digger communism was even further from the contemporary social possibilities and was, moreover, inspired by evangelical Christian convictions similar to those inspiring medieval heresies.

In the French Revolution, the parallel to the Leveller organization was the sans-culottes movement and the clubs of the Paris sections, representing, like the Levellers, the radicalism of the preindustrial populace. If Protestant millenarianism and the idea that the English nation was God's chosen people were the distinguishing marks of the Puritan Revolution,[2] in France the characteristic element was a combination of Enlightenment idealism and the myth of Paris as the navel of human society. In fact, the artisans and shopkeepers of Paris had largely been organized to serve the royal court, where the monarch explicitly identified the state with his person. In every French revolutionary enactment, the Parisian commoners, having deposed a royal despot, acted on the exalted notion that *they* incarnated both France and mankind, the difference with the Bourbons being that the religion of the Revolution, as Michelet pointed out, was not Christianity but Reason, Justice, and Fraternity. In the popular tribunes of the Revolution—Danton and Jacques Roux, for example—and in the social prophets of social romanticism a half century later, we find the creators and re-creators of this revolutionary religious conviction.

From Arcadian Dreams to Socialist Prometheanism

The modern Left inherited not only the social revolutionary tradition of the great national upheavals, but also, as we have seen in the case of Digger communism, the dreams of a perfect society, of a return to the abundant innocence of Eden, that haunted medieval society. Such visions stimulated pacific movements for evangelical poverty and a communism of goods like the thirteenth-century Waldensians as well as militant ones like the fourteenth-century English peasant uprising of Wat Tyler, based on the Christian "vision" of Piers Plowman, and the fifteenth-century Hussites. In the wake of the great social and political transformations that ushered in industrial society, these dreams recurred, founded less on interpretation of holy writ than on the untested potentialities of the post-revolutionary age: the presumably vast productivity available through the unleashed Prometheus and the apparently blank page open to humanity after the deconstruction of the old regime. Inspired by ideals of equality and social justice, Saint-Simonians and Owenites planned the economic organization of the new society on the basis of the cooperation of all its productive forces—factory workers, engineers, and capitalists. Fourierists worked toward decentralized units of combined agricultural and industrial production, but put more emphasis on the psychological aspect: fitting personality types to particular kinds of work, and encouraging the pacific development of instinctual and aesthetic capacities.

Alongside such utopian dreamers, a more practical Left used the Promethean values of equality and social justice and the Promethean ideal of *Homo faber* to demand basic political and economic reforms. This Left was oriented to the needs and dissatisfactions of the workers of the emerging industrial society. More equality meant, in the first place, universal manhood suffrage and a graduated income tax. Social justice meant an amelioration of the harsh lot of the working man: the right of workers to organize and negotiate working conditions and wages, to demand a larger share of the wealth they created. Supporting such rights was the notion of the worth and dignity of labor. In this new interpretation of *Homo faber,* liberal ideas about labor and property were given added meaning by the increasing consciousness of the laboring class itself about its identity and worth.[3] Nonetheless, socialism before 1848 was rarely based on factory workers, who were numerous only in England and, even there, less inclined to social radicalism than were artisans in traditional trades. [4]

While Jacobin socialism in France and Chartism in England tended to limit themselves to these principles and this valorization of the working class, Karl Marx's celebration of the industrial worker as the inheritor of the bourgeois in the remaking of modern society went much further. Marx postulated a dialectical transformation of the central project of modernism through the revolutionary self-transcendence of a proletarian *Homo faber.* Leszek Kolakowski has accurately identified the Promethean idea permeating Marx's work as "faith in man's unlimited powers as self-creator, contempt for tradition and worship of the past, history as man's self-realization through labour, and the belief that the man of tomorrow will derive his poetry from the future." While admitting that Marx's Prometheanism revealed a "lack of interest in the natural (as opposed to economic) conditions of human existence, the absence of corporal human existence in his vision of the world," Kolakowski highlighted the similarity between the equally antinaturalist Prometheanism of capitalism and that of Marx:

> Marx was certain that the proletariat as the collective Prometheus would, in the universal revolution, sweep away the age-long contradiction between the interest of the individual and that of the species. In this way, too, capitalism was the harbinger of socialism. By smashing the power of tradition, brutally rousing nations from their slumbers, revolutionizing production, and liberating fresh human forces, capitalism had made a civilization in which man for the first time was able to show what he could do, although as yet his prowess took non-human and anti-human forms.[5]

When the socialist movement arose in mid-nineteenth-century Europe to fulfill the social side of the revolutionary expectations aroused in 1789, it appeared as the successor to French Jacobinism and radical Protestantism. Much more than its predecessors, it based itself, in theory, on the achievements and aspirations of a modern social and economic order. It appealed to a notion of the oppressed proletariat that was explicitly destined, in its Marxist formulation, to build on the accomplishments of the bourgeoisie.

Nonetheless, the Marxist revolutionary idea was rooted, more than in Hegelian metaphysics and bourgeois political economy, in the fusion of chiliastic populism and nationalist sentiment that had impelled all the great revolutions of modernity. Socialism's emotional appeal to workmen slowly moving from cottage industry and artisanry to factories remained based both on earlier solidarist utopias of the preindustrial common people, and on popular revolutionary myths of the exalted nation in arms.

In France, such a myth arose from memories of the militant phase of the Revolution of 1789–94. This was surely the basis of the Paris Commune of 1871, whose Blanquist vanguard consciously revived many of the customs and slogans of 1793, including the revolutionary calendar and the cry of *la patrie en danger*. In other words, while French Marxist or Blanquist theories of the proletariat may have provided lawyers, schoolteachers, doctors, and religious folk with the modernist ethical and historicist justification for hurling themselves, in the name of socialism, into the political arena, it was largely the persistence of the revolutionary myth in the lower orders that gave them the necessary popular support to obtain office.[6] Mutatis mutandis, the same held true for Italy, Germany, England, and other European countries. Once in office, of course, the considerable material advantages accruing to the politically successful in parliamentary systems insured that socialist politicians—notwithstanding ideological pronouncements intended for their followers—restricted their activities to reforms of existing structures.

Behind such reformist practices, national revolutionary myths continued to be the source of mass militancy of both Left and Right in the modern era. They served as screens which permitted the imagined resolution of social frustrations through a womblike immersion in linguistic, cultural, and often religious identification at the level of the nation-state. What distinguished Left from Right was the assumption in leftist movements of a universal human dignity, equality, and fraternity underlying the national myth of solidarity, an assumption rooted in the Enlightenment philosophical presuppositions that dominated bourgeois consciousness in the eighteenth and nineteenth centuries. Absence of this assumption in rightist mass movements has permitted them both a bellicosity and an intolerance to ethnic or religious minorities that is not normally found on the Left.

The gaining of power by the reformist Left in the last century—municipally, nationally, or regionally—occurred, then, largely through a reawakening of feelings of injured national pride, the reaction to particularly vicious, self-centered, or stupid practices of conservative or liberal regimes: for example, the catastrophic results of world wars and the menace of militarism (Dreyfus Affair) or of fascism (Popular Fronts in Spain and France). Whenever they gained power, these reformists were usually able, given the resurgence of the revolutionary myth, to counter the immediate political threat from the Right, but they displayed notorious incompetence in dealing with the economy—the French Popular Front being typical in this respect. In other words, modern socialism has an adequate, if spotty, record in turning back the menace of brute reaction, but a very bad one in revolutionizing bourgeois society. This is why in France, after the final active replay of 1789 in the Paris Commune of 1871, the Left was only effective defensively—against militarist reaction in the Boulanger and Dreyfus affairs and against French fascism in 1934–36.

Anatomy of Defeat

The inability of Marxism to unleash the world revolution promised by its founder, and of the social-democratic Left to go any further than the defense of civil society and the bourgeois republic, is overdetermined. Two components of that failure have to do with the sociology and potential historical role of Marxism's chosen agent for revolutionary change, the industrial proletariat. A third has to do with Marxism's productivist values, which had too much in common with those of the capitalism it tried to overthrow to permit a major new historical departure for human society.

While Marxist socialism and social democracy, seen in the light of French and English national revolutionary millenarianism, continued the work of Dissenters, Chartists, radical republicans, neo-Jacobins, and social romantics, they did so with a new constituency—the factory workers (instead of the preindustrial *couches populaires*)—and a new grief: capitalism instead of the remnants of feudalism, monarchy, and imperialism. Shifting their source of support from the preindustrial popular strata to the industrial workers thus seemed to give socialists a firmer footing in the modern world, but there was a problem: the new proletariat was considerably less likely than the older popular classes to demand *active* democratic participation or even to be in a position to hold its "leaders" to any accounting of responsibility.

The industrial proletariat was inadequate to its "historic task" in another, more profound sense as well. For the Marxist notion of fundamental historical change was premised on the notion that within an existing system of production and exchange, a group would develop whose fundamental perspectives and interests were antithetical to that of the system as a whole and superior to it in some world-historical sense. As the existing system decayed internally, this new group would prove resilient enough and conscious enough of its own interests to posit a new social model, a "utopia" in terms of the older system, which would be the basis of a radically new departure in world history. In relation to the class of feudal warrior-landlords that dominated the European landmass between the end of the Roman imperium and the revolutions of modernity, the bourgeoisie was such a new group, in the sense that its entire way of life and values were fundamentally at odds with those of the feudal aristocracy, and economically progressive by comparison with it. Even the preindustrial artisanry, however, whose combativeness in the national revolutions of modernity had led early socialists to invest it with millennial hopes, had been retrograde in relation to the commercial bourgeoisie, comparable to the (relatively) free peasantry that sometimes resisted the rise of feudalism in late medieval Europe. And the industrial proletariat was simply a subordinate class of the capitalist system, similar to the medieval serfs in their relation to the dominant class.

Thus the values of most members of the surviving working class, mired in the middle-class pattern of "work and consume," hardly differ from those of their employers. They simply have a lot less wealth at their disposal. Under conditions of great hardship, one might expect discontent and perhaps revolt from oppressed workers. But the modern proletariat was no more capable of ushering in a new world than the medieval serf. Indeed, it is noteworthy that the millennialist dreams of a perfect society arose in European society in two widely separated periods: in the two hundred years from 1350 to 1550—when movements of oppressed peasants and artisans threatened by Christian feudalism, such as the followers of Wat Tyler in England and Thomas Münzer in Germany, used Christian eschatological doctrine to justify revolt—and in the early nineteenth century, when artisans and small businessmen threatened by the new capitalism (Cabet, Fourier, Leroux, Weitling) created "utopian" socialism. The latter movements, however, which flourished in the aftermath of the French Revolution, when nationalism and capitalism still had a progressive face, withered in the wintry climate that followed the failed revolutions of 1848. From the 1860s on, capitalist industrialization pushed increasing numbers of artisans and peasants into factories. And it was only then, as the dawn of the twentieth century approached, that socialism came to base itself not on the artisanry but on the industrial proletariat.

Outside of moments of social collapse, the tendency of propertyless factory workers to political passivity as well as their inclination to ape the capitalist propensity to focus on earning and spending, insured that the function of the "proletariat," despite the Left's ideological bluster, was simply to give passive support—and pay dues—to organizations claiming to act in their name for higher wages, expanded suffrages, and a modicum of social insurance. This passivity was formulated theoretically in Robert Michels's "iron law of oligarchy," the tendency of mass parties aiming at an extension of democracy to develop an antidemocratic, oligarchic leadership that manipulates party procedures to stay in power.

The leaderships of large socialist parties have in fact been notoriously oligarchic in their relation to their constituencies. Moreover, while a few socialists, before and after World War I, took their ideas seriously enough to be murdered for them—Jaurès, Liebknecht, Luxemburg, etc.—most did not, and even in revolutionary moments such as 1918–19 played the double game of using their old mass support, now largely revolutionized, to suppress the revolution (on grounds of "adventurism") and to bring back the old elites. At *un*revolutionary moments, the most socialists had to offer was a more friendly look and a more progressive rhetoric at election time than their conservative, often reactionary, political opponents. Once in power, they simply implemented the most recent version of liberal modernist economic wisdom, which was Keynesian from about 1935 to 1975, and has been Hayekian or Thatcherian since 1980.

The apparent exceptions to this are the communist regimes that issued from the Russian and Chinese revolutions of the first half of the twentieth century, which merged Marxism with a vitalist ethic that in some ways contradicted Marxism's dialectical materialism. As I have suggested, these regimes turned out not to be exceptions at all, but rather evidence of the inadequacy of even revolutionary Marxism to advance beyond the givens of modernist political economy and rule by economic elites.

The communist movement began in Europe around the turn of the twentieth century as a response to the Marxist revisionism that first permitted revolutionaries to participate in bourgeois governments.[7] Common to both revisionist and orthodox Marxists was the idea that socialism and communism would be built on the achievements of the most technologically advanced capitalist economies. Only in backward Russia, however, did Marxist communists, under Lenin's leadership, succeed in taking over a large country, using a centralized, authoritarian party structure that was to be fatal to the traditional relationship between the Left and the cause of freedom. Fatal, because Lenin's Bolsheviks, destroying Russian democracy in the name of the dictatorship of the proletariat, conflated the latter with the dictatorship of the party, and because the emergent party dictator, Stalin, had no interest at all in democracy and even less in world revolution.[8]

Thus in Russia, and later in China, centralized, authoritarian Marxist parties took power in countries where war and imperialist intervention had undermined old, semifeudal agrarian empires which had haltingly begun to modernize. Marx, of course, had hypothesized that the socialist revolution would be the achievement of an educated industrial working class in an advanced capitalist economy. We have seen why that was unrealistic in terms of his own theory of historical change. What happened in Russia between 1914 and 1917 and in China between 1933 and 1945 was that wars waged by aggressively militarist capitalist states—Germany and Japan—had produced a complete breakdown of the social and economic structure of agrarian-based empires they attacked, leading to massive army mutinies and peasant revolutions. In both Russia and China, tightly organized communist parties took power on the backs of such social revolutions and guided them first in the direction of a redistribution of land to the peasantry, then to a planned state capitalism that celebrated heroic workers, collectivized the peasants, and threw dissidents into work camps, and finally to the abandonment of planning and the introduction of market capitalism.[9]

Apart from the utter inadequacy of the agent selected by modern socialism to change the world and the opportunist propensities of its leadership, the collapse of Marxist communism and the impotence of European social democracy in the past half century are rooted in a double inheritance from their origins in the European revolutionary Left.

On the one hand, this Left has been unable to move beyond the shibboleths of modernity that presided over its birth: the linking of political ideals of freedom and fraternity to economic and philosophical ones of productivity and instrumental rationality. The incompatibility of these various perspectives was predictable in the Left's origins as the offspring of two essentially mismatched progenitors: modernizing reformers and premodern masses. That this incompatibility has survived into the present *post*-modern age is a tribute to the stubborn persistence with which the Left's leadership—despite fundamental changes in the character of its mass following—has clung to its modernist agenda, an agenda that had become distinctly out of date by the eve of the twenty-first century.

On the other hand, there is the Left's birth legacy in the great national revolutions that shaped the modern era. This legacy was invaluable for developing a more than local or regional social and political solidarity in the populations the Left had to mobilize to gain national power, but it has proven a ball and chain in the current era, when the basis of socioeconomic power has moved from the national to the international arena and fundamental change can only be achieved at the supranational level. It is unlikely that modern social-democratic parties will be able to break out of the frameworks given them by national traditions in order to confront the challenges of a global, multinational economic order.

In fact, even what had appeared to be the Left's lasting achievement, the creation of a modern welfare state guaranteeing material security as well as democratic freedoms for the masses, has proven ephemeral in recent decades. For the evolution of liberal capitalism, which the Euro-American welfare state never challenged, has eliminated the conditions that had made that state possible.

Downsizing, the "End of Work," and Job Export

In recent years a number of insightful analyses of the evolution and meaning of work in our high-tech age have postulated the rapid diminution, or even disappearance, of traditional salaried labor and have broached the question of its effects on mentalities and culture generally.[10] The consensus seems to be that in North America and Western Europe most jobs in production and distribution have been either eliminated by automation and computerization or exported to cheap labor areas or simplified to such an extent that relatively inexperienced people can be hired on a temporary basis, and dismissed when demand slackens or a new wave of computerization makes their jobs altogether superfluous. Apart from enabling the "downsizing" of most of the regular employment in industrial production, technology has in recent years invaded the distribution and service sectors, permitting, for example, the increasing replacement of bank tellers and railroad ticket window agents by computerized machines.[11]

Those forced out of jobs have suffered major losses in income, self-esteem, and sense of social belonging, but they have not, by and large, joined the ranks of the unemployed. Particularly in the United States, where unemployment insurance is low and runs out quickly and where welfare provisions are close to nonexistent, they have either taken on insecure, poorly paid temporary work in the branches they used to work in,[12] or they have joined the swelling army of the tertiary "service" sector, as cleaning workers, information consultants, household personnel for the wealthy, servicemen and repairmen, etc. In Europe the better social security net permits a higher unemployment rate (10 percent for the European Union), but there, as in the United States, social exclusion and homelessness are much more evident than a generation ago.

Although mostly working conditions and pay are worse than ten or twenty years ago, some 20 percent of the work force—in general those workers with higher education, analytic capacities, and skills in the manipulation of symbols—enjoy better incomes than ever: consultants, lawyers, computer programmers, top managerial personnel. With huge salaries, however, come stress levels comparable to those struggling for a living. Indeed, those at the very top justify their ever-increasing salaries by the precarious nature of their employment in the age of mergers and acquisitions. But those below the top 20 percent have the same stress and are often forced to work longer for less money.

Thus work has not ended and will not end. But, because of changing technologies and mounting competition for investments, the nature of work has been revolutionized in recent decades. The contractual conditions under which employees agree to work has correspondingly changed drastically. Partly through computerization and partly through a steady expansion of investment in the Asian and eastern European periphery of the capitalist world system,[13] what we might call the "imaginary space" of capitalism has expanded steadily, to the benefit of employers seeking cheap labor and to the detriment of workers seeking better wages and job security.

As early as a century and a half ago, it was a commonplace of intelligent social observers that capitalists were constantly on the lookout for cheap labor. They had no qualms about abandoning work forces that had become too dear and investing capital elsewhere, if necessary in other countries. In the 1830s the historian Michelet noted the tendency of English capitalists to move factories to Ireland, and he predicted they would move elsewhere if labor became expensive there too. Nonetheless, before the second half of the twentieth century, national boundaries tended to form a barrier to capital, since communications and transportation, though steadily becoming easier, were still far from the instantaneous telecommunications and rapid air transport that subsequently developed. Moreover, problems of political control and language often made denationalizing capital a costly and risky affair. Thus most of the search for cheap labor by even the largest companies went on within nation-state boundaries This meant that trade union efforts to defend the working man against such dangers to job security and decent wages could plausibly and effectively restrict organizing to the national scene, within which they might have a fighting chance against the power of capital. Unions were at most nationwide, and left-wing parties, whose political goals were often aligned with those of unions, were national parties.

Nonetheless, capitalists eager to gain a competitive edge by cutting wage costs always found it far easier to relocate than did organized workers, and the larger the national space, the easier it was for capitalism to evade organized labor, the harder for workers to defend their interests. Thus the congenital weakness of socialism and the union movement in the United States is partly explained by the relative ease of capital in escaping from organized, demanding, and often violent work forces within the vast spaces of continental North America. The contrast is striking between this continental dimension within which American capitalism was able to develop and the relatively restricted size of the dozen or so major European capitalist powers.[14] In the first half of the twentieth century, for example, the American textile industry moved from the unionized Northeast to the socially undeveloped and impoverished South. In the last third of the century, most of the automobile industry, whose well-paid workers belonged to one of the most radical unions in the United States, relocated from the Flint-Detroit area primarily to Asian and European assembly sites, compelling unemployed American workers to take on poorer paying jobs, mainly in the South. To move a factory as far away from Belgium—a comparable old industrial area in Europe—as the Deep South is from the textile mills of New England, one would have to relocate in Algeria.

Because of the absence of any social or political infrastructure and the continental size of the country, American workers have usually been powerless to do anything about this situation. If, as liberal theorists argued in the sixties, democracy depends on a kind of social and economic pluralism in which the interests of labor and capital have a more or less equal footing, then this kind of democracy never really existed in the United States. In fact, simply because of the geographic breadth and depth of the United States, one might say that the system of representative democracy has served there as a screen for an economic power over the citizenry more consistent with authoritarian empires than with the liberal nation-states of modern Europe.

Nonetheless, from the thirties until the mid-seventies, under the shock of depression, world war, and a postwar tide of rising expectations, a political establishment fearful of social chaos and revolution installed the rudiments of a welfare state in the United States. Unions received national protection; social security supplied minimum pensions, unemployment, and welfare rights; and, increasingly during the sixties, the civil rights of black people were guaranteed. Real wages and living standards after 1945 increased considerably, driven by the labor-dependent postwar reconstruction and expansion of capitalism.[15]

In Europe, where working-class resistance to capitalism had early created socialist parties to protect the common interest, the welfare state had deeper roots. It originated in social legislation to protect workers against unemployment and ill health in Bismarckian Germany, clearly measures intended to reduce the support of industrial workers for revolutionary socialism; in the 1920s these measures were extended under social-democratic governance in Central and Western Europe to include housing projects for the poor to take the place of insalubrious proletarian slums. As I have indicated, after the deprivations of the depression and the multiple traumas of the Second World War, European elites accepted further social legislation as necessary to restore national social cohesion. Moreover, until the 1980s they viewed communism, which in principle offered total protection for the working man, as a serious social threat: powerful communist parties were for a while the largest political groupings in France and Italy, garnering a quarter to a third of the vote. The only trump card available to the liberal capitalist powers was the welfare state, which gave workers a higher living standard than that enjoyed east of the Elbe, almost as much security, and also offered democratic freedoms. Moreover, such welfare states, despite their high taxes, were congruent with capitalism's need for placid workers who could purchase much of what they were producing under Fordist conditions of mass production.

Neoliberalism, Social Dumping, and the Demise of Homo faber

The European and American welfare states, though supported by the Left, fitted into the social strategy of postwar capitalism. They were, however, also a result of conjunctural and structural changes in the system of production. Further changes made them an unnecessary burden.

Capitalism recovered from the crisis of the thirties largely through the war economy triggered by the global conflict of 1939–45 and through the wholesale reconstruction of European economies after the devastation caused by that war. War economies under advanced capitalism amount to a kind of socialism for the rich, with a significant trickle-down effect for the rest of the population. Both the war economies and the welfare states that accompanied them required the acceptance, by traditional capitalist circles, of a considerable amount of government intervention and regulation of economic life, undertaken under more or less Keynesian principles, which supported vigorous government intervention and, in periods of recession, deficit financing as pump priming for the economy. Thus it was that, during the postwar continuation of the U.S. war economy, welfare institutions were established in North America and noncommunist Europe, institutions that in many European countries merited the appellation of a welfare state. In the United States, the war economy endured for more than three decades after 1945, since the cold war (along with the Korean War at the beginning and the Vietnam War toward the end) gave it new life. (Even President Eisenhower acknowledged the dominance in America of a "military-industrial complex.")

The winding down of the Vietnam War in the early seventies, however, considerably reduced military expenditures in the United States. Ominously, for the welfare state, this curtailing of government subsidization of "defense" industries coincided with the oil crisis of 1974, the breakdown of the Bretton Woods agreements on currency regulation, and the emergence of Japan as a fierce competitor to Euro-American capitalism. The prolonged period of economic control of the capitalist world economy by the U.S. superpower drew to an end in the 1970s, and with it the social truce with the laboring classes that the welfare state had represented.[16] An additional reason for the increasing dissatisfaction of corporate capitalism with the welfare state was the profit squeeze caused by the combination of increasing competition, high taxes, and the militant wage demands of labor at a time when it was in short supply.

In England under Thatcher and in the United States under Ronald Reagan, Western capitalism—exploiting a conservative mood in an electorate frightened by the political and cultural radicalism of the youth of the sixties and seventies—embraced the antiwelfarist, anti-Keynesian principles of Milton Friedman and Friedrich von Hayek. As against Keynesian and social-democratic ideas that society could be shaped in a humanitarian direction by collective intelligence, the new conservatism advocated a return to nineteenth-century liberal economics: the apotheosis of market relations between individuals as the only sacrament of the social nexus, the celebration of individual calculation of advantage as the exclusive motor of economic progress—a position that became known as neoliberalism. Neoliberals viewed welfare provisions as a useless tax burden, increasing the cost of labor and in any case incapable of relieving social ills, which the unfettered growth of capitalism alone could accomplish. Supplementing this ideological revolt against the welfare state was the technological revolution of automation and computerization, which permitted wholesale replacement of experienced but costly workers by machines, quick global coordination of "flexible" production and distribution, and the near-instantaneous execution of financial operations.

Under these ideological and technological conditions, capitalism has become, in the last quarter century, more predatory than ever. Given the redistribution of wealth to the managerial and proprietary strata, given also the huge amounts of money in the pension funds of governments and large corporations, shareholder capital has expanded at the expense of banking capital, and multibillion-dollar corporations competing for the shareholders' favor are continually on the lookout for short-term fixes—takeovers or mass firings—that may increase their profit margins or, at least, their prospects of increased profits. Popularity of a company among shareholders—and among the neoliberal agitprop journalists who shape shareholder opinion—will usually rise after wholesale firing of personnel and a merger with, or acquisition of, a competing company.[17] Such dog-eat-dog capitalism has the built-in limitations of any closed system consuming itself.[18]

The indefinite continuation of such short-term fixes thus depends on market globalization, the steady expansion of large-scale capitalist enterprise into areas previously closed to it by trade barriers.[19] This has been the raison d'être of the International Monetary Fund, the World Bank, the World Trade Organization, and the European Union. Within the core area of global capitalism, these organizations have functioned as watchdogs to prevent any restoration—or even any popular defense of—the institutions of the Euro-American welfare state, universally condemned by neoliberal ideologists as archaic. They have also written the rules governing the deregulation and privatization of public services, permitting the expansion of capital investment in everything from education to energy utilities and public transportation. They have been equally important in capitalism's peripheral areas, forcing countries like India to surrender government control over key sectors of the economy to obtain loans and favorable terms of trade, thereby incorporating ever larger parts of the global economy into the area dominated by transnational corporate capitalism. The North American Free Trade Area (Nafta), created under the Clinton presidency has served as a model for this expansion, and it was the clear intent of the leading spirits of the WTO, at their failed Seattle meeting of November 1999, to replicate this accomplishment on a global scale.

This new conjunctural phase of capitalist ideology had begun well before the final collapse of the Soviet empire. From the early eighties on, the Euro-American welfare state was undermined by three new strategies of enterprises seeking to cut wage costs. While these strategies were first justified and spurred on by hard-nosed American neoliberal economic theorists like Friedman, they had their European equivalent in followers of von Hayek, the totem ideologist of British conservatism.

One technique, technological and administrative, was innovated in Japan, particularly by the Toyota company. It was alleged to be more efficient than the centralized, assembly-line system of production in one large company. On the one hand, labor costs were reduced by replacing as many workers as possible with automated and computerized production, and "encouraging" the survivors to use their own ingenuity to work more efficiently in small production teams, each with group responsibility for a major part of the final product. On the other hand, as many components as possible were purchased from smaller subcontractors, where interfirm competition kept wages at a much lower level than what was paid to the rump work force of the main company. This tactic cut the cost of those components for the subcontracting mega-enterprise.[20]

The other two strategies had to do with the globalization of capital, through multinational and transnational corporations.[21] One was job export, sometimes called social dumping. Corporations exported capital and production much more extensively than was possible earlier to cheap labor areas in Asia or eastern Europe, where little or no social security costs ate into company profits. When it was a question of heavy consumer hardware, such as cars or refrigerators, this displacement was partly intended to supply the local market for such products, but in many cases, as in automobile production, it might concern components for the product that could be produced so economically elsewhere that the cost of shipping them back to a central assembly point was more than compensated for.[22] In the case of the lucrative and growing electronics industry, goods were rarely so heavy that shipping costs precluded delocalization of production to other countries, as the employees of the Dutch electronics giant Philips have learned to their sorrow.[23] Such delocalization was easiest when it came to routine administrative paperwork, earlier done by workers in the main office of a concern and now prepared by computer. For example, in the case of bank statements, the data could be sent electronically to skilled computer workers in the Indian city of Bangalore (whose high-tech companies pay their programmers a fraction of their Western counterparts' salaries) and the statements relayed instantly via telecommunications to the main bank offices in Europe and North America.

The final strategy was simply legalized extortion. Using as arguments the ease of dumping jobs in low-cost areas of other nations and continents, captains of industry, in countries where their political representatives were not already empowered to help them cut wages, blackmailed social-democratic and Christian-democratic governments into cutting both social insurance premiums and taxes under threat of further increases in the politically sensitive unemployment rate. From the 1980s on, it was a foregone conclusion shared by the entire political establishment that the Euro-American welfare state would have to be eliminated or reduced to "minimal" proportions because of the inability to continue supporting the unemployed, the ill, and the aged. This inability was partly because of the increased number of those excluded from a normal work life by the computerization of production and distribution and by social dumping to other countries, and partly because of the reduced resources of the state imposed by neoliberal budget cutting. In any case, the obvious solutions to these problems—redistributing work by cutting the workweek, raising taxes on the wealthy, and fining social dumping—were excluded by the social-democratic establishment as contrary to contemporary economic principles, and indeed any attempt to implement such solutions within the traditional nation-state framework was indeed out of the question, because of the inevitable and prohibitive sanction of large international investors and the international banking and trade organizations that represented them.[24]

What effect have these changes had on the central ideal of modernity, *Homo faber*?

Under the welfare state, two contradictory ideologies were encouraged, one supporting *Homo faber,* the other undermining him. Supplementing liberal utilitarianism's ascetic idealizing of *Homo faber* was the social-democratic celebration of the dignity of labor. Intended to provide cradle-to-grave security for honest workers, the welfare state was established for presumably hard-working proletarian families by parties that claimed to represent them. Its underlying premise was not the boondoggling subsequently associated with it by conservative ideologists, but the need to protect the laborer because of the ethical value put on his work. This ideal of work was imbedded both in a philosophical valuation of *praxis* (imported from Greek and Renaissance philosophy into Enlightenment thought) and in Christian notions that asceticism was good and leisure and luxury were sinful, notions that crystallized in the seventeenth century into the Protestant work ethic and that, as mentioned, subsequently found their place in liberal utilitarianism.

Paradoxically, however, the growing security and affluence that were guaranteed, for a time, to working men and women brought them into the middle-class mentality of consumption, which reduced labor and productivity from a social ethic to a mere means to the good life. Working people were encouraged to buy homes, automobiles, and household appliances, and, by omnipresent advertising, to aspire to a wide range of initially non-essential consumer goods that rapidly became an indispensable part of the standard of living. Consumption as a goal largely replaced the work ethic, as indeed it had to if the goods produced by Fordist capitalism were to be sold.

In the past two decades, the expansion of neoliberal capitalism has eliminated both the dignity of labor—which has ceased to be secure, regular, well paid, and limited to daytime hours—and the welfare state.

Those who have had to suffer this expansion in areas peripheral to Western "core" capitalism, like the peasants of Chiapas, Mexico, and of India, are bound to view the "modernize or die" dictates of capitalist agriculture no more favorably than the Russian peasants who underwent collectivization as part of the Soviet Union's state-capitalist industrialization in the 1930s. But by virtue of this combination of economic cannibalism and continual expansion, the economic strongholds of neoliberal capitalism have managed, amid growing chasms between rich and poor and rampant personal insecurity, to maintain a fragile equilibrium.

In the United States, repeated "downsizing" operations, which have in most cases increased the value of an enterprise's stock shares, have not produced the kind of unemployment common in Europe.[25] In the absence of any adequate unemployment or welfare insurance, the millions of workers thrown on the garbage heap have been forced to take work at lower wages, frequently in evanescent service occupations. To continue to purchase houses, cars, and appliances, housewives, hitherto able to devote themselves to the upbringing of their children, have often had to join their husbands in the myriad of marginal employments paid for, poorly, by the wealthy: housecleaning, supermarket delivering, gift wrapping, temporary clerking, gardening, minor repairs of house and auto, etc. In Europe, where welfare systems were more firmly implanted, the tendency has been slowed by existing social protections, but unemployment is high (10 percent in the European Union) and destructive of personal identities. As in North America, a growing human detritus has been thrown on the streets, homeless, in abysmal poverty and disorganization.

The Twilight of the European Left and the Humanitarian Drift of European Social Democracy

I do not wish to denigrate the accomplishments of the European Left. It has for a century and a half represented the aspirations of tens of millions of men and women toward a better life, and it has been the medium through which they have struggled to obtain it. Where the Left has been able to build on the principles of democratic revolutions, as in Western Europe, it can justly lay claim to having extended suffrage and defended legal equality and humanitarianism against militarist and nationalist reaction, sometimes brilliantly (in the Dreyfus Affair and the Front Populaire, for example). However, the political Left has been only marginally effective in its effort to combine freedom with social justice. And its contemporary ineptitude has profound roots.

First, the Left has but rarely attacked the problems of formal democracy, party oligarchy, and bureaucratic government: how to alter a political structure that often limits the rights of the overwhelming majority of citizens to choosing between brands X and Y at election times, how to cope with party organizations that seem to be expert at manipulating and maneuvering around the supposedly democratic organs of the membership (to say nothing of the democratic interests of their voters), and how to deal with the entrenched bureaucrats and corporate lobbyists whose professional skill in outmaneuvering even parliamentary majorities is awesome. In other words, how to move from the lust for patronage and booty that characterizes all mass parties and large bureaucratic structures to some form of genuine democratic control over public life, in which leaderships would be accountable to their members and constituents, and their policies would be the outcome of wide public debate.

A second problem area is that of creating an indispensable international economic and social program for parties which are purely national and which, moreover, have been notoriously ineffective even at that level.

Various aspects of the changed world of the past quarter century have altered the character of the Left as well. Given the rapid diminution of its proletarian base, the Left has found a new constituency in the massive, insecure, but educated white-collar and intellectual strata. In this new context, the economic programs and rhetoric of the Left parties, keyed to the modernist stakes of a hundred years ago in a postmodern world, are increasingly outdated and irrelevant. In particular, the productivist ethic of the traditional Left and the value of growth for its own sake have become obsolete and ecologically dangerous justifications for not rocking the boat of the global capitalist economy.

Indeed, in its effort to prove its trustworthiness to neoliberal capitalist circles, the government of Tony Blair has adopted their language. Its *Annual Report* of 1998 began: "Changing a government is like sweeping away the entire senior management of a company."[26] That this rhetorical gesture is matched by serious commitment was made clear at the March 2000 Lisbon economic summit of the European Union, presided over by Blair and Schröder, which produced, according to the *Financial Times* of March 25–26, 2000, "a corporate plan for corporate Europe." In an appreciative editorial in the same issue, the *Financial Times* dismissed as a 1968-style "rant" an appeal by Nicole Fontaine, the Christian Democratic(!) president of the European Parliament for a curb on the "ruthless pursuit of profit at the expense of working men and women," and concluded that "the board of Europe Inc. made it clear this week that [such ideas] should no longer interfere with the business of business."[27]

To compensate for their abandonment of any plausible goal of economic transformation, in fact their total devotion to neoliberal interests, the large European parties of the democratic Left have adopted two strategies to distinguish themselves from their conservative opponents. One is to try to modify, without seriously attacking, the ground rules of globalized neoliberal capitalism in the direction of a humanitarian and ameliorative concern for its victims. For example, whereas conservative liberals, who are in general opposed to all government intervention in corporate policies and in market relationships, support mass dismissals to cut costs and improve profits and stock exchange ratings, social democrats deplore such dismissals (although they rarely deny their legitimacy)[28] and favor government subsidies for low-paid extra jobs of public utility, such as (in the Netherlands, for example) additional ticket collectors in mass transport. In France, where there is a powerful tradition of state intervention in economic life, the more daring social democrats (pressured by the Greens) have gone as far as legislating a thirty-five-hour workweek to absorb some of the unemployed. Nonetheless Keynesians on the social-democratic Left, who advocate systematic regulation of the economy to stimulate demand, are now marginal figures, excluded even in France from key positions, and the dramatic forms of government intervention they represented in the heyday of the welfare state have become invisible. The result of this economic conformism has been the forfeiture of any kind of critique of neoliberal capitalism to parties to the left of the social democrats: communist, Trotskyist, Green-left, and simply socialist. In a number of Dutch cities, voters for the Green Left and the left-wing Socialist Party are now more numerous than those for the social-democratic Labour Party.

The second tactic of the moderate Left is to embrace sociocultural issues, such as women's right to choose abortion, gender equality, gay rights, environmental protection, and multiculturalism—that is, opposition to racism and xenophobia—where a contrast with conservative positions continues to be noticeable. Given the surrender of efforts to oppose neoliberal economic policies, such issues have become the basis of coalitions between social democrats and liberal-democratic or Green parties in a number of European countries. In 1999, such coalitions were in power in France, Germany, Italy, Belgium, and the Netherlands.[29] In England, alliance with the liberal democrats was made unnecessary by the "first past the post" district election system, which usually gives a hefty parliamentary majority to either Labour or the Conservative Party. In the present case, it was also superfluous because the "Third Way" Labour Party of Tony Blair, in its quest for middle-class votes, had already incorporated much of the political program of the small Liberal Democratic Party and had, by its strong advocacy of market capitalism and its condemnation of the welfare state, made itself attractive to disillusioned, but European-oriented, voters of the Conservative Party as well.

European social democracy's tendency to conceal its impotence on bread-

and-butter issues by embracing humanitarian causes of a sociocultural character has nowhere been more obvious than in its fervent support for intervention to halt ethnic cleansing in Kosovo and promote European multiculturalism. The NATO bombing of Serbia, ostensibly to prevent a Serb genocide of the Kosovar Albanians, occurred during the spring 1999 election campaign to the European Parliament, and effectively served to obscure the potential significance of those elections from the European public.

If the predominantly social-democratic governments of the European Union had wanted to democratize the Union's governance by increasing the influence of its featherweight parliament, if they had wished to implement the program for a Social Europe to which they had long paid lip service (by enacting Europe-wide minimum wages, social security networks, pensions, and medical care), the European parliamentary elections were a perfect moment to do so. Corruption scandals exposed by left-wing members of the parliament had forced the European Commission, its executive organ, to resign en masse, and leftward shifts in the European electorate had been visible since 1995.

But an election victory of the European moderate Left on a Social Europe program would have forced it into a confrontation with U.S. and European capital, the IMF, the World Bank, and the WTO. Having long embraced the Thatcherian TINA principle ("There Is No Alternative" to market capitalism and neoliberal ideology), most European social-democratic parties had no stomach for such a confrontation. During the spring of 1999, when European voters might have been debating these issues, Tony Blair and Gerhard Schröder, leaders respectively of the British Labour Party and the German Socialist Party, were grabbing the headlines with militant rhetoric about Europe's "humanitarian" mission in Kosovo, resulting in the military intervention whose splendid achievements in ending ethnic hatred in Kosovo are now part of history.[30] Meanwhile, so few people were aware there was a European election going on that fewer than 50 percent of them voted, and the majority of those who did vote empowered Europe's conservative parties.[31]

Thus, despite its recent national electoral successes, European social democracy has rarely been weaker than it is today. This febrility has three elements. One is its inability to provide anything more than a cosmetic remedy to the increasing gulf between rich and poor, inevitable in terms of its neoliberal capitalist orientation. This gulf is growing not merely between "northern" (core) and "southern" (peripheral) states, but within the core states themselves. A second is its incapacity, given its productivist premises, to reverse the globally dangerous degradation of the earth's environment.

The third is the weakness of the nation-state as a whole. This weakness, an inevitable consequence of globalization, is the framework for the first two problems I have signaled.

The enfeeblement of the nation-state in an age of global market capitalism is a commonplace of contemporary political discourse. One sign is the literal breakup of once all-powerful national governments. Manifestations of this are contradictory, some of them being a resurgence of ethnic regionalism—usually representing conservative local social or economic forces, but sometimes, as in Scotland and Catalonia, of a leftist-populist character that is clearly more radical than the national socialist parties—while others are a direct reflection of quasi-autonomous regional capitalism, as in the area of southeastern France and northwestern Italy.[32] Another symptom of this enfeeblement is the virtual impossibility of even the more left-wing social-democratic governments such as the French (in which Socialists ruled together with Communists and Greens) to break with the model of a global market economy propagated by the multibillion-dollar transnational corporations and their financial and commercial organs: the IMF, the World Bank, the WTO, and the European Commission. These forces exercise so much influence in every country that defiance of their strictures against government regulation, more than minimal welfare provisions and deficit financing brings penalties no social-democratic government finds acceptable.

Even before this undoing of the nation-state and traditional social democracy by globalization, a troubled relationship prevailed between nationalism, an ideology of collective identity, and the individualist capitalism it stimulated. Liberal individualist advocates of capitalism cared little for solidarity and social justice, viewed freedom strictly in terms of the free disposal of property, and measured rationality and productivity by the increase in the individual wealth of property holders through a free market. They condemned social control, beyond the maintenance of legal equality, as an unjust expression of collective power: authoritarian, collectivist, irrational, and unproductive. Reducing reason to instrumental efficiency, this denigration of the social undermined the popular solidarities and the sense of injustice that had survived under the old regimes and had been an indispensable source of the revolts against them. Abandoning the social nexus may have been convenient to the economic individualism that created a capitalist order on the ruins of absolute monarchies, but it was destructive of the notion of political obligation necessary to the cohesion of even a liberal-democratic state.

Indeed, the classic historian of liberal individualism, C. B. Macpherson describes "the dilemma of modern liberal-democratic theory" in these

terms: "it must continue to use the assumptions of possessive individualism, at a time when the structure of market society no longer provides the
necessary conditions for deducing a valid theory of political obligation
from those assumptions. . . . the maturing of market society has canceled
that cohesion, among all those with a political voice, which is a prerequisite for the deduction of obligation to a liberal state from possessive individualist assumptions."[33] To return to the guiding metaphor of this book:
when one posits the market-oriented social order as the sole acceptable
framework for the Promethean ethos, solidarity with the common good,
without which Prometheus would never have sacrificed himself, expires in
the process.

This brings us to the neoliberal capitalism I have mentioned. First formulated ideologically by English and American capitalism in the 1970s and
1980s, it has done its best, in its quest for continual global expansion, to undermine local economic models opposed to it. This has meant the demise
not only of Keynesian-based welfare systems, such as in Scandinavia, but
also of competing capitalisms, such as the German "Rhenish" model of co-
determination of corporate policy by management and union.[34] How much
of Rhineland capitalism still exists is, of course, debatable. An example of a
purported "Anglo-Saxon" attack on the Rhenish model is the 1999 takeover
by the Anglo-American telecom corporation Vodafone of its German rival
Mannesmann. While the defense of Mannesmann was conducted specifically in the name of the German model of co-determination, with a very
strong union protest, an insightful column in *Le Monde* of November 23,
1999, pointed out that the German corporate culture of the 1990s had been
thoroughly Americanized, and that union representation in German corporations had become no more than a fig leaf for the same kind of "lean management" that had resulted in massive downsizing elsewhere in the world.[35]

The public reactions to the terrorist attacks on the United States in September 2001, followed by war in Afghanistan, resulted in a temporary
reinforcement of the authority of the national state and a brief abandonment
of neoliberal antistate ideology in the heartland of world capitalism. Inspired by anxiety about anthrax and by fear, carefully cultivated by the government, of new attacks, some 88 percent of the American people supported
the Bush administration's "war on terrorism." The congenital suspicion of
"big government" became a minority sentiment, flag-waving and chants of
"U.S.A." were ubiquitous, and the Bush administration competed with the
Democratic majority in the senate in sponsoring large spending bills to
help New York rebuild its devastated downtown and to rescue the United
States economy from recession. Considering the huge amounts earmarked

for military hardware, it seemed as though the military-industrial state had a new lease on life.

It became quickly evident, however, that, while the government was willing to apply Keynesian principles to production for the military and to extend huge tax breaks to the rest of ailing corporate America, there was to be no return to welfare state protection—"handouts" to the unemployed and the indigent. Even the promised aid to New York City was reduced, two months after the attacks, by 45 percent.[36] Thus behind the mask of "compassionate conservatism," the administration's Scroogist neoliberalism remained. And the ideological fig leaf of a restored welfare state showed its ephemeral character. Assuming the present world recession does not deepen into a thirties-style depression, the trauma of September 11 is not likely to be followed by change in the fundamental direction of global society.

As multinational corporations flex their muscles globally, and as the IMF, the World Bank, and the WTO lay down guidelines for loans and investments that make a mockery of national sovereignty and humiliate those who long struggled for workers' rights through socialism, growing hordes of insecure, temporary workers, drifting from job to job, are manipulated into consuming more than they need or can afford by the media-magnified lure of the fabulous living standards of the wealthy, and by advertising, all of which leads them to associate sex, power, popularity, and prestige with the right brand of cars, soap, and beer.[37] There are, then, compensations for the loss of a fixed employment, poorer working conditions, and the disintegration of the social nexus. Television and the shopping mall offer the masses the bread and circuses of a consumer society. For a more restricted group, Internet commercial sites offer the illusory enchantment of the global village. The function of consumerism as a surrogate for the lost dreams of socialism, and the questionable effectiveness of this placebo, are the subject of the next chapter.

chapter three

Consumer Paradise:
Another Failed Theodicy

All things are sold: the very light of Heaven
Is venal; earth's unsparing gifts of love,
The smallest and most despicable things
That lurk in the abysses of the deep,
All objects of our life, even life itself,
And the poor pittance which the laws allow
Of liberty, the fellowship of man,
Those duties which his heart of human love
Should urge him to perform instinctively
Are bought and sold as in a public mart
Of undisguising selfishness, that sets
On each its price, the stamp-mark of her reign.

SHELLEY, *Queen Mab*

The United States now has the highest obesity rate of any industrialized nation in the world. More than half of all American adults and about one-quarter of all American children are now obese or overweight. Those proportions have soared during the last few decades, along with the consumption of fast food. The rate of obesity among American adults is twice as high today as it was in the early 1960's.

ERIC SCHLOSSER, *Fast Food Nation*

The Consumer as Promethean Hero

THE CONTEMPORARY DOCTRINE of consumerism, the popular face of capitalist individualism today, seems closer to older cultures of aristocratic opulence than to the Promethean work ethic, and its full expression is limited to an envied and imitated minority. Nonetheless, at the beginning of the third millennium, the ideology of style, power, and wealth of contemporary consumer society—the perfect accompaniment of capitalist individualism and the only ideology to survive the debacle of the welfare state—

has taken the place of the moribund collective ideologies of nationalism and socialism as a reified Prometheanism. In a review of a book on the rise of the free market in Europe—seen as an unintended consequence of medieval strife between church and state—we find one of a litany of celebrations at the turn of the millennium, of the success of liberal capitalism in vanquishing all competitors. The reviewer, Martin Wolf, agrees with the author (Deepak Lal) in attributing "Promethean growth—the progressive rise in real incomes of the modern age" to "the distinctive beliefs of the west," which he summarizes in one word: "individualism." From "individualism tempered by guilt" arose first Protestantism, then "Promethean growth" (capitalism), and then, "with the 'death of God' and so, of guilt, contemporary hedonism" (consumer society).[1]

The reach of capitalist ideology is thus not limited to those with the income to compete in the consumer rat race. If its full expression is restricted to a small minority of millionaires and billionaires,[2] its appeal as an ideology pushed by omnipresent advertising and by peer pressure extends far beyond that circle. In our contemporary postindustrial society, where it helps drive millions living in daily fear of downsizing to ruthlessly competitive overwork,[3] consumer ideology can be seen as the contemporary middle-class equivalent of what Ernest Gellner refers to as industrial society's "favoured mode of social control . . . universal Danegeld, buying off social aggression with material enhancement."[4] Gellner also signals the "greatest weakness" of this method: "its inability to survive any temporary reduction of the social bribery fund, and to weather the loss of legitimacy which befalls it if the cornucopia becomes temporarily jammed and the flow falters."[5]

Although this ideology is the principal surviving justification for the harshly competitive neoliberal version of *Homo faber,* it is incompatible with virtually all of the humanist values attached to the Promethean ethos, apart from the "freedom" to own, flaunt, and dispose of property. Here, as elsewhere, the myth of Prometheus has been invoked to legitimize an ideology which, intended to give meaning to the sacrifice and pain caused by modernization, has undermined the ethical values associated with Promethean productivity. And, as Gellner indicates, a major economic downturn could finish it off.

The shock troops of modernity are then no longer the heroic workers of industrial capitalism, but heroic consumers. As the ebullient James B. Twitchell puts it, "Man (and woman) is not only *homo sapiens* or *homo ludens,* or *homo faber* but also *homo emptor.*"[6]

The significance of this shift cannot be underestimated. Before the First World War, the consumption pattern of workers—even factory workers—

was largely premodern, involving "domestic production, for example making clothes, growing vegetables, raising animals, making one's own entertainment."[7] Such a traditional pattern was understandable, considering the largely rural origins of the new European and American factory workers. There were of course some significant exceptions, such as the widespread purchase of factory-made textiles by workers, which the French historian Michelet noted in the 1840s.[8] But in general, the preindustrial consumption pattern of ordinary people was in harmony with an epoch in which the major items of production were capital goods (railroads, for example) rather than consumer products, and poorly paid factory workers neither could nor were expected to consume what they produced.

As we have seen, during the epoch of Fordist production the preeminence of the work ethic began to coincide with large-scale consumption of mass-produced industrial goods. Indeed, if the mountain of goods turned out by assembly line workers were to be sold, they had to be consumers as well as producers.[9] The double function of the worker was recognized by Henry Ford himself, who paid his workers high wages in the expectation that they would purchase the cars they made.[10] At the same time, "human engineering"—Taylorism—increased both the productivity and the alienation of the industrial work force.

Fordist mass production also coincided with the period of the twentieth century's two world wars and the ensuing cold war: roughly 1914–75. Free-trade liberalism had by the turn of the twentieth century already succumbed to the imperialist rivalries of the great powers, and the war economies and economic crisis during the earlier phase of Fordist/Taylorist production prepared post-1945 Western mentalities for the role of the state in regulating the economy and in guaranteeing a broader distribution of wealth. Indeed, most of the new political responses of the interwar years acknowledged the need, in the light of the unprecedented suffering caused by the First World War and the economic collapse of the 1930s, for the state to control the economy. The transformation of traditional authoritarianism into the total state systems of Nazi Germany, Fascist Italy, and Stalinist Russia was mirrored, among parliamentary democracies, in the Keynesianism of the American New Deal and the French Popular Front.

During the prolonged tension with the Soviet Union that followed World War II, Western democracies created a system that combined state regulation of the economy with redistributive principles and social security: a cocktail of measures designed not only to avoid the maldistribution of wealth and the runaway speculation that had led to the Great Depression but also to neutralize the challenge of international communism. Born out of forty years of suffering, the post-1945 welfare state gave an unprecedented envelope of security to the growing prosperity of the European and American working class. It also gave a new breath of life to international capitalism.

Fordist production had contradictory implications for the status of the factory proletariat. On the one hand, it led to a steady breakup of traditional working-class communities and a considerable increase in alienation from monotonous and repetitive labor; on the other hand, it gave the workers material betterment and, after a phase of bitter corporate resistance, established large industrial unions as their privileged representatives: thoughtful managers came to understand that "responsible" union leaders were the best guarantee of peace on the factory floor. Moreover, the Fordist welfare state's apportionment of middle-class conveniences to the proletariat bound them to their novel comforts as to a new religion, via the deployment of the commercial paraphernalia of the twentieth century's mass consumer society. A sophisticated advertising industry that combined Barnum and Bailey spectacles with the tricks of snake oil salesmen encouraged and facilitated the acquisition of consumer goods through chain stores, supermarkets, and shopping malls; credit agencies distributed plastic cards that took the place of money. Increasingly, despite the surface hegemony of the work ethic, working and middle-class masses were exhorted, by all the psychological cunning known to Madison Avenue's bright young men, to center their lives around consumption.[11]

This switch in the focus of life from producing to consuming, despite its cultic aspects, was supported by ideological argument that justified acquisitive behavior in terms of rational idealism. The consumer's engrossment with how to spend his money—how to choose between competing products and brand names[12]—became embedded in liberal ideologies and mentalities as a freedom as fundamental as the choices of free agents in the free market to buy and sell everything from labor power to advanced weaponry.[13]

The ideological liberalism underpinning consumerism—indeed, the identification of the indefatigable consumer as a Promethean hero as important to the modern age as the indefatigable producer—has been explained succinctly by Don Slater:

> Liberal tradition connected material gain, technical progress and individual freedom through the motivation of the *pursuit of self-interest.* This laid the basis for a "democratic" heroism: in the individual's most banal and previously undignified desires (for comforts and for wealth, for trade and for industry) could be discerned the heroic will and intelligence that could transform nature and society and bend them both to mastery by the freely and privately

chosen desires of the individual. The consumer is heroic because he *(sic)* is rational and autonomous and because only his self-defined needs can give legitimacy to economic and social institutions.[14]

Liberal ideology's heroic consumer is thus the perfect counterpart of the heroic entrepreneur of nineteenth-century mythology and the heroic worker of Fordist and Stakhanovite legend.[15] In fact, of course, as with much other ideological hype justifying the ravages of modernity, the reality is far from rationality, autonomy, or heroism. And the path to the present Babylonic standard of enjoyment, by the 20 percent of the world's population that can afford weekly visits to the shopping mall, has never been without resistance.

Critics of Consumption

Western culture has always had an element of hostility to materialism and pleasure seeking, evidenced in the disdain of Roman stoics for Epicureanism, and the hatred of church fathers like Tertullian for sensuality and display. Medieval Christianity experienced repeated waves of internal reformers who attempted to return the errant clergy, by the establishment of new monastic orders, to the gospel of poverty. Outside the clerical order, antimaterialist evangelical sects such as the Waldensians were condemned by the church as heretical because they attempted to introduce this gospel, and its practical implications, to the laity. In the late Middle Ages, ascetic zealots savagely attacked the luxury-oriented lifestyle of wealthy burghers, aristocrats, and even bishops in word and picture. The paintings of Hieronymus Bosch and Pieter Breughel, inspired by evangelical antimaterialism, depicted that lifestyle as degenerate, the work of the devil and his minions.

The Reformation, particularly in its Calvinist manifestation, institutionalized this attack. Calvinism, returning to Augustinian doctrines of predestination, instilled a fear of eternal damnation in its adepts for living anything but a life of worldly asceticism, but the emphasis on *this* world, as Max Weber astutely pointed out, made of the hell-fearing Calvinist a model capitalist: one who not only strove for a maximum profit but who could do so in good conscience as long as he plowed it back into his enterprise and refrained from enjoying it personally. High rates of profit and the exploitation of others could be seen as a sign of divine election, if one worked incessantly for the increase of a divinely created material order, lived ascetically, and accepted the tenets of the Reformed Church.

Calvinist/capitalist asceticism, however, while it discouraged consumption by the true believer, implied that someone, somewhere, had to be

ruining his chances in the hereafter by consuming immoderately. Such indifference to salvation was structured in two models of excess which, evading the chastisements of puritanical Christianity well into the age of heroic
modernity, paved the way to a modern consumer society: the worldly consumption patterns of aristocratic elites and the periodic binges associated
with the seasonal festivities of the traditional rural social order.[16] Both models tended to undermine Christian restraint among the laity (and even
among the princes of the church), the aristocratic one frequently serving—
especially in France and Italy—as a sumptuary standard for upwardly mobile bourgeois and petty bourgeois, and the carnivalesque binges serving as
a shield for the traditional popular classes against the rigors of evangelical
asceticism. Satirizing these kinds of excess was a common sport among secular nineteenth-century intellectuals skeptical about the claims of modernity. Gustave Flaubert, for example, placed the petty-bourgeois emulation
of aristocratic luxury at the heart of his heroine's tragic demise in *Madame
Bovary* (1857), and in his private letters he ridiculed carnival and other popular festivities. The Belgian painter James Ensor skewered the commercialism of late-nineteenth-century carnival in his grotesquely sad *Entry of Christ
into Brussels,* and the figure of a Christ whose message of freedom is condemned by the materialist powers of this world—including the church itself—is at the heart of Dostoyevsky's "Legend of the Grand Inquisitor" in
The Brothers Karamazov. Once the age of mass industrial production had
begun, however, seasonal festivities as well as upper-class opulence would
have to be made compatible with the ideals of liberal capitalism for consumer society to take off.

The ideological prerequisite for such integration was the philosophical
individualism that underlies the liberal tradition, from Hobbes through
Hume and Adam Smith to the English utilitarianism of Bentham and
Malthus. This tradition's ultimate celebration of the consumer in terms of
the rational autonomy of marketplace negotiators was premised on the dismissal of any collective or social definition of needs, that is, any definition
external to the individual.[17] But to achieve such dismissal, to reach the contemporary triumph of a society built on the apparently unlimited needs of
individual consumers, there were also historical and material prerequisites.

Historically, public opinion had to be convinced that the collective
("holistic," to use Louis Dumont's term) incarnations of the Promethean
spirit that had long overshadowed capitalist individualism—nationalism
and socialism—were both obsolete and immoral. It is ironic that this obsolescence was alleged to be proven by the successful end of a fifty-year
struggle undertaken by nationalists and socialists allied with liberal capi-

talist individualists (the alliance that called itself Western democracy) against the totalitarian deformations of the collective Prometheus: Fascism and Stalinist Communism. For once this struggle was won, social philosophers newly converted to liberal individualism argued that both traditional nationalism and the socialist welfare state, insofar as they presupposed super-individual collectivities which could limit individual freedoms and pretend to shape social development, were the seedbeds of the slain totalitarian Hydras.[18]

Alongside this ideological offensive, at a less theoretical level, multinational corporations and the various international agencies that represent them—the World Bank, the IMF, the WTO, and the European Union—used, as we have seen, the club of globalization to bludgeon the erstwhile ideological partners of liberal individualism into submission. And at the most material level, two aspects of the technological revolution that made the sale of factory goods to a broad internal market necessary for the survival of capitalism have been crucial to the development of a globalized consumer culture: on the one hand, computerization of production, distribution, and exchange; and on the other, the development of mass media, first those of print and, in the last half century, those of electronic communication, to spread the gospel of what James Twitchell calls "Adcult."

Notwithstanding the ideological and material triumphs of liberal consumer culture in recent decades, the historical evolution toward our contemporary consumer Stakhanovism has been accompanied by a drumfire of criticism comparable to that which condemned the ancient and not-so-ancient prototypes of the acquisitive society. In the nineteenth century, some critics—Dostoyevsky, for example, or Tolstoy, or the French priest Félicité de Lamennais, or the Scottish essayist Thomas Carlyle—drew on traditional religion, condemning the acquisitive impulse in modern society in terms of a Christian standard of brotherhood and purity. Others, like Flaubert and the Goncourt brothers, or, in England, the pre-Raphaelites and Oscar Wilde, ridiculed the incipient philistine culture of consumption from an elitist, aristocratic standpoint which they integrated with the doctrine of art for art's sake.

Many of the early critiques, however, represented social versions of the Promethean ethos. For example, romantic attacks on the slothful luxury of wealthy parvenus were based (differently according to country and movement) on some combination of the Rousseauian return-to-nature philosophies of the late Enlightenment, the collective idealisms of national revolutionary movements (particularly the French, German, and English), and artisan or utopian socialism. Among post-romantic critics a growing number, translating Christian ascetic standards into secular idealism, were inclined to condemn the acquisitive impulse in the light of a heroic purity they associated with the French revolutionary tradition. Zola's *Le ventre de Paris* is an excellent example of the latter. The basic symbolism that runs through the novel, that of the fat (*le gras,* the materialist pleasures of carnival) versus the thin (*le maigre,* the ascetic idealism of Lent), characterizes the opposition between the materially satisfied, politically craven shopkeepers of Paris's central market district during the authoritarian Second Empire and an escaped political prisoner who tries to launch a revolutionary conspiracy to reestablish the French Republic.

Nonetheless, the consumer ideology pilloried in Zola's novel is quite traditional (the hero's tale of his harrowing escape from imprisonment is listened to somewhat absentmindedly by his pork-butcher brother and his sister-in-law, who are stuffing blood sausages as he speaks). Moreover, while avid commercialism is characteristic of Zola's shopkeepers, it hardly affects his artisans and peasants, who may be drunkards (as in *L'assommoir*) or greedy brutes (*La terre*) but normally die in destitution or violence, not in luxury. When Zola described the new department store in *Au bonheur des dames,* it was clear that he saw the delirium of the horizonless consumer paradise as limited to wealthy females. Meanwhile, the capitalists in his novels, while prepared to give their spouses the good life, were models of heroic asceticism in their total devotion to their enterprises.[19]

While Fordist capitalism evoked mass consumption, advertising, and social conformity in the interwar period, the principal aspect of mass society noted by intellectuals and artists before the mid-twentieth century was not in the area of consumption but in that of production. A number of films of the twenties and thirties reflect this awareness of the heightened alienation of factory labor under the new dispensation: in Germany, Fritz Lang's *Metropolis* showed factory workers as hardly more than slaves; in France, *À nous la liberté* shows workers fleeing the factory into a pastoral idyll; in the United States, Chaplin's *Modern Times* equally emphasized the little man's flight from a work life reduced to the interminable repetition of assembly line production. But the political and economic turbulence of the period before 1945 diminished the visibility of the changing consumption horizons of the proletariat. Indeed, war, depression, political turmoil, and social conflict imposed such new hardships during this period that the significance of innovations like Ford's effort to sell his cars to everyone (mirrored in Nazi Germany by Volkswagen—the "people's car") seemed of secondary importance.

The cornucopia of consumer goods characteristic of North American (and subsequently European) mass society and mass culture was recognized and analyzed by sociologists only after the Second World War. Even then, the focus of most social theory was for several decades on the alienating nature of industrial—or white-collar—work, rather than on the apparently unlimited appetite for worldly goods that was being nurtured together with mass production. Marxists, for example, whether they chose to emphasize the mature Marx's castigation of the fetishism of commodities in *Capital* or the young Marx's exploration of humankind's "species being," normally focused on the inhumanity and irrationality of capitalist production and exchange, while assuming that only socialism could end alienation and supply impoverished masses with a secure supply of useful objects.

The most advanced Marxist critique of bourgeois society was that of the Frankfurt School, a group of Hegelian-Marxists, largely Jewish, who fled Nazi Germany in the 1930s and, after a few years in Paris, were able to continue their work at Columbia University in New York. Between 1930 and 1970 the Frankfurt School, impelled by the failure of the socialist and communist Left to halt Nazism and by the horrors of the Second World War, vastly extended the breadth and depth of Marxist thought to make it broadly compatible with the critical aspects of Freudian and modern philosophical thought. While, for example, Max Horkheimer and Theodor Adorno developed from their early Marxism into a full-scale critique of the Enlightenment's notion of rationality (*Dialektik der Aufklärung*, 1945), Herbert Marcuse went furthest in integrating Marxist ideas of alienation with Freudian notions of sexual repression and sublimation in a tour de force that embraced the entire tradition of European high culture (*Eros and Civilization*, 1955).[20]

Alert to the irony of history, Marcuse argued (in *One Dimensional Man*) that advanced bureaucratic capitalism used consumer culture to pacify alienated humanity by the appearance of freedom. Technological progress created "unfreedom—in the sense of man's subjection to his productive apparatus—[which] is perpetuated and intensified in the form of many liberties and comforts."[21] The liberties were thus illusory, since they signified "a contraction rather than extension and development of instinctual needs," working "*for* rather than *against* the status quo of general repression."[22] Marcuse called this "repressive desublimation" and saw it as a basic component of "the authoritarian personality of our time." In the workplace, "the reduction of dirty and heavy physical labor" was accompanied "by the availability of cheap, attractive clothing, beauty culture, and physical hygiene; by the requirements of the advertising industry, etc. The sexy office and sales girls, the handsome, virile junior executive and floor walker are highly marketable commodities, and the possession of suitable mistresses—once the prerogative of kings, princes, and lords—facilitates the career of even the

less exalted ranks in the business community." Marcuse also saw desubli-
mated instinctual gratification in the manipulation of recreational artifacts:
"racing the outboard motor, pushing the power lawn mower and speeding
the automobile." And he added: "This mobilization and administration of
libido may account for much of the voluntary compliance, the absence of
terror, the pre-established harmony between individual needs and socially-
required desires, goals, and aspirations."[23]

Ever more explicitly, Marcuse linked the baubles of a high living standard to the repression, indeed the redefinition of human instinct. In *An
Essay on Liberation* (1969), he wrote:

> The so-called consumer economy and the politics of corporate capitalism
> have created a second nature of man which ties him libidinally and aggres-
> sively to the commodity form. The need for possessing, consuming, han-
> dling, and constantly renewing the gadgets, devices, instruments, engines,
> offered to and imposed upon the people, for using these wares even at the
> danger of one's own destruction, has become a "biological" need in the sense
> just defined. The second nature of man thus militates against any change
> that would disrupt and perhaps even abolish this dependence of man on a
> market ever more densely filled with merchandise—abolish his existence as
> a consumer consuming himself in buying and selling. The needs generated
> by this system are thus eminently stabilizing, conservative needs: the
> counter-revolution anchored in the instinctual structure.[24]

Marcuse's thesis did not seem persuasive when first published. The link
he postulated between relaxation of prohibitions on sensual experience and
integration to a repressive social order appeared to be belied by the youth revolt of the sixties, whose challenge to authority was tied to a far-reaching
"desublimation," mediated by drugs and pop music, of experience and social
relations. But since the antiauthoritarian sexual revolution, we have seen
how most of the attributes of the youth culture of that time (clothing styles,
pop music, and the desire for early freedom from parental restraint and mobility) have been brought into the commercial sphere to fuel the consumer
splurges of yuppies in the eighties and nineties.[25] Commercial colonization
of the minds of youth has not, of course, been limited to the affluent middle
class. The marketing of expensive brand-name sportswear has been aimed in
particular at impoverished minorities, in the conviction that once sold, they,
and their brand-bound sports heroes, would drag middle-class adolescents
with them. Naomi Klein writes of "inner-city kids . . . stabbing each other
for their Nike, Polo, Hilfiger and Nautica gear" and observes that "these

fashion labels sold disadvantaged kids so successfully on their exaggerated representations of the good life—the country club, the yacht, the superstar celebrity—that logowear has become, in some parts of the Global City, both talisman and weapon."[26]

Even the sixties-style consumption of soft (and not so soft) drugs, if still illegal in most countries, remains an important black-market component of consumer culture, and the "liberated" sexual mores of the sixties are commercialized in the Internet marketplace of the new millennium by tens of thousands of well-established pornographic websites. Marcuse's thesis that the material advantages of contemporary bourgeois society brought about a desublimation of instinct, and that in buying off rebellion this desublimation served repressive ends, anticipated by three decades Ernest Gellner's apt description of consumer culture as a "universal Danegeld."[27]

Outside the sphere of Marxist thought, analysis and critique of consumer culture took off largely after 1970, but there were important precursors. In 1899, Thorstein Veblen emphasized the significance of social envy in the process of conspicuous consumption, though his analysis was, understandably for his time, focused on these processes among the wealthy.[28] In the early twentieth century, the most profound critique of bourgeois society came from anthropologists, for example Marcel Mauss, whose insight into gift-giving as a social tie characteristic of most cultures relativized and de-essentialized the acquisitive individualism assumed by most liberal theory as the basis of bourgeois political economy. Karl Polanyi's *The Great Transformation: The Political and Economic Origins of Our Time* (1944), a work often referred to by contemporary non-Marxist critics of capitalism, cites similar findings by Malinowski to attack the foundations of liberal theory. While anthropological theory undermined the liberal idea that possessive individualism was the cornerstone of human nature, however, its view of contemporary consumer society has generally tended more to describe the social ties created by consumption patterns rather than to analyze them critically. This is certainly the gist of Mary Douglas's *The World of Goods* (1979) and of the popular *AdCult* by James Twitchell (1997).

Where non-Marxist intellectuals criticized contemporary conformity and alienation as reflecting a defective social structure, they often identified mass society and mass culture (rather than capitalism) as the culprit. Before 1970, however, like the Marxists, they infrequently discussed consumer society directly. Two major exceptions, sociologists who focused on the significance of consumption in the emerging postwar world, were Ernest van den Haag and David Riesman.

Van den Haag's essay of 1957, "Of Happiness and Despair We Have No

Measure," is an excellent example of the perceived link between Fordist mass production and the new mass consumer market. Van den Haag's perspective, like that of the Frankfurt School, is that of the traditional elite culture (he cites, for example, Shelley's "In Defense of Poetry" to advance his argument, just as Marcuse cites Rilke in *Eros and Civilization*). Unlike Marcuse, Horkheimer, and their colleagues, however, van den Haag specifically relates contemporary culture not to capitalism but to the joint rise of mass production, mass society, and mass culture. He is particularly concerned about what he sees as a flattening of taste and values coming from the mass media and advertising. While he exonerates advertisers from the charge of conspiring with "wicked capitalists . . . and mass media [to] debauch the original good, natural taste of the masses," he does in effect accuse them of pandering to a lowest common denominator for the sake of mass commercialism, and in so doing he makes the connection, reasonable for the mid-twentieth century, between Fordist production and mass consumption: "It does not matter what people want to buy as long as they want to buy enough of the same thing to make mass production possible. Advertising helps to unify taste, to de-individualize it, and thus to make mass production possible."[29]

Mass consumption, then, is an aspect of modern society that is symbiotically tied both to mass production and to modern mass media, and van den Haag's critique approaches prophetic proportions when he considers the destruction of individuality in the resultant mass society. Standardized production depends on repression of one's individuality both as producer and consumer; "assembly-line shaping, packaging and distributing of persons, of life" permeates material existence, destroying individual identity:

> Most people perch unsteadily in mass-produced, impermanent dwellings throughout their lives. They are born in hospitals, fed in cafeterias, married in hotels. After terminal care, they die in hospitals, are shelved briefly in funeral homes, and are finally incinerated. On each of these occasions—and how many others?—efficiency and economy are obtained and individuality and continuity stripped off. If one lives and dies discontinuously and promiscuously in anonymous surroundings, it becomes hard to identify with anything, even the self, and uneconomic to be attached to anything, even one's own individuality.[30]

Van den Haag's critique, focused as it is on the connection of consumer society with mass production, is not as advanced as that of David Riesman's *The Lonely Crowd,* which appeared seven years earlier, in 1950. Riesman not only anticipated the new consumer society of the end of the century, he related it, by implication, to a post-Fordist production system, in which productivity as the center of individual existence had been replaced by consumption. His framework, however, was clearly that of economic modernization, linked to a loosely Freudian notion of personality.

The Lonely Crowd concerns "two revolutions and their relation to the 'mode of conformity' or 'social character' of Western man since the Middle Ages." The first such "revolution," occurring roughly between 1450 and 1950, marked a sharp departure from "the family and clan-oriented traditional ways of life in which mankind has existed through most of history." More or less equivalent to what I have discussed above as the ascent of Promethean modernity, this transformation was embodied in "the Renaissance, the Reformation, the Counter-Reformation, the Industrial Revolution, and the political revolutions of the seventeenth, eighteenth, and nineteenth centuries." While still going on in 1950, according to the author, that upheaval in humankind's ways of thinking and acting was in the most advanced parts of the world—particularly in the United States—being replaced by "another sort of revolution, a whole range of social developments associated with a shift from an age of production to an age of consumption."

Riesman related these two revolutions to changes in basic social psychology by distinguishing three underlying personality orientations. Before the revolutions of modernity, a tradition-directed personality characterized the immemorial village and feudal cultures of humankind: the wisdom of one's ancestors conveyed to farmers, hunters, and warriors the socially acceptable values, thought, and behavior. An inner-directed personality, in which values transmitted to the youth by parents alone were internalized as a "psychological gyroscope," typified the new elites during the first revolutionary epoch that stretched from the Reformation to the establishment of a Fordist industrial system. The basic value in this epoch was productivity. The second revolution saw the dominance of the type of personality congruent with what we might call postindustrial, or perhaps postmodern, society: the consumer. Riesman argued that beginning in the mid-twentieth century, when the easy abundance produced by the industrial revolution reduced the need for productivity as a crucial character trait, a transition was made to the other-directed personality, in which parents counted for less than peer groups in orienting values, and fashions of consumption became more important to social cohesion than modes of production.

Alongside of the historical ideal types of tradition-directed, inner-directed, and other-directed societies, Riesman postulated another, overlapping, triad of what he called universal ideal types: that of the adjusted, anomic, and autonomous personalities. Riesman was clear about his preference for the autonomous character. Although he granted that each of the universal types could be found in each of the three historically based societies, not surprisingly he saw an elective affinity between the autonomous personality and the epoch characterized by inner-directedness. Central to his concept of autonomy was the notion that human beings could "imagine being somebody else" than what they were socially shaped to be, could assess whether they found that "somebody else" desirable and, if they did, direct their existences to attaining it.[31] Though autonomy was incompatible with tradition-directed societies, a limited but significant number of autonomous personalities came to flourish in the inner-directed era that began with the technological revolutions and the European Renaissance and Reformation of the early modern period, partly because the new technology allowed for an increasing differentiation of human activity and an accompanying "leisure to contemplate change," partly because the vast expansion of knowledge permitted the contemplation of other historical and geographic conditions. The Renaissance, when "a richer picture of the past made it possible to live toward a more open future," was a particularly powerful motor for the autonomous personality, as was the prospect of creating an industrial society out of an agrarian, feudal one.

While Riesman refrained from the kind of pathos expressed by van den Haag or the sweeping philosophical critique of the Frankfurt School,[32] his own more or less traditional elite values came to the fore in these remarks on human autonomy, and in others on the cultural protagonists of modernity—representatives, in my terms, of the Promethean ethos of productivity and creativity. All of Riesman's specific references, however, relate the autonomous personality to inner-directed societies. When he discussed the possibility of autonomy in the new historical phase of other-directed societies (when consumers would be replacing producers as ideal types,) he foresaw great problems. The tolerant, laid-back pluralism of modern society allows all sorts of niches, he argued, for peer-group formations which, while conforming unproblematically to one another, could give themselves the "illusion of attacking an allegedly dominant majority of Babbitts." The nonconformist or eccentric in an other-directed society "must, like a movie star, accept the roles in which he is cast, lest he disappoint the delighted expectations of his friends."

For Riesman, the transformation of "efforts at autonomy" into cues for peer-group behavior signifies the degeneration of such efforts into "other-directed play acting." Accordingly, the only creative figures he mentions in his section on autonomy in other-directed society are those who anticipated the problem of group-oriented conformity in their analyses of the future of democracy: Tocqueville, John Stuart Mill, and, in the twentieth century,

Sartre, Simone de Beauvoir, Erich Fromm, José Ortega y Gasset, and Bertrand Russell.

Let us recall that for Riesman other-directed man is man the consumer, and that the fundamental economic and technological transformation he saw as underlying the development of other-directed humanity is indeed that which we, fifty years later, have come to recognize as the shift from a Fordist industrialism, with a fundamental commitment to productivity, to a postindustrial consumer-oriented society. In this context, the emphasis in liberal ideology on the rationality and autonomy of the "heroic" consumer has a particularly hollow ring to it. To the contrary, the present society built around the values of consumership, in which the rituals of common and competitive consumption constitute the principal bond tying together those with enough income to participate in the globally dominant social order, allows, as Riesman perceived, precious little room for autonomy or heroism.

No doubt, the consumer society of today is, in the details of its consumption patterns, more varied and less conformist than that developing in mid-century under Fordist conditions of mass production, the moment of Riesman's book. The post-Fordist revolution in production methods—computerization plus flexibility of labor—permits companies to make profits on a considerably more variegated supply of products, produced in smaller quantities, and this feeds into customer desires for distinction. If, however, instrumental rationality and a degree of autonomy remain indispensable for the construction and administration of global enterprises like Microsoft and IBM, other human qualities come to the fore in the consumers of their products.

Consumer society activates and gives satisfaction to a peculiar combination of individual and social needs. At the individual level, commercialism caters to a desire for cultural distinction that serves as a screen for less avowable impulses of acquisitiveness, envy, lust and aggression.[33] At the collective level, a certain emphasis on altruistic values of group bonding and multiculturalism serves to mask and sublimate group hatred of otherness. Indeed, in this most competitive society, those who believe devoutly in the individualism of market and property relations and oppose any measures of social control over them as contrary to nature are daily confronted with the anthropological needs of the species for social cohesion, nurturing, and solidarity as well as for the exclusion and destruction of otherness. Often only intuitively aware of what they are doing, advertisers, politicians, and publicists weave such social needs, as Marcuse saw nearly four decades ago, into sublimated versions of the more questionable urges for sex, power, and aggression.

Consumer Society as Carnival

It is particularly in the exploitation of this anthropologically comprehensible witches' cauldron of private and collective passions that we find the much vaunted "carnivalesque" aspects of consumer society. Mike Featherstone, a leading theorist of consumer society, borrows from George Bataille's notion that human societies confronted with a surplus of production over immediate needs "manage" this surplus by destroying or squandering it in "games, religion, art, wars, death" and through rituals of "gifts, potlatch, consumption tournaments, carnivals and conspicuous consumption."[34] While Bataille sees capitalist societies as channeling economic surplus (which he called the *part maudite*) into unending economic growth, Featherstone argues that contemporary capitalism retains for its own purposes the core of the archaic celebrations referred to by Bataille and other anthropologists, insofar as it "produces . . . images and sites of consumption which endorse the pleasures of excess [and which] favour blurring of the boundary between art and everyday life." In the framework of such blurring, Featherstone offers us an intriguing postmodern sociology of consumer culture: not only are distinctions between high and popular cultures done away with, but capitalist society shows its retention of the archaic. He proposes a fourfold inquiry into:

> (1) the persistence within consumer culture of elements of the pre-industrial carnivalesque tradition; (2) the transformation and displacement of the carnivalesque, into media images, design, advertising, rock videos, the cinema; (3) the persistence and transformation of elements of the carnivalesque within certain sites of consumption: holiday resorts, sports stadia, theme parks, department stores and shopping centres; (4) its displacement and incorporation into conspicuous consumption by states and corporations, either in the form of "prestige" spectacles for wider publics and/or privileged upper management and officialdom.[35]

"Prestige spectacles" indeed. Social historians of traditional European popular cultures will find this familiar territory. For example, in medieval and early modern times, marketplaces were also the sites of public executions, which were public spectacles accompanied by feasting and revelry comparable (though with a more predictable ending) to the gladiatorial combats of ancient Rome and the boxing matches of today. As the insightful Robert Kaplan remarks on the bloody combination of boxing, karate, and wrestling ("extreme fighting") that seems to be the latest fad among lower-middle- and middle-class spectators who want to "see blood": "The mood of the Colosseum goes together with the age of the corporation, which offers entertainment in place of values."[36] From the unmasked bloodthirstiness of spectators at a boxing match to the projected group aggression of the national or international football or soccer match is a short step. Both are arenas in which aggressive impulses, frustrated by jobs and family situations that require self-control, civility, and group conformity, can be projected into a situation closer to the ancient mutual slaughter of rival clans than anything—apart from hand-to-hand warfare and adolescent gang violence—in modern life.

Since important sports competitions are spectacular occasions for advertising, whereas warfare and gang violence generally are not, only the former are systematically encouraged and integrated into the consumerist *société de spectacle*.[37] In the post–September 11 political mood in the United States, nonetheless, the militarist hype at the 2002 Super Bowl (Fox TV showed repeated shots of U.S. troops watching the football game from Kandahar) has caused one critic to reflect on the way the Super Bowl had "always warmly embraced America's wars." Geov Parrish reminds us, for example, that at the 1991 game, which coincided with the opening salvos of the Gulf War, "pregame and halftime ceremonies . . . plant[ed] wet fat kisses on the war that was at that very moment massacring hundreds of thousands of Iraqis." He underlines the interchangeability of "patriotism and warfare and corporate branding" in the "jingoistic" advertising during the 2002 spectacle.[38]

Such integration of war, sport, and commercialism reveals vividly the moneyed interests invested in the passion of group violence. Twitchell used the term "carnival of commercialism" to describe the advertising during the Super Bowl, where, on one occasion, television viewers were exposed to commercials and promos during twenty minutes of a forty-five-minute stretch.[39] The intensity of this merchandising can be gauged by the fact that the $40,000 per second cost of Super Bowl TV advertising that Twitchell mentions in his book of 1996 had four years later grown to more than $70,000.[40] On the day before the 2000 Super Bowl, the pre-fight publicity for the four-minute Tyson-Francis boxing contest generated £12 million (about $20 million) from a million pay TV spectators, roughly twice the income from the sale of 21,000 seats at the spectacle itself. "The fight—made possible by Jack Straw, home secretary, allowing the convicted rapist [Tyson] into the country in the interest of business—confirmed Tyson's marketability in Europe," according to the *Financial Times* of January 31, 2000.

Carnival, of course, is an ancient festivity commemorating death and rebirth. One wonders if international athletic competitions such as the Olympics, which consciously revived the games of ancient Hellas, may not function to reinforce social cohesion in a way similar to the ritual sacrifices of antique religion. There may, then, be a certain archaic logic in the fact that top professional athletes, the global image of gleaming health and physical perfection, are four times more likely to expire of heart disease before the age of forty-five than their compatriots. The tribal deities they are being sacrificed to, however, are not the ones of Olympus but those of Mammon and the golden calf. The athletes' frequently untimely demise comes from the chemicals they are doped with by trainers, managers, and owners eager to enhance their income through the victories of their lads and lasses, which reinforces Twitchell's point about the intersection of carnival and commercialism in sports spectacles.

Nonetheless, Mike Featherstone's erudite celebration of consumer culture focuses not on the spectacular commercialism attached to major athletic competitions but on the allegedly carnivalesque aspects of the contemporary shopping experience. Featherstone has been sensitized to the historical source and significance of these phenomena by scholarly studies of "the tradition within popular culture of transgression, protest, the carnivalesque and liminal excesses," including Mikhail Bakhtin's book on Rabelais, Peter Stallybrass and Allon White's book on the transgressive elements of English culture,[41] and Victor Turner's work on the rites of passage of tribal communities. This tradition, found in "carnivals, fairs and festivals," inverted the official culture of civilized controls symbolically, and in so doing transgressed it, favoring "excitement, uncontrolled emotions and the direct and vulgar grotesque bodily pleasures of fattening food, intoxicating drink and sexual promiscuity." Such carnivals, fairs, and the like are characterized, according to Featherstone, by "*liminal* spaces, in which the everyday world was turned upside down and in which the tabooed and fantastic were possible, in which impossible dreams could be expressed." Further borrowing from the ideas of Turner, Featherstone discerns the presence within such spaces of "*anti-structure* and *communitas,* the generation of a sense of unmediated community, emotional fusion and ecstatic oneness."[42]

While he grants that there was a certain resistance to such popular feelings of exaltation in "the state" and "the emerging consumer culture industries and 'civilizing processes'" in the Britain of the eighteenth and nineteenth centuries,[43] it appears to be precisely the merit of the consumer culture of the twentieth century to have reintegrated such archaic impulses for liberation and transgression, thus compensating for the increasing repression of impulse in the productive process and in normal social intercourse:

For those people, especially in the middle classes, who were developing bodily and emotional controls as part of civilizing processes, sites of cultural disorder such as fairs, the city, the slum, the seaside resort, become the source of fascination, longing and nostalgia. In a displaced form this became a central theme in art, literature and popular entertainment such as the music hall. It can also be argued that those institutions which came to dominate the urban market-place, the department stores plus the new national and international exhibitions, provided sites of ordered disorder which summoned up elements of the carnivalesque tradition in their displays, imagery and simulations of exotic locations and lavish spectacles.[44]

At this point, Featherstone works Walter Benjamin's analysis of the nineteenth-century Parisian arcade—a shopping mall *avant la lettre*—into his analysis. Lyrically, he invokes a dreamworld of luxury: in the world of aestheticized commodities first identified by Benjamin, "the department stores, arcades, trams, trains, streets and fabric of buildings and the goods on display, as well as the people who stroll through these spaces, summon up half-forgotten dreams, as the curiosity and memory of the stroller is fed by the ever changing landscape in which objects appear divorced from their context and subject to mysterious connections which are read on the surface of things." The daily life and landscape of the world's metropolises becomes aesthetic as new technologies allow for the penetration of industry by art, through increased employment in "advertising, marketing, industrial design and commercial display." Yoking Benjamin to the postmodern celebratory lucubrations of Jean Baudrillard and Fredric Jameson, Featherstone stresses the "immediacies, intensities, sensory overload, disorientation, the *mélée* or liquefaction of signs and images, the mixing of codes, the unchained or floating signifiers of the postmodern 'depthless' consumer culture where art and reality have switched places in an 'aesthetic hallucination of the real.'"[45]

No doubt, there is some hallucinating going on here. But one cannot avoid the sentiment that the hapless Benjamin, had he survived his flight across the Pyrenees in 1940, would surely have remarked that "depthless"—whether modifying "postmodern consumer culture" or anything else—is synonymous with "superficial," and that he would have viewed his being attached as the ideological totem to this carnivalesque procession of grotesque jargon as resembling nothing so much as James Ensor's *Entry of Christ into Brussels*.[46] This feeling of being sacrificed on the altar of a triumphant modern mass culture would probably have been intensified had Benjamin seen that his presumed "celebration of the aesthetic potential of mass culture and the aestheticized perceptions of the people who stroll through the urban spaces of the large cities" was to be seen as the basis for subsequent scholarly emphasis on "the transgressive and playful potential of postmodernism."

Let us turn back from this co-opting of Benjamin (not to mention Bakhtin and Turner) into postmodern theory, to the more serious act of usurpation: the attempt to smuggle all manner of transgressive, carnivalesque elements into the "depthless" consumer culture of our day. One need only look at a contemporary carnival celebration, at least at one such in northern Europe, and compare it with historical descriptions of carnival to see the "depthlessness" of the postmodern celebration of "transgressive" elements in contemporary consumer culture.

The spuriousness of such an assimilation of the shopping mall to the carnival culture of premodern societies is evident, for example, from Alain Faure's overview of the fate of carnival in nineteenth-century Paris.[47] The French Revolution had inspired, despite the bourgeois intentions of its leading figures, a spontaneous rejuvenation of the traditional popular culture of town and village, after centuries of persecution by state and church.[48] This continued, irrepressibly, during the post-revolutionary restoration of monarchy. In the carnivals of the decades before the revolution of 1848, Parisians actually did invert, for a few days, their social identities and transgress official codes of behavior: the poor dressed up as aristocrats, the aristocrats as beggars; all official eminences of church and state were lampooned; morality was abandoned. Violence was always latent, and sometimes significantly more than that. The carnival season of 1820 saw the assassination of the successor to the Bourbon throne, setting off a wave of political repression that ultimately led to the revolution of 1830. The Brussels carnival of 1830 was the stage for the Belgians' revolution of that year, their declaration of independence from the Netherlands. The Parisian carnival of 1831 was the background for anticlerical riots which resulted in the pillaging and destruction of the palace of the archbishop. The revolution of 1848, though directly provoked by the prohibition of a political meeting for reform, also occurred in February, the month of carnival.

Everything changed after the triumph of bourgeois conservatism during the Second Republic and the Second Empire. In the middle of the nineteenth century the bell of reaction tolled everywhere in Europe, not just in France, and the rejuvenation of the popular culture that had occurred after the French Revolution gave way to the reimposition of iron laws and repressive civilizing processes. The suppression of the Paris Commune of 1871, a final outburst of mass transgression, signaled the end of the age of French revolutions and of the popular cultures that had merged with them. Pre-1914 photos of carnival processions in Paris reveal a passive populace watching from the sidewalk, completely cut off from the "official" celebration, as large, commercially sponsored floats (there was one for Michelin tires in 1911) slowly, and with forced enthusiasm, wind their way down the grand boulevards.[49] Apart from the clothing, one could be watching a contemporary American Thanksgiving Day parade.

Carnivalesque Transgression or Social Integration?

To suggest that the spirit of carnivalesque transgression has been reincarnated in the contemporary department store, shopping mall, or Thanksgiving Day procession is absurd for anyone who has noticed the omnipresence of brand names and chain stores, the purely mercantile nature of the enterprises involved and the strict prohibition on any breakdown of "civilized" behavior. Even Featherstone, who argues that the imagery of urban spaces, theme parks, and museums invokes, in a postmodern manner, "pleasure, excitement, the carnivalesque and disorder," reminds us that "to experience them requires self-control and for those who lack such control there lurks in the background surveillance by security guards and remote-control cameras."[50]

This presence of the iron fist behind the "carnivalesque" commercialism of our malls and Disneylands reminds us that in our society the mores of consumption are structured and encouraged by global corporations, whose wealth may be measured by the fact that the two hundred richest captains of industry control more property than two billion of their less fortunate contemporaries.[51] The power and influence over our lives of these men and the corporations they run are so great that it is hardly an exaggeration to say that the shreds of formal democracy left to us exist only by their grace. When, for example in Chile in 1973, a democratically elected government presented a threat to the interests of one of these mega-corporations, it was deposed by an American-supported coup d'état and replaced by a military dictatorship that left the running of the economy to the "Chicago boys" of Milton Friedman, a fate barely escaped by Hugo Chavez's Venezuela in April 2002.

I have indicated above the disadvantages of this system, not merely in "peripheral" societies crushed by it, but even in its North American and European "core": growing insecurity and marginalization of downsized former factory and office workers; increasing numbers hired on a "flexible" part-time and temporary basis, with poor wages, no benefits, and a dim future; and longer working hours and an ever growing army of working mothers to purchase the many commodities that modern advertising and peer pressure transform from luxuries into necessities. In Europe, where a remnant of the welfare state continues to exist, 10 percent of the work force are unemployed, with increasing pressure to force the unemployed either into poorly paid jobs below their qualifications or into the ranks of the excluded and homeless. Apart from the beneficiaries of inherited wealth, only a minority of the Euro-American population—the 20 percent that consists of well-trained professionals, including lawyers, doctors, managers, and the "symbolic analysts" celebrated a decade ago by Robert Reich—can enjoy without anxiety, with a sense of a personal future, the splendors of consumer society.

That the world until recently largely accepted this situation without significant demurral or dissent, to say nothing of revolt, that we have rarely challenged the way this mess of pottage has disguised itself as the latest embodiment of Promethean creativity and autonomy, is explicable partly through the exhaustion of all other ideological formulations of that ethos, and partly through the defenses that have justified its ways to humanity. These defenses have been, on the one hand, invisible, and on the other, so candy-colored and attractive we hardly know that, inside the tasteful packaging and behind the delicate aroma, what is hitting us is the excrement of an industrial machinery that operates for its own sake. The invisible defenses have been the enormous deployment of lobbyists and policy makers who constitute the real power that shape legislators and governments to their will. The visible, candy-colored parts have been the "carnivalesque" mass media of newspapers, glossy magazines, and TV, whose enserfment to the advertising agents representing multibillion dollar corporations Twitchell documents in breezy, hip prose.[52]

Those who are aware of the historical significance of carnival as subversive of both established political authority and conventional sexual morality will therefore question this equivalence. It is of course true that the cornucopia of consumer goods the admen have encouraged us to view as a necessity also comes in attractive social wrapping paper. Twitchell himself, like Mary Douglas, sees consumer society as anthropologically explicable: the common experience of consuming commodities and reading, watching, or listening to advertisements is the ritual glue that holds together modern culture. For those who live outside of, or on the margins of, the consumer paradise offered by the modern shopping mall, the existence of those colorful transformations of the department store has the cultic significance and mysterious power that once attached to the imposing castles of medieval noblemen and the vaulted interiors of gothic cathedrals. If there is anything to the analogy between contemporary commerce and traditional culture, it is therefore not in the realm of transgression theory but in that of social integration: like many popular culture rituals, the much publicized pleasures of buying and owning expensive cars, designer clothes, and the latest electronic gadgetry function as a social glue. But expensive commodities, beyond the connotations of power and sexual attractiveness advertisers teach us to associate with them, also serve as a safety valve for unsatisfied passions, signifying the ultimate in (barely) sublimated sensuality. And the vicarious participation of millions, thanks to television, in the Homeric competitions of professional sports teams—accompanied, for those in actual attendance, by occasional orgies of empathetic violence—leave little doubt that the Roman imperial tactic of bread and circuses to distract the masses has not been forgotten.

These various side effects of our contemporary consumer society suggest that rather than being a carnivalesque end of history, it is a dead end for humanity, in the most literal sense. On the one hand, anything recognizable as a human future is lost in the orgies of acquisitiveness of the few, seen against the increasing misery of the many; on the other, enlargement of the present post-Fordist consumer paradise to the three-quarters of the human species presently outside it would see us all expire in the vastly expanded pollution of air, earth, and water.

Even without such expansion, however, the level of consumption of food and raw materials in the American consumer economy is an absurd and dangerous waste of resources. Stimulated by the increasingly concentrated agro-industry, the high-protein diet of Americans, stuffed with hormone-inflated beef and factory-prepared fast foods, has four serious consequences: massive obesity, diversion of grain products to cattle feed rather than feeding of the world's poor, ecological disasters (overproduction of animal wastes that pollute land, air, and water, and health disasters like Creutzfeldt-Jakob disease and *E. coli* pathogens, inherent in the methods of industrial farming), and, socially, the destruction of small-scale farming.[53] The enslavement to the automobile, and in particular the prestige of expensive gas-guzzling sport-utility vehicles,[54] guarantees the profits of automakers and oil corporations, the impoverishment of public transportation, and a U.S. contribution to global warming (25 percent of world CO^2 pollution) that is four times the global average per head of population.

Oil, Growth, and Unsustainability: Seedbeds of Terror and Totalitarianism

Independent of planetary pollution and the health dangers of industrial farming, the quest for a secure supply of the resources necessary to assure continued "growth" (and thus to guarantee an ever expanding consumption) creates global tensions that could lead to the totalitarianism foreseen by Orwell in *1984*.[55] This is an extreme assertion, but a brief look at the background of the terrible events of September 2001 will support it.

In a country whose oil reserves diminish daily, consumer capitalism's ideology of continual growth—mirrored in the individually felt need for more and more—creates an increasing dependency on foreign oil. In turn, it is resentment at the decades-long diplomatic and military pressure to create a "friendly" environment for Western oil companies in the Middle East and the Caspian Sea region which motivated both the terrorist offensive against the United States and the reaction of the Bush administration to it. In other words, the needs of U.S. consumer capitalism nurtured the Middle East conditions that created the terrorists, and continuation of that capitalism could necessitate a permanent state of war and a police state.

The needs of the American economy for foreign oil are apt to increase. United States reserves are being rapidly depleted, and a country that fifty years ago seemed to have more than enough resources to fuel its economy can now supply only half of what it needs; 25 percent of its oil consumption is imported from the Middle East. In fact, world oil reserves cannot last more than another few decades; the discovery of new reserves is declining steadily, and predictions of specialists are that before the present decade is out, oil prices are likely to increase sharply.[56] This is the background of every American action in the Middle East. And of the terrorist acts that shattered the confidence of the American people on September 11 2001.

The terrorism presumably came from Al Qaeda, a powerful, international network led by shadowy Saudi Arabian and Egyptian Muslim fanatics, fueled by Saudi money and inspired by hatred of U.S. hegemony in the region. While Bin Laden and his associates were no doubt motivated by Islamic fundamentalism, their convictions were nonetheless embedded in the cultural, political, and economic matrix of the Middle East. The latter was complex, rooted in an Arab civilization that was in full bloom during Europe's dark ages and understandably resentful of a recent history of foreign domination.

A brief historical digression.

After the collapse of the Turkish empire early in the twentieth century, British and French neocolonialist mandates in former Turkish provinces were followed, after World War II, by indigenous attempts to combine local nationalist aspirations with a mix of pan-Arabic and Muslim ideologies. In several cases (Egypt, Iraq, Syria, and Libya, for example) military takeovers, with a veneer of national socialist ideology, were the result. Nasser's nationalization of the Suez Canal in 1956 led to British, French, and Israeli military intervention the following year. In Iran and Afghanistan, secular states supported by the Soviet Union but opposed by Islamic fundamentalist nationalists were undermined by the United States. In 1953 in Iran, America punished the modernizing Mossadegh for the 1951 nationalization of the oil fields by orchestrating, with the British, a coup to bring in the Shah;[57] in Afghanistan it supported an Islamic rebellion against the Russians in the 1980s which, after prolonged civil war, ended in Taliban rule. In other cases, however, particularly in oil-rich Saudi Arabia, Kuwait, and the United Arab Emirates, local sheiks, emirs, and royal families with pedigrees from the Ottoman feudal empire were kept in place against secular and religious nationalists by Western, and particularly American, interests.

The United States developed a threefold strategy in the Middle East after the Second World War: securing unhindered access to the region's oil reserves, increasingly important as U.S. reserves thinned out and America became dependent for a quarter of its oil supplies on Saudi oil; opposing Russian political influence in the region; and protecting the Israeli state, a pro-American enclave in a largely hostile Arab sea. All three of these strategies contributed to the focusing of Al Qaeda's terror on the United States.

The goals of securing Middle East oil for American consumers and of opposing Russian influence led to a permanent deployment of American naval and air power in the region, with bases in Saudi Arabia and military dependencies in the Persian Gulf.[58] These goals lay, as mentioned, behind the CIA's overthrow of Mossadegh, behind the U.S. role in the Afghan civil war of the 1980s, and behind the war against Saddam Hussein's Iraq in 1991.[59] Such interventions have not made the United States loved in the Middle East, not even by its business partners.

While the economic elites of the Gulf states are themselves largely conservative capitalists, dependent for their wealth on sale of their oil to the West and for their political preeminence on U.S. military support, most of them remain devout, traditionalist Muslims with extremely mixed feelings about the source of their riches. Just as Christian and Jewish capitalists in the West try to quiet public criticism of their enormous wealth (and perhaps their consciences) by gifts to schools, orphanages, and charitable foundations, so do Muslim ones in Saudi Arabia fund orphanages and schools in poorer Islamic countries—Pakistan, for example, where the Saudi-funded Koran schools (madrasas) nurture hate for the West and Israel and reverence for Osama bin Laden.[60]

Bin Laden himself is a wealthy Saudi dissident, one of many children of the founder of the largest construction firm in the country. His complex antipathies are no doubt shaped by the fact that his family is Yemenite by origin and outside the main stream of Saudi elite society, but it is important that he first rose to prominence in the CIA-sponsored Mujahideen guerrilla against the Soviet occupation in the 1980s. In this respect, he is a perfect example of what Chalmers Johnson calls "blowback,"[61] the recurrent phenomenon of U.S. protégés turning against it when they feel betrayed.

Having devoted both life and fortune to the fundamentalist cause, Bin Laden combined religious, political, and historical resentments in his sense of betrayal. Bernard Lewis writes that Bin Laden's admitted grievances were "America's presence in Arabia during the Gulf War—a desecration of the Muslim Holy Land—and America's use of Saudi Arabia as a base for an attack on Iraq."[62] But for an Islamic purist prepared to give his life and his fortune to eliminate infidel communists from Muslim Afghanistan, the maintenance in power of a decadent Saudi elite by American money and arms must have been galling, particularly in view of the unwavering American support for a Jewish state viewed as occupying the territory of another Islamic people.[63] If Bin Laden's fundamentalist terrorism has proven so popular with Islamic masses throughout the Middle East, it is because the United States, in its zeal to retain control over the area's oil riches, has consistently excluded every other path to collective dignity in the Arab world, from moderate nationalism to Soviet-aligned radicalism, supporting only corrupt dictators and feudal monarchs feared and hated by their subjects.[64]

Under these circumstances, militant opposition to American hegemony in the Middle East is inevitable. If it were not stained by the blood of the innocent, such resistance would even be desirable for the human dignity of those who suffer that hegemony. The fundamentalist fanaticism that inspired the September 11 attack was in that respect almost as much a tragedy for the cause of resistance to the imperialist shield of consumer society as it was for its victims and their families. Terror against civilians degrades the humanity of the perpetrators as well as of their targets. But even if the United States–led military force in Afghanistan kills every member of Al Qaeda, resistance to that hegemony—armed or unarmed, cruelly violent and counterproductive like the World Trade Center attack or more political in nature—is likely to persist.

For if the dominant forces in the United States want to retain the indispensable supply of Middle Eastern oil for continued expansion of U.S. consumer society and the world economy, they can do little else than maintain U.S. military control over the principal oil-producing or oil-transporting states (Afghanistan potentially belongs to the latter). This is why Bush, Vice President Cheney, and Defense Secretary Rumsfeld warned repeatedly in the midst of the debacle of the Taliban in November 2001 that America's Middle Eastern "war against terrorism" would not end with Afghanistan. The consumer capitalism that is now the basis of neoliberal ideology, given its fetishism of continued growth, must expand or die. To guard against the continual menace of terrorism, permanent war may be necessary, and a police state may be needed to enable the conflation of political dissent with terrorism. The USA Patriot Act could be only the beginning, unless we change course.

§ § §

To sum up: The moral indecency of expanding inequalities in a world of material abundance is inseparable from two other unpleasant consequences of our growth fetishism: the suffocation of democracy in the imperial defense of consumer society, and the incompatibility between the pillaging of planetary resources and the survival of humankind. Realization of this link is the beginning of wisdom about the future of Promethean man.

In the second part of this book, I discuss alternatives to the abasement of the Promethean ideal in modern commercial society. Before considering these alternatives, however, I examine the relation of our consumer society to earlier productivist ideals and broach the vexed question of human needs. In particular, I contest the liberal theory of needs that underpins both producer- and consumer-based modernity—the idea that such needs are individually determined by rational calculations of utility and are in principle insatiable.

PART II

PROMETHEUS REDEEMED

What the inventive genius of mankind has bestowed upon us in the last hundred years could have made human life care free and happy if the development of the organizing power of man had been able to keep step with his technical advances. As it is, the hardly bought achievements of the machine age in the hands of our generation are as dangerous as a razor in the hands of a 3-year old child. The possession of wonderful means of production has not brought freedom—only care and hunger.

ALBERT EINSTEIN, letter to the Disarmament
Conference of 1932

chapter four

Theoretical Interlude:
The Question of Needs and Nature

The artist distinguishes where the conqueror levels. The artist who lives
and creates on the level of the flesh and passion knows that nothing is
simple and that the other exists. The world of the artist is one of live debate and understanding. The conqueror wants the other not to exist; his
world is a world of masters and slaves, the very one in which we are living.

ALBERT CAMUS, "The Artist as Witness of Freedom"

IN CONTEMPLATING the modern avatars of Prometheus as they emerge
at successive historical moments, we cannot help but notice a marked degeneration from the "party of humanity," as the European Enlightenment
was called, to today's consumer society: a steady erosion of the founding
ideals of reason, creativity, and social justice and a disquieting increase in
both bureaucratic domination and the stimulation of individual greed and
hunger for power. No doubt this has to do with the increasing hegemony
of state-supported market capitalism over all competing forces. Within the
coalitions of technocratic reformers and millennialist populists that sustained all the putative collective liberations of humankind's Promethean
energies—from the English and French Revolutions through the nineteenth century's republican and authoritarian nationalisms to European socialism, the Fordist welfare state, and contemporary consumer society—
the growing power and predominance of global capitalism, its capacity to
corrupt its opposition, to mask its iron fist in a panoply of velvet gloves,
has been unmistakable.

More recently a second, more dramatic, shift, represented by the globalized, neoliberal "new economy" and by its British and German social-
democratic clones, "New Labour" and *die neue Mitte,* was touted as signaling
a new and better world. Under the impulse of cybernetic technology, which
eliminated much work and many workers, and of postmodernist theory,
which aestheticized commodities and relativized rationality, this shift was
presented as reflecting an earthquake in contemporary identity. Apart, however, from the use of computer programs to "flexibilize" mass production

and facilitate international speculation, and the novelty of making social democracy an indispensable public relations front for neoliberal capitalism,[1] the "newness" appeared to consist in the alteration of Promethean character from ascetic producer, the soul of successive industrial revolutions, to hedonistic consumer—the crucial actor in today's global market economy. While that change has been significant, its importance has been exaggerated.

Both the productivist and the consumerist norms of Western society derive from the possessive individualism of Thomas Hobbes, whose theory was developed by the laissez-faire liberalism and utilitarianism of Adam Smith and Jeremy Bentham and, in the past century, by the economic theories of Friedrich Hayek and Milton Friedman. This individualism, which has led to a mounting social inequality and impending ecological disaster, constitutes a dead end for human thought as well as for society.

I shall forbear from reiterating the many theoretical attacks on possessive individualism and note simply that its tenets, including the argument against social restraint on individual market choice, have been refuted or relativized throughout the last two centuries by philosophers, social theorists, and historians for its one-sided assumptions about human nature and its neglect of a wide variety of human capacities.[2] I shall add to this critique three historical and psychological reflections. First, concerning the apparently contradictory types of the producer and the consumer, I will suggest an underlying continuity and unity between them as well as between the antinomies, parallel to those types, of modern and postmodern, Fordist and post-Fordist, and inner-directed and other-directed versions of Promethean humanity. In this framework, I shall discuss the supposed conflict between liberal individualism and the collectivism of social regulation as well as the theoretical fault lines that make free-market individualism an inadequate basis for the continuation of human civilization, indeed, for any seriously considered freedom or autonomy. Second, I shall propose, as the litmus test for a global culture that combines sustainability, freedom, and solidarity, the compatibility of such a culture with basic human needs, as these can be discerned through anthropological, depth-psychological, and historical insights into our nature and capacities. Finally, in the context of this question of needs and nature, I will examine the theory of the psychoanalyst Ernest Schachtel, a creative critique both of Freudian assumptions on human nature and of consumer society.

Ideals of Consumption and Production

The austere producer of the early stages of capitalist accumulation, inspired by religious or ideological asceticism to abstain from worldly pleasures, was not merely condemned by the gradual spread of cultural enlightenment and sexual liberation, he was by temperament inadequate to the consumption of the oncoming mountains of inexpensive goods to be produced by industrial modernity in the twentieth century. In this sense, the celebration of the heroic consumer as a second incarnation of capitalist man signified an indispensable evolution of modernist values. Yet one can easily exaggerate how much has changed. Instead of a radical rupture from producer to consumer models, a long-term perspective might view the development from the one to the other as based on a unilinear development of two interrelated ideas that were implicit in Protestant asceticism and explicit in the instrumental rationality of both the Enlightenment and liberal utilitarianism: possessive individualism and the striving for mastery of nature.

The historical rise of possessive individualism is marked by paradox, and its theoretical foundation is racked by internal contradiction. For example, the argument against social constraint on market transactions is rooted in the denial both of society as a real and legitimate force and of any human nature that might dictate a fixed set of needs. Historically, this polemic against social restraint appears to have been equally important in the deployment of those collective enthusiasms that were necessary for the abolition, in the name of "the wish to be free,"[3] of feudal despotism. In fact, however, as I indicate in Chapter 2, such social movements had historical roots in premodern popular collectivities that used the moment of weakness of old regimes to reassert long-suppressed solidarities and, together with modernizing elites, to launch revolutions which—they thought—would reestablish those solidarities. In other words, without the collective mentalities, energies, and hopes of premodern social strata, capitalist Prometheanism— the "Unbound Prometheus" of David Landes's classic work on the industrial revolution[4]—would never have been able to recreate society in the name of possessive individualism.

This tension within the soul of the modern Prometheus between, on the one hand, an impulse of individual aspiration—for personal creation, higher knowledge, refinements of taste and imagination, productivity, profit, perfection, beauty, or some existential combination of all of them— and, on the other, a collective aspiration of masses of ordinary people for control over their lives and for liberation from the poverty, insecurity, and subjection they associate with traditional authorities has, as I have indicated, been reified in a number of ideologies and institutions. The outmoded utopias of the modern world—nationalist, liberal capitalist, and socialist—have all been built out of some aspect of this tension.

Free-market ideologists celebrate, as the basis of today's consumerist utopia, rational individuals deciding what transactions are useful to them, and at what price. Tension between the individual and the collective, they allege, characterizes the struggle between capitalist economies based on individual choice and "archaic" collective controls (governmental regulation, the welfare state). The briefest examination of this tension in contemporary society reveals it to be largely ideological hype. No doubt, historically, the "freedom-from" aspect of economic individualism was important in setting off masses of shopkeepers and nascent entrepreneurs against the corporate authoritarianism of feudal absolutism. And it is evident that the Promethean ethos inspired much of the individual genius that created the modern world. Nonetheless, it is arguable that this individualist aspect of the Promethean ethos was more prominent in the world of thought and aesthetic creation than in that of economic striving. In fact, creative intellectuals have more often found themselves in conflict with authoritarian political structures than have capitalist entrepreneurs who, from the age of princely absolutism to General Pinochet, have usually been able to demonstrate their usefulness as moneylenders or economy builders to despots.[5] In contemporary social conflicts, allegedly between proponents of individual economic freedom and obsolete collectivist ideologies, the reality is that the stigmatized representatives of collectivism are largely the inheritors of the popular revolutions that gave birth to the modern world—citizens' organizations (NGOs) for global equality, human rights, and sustainability, trade unions and parties of the Left, and national or ethnic units defending democratic decision making against corporate extortion—and that the global capitalism they struggle against has as much in common with individual entrepreneurs or rational consumers as a killer whale does with the minnows it devours.

Indeed, while the spokesmen for individualist theory attack efforts to impose collective restraints on the marketplace, those who subsidize such spokesmen represent multinational corporations whose wealth and bureaucratic structures are more powerful than all but the world's largest nations. The neoliberal strategy for preventing political decisions contrary to the interests of those corporations is, apart from threats of capital flight, two-fold. Neoliberals claim that their program is the only protection of middle-class investors, entrepreneurs, and consumers. And they argue that what is good for the world's economic giants is good for everyone: only the unimpeded capacity of corporations to take over each other, to maximize their profits, to downsize and "flexibilize" their work forces, and to sell and advertise their products with as little description of their contents and effects as possible will guarantee the "robust" growth that may ultimately trickle down to the lower orders. Meanwhile, the actual field of choice of individual producers or consumers of commodities is more hemmed in by the economic weight of multinational corporations than by the taxing and regulation of governments.

Although economic and social life has undergone fundamental transformations since the Hobbesian formulation of possessive individualism, the theory and its psychological presuppositions have hardly changed.[6] Despite the hoopla about the shift from producer to consumer—and from inner-directed to outer-directed, from modern to postmodern—the self-abnegation of the early capitalist and the unlimited self-indulgence required of contemporary consumers have a common core. Both are founded metaphysically on a dichotomization of subjective mind and objective nature akin to that of Descartes. They oppose the human individual to both society and the natural environment, and consequently reject any notion of social or natural constraint. Psychologically, they both suggest covert deification of the human subject, akin to what Freud calls narcissism, and Schachtel, secondary autocentricity.[7]

The psychology underlying Max Weber's *Protestant Ethic and the Spirit of Capitalism* confirms this for the compulsive early capitalist. Measuring himself against an all-powerful creator, Calvinist man called himself a worm but nonetheless had to convince himself, to avoid the prospect of eternal damnation, that he was inspired by the iron will and creative power of God Almighty; he could find evidence of this will and power in his worldly success as a self-denying entrepreneur. His distant descendant, the mall prowler, in rejecting any natural or social limitation on his propensity to consume, displays a similar need for self-deification, but now through unceasing gratification of impulses (defined as needs) rather than through heroic denial.

There may be some major differences between the deferred gratification of the early capitalist and the instant gratification of today's consumer, but they are less than they seem, more a result of secularization and the collapsing of time perspectives than anything else, since the consumer simply expects the blessings of paradise now instead of in the afterlife awaited by his Calvinist ancestor, just as the investors in Internet stocks in the year 2000 counted on an immediate multiplication of their wealth. Paradoxically, however, neither as an inner-directed ascetic producer nor as an other-directed hedonistic consumer/investor can the modern individualist be conceptualized outside a collective social framework of norms, values, and mentalities; and even in its most anti-collectivist neoliberal dispensation, this collective framework—the rules and institutions of economic life—gives much less scope to individual deployment today than it did two hundred years ago.

Thus the basic conflict of our age is not between economic individualists and self-perpetuating political collectivisms. While neoliberal capitalism and consumer culture both assume that freedom and autonomy derive from individual market transactions based on individual choice, that such choice is made on the basis of rational considerations of utility, and that the needs satisfied by individual choices and transactions are nonsocial, nonnatural, and insatiable, in fact this individualism is simply used as a screen to justify the "insatiable" needs of large capitalist enterprises to expand production and sales indefinitely, needs justified by the assumed beneficence of "growth."

As the Club of Rome report warned three decades ago, if this kind of compulsive growth is not curbed, the days of humanity and perhaps of life on earth may be numbered. Possessive individualism is completely self-serving and highly dangerous, since constraints on the individual consumption of ongoing productive "growth," apart from the Malthusian limits that science and technology appear to have made obsolete, can never be found in purely individual considerations of utility, whereas without such constraints the irreparable poisoning of the water, air, and earth on which future generations depend is inevitable.

Conversely, such constraints are incompatible with the continued survival of capitalism, which, as Don Slater has observed, "could not survive the restriction of need."[8] The character of individual choices, the meaning of human autonomy and freedom, the apparent insatiability of human needs, indeed the question of whether humankind has a "nature" and if so what that may be, thus become essential problems, whose resolution affects the future of humankind.

The critics of liberal utilitarianism mentioned above differ on many points, but they agree that the individualism on which liberal capitalism is founded is mythical to the extent that individuals exist only by virtue of their embeddedness in society. It is this social embeddedness that constitutes our "species being," to use the young Marx's term, and our choices about purchasing and consuming commodities have only the appearance, not the reality, of autonomy, since they are powerfully conditioned by the social influences emanating from that embeddedness. In other words, individual human intelligence, psychology, and ethics are exclusively formed in a social nexus.

This nexus begins with mother-child nurturance, moves through other early family relations that model emotional development as well as the development of language and gesture, proceeds to the influences of peers and teachers, and ends in the complex web of relations created by work, love, friendships, recreation, group mentalities, and social and political organization. This is not to say that freedom and autonomy do not exist, but merely to note that they develop only within, and not independently of, the solidarities created by the social nexus, and that the kind and degree of freedom and autonomy available to individuals will depend on the quality of that nexus.

When we trace the evolution of Promethean modernity's central values of freedom and creativity from the Reformation to consumer society, we discern an interesting curve. In the early modern era, when the overarching social frameworks were those of politico-religious despotism and social traditionalism, the sources of Promethean renewal were necessarily either oppositional or maverick. Church reformers in most of Western Europe found support in dissident social groups among the peasantry, city folk, or nobility. Concomitantly, independent-minded artists, scientists, and philosophers obtained minimal breathing space either from mercantile elites of city states seeking self-celebration through patronage of the arts (the Renaissance) or from enlightened absolutisms attempting to organize knowledge in the struggle for power. All such individuals, as soon as their creativity produced unorthodox religious, scientific, or philosophical insights, needed powerful protectors if they were to avoid persecution by orthodoxies of state or church, and such protection normally emanated from elements of the old regime that were jockeying for position against one another.

With, however, the social explosions that marked the demise of old regimes in one part of Europe after another—explosions which, I repeat, were essentially eruptions of communities of long-suffering peasants and artisans, delighted to find a part of the educated elites on their side—the post-revolutionary dispensation revealed a division within Promethean modernity: a continual tension between the individualism embraced by middle-class elites and the social norms of the new democratic collectivities, born out of the fusion of revolutionary idealists and traditional popular solidarities. This fusion went successively under the flags of the nation, the republic, and the working class.

At the end of roughly two centuries of this friction, centuries scarred by global wars and economic crises but spurred on by accelerating processes of industrialization and rationalization unleashed by the new economic elites, the last of the democratic solidarities, that of the national welfare state, has been subjugated by the planetary proliferation of market capitalism, victorious over all its opponents under the banner of personal freedom. In the place of the collective guarantee against poverty and illness of the social-democratic welfare state, we now have the individualist consumer culture that purports to be the end of history.

Yet, though Margaret Thatcher, the Cato of the myth of possessive individualism, might declare, "There is no such thing as society, only individuals and their families,"[9] reality was elsewhere. As legions of sociologists and anthropologists have pointed out, the vaunted freedom and autonomy of the modern consumer are shaped by the corporate giants that control the media (and more or less own the planet) just as much as the beliefs of credulous peasants were by the all-powerful feudal Catholicism of five centuries ago.

Indeed, what holds the system together is that the advertising and the identity-defining media narratives of TV, film, and glossy magazines neither propagate the rational autonomy of individual choice nor reject, as does possessive individualism, the assumption of social needs, but actually provide surrogate satisfactions for a panoply of social and nonrational instinctual needs in the hapless consumer. In such narratives, the consumer's needs for love, friendship, and social esteem—as well as his or her fantasies of sexual pleasure and total power—are exploited by the repeated presentation of commodities whose possession, it is whispered, will bring satisfaction. Meanwhile, we are conditioned to spend most of our free time watching or reading the very media that convey these messages, thus restricting our capacity to obtain these feelings to the virtual reality of the media, and limiting our autonomy to deciding whether Brand A or Brand B will deliver the better illusion. As Don Slater puts it, "With the decline of traditional social information systems such as religion, politics and the family, advertising fills the gap with its privileged 'discourse through and about objects.' Advertising offers maps of modernity, maps of the social order that are no longer available from traditional sources."[10]

The deadly aim that omnipresent advertising takes at our social-psychological needs, and the rather consistent social narratives we are fed by TV films and serials, are thus a covert admission that, contrary to the stated ideology, we do have a nature and we do have specific social needs which our present social order does not normally satisfy. Indeed, it is not from rational calculations of utility that advertisers earn their billions but from manipulation of our unsatisfied social and emotional needs.

In fact, these needs can never be satisfied in a system which in principle ignores and denies them, since such denial is what drives their apparent insatiability. To understand this, we need only reexamine the opposition—common to Marxist and non-Marxist economics—between the exchange value and the use value of goods. On the one hand, in settings where the social character of individual needs is accepted, use value will be the principal criterion for commercial exchange. This was true until the nineteenth century for the vast majority of humankind, and it is still the case for probably more than half the globe's population that buys its goods in the rural village markets of Asia, Africa, and Latin America, markets where goods are produced, exchanged, and consumed because they satisfy basic human needs. Marx's code for this use-orientation of commodities was C-M-C (commodity-money-commodity). One sold a commodity in the marketplace to have the wherewithal to purchase another one. The goods so acquired may have been chosen because of individual taste, but the group mentality conditioned individual choices about what could be sold as a commodity and what not, and which commodities were desirable and which not. Money-based market operations were limited to facilitating such choices. Land, for example, was largely considered inalienable in Europe until the end of the Middle Ages, and struggle over the village common land prevailed throughout the early modern period. Even today, while most kinds of services are freely sold, certain kinds of merchandising—for example, selling one's body to give sexual pleasure to others—remain prohibited by group mentalities and residual religious codes. In all cases where exchange was established primarily to facilitate the acquisition of useful goods, social limitation on consumption was implicit.

On the other hand, where the basic model of commercial exchange follows the principles of capitalism—that is, where goods are seen in terms of their exchange value rather than their use value, and the goal of commercial transactions is not the acquisition of use values, but the increase in total wealth of the seller (money-commodity-money, or M-C-M)—the sky is the limit. This transformation of economic activities from the production of use value to the increase in abstract wealth wrenches work, exchange, and consumption from the social nexus in which it was—and at a residual level, continues to be—embedded, and makes of the totality of economic existence a strictly individualist undertaking. What motivates the basic exchange model of capitalist enterprise, the unlimited desire for money, the symbol of abstract wealth, infects the market for consumer goods as well. This hypostasis of exchange value (M-C-M instead of C-M-C) carries with it a celebration of the isolated individual, of the rational autonomy of his or her tastes and choices. I have argued that narcissism and manipulation, common to both the productionist and consumerist models of modern capitalism, are more suitable concepts for describing this individualism than autonomy. In any case, it is the equivalent, in economic life, to the transformation, signaled by Weber, of the Calvinist's cloak of asceticism into the iron cage of the modern world.

To establish what kind of human social needs and capacities are being denied by—indeed are incompatible with—the fetishizing of commodity exchange, we are obliged to consider the thorny question of human nature, a subject largely tabooed in contemporary philosophical discourse as incompatible with the postmodernist rejection of "essentialism." There are excellent reasons for refusing that rejection. When truth is defined either in terms of the poetics of textuality or as what is empirically verifiable, serious consideration of human nature, norms, and needs seems to be dispatched to an obsolete realm of metaphysical absolutes, but this dismissal disregards the distinction between philosophical purity and the concrete world of human action. In that world, relative and provisional hypothetical constructions are indispensable to the planning or projecting of any part of our existence whatever, personal or social. In fact, essentialism creeps into the philosopher's language whenever he or she uses nouns, and no government, party, multinational corporation, or advertiser can evolve a strategy without at least provisional assumptions about human nature.

In examining some relevant anthropological and psychological data on this subject, I wish to focus on how human needs are, and are not, satisfied in today's global consumer society. I shall first present a summary consensus of what we might call a psychoanalytically informed anthropology of such needs and capacities, and then, to return to the question of the Promethean spirit, discuss one particular psychoanalytic approach to them, that of Ernest Schachtel. Schachtel's concept of an allocentric mode of perception, which translates in philosophical terms as the capacity to recognize and cathect with "otherness," tells us much about the sources of creativity, and can be used as the basis for theorizing novel forms of group and personal identity.

Psycho-anthropological Summary

Cultural anthropologists and ethnobiologists seem to be in general agreement, on the one hand, that through its genetic endowment, humankind shares a number of instinctual needs with other primates; on the other, that through its language and its advanced conceptual capacities, our species has developed additional needs that are largely absent in the animals closest to us. In satisfying these basic needs, human beings, unlike other animals, do not have instinctually fixed ways of behaving, and it is probably more reasonable to describe our needs as impelled by drives or capacities rather than instincts.

Drive-impelled needs fall into basically two categories: those that pertain to the preservation of the individual and those that pertain to the propagation of the species. Biological urges to eat when hungry, to find protection from cold and inclement weather, and to defend oneself against life-threatening attack answer to an individual requirement of self-preservation. In contrast to other animals, however, whose manner of satisfying these individual needs is programmed instinctually at birth, our ways of doing these things has always been conditioned by a social nexus, provided in the first instance by maternal nurturance during the necessarily long (compared with other mammals) period of dependency before the human young become physically mature, and in the second place by the language and collective mentalities, related to this long nurturant period, that we use to organize experience and store knowledge.[11]

Anthropologically, the near universal presence in human settlements of patterns of work and fighting, reflections of the instinctual need and capacity for individual self-preservation, reveals the essential importance of the social framework. While work has been necessary to obtain the wherewithal for individual survival—food, clothing, and shelter—modes of work have always been social.[12] From hunting, gathering, and tool-making to the cultivation of the earth and to the transformation of raw materials by artisan and factory production, human societies have refined the need of physical survival into the need to transform nature so as to make its benefits more regularly available through systematic labor.

All of this was driven by the impulse and the capacity to understand the workings of nature, a capacity unthinkable without social communication. The myth of Prometheus attributes to a single divine individual a central aspect of this mastery of nature, the appropriation of fire, but in fact this sort of work has always been carried out in the context of collective mental frameworks, and innovations were transmitted between individuals and generations by that instrument of collective memory and social reason: language.

While the drive for individual self-preservation is normally satisfied in a social context, the drive to propagate the species—manifested in the urge to procreate and in the pleasures of nest building, nurturance, and family and clan life—demands by definition a social solution. It is also the source of human culture. Given language-based human capacities to plan work, to fantasize pleasure, and to imagine the future, various cultural impulses arise that merge with—and in some cases modify—human instincts of species preservation: the urge to live in society; to rediscover, in the mature physical relation to a sensuous love object, the fusional state of maternal nurturance (Freud/Rolland's "oceanic feeling");[13] to have groups of friends; to identify with and defend collectively clan, peer group, tribe, village, city, or nation; to plan hunting expeditions, design houses and cities, conquer nature, and subdue other human beings.

Because of the human capacity to conceptualize and to wonder about both the origins and the death of individuals and communities, cultures tend to fantasize about the relation of man to nature and the supernatural order of things. In all cases, fantasies and speculations about the natural and the supernatural are socially conditioned; in fact they are crucial to the establishment of group and individual identity.

Religions, rituals, and mentalities, often originating in cults of ancestor worship, thus stabilize group identities and tend to prohibit and punish deviations from the group's moral code, particularly in matters of sexuality and interpersonal violence. Such identities correspond to Riesman's tradition-directed societies. Following Riesman's typology further, one might argue that in the subsequent, inner-directed phase of Western culture (characteristic of the elites of the early modern period), large-scale internalization of such prohibitions made direct communal pressures superfluous.[14] In this phase, for reasons discussed above, Promethean creativity became more widespread and less subject to drastic punishment. Whether the phase beyond such internalization is better characterized as other-directed or as autonomous is a moot question, but it is clear that only in more advanced cultures—cultures that have not only relinquished traditional religions and mentalities as standards of conduct but also relaxed the rigid superego controls developed in the inner-directed period—do we find liberation from customary norms. (In the area of sexual behavior, for example, we find social acceptance of adolescent sexual experimentation and of heterosexual partnership instead of marriage, and legitimation of alternative forms of sexual desire that do not lead to procreation: homosexuality and lesbianism.)[15]

Advanced cultures must, of course, also cope with the social pathologies induced by large-scale problems of anomie and social exclusion. The procreative urge can take the deviant reified forms of the Don Juan in eternal search of copulatory pleasure or, when combined with patriarchal contempt for women, of the rapist; serial killers can emerge from pathological inversions of the impulse to self-defense. But the non-anomic, social frameworks of these drives shape the capacities to work, to make love, and to defend oneself against aggression. The social conditioning of instinctual needs variously expresses, sublimates, and represses them. Feelings of affection and solidarity with others in courtship, family life, and friendship express such needs, as do the pleasures of creative labor and the brotherhood of warriors. Intense aesthetic or religious experiences and some kinds of intellectual work sublimate them.

Repression of instinctual impulse, necessary for the maintenance of any degree of social order, generally increases with the complexity of cultures and goes under the banner of the "civilizing process." Freud's anthropological speculations on the origins of society located the origins of the "tradition-directed" personality type, as David Riesman subsequently called it, in the transfer of the punitive authority of clan patriarchs to collective mentalities. This authority, Freud suggested in *Totem and Taboo,* centered on the patriarchal leaders' efforts to obtain sexual control of women and to keep male offspring from challenging this prerogative. Whereas violations of the moral code imposed by primitive authorities gave rise to feelings of shame—dishonor in the eyes of significant others—individual internalization of such authority in more advanced cultures (Freud's "superego," Riesman's "inner-directed type") leads to feelings of guilt about real or fantasized rebellion.

Transposition of such archaic patterns of repression into the highly complex civilizing processes developed by modern religious and political authorities can, as Freud indicated in *Civilization and Its Discontents,* lead to the deformation of instinctual aggression into socially sanctioned psychological cruelty or, in extreme cases, into physical cruelty and even mass murder, carried out in the name of a threatened collective identity. Herbert Marcuse, in *Eros and Civilization,* developed the notion of "surplus repression," a degree of repression not necessarily required for the maintenance of a developed civilization but indispensable to the stability of particular systems of domination.

Some degree of repression will of course always be necessary in human culture, but Marcuse was certainly correct in indicating the social parameters of that repression and denouncing it where tied exclusively to domination. There are two essential questions: To what extent may such domination, at a particular historical moment, actually be superfluous in terms of the technological and social possibilities of non-repressive need satisfaction? And, more fundamentally, how do we define such needs at a cultural level, that is, at a level more advanced than the biological needs of the human species for individual and collective self-preservation?

As I have indicated, we are not talking here about purely instinctual needs, but about characteristic capacities and needs that have evolved from the biological-social constitution of the human species: primarily the capacity and need to communicate through language thoughts and speculations about human identity and about the natural and the supernatural worlds. Let us call this the identitarian impulse. Psychologically, it has a negative, regressive aspect, insofar as it is based on a quest for womblike security (what Schachtel calls the "embeddedness affect") and leads to hostility to other human identities, and a positive aspect of social creativity and potential openness: one can only acknowledge and explore sympathetically the identity of others if one is aware of one's own.

In its more positive aspect this identitarian impulse constructs cosmological narratives to explain the origins and destiny of the group. These arise out of speculations on the origins of things and the coming of death, that is, out of notions about the organization of the visible world in which natural mortality is built into a larger scheme of the organization of things. There is a grain of truth in the outmoded Comtean idea that these speculations and notions first take the form of religions, rituals, and mythic mentalities and subsequently of philosophical and scientific speculation. Comtean positivism fails, however, in its assumption that this sequence, allegedly consigning value frameworks to a prehistory of superstition and metaphysical beliefs, means progress toward scientific truth. For what we see throughout the development of thought, from totemic religion to postmodern philosophy, is its enduring encapsulation by value-impregnated mentalities, paradigms, and discourses that give the cachet of "good and reasonable" to some ways of thinking and deny it to others.

A second near-universal human capacity, intricately tied up with the identitarian impulse, is the play impulse, which, though rooted in biological drives, goes beyond them. It is based partly on the proprioceptive pleasure of exercising mind and body,[16] and partly on the sublimation of mixed impulses of sex and aggression, as in competitions of physical or mental superiority (and in foreplay). In addition to these sources, however, the play impulse is also founded on what Schachtel calls the activity affect, an impulse to explore reality beyond the immediate requirements of biological need satisfaction.

I mention the identitarian and the play impulses together because the arts originate and develop from a combination of these two general characteristics of human cultures. That is, music, literature, and the visual arts begin at the intersection of religious awe, social identity, and creative play, whether in cave drawings, bardic poetry, Greek drama, monastic chants, mystery plays, temple carvings, or cathedral decoration. In the modern world, neither the transformation of traditional religious mentalities into "rational" economic and political ones nor the ongoing secularization of the arts can efface the essentially religious forms of identity and conviction that persist in the modern (and postmodern) ideologies, discourses, and paradigms of aesthetics and social thought.

Through this rapid survey of the biological, historical, and social frameworks of human nature, we have returned to the sources of human creativity and their potential renewal: the main subject of this book. Artistic innovation, arising at the intersection of the play impulse and cultic social identity, is a prime example of the Promethean ethos. Instances of such innovation are the incredible flowering of human culture in the Greek city-states and in the European Renaissance, as well as the more recent expressions of Promethean creativity in Western modernity. Although creativity has always had to struggle against institutional and ideological restraints, the latest straitjacket, the neoliberal political and economic order that now rules the world, is a dead end for culture as well as humanity. Claiming the aura of Prometheus, it simultaneously denies the social and biological needs of humankind, provides illusory, surrogate, satisfactions for them, and condemns a large majority of men and women to a meaningless, servile existence as the suppliers of a Disneyland version of happiness for a minority.

Meanwhile, premised on our allegedly insatiable appetite for junk food and junk gadgetry, the hunger of large enterprises for "growth" dominates our everyday existence, propagating the extension of a culture of alienated labor and involving in the United States longer workweeks for everyone.[17] All this so that citizens can have the wherewithal to purchase and repurchase throwaway production: microwave ovens that spare us the experience of preparing our own food, television sets that vomit forth plastic ways of life and incitations to purchase yet more gadgetry, automobiles whose power, speed, and newness substitute for the spontaneity, creativity, and youth our working and domestic lives seem designed to destroy. Such perpetual motion wastage goes on while basic human needs like health care and drinkable water take a backseat,[18] while the economics of globalization and post-Fordist production widens the gap between rich and poor, while environmental pollution further undermines our future, and while the material potential for a fairer, simpler life for all humankind is being squandered.

I make no pretense to originality in this critique. Many people recognize that our existing consumer society and the economic machine that powers it must be opposed, and militantly, if humanity is to survive the coming century. We lack, however, a notion of what might constitute a step beyond the false Prometheanism we see around us, a notion that might build on the global achievements of the last stage of Promethean man to radically recast the bases of our social order. New utopian concepts are only beginning to emerge, concepts designed to carry the human species beyond the deformed Prometheus of contemporary productivist and consumerist ideals. I shall offer one of my own in a later chapter. It will postulate the necessity of combining a sustainable social identity with personal freedom and with the recognition of "otherness"; a crucial element in this concept will be the theory of allocentric perception of Ernest Schachtel.

Schachtel's Theory: Activity versus Embeddedness

Ernest Schachtel's *Metamorphosis: On the Development of Affect, Perception, Attention, and Memory* (1959) is a high point in the wave of neo-Freudian theorizing which, challenging Freud's ideas, transformed psychoanalysis from a therapy subserving social adjustment to a radical critique of society. While many of Freud's concepts were revolutionary, and while he attacked, as did Darwin and Nietzsche before him, shibboleths of Western culture concerning human nature, sexuality, the family, and religion, Freud was very much a Central European bourgeois. His subversions affected the packaging of Western morality more than its substance. Like the Victorian protagonists of the bourgeois "civilizing offensive," but perhaps more subtly, he argued for the primacy of the rational ego over irrational id-drives, seemingly convinced that those two aspects of personality were in fundamental conflict. His therapy aimed at making his patients more effective workers and better spouses, partly through the mending of object relations disturbed in childhood, via the transference relationship to the therapist, and partly by developing the sources of self-comprehension.

Freud's theory, while daring for its time, was actually patriarchal to the core: it focused on the conflicts of sons with fathers and aimed at their pacific resolution within a new paternal authority. Neither wives nor daughters played an important role in it, except to the extent that the central Oedipal conflict between adolescent sons and fathers was assumed to hinge around their mutual competition for the mother. While Freud recognized the intimate love of mothers and sons in the first years of life as a source of infantile personality development, this early "oral" stage was overshadowed by subsequent stages of paternally determined anal repression and genital expression. Freud's indifference to the actual condition of the female half of the human species is evident from his notorious theory that women's personalities are dominated by penis envy.[19]

Even during his own lifetime, disciples closer than Freud to the circles of dissident modernism—genial figures such as Carl Jung, Otto Rank, Alfred Adler, Wilhelm Reich, and Otto Gross—questioned these conformist aspects of his theories, particularly with regard to women.[20] In the interwar years, after the carnage of 1914–18 had shattered Europe's Victorian consensus, dissident modernism became more widespread, and so did dissident Freudianism. Starting from the research of Freud's daughter, Anna, into infantile development, an English school of psychoanalysis—Melanie Klein, John Bowlby, Ian Suttie, and others[21]—revised Freud's theory of personality development by focusing on the crucial importance of the mother-infant relationship for developing both a healthy personality and the joined powers of emotional and rational comprehension.

While a French school around Lacan attempted its own revision of Freud, emphasizing the infant "mirror" relation of child and mother as a basis for the subsequent role of the father in introducing the child to rational thought, two German-Jewish analysts close to the Frankfurt School, Erich Fromm and Ernst (later Ernest) Schachtel, offered the most radical correction to Freud's patriarchal bias while bringing psychoanalytic theory into the ambiance of critical social theory. Fromm's accomplishment was more in the area of cultural history, the study of the matriarchal aspects of Western myth and culture.[22] Schachtel's work, part of which reappeared in Herbert Marcuse's *Eros and Civilization,* reexamined, on the basis of careful studies of childhood development, Freud's assumptions about human nature.[23] Like Fromm and the British school, Schachtel argued against Freud's neglect of the mother's importance in defining a child's personality.[24]

Schachtel's main theoretical point of departure was a critique of Freud's notion that the two basic forces guiding mental activity, the pleasure principle and the reality principle, were irreconcilably opposed. Freud, he argued, was wrong in juxtaposing as mutually exclusive, on the one hand, the requirements of work and civilized society—the reality principle—and, on the other, the instinctual drive to seek immediate gratification of impulse— the pleasure principle. Apart from positing instinctual behavior as irrational, Freud understood the drive for immediate gratification as actually a need to relieve tension and return to a tensionless, quiescent state (p. 151).[25] He thought this was so, for example, in the case of the hunger impulse of the infant, and in the desire for adult sexual congress. In all such cases, the desire to return to a tensionless condition, according to Freud, was an obstacle to an efficient coping with natural and social reality, for which the human ego had to develop rational ways of working and of administering its relations to the object world.

The creative achievements of human culture were, then, largely contingent on the supremacy of the reality principle over the pleasure principle—of reason over instinct. Freud did, of course, acknowledge that such creativity amounted to a kind of kidnapping, or harnessing, of instinctual energies which, if left undisturbed by the ego, would only lead the individual back to quiescence. And he recognized the arts and philosophy as non-utilitarian sublimations of instinctual forces. But the basic opposition between the more animalic aspects of human drives and the reality principle of human culture persisted in Freud's notion that behind the quest for pleasure was actually a death instinct, inherent in all life and ever more present in the evolution of advanced civilizations, a death instinct that he saw as surfacing in the great wars and totalitarian adventures that overshadowed his last decades.[26]

Schachtel, while accepting many of Freud's theoretical presuppositions, rejected his metapsychological theory of the conflict of the pleasure and reality principles. He did not deny that neonates appeared to want to satisfy tensions like hunger in order to return to sleep, that they displayed an impulse to return to the completely passive, protected existence of the maternal womb. Schachtel called this aspect of existence the "embeddedness affect," and he agreed that it was a recurrent and necessary phenomenon throughout human life (pp. 29, 31, 74–75, 151). But, he argued, close observation of human infants showed that neonates, alongside this embeddedness affect, exhibited from birth an instinctual desire for active pleasure in nursing, "in being held, turning toward the warmth of the mother's breast, touching and sucking and tasting and swallowing," and, he maintained, this active pleasure was quite different from "the negative pleasure of relief from tension" (p. 123). Schachtel saw this as the initial manifestation of an "activity affect" that was just as biologically grounded, in his view, as the embeddedness affect.[27] It was in this inborn capacity for active pleasure that Schachtel found the roots both of human creativity and of the subsequent development of human reasoning powers.

Schachtel understood the early, prerational, period of human development to occur under the hegemony of the proximity senses of taste, smell, touch, and proprioceptive experience, which were the framework of both the embeddedness and the activity affects in the first few years. Using a wide range of evidence from experimental psychology, he pointed out that where the infant is visually or aurally stimulated, it is in terms of pleasant or unpleasant colors and sounds. Only later does it recognize and classify the world of objects, transmitted by the distance senses. Such recognition and classification, which provides the basis for rational distinctions, develops,

Schachtel argued, long after the phase of infantile experimentation with its visual capacity so as to be able to identify the mother's face, and after the infant begins to comprehend sound in terms of language. Its early dependency on the proximity senses builds up to what Schachtel calls the perceptual mode of "primary autocentricity," in which sense information is interpreted in terms of pleasure and displeasure, and objects, insofar as they are perceived as independent of the subject, are understood as existing only for the satisfaction of the infant's needs.

Even in this stage, however, the infant, according to the ethnobiologists cited by Schachtel, displayed an active striving to find out more about the object through the senses of taste, touch, and smell, which was incompatible with Freud's notion of the pleasure principle as a mere quest for tension-reduction. Subsequently, from the third or fourth year on, the distance senses of sight and hearing, on which a conceptual grasp of the world depends, gradually come to dominate over the proximity senses. This conceptual grasp of the world developed in two opposed ways. To the extent that the activity affect predominated, the revelation of the object world would occur in terms of what Schachtel called "allocentric" perception: the discovery, exploration, and understanding of "otherness." To the extent that one learned to use the world exclusively in terms of one's subjective needs, Schachtel saw a continuation of the infantile embeddedness affect, and he called this perceptual mode "secondary autocentricity" (pp. 166–212).

All of this, however, occurred, and could only occur, in the social context of the infant's social relation to a nurturant figure. Schachtel understood the phylogenetic origin of human society in terms of the prolonged period of dependency of the human young on such nurturance, a phenomenon that went together with the larger and more refined structure of the human brain when compared with other primates.[28]

Schachtel's juxtaposition of passivity and creativity—which in the adult is expressed in the opposition of secondary autocentricity (based on a continuation of the embeddedness affect) against allocentric perception (rooted in the activity affect)—contains a powerful dimension of social criticism. It also suggests that there is a basis in our instinctual endowment for an alternative to the present martyrdom of Prometheus on a mountain of superfluous consumer junk, a different order of things in which we might exponentially increase our creative capacities to explore and enjoy both the world and human otherness, and in which basic human needs could be satisfied without extremes of wealth and poverty and without the menace of ecological catastrophe.

Secondary autocentricity is not presented as exclusively negative in

Metamorphosis. Rather, Schachtel sees it as necessarily developing conjointly with allocentric perception. Secondary autocentricity, in relating sense perception to the needs of the subject, responds to the need of allocentric perception for formal organization of its discoveries of the world, that is, for the organization of such sense perception into more or less lasting frameworks of language, concepts, and mentalities. The problem is that, once categorized, the achievements of autocentricity tend to become institutionalized obstacles—reifications—that overshadow the allocentric capacities. "While man could not live without the perspective of this secondary autocentricity," Schachtel writes, "it can block his view of reality and lead to stagnation in a closed, autocentric world. Whether and to what extent he can transcend secondary autocentricity and retain or expand his world-openness is therefore crucial for his experience of other people and of the world around him" (p. 166).

The two most general examples Schachtel offers of the negative effects of secondary autocentricity are, on the one hand, what we would call the pleasure-pain calculus of utilitarian philosophy and, on the other, the construction of cocoonlike social or cultural identities, extensions of the embeddedness affect of infancy. He does not specifically define the first of these as utilitarianism, but it is clear from his psychological description that this is what he means: "Objects are most frequently perceived from the perspective of how they will serve a certain *need* of the perceiver, or how they can be *used* by him for some purpose, or how they have to be *avoided* to prevent pain, displeasure, injury, or discomfort. . . . When the object is perceived in this way then the predominating feature of the perception is not the object in its own right, but those of its aspects which relate to the perceiver's more or less conscious feelings of the need or purpose which the object is to serve, or of the fear which makes him want to avoid it" (p. 167).

I must emphasize that there is no absolute opposition in Schachtel's theory between this utilitarian view of the object world and the early exploration of the object world carried out by the child's activity affects. As I have indicated, Schachtel views the activity impulse as evolving conjointly in the young child with the autocentric senses and subsequently with secondary autocentricity, whose frameworks become indispensable as the point of departure for the deployment of the allocentric mode in ever more subtle explorations of otherness. His critique of secondary autocentricity is thus directed neither to the objectification and categorization of the world it brings about nor, in principle, to the social frameworks it creates—that would be akin to a Nietzschean denunciation of society as such—but is limited to the prevalence of situations in which it dominates and suffocates the activity affect and the allocentric mode—Schachtel's technical terms for what I have called the Promethean ethos. (In fact, Schachtel's juxtaposition of allocentricity and secondary autocentricity basically corresponds to what I have presented, in another rhetorical mode, as the relation between the Promethean ethos and the ideologies and institutions of modernity.)

The utilitarian reduction of objects to servants of the subject's needs can occur in two distinct cases, both of them involving the reification of the object world: where one views the natural world as an object of scientific research and technological manipulation, and where one views other persons autocentrically as objects of use. In both of them, this reduction of the object world to a set of useful things devoid of sentient qualities and subjective experiences in their own right signals a fundamental estrangement of human subjects from their social and natural world. The young Marx, cited by Schachtel, argued, for example, that the perspective on the world of nature as an object of use is a crippling limitation on sensory experience: "The sense dominated by the raw, practical need is a limited sense only. For a starving man the peculiarly human form of food does not exist, but merely the general quality of food. It could be just as well food in the rawest, most primitive form. His eating activity would be in no way different from the animal's feeding. A man worried, in need, has no sense for the most beautiful spectacle. The dealer in minerals sees only their mercantile value, but not their beauty and their peculiar nature and quality" (p. 168).[29]

Not only the starving man and the dealer in minerals focus one-sidedly on the utility of natural objects. So do many, though not all, scientists and engineers, when they use objects to test hypotheses or manipulate objects with the goal of improving predictability, control, and efficiency. In this kind of "operational" knowledge, the object simply becomes a means to a given end, which might be the development of more efficient energy resources, or the predictability of the weather, or an improvement in construction methods, or an increase in the profit margin of an enterprise. In these cases "perception," Schachtel writes, "may . . . become almost an act of aggressive violence in which the perceiver, like Procrustes with his hapless victims, cuts off those aspects of the object which he cannot use for his purposes. Instead of approaching the object with complete openness and receptiveness, he approaches it with the determination to see how it will fit into this or that scheme which he has in mind, or whether he can produce this or that effect on it or with it." (p. 171)

While this kind of science may indeed by useful for given social goals, it normally involves a willed ignorance of those parts of reality that are not easily quantifiable. The economist Dominique Méda, for example, writing about the definition of wealth in the history of economic science, indicates a point at which Malthus redefined the concept of wealth in strictly material and quantifiable terms, because a broader, more traditional use of the term to include social and moral well-being could not be applied to the utilitarian mathematical schema he was working with. The result was that the discipline of economics developed from Malthus on without any possibility of balancing quantifiable (usually material) and nonquantifiable (often immaterial) results of economic activity, or even of discussing the latter.[30] Less theoretical cases are those in which nuclear or genetic scientists have gone ahead with research whose larger social implications were left undiscussed, or where the planners of large-scale programs of hydroelectric power ignored grave social and ecological consequences—for instance, the forced migration of millions of Indian peasants to urban slums.[31]

As to the perception of human beings as "objects of need, fear, or use for some purpose," a principal example for Schachtel is the view of other persons "primarily in terms of their social position, status, 'importance,' and . . . in terms of their usefulness as employees or customers or business contacts" (p. 173). Viewing others in terms of status can take the form of wanting to associate oneself with important people or celebrities, or simply with the "'right' kind of people," as a means of social advancement. In all such cases, autocentric perception is not "receptive to the other person as a human being, but primarily to the . . . signs which will indicate . . . whether this person is or is not 'worth while' in terms of the perceiver's scale of desirable social position and status." Another form of the status quest is the search of dependent persons for powerful parentlike figures, which is frequently at the basis of the specific relation of the analysand to the psychoanalyst. Common to all such cases is the inability really to see the other: "The autocentric perspective of the dependent personality usually is the result of a narcissistic attitude which blocks the full view of the other person and limits perception to those (real or distorted) aspects which have a bearing on the neurotic demands and fears of the perceiver. He is looking *for* something in the other person rather than looking at the other person. What he is looking for is determined by what he wants to get from the other person and/or what he is afraid of" (p. 175).

The view of others in terms of their usefulness as employees and customers signifies the reification of, respectively, the producer and the consumer, discussed above. In the first case, which is the psychological analogue of Marx's labor theory of value, one sees one's productive power, or that of other persons, as a commodity; in the second, one views oneself or the other as a potential buyer of commodities. Schachtel's most extreme example of the view of the worker as a use object is the slave economy, where slaves would be appraised like beasts of burden. But, he argues, "it is equally apparent when in hiring a worker the only perspective from which he is viewed is whether his actual work output will contribute to the greatest possible profit" (p. 174). In a critique of the alienation of white-collar and managerial workers that parallels that of C. Wright Mills in *White Collar,* Schachtel notes the increasing tendency, in the job market for higher positions, to scrutinize the personality of the applicant not only in terms of the traditional criteria of physical condition, qualifications, and diligence, but also as a use object.[32]

Secondary autocentricity is particularly evident in a post-Fordist consumer society in the viewpoint of "the salesman and the advertiser who 'size up' the customer . . . looking for the weak spot which they can exploit in order to persuade him to buy their product." The close fit between secondary autocentricity and the commodification of the world in consumerism is also apparent in the widespread view that workers—particularly white-collar, managerial, and professional employees—have of themselves "as an object on the market whose value depends on how much he is 'in demand,' an object to be used by other for their ends as he uses them for his" (p. 174). Consumer society is in fact a perfect example of "the secondary autocentricity of the adult's world of 'objects-of-use,' in which all objects are reduced to and exhausted by the familiar labels and reactions the culture provides for them." Consumer society is thus an archetypal cocoon of secondary embeddedness: "While the 'cocoon' at which he arrived is larger than the womb was, *and while within it there are many more objects than the infant ever dreamt of,* they have lost their aliveness, just as the man who has 'matured' to the state where he does nothing but contribute to the protective uniformity of the cultural cocoon has lost his enthusiasm, his capacity for growth, the essential and specifically human capacity to remain open toward the world, that is, to transcend a closed pattern of reactions and thus to encounter and perceive the new" (p. 185; italics added).

This cultural cocoon is the second principal manifestation of secondary autocentricity. Like the utilitarian reduction of the object world to serve the subject's needs, the quest for a closed social identity leads, Schachtel argues, "to the experience of any new stimulus or any change as something disturbing and to be avoided" (p. 176). Religious fundamentalisms, xenophobic nationalisms, peer-group mentalities,[33] and some ethnic or other ideological identities are examples of such cocoons, hypostatized extrapolations from tribal or village identities destroyed by religious and political centralization. In important ways extensions of the infantile impulse to return to intrauterine embeddedness,[34] such social identities based on secondary autocentricity are characterized by quick recognition of familiar categories, which reassures the subject that everything is as it should be. To escape the boredom that results from prolonged immersion in the familiar, those enveloped in such identity cocoons have recourse, writes Schachtel, to "the quick succession of a variety of familiar or easily labeled perceptions, or, as in many entertainments such as detective stories, television shows, etc., by the rearrangement of familiar elements in such a way that some suspense or surprise is effected, without deepening or adding to the substance of the perceiver's experience" (p. 177).

In contrast to the conformity and passivity of social constructions built on secondary autocentricity, Schachtel cites the experience of "the great artists, poets, scientists, and the great masters in the art of living, and . . . of quite a number of people in moments of being fully alive and fully turned toward the object of their perception (i.e., without wanting to *use* it and without being in need of it, that, is, dependent on it)" (pp. 176–77). In such cases, allocentric perception

is characterized by an inexhaustible and ineffable quality, by the profoundest interest in the object, and by the enriching, refreshing, vitalizing effect which the act of perception has on the perceiver. . . . [F]ully allocentric perception (especially of nature, people, and the great works of art) always breaks through and transcends the confines of the labeled, the familiar, and establishes a relation in which a direct encounter with the object itself, instead of with one or more of its labeled and familiar aspects, takes place. . . . In the moments of allocentric perception at its fullest we always are at the frontiers of our familiar world, breaking through the enclosing wall of explicit or implicit labels and encountering the inexhaustible other, which transcends all labels with which man tries to capture and tame it, so that he may use it and so that its unfamiliarity will no longer disquiet him. Allocentric perception, thus, always transcends, in some respect, that part of the labeled, traditional, cultural world with which the perceiver is familiar. The more original the mind and personality of the perceiver is, the greater is the likelihood that what he perceives will transcend *"reality"* as known in the everyday currency of his culture. (pp. 176–78)

In his celebration of allocentric culture heroes, Schachtel betrays a certain ambivalence with regard to the ordinary run of humankind. On the one hand, he seems to be talking primarily about "the never ending struggle of the poet, the writer, the artist" to record their "allocentric vision of the true object." In this light, his description of normal social existence built around secondary autocentricity reads like many other condemnations of mass society by 1950s intellectuals who identify with elite culture. On the other hand, Schachtel argues that allocentric perception, based on the activity affect and universally evident in the period of childhood exploration of the world, is not the characteristic of a small number of geniuses but is implicit in the human condition.

In fact, Schachtel touches here on the fundamental philosophical controversy over the relation of subject and object in the modern world, the dispute over the nature of the human mind and its relation to objects of perception. In the tradition emerging from the Cartesian *cogito ergo sum,* the essential characteristic of human beings is their capacity to conceptualize themselves and in so doing define themselves in opposition to the external world. Out of this presumed opposition comes the struggle to master the object world external to the thinking subject. Both nature and other men are viewed as objects to be understood and exploited. The political theory of Hobbes, the scientific epistemology of Bacon, the utilitarianism economics of Bentham, Malthus, and Ricardo, all presuppose the mind/nature split formulated so trenchantly by Descartes.[35]

Behind this philosophical assumption is the Judeo-Christian cosmology that opposes a transcendent, all-powerful and omniscient deity to the world of nature that it has created and may someday end. Man, in this cosmology, is the steward and representative of the divinity, representing it in its overlordship of the natural world and, if inspired by correct belief, able to join it after death. The political philosophies of Christian absolutism assumed this cosmology when they put in parallel the domination of God over man, moral intelligence over animal impulse, man over nature, lords over peasants, male over female, parents over children, and teachers over pupils.[36]

Contrasting with this is another cosmology, found in Indian religion and in the pre-Christian peasant religions that still influence folk belief in some parts of the world, which reflects the immersion of traditional agricultural societies in a powerful natural world, a world perceived as capricious, alternately nurturant and punitive. Here the relationship of nature, humankind, and the supernatural is seen as a continuum. As befits agrarian cultures dependent on the eternal return of the seasons, the passage of time, which is viewed in the Judeo-Christian scheme as linear, with a beginning and an end, is seen as cyclical. Man and the divine are both understood as rooted in nature rather than standing above and in opposition to it. Related to this mentality are certain mystical undercurrents of the Christian tradition itself, such as that of Jacob Böhme, which resurfaced in English and German romanticism as well as the pantheist philosophy of Spinoza and the dialectical philosophy of Hegel and Marx.[37] The latter in particular aims at the reconciliation, through the notion of dialectical development, of man and nature and of subject and object.

Schachtel's notion of allocentric perception is a nuanced psychoanalytic appreciation of this latter tradition. Impelled by the activity affect, allocentricity explores the object, seeks to understand it from the inside and to merge with it. This quest for the reconciliation of subject and object challenges the rigid Cartesian premise of an opposition between subjective mind and objective nature. It is opposed to the utilitarian approach manifested in secondary autocentricity, as well as to the cultural embeddedness of inward-turned identities that is the other expression of secondary autocentricity.

Allocentricity thus represents an empathic aesthetic, affective, and intellectual understanding of "otherness" both of the natural environment and of the human world. Schachtel cites, for examples of the painter's need to understand the object by identifying with it, Dante ("Who paints a figure, if he cannot be it, cannot draw it"), Cezanne ("Nature out there and in here [he hits his forehead] must penetrate each other"), and Braque ("One must not just depict the objects, one must penetrate into them, and one must oneself become the object"), as well as the principles of Japanese and Chinese art. He distinguishes, here and elsewhere, this allocentric "oneness" with the object from the "oneness" of infantile autocentricity. Whereas the latter, focused on the proximity senses, reduces the experience of the object world to "states of the perceiver's comfort or discomfort" and "antedates the experience of "I" as separate from the world," allocentric experience "presupposes a temporary eclipse . . . of all preoccupations with self and self-esteem, and a full turning towards the object. . . . The oneness of allocentric perception leads not to a *loss* of self, but to a heightened feeling of aliveness" (p. 181).

Schachtel differentiates his theory of perception from that of Freud (and of cognitive psychology generally) in arguing that the latter does not take allocentric perception into account. Freud (in *Civilization and Its Discontents*) does discuss the experience of oneness with the outside world in the "oceanic feeling" of fusion with the universe, known to mystics and to lovers. Schachtel questions, however, Freud's attribution of this sense of fusion with otherness exclusively to a recurrence of the infantile experience of identification with the body of the mother.

While Schachtel agrees with Freud that the impulse to restore unity with the object world has its origins in separation from the mother, he argues that such unity can be attained "not only in a regressive way, by the wish to return to the womb, but also in a new way, on a higher level of development, by loving relatedness to others and to the world." In the latter case, "the oceanic feeling borders on the experience of oneness in allocentric perception." Objects, whether they are other persons, natural phenomena, or works of art, are then not perceived in isolation "but as containing in [them] the *mysterium tremendum* of life, of being. . . . [T]he relatedness to a particular, very concrete object in fully allocentric perception is also always a relatedness to something more than just an isolated, separate, single object" (pp. 182–83).[38]

The oceanic feeling, then, can signify in the child both regressive fusion with the mother's body (embeddedness affect) and the pleasurable exploration of the world (activity affect). In both cases, the infant expresses these affects through the perceptions of the proximity senses (primary autocentricity), though the growing child, in whom seeing and hearing gradually replace the dominance of taste, touch, and smell, gradually separates himself from, and becomes highly curious about, the external world (allocentric perception). Schachtel compares "the childhood period of openness toward and fascination with a yet unlabeled environment" to the "playful learning" of other "higher animals" and he sees as the link between humankind and this animal world "an innate behavior pattern to which is entrusted the essential task of acquainting the organism with the larger environment (compared with the protected maternal world) in which the adult organism will have to live" (p. 186).

Schachtel's primary concern is with the frequent loss of allocentric capability in adulthood. He raises the problem of the widely varying quality of adult experience, the question of why "some people are always interested, capable of fresh allocentric perception, while others live in an indeed closed world in which nothing vital or new every happens." And, after noting that some adults who live in the cocoon world of secondary autocentricity can experience a reawakening of allocentric perception,[39] he cites evidence that in man as well as in some mammals there are tendencies "both . . . to seek the new and to be afraid of it and avoid it." He notes the sharp swing in allocentric capacity through the life cycle: avoidance of the new in infancy, strengthening of the tendency to explore the new in childhood, and a return, in animals and in many, but not all, human beings, to avoidance of the new in adulthood. The "cocoon aspect of civilization" is thus normal for those who simply evolve "from the primary embeddedness in the womb and in the world of the mother to the secondary embeddedness in the culture, usually in the subculture of the particular social group to which [they] belong . . . from the primary autocentricity of the infant's perceptual world to the secondary autocentricity of the adult's world of 'objects-of-use,' in which all objects are reduced to and exhausted by the familiar labels and reactions the culture provides for them" (p. 185).

Schachtel views this closed adult world of secondary autocentricity and embeddedness—the world I have described above as that of reified institutions and ideologies, created by the Promethean ethos but suffocating to it—as doubly rooted in human culture. On the one hand it is the result of the social pressures of parents, pedagogues, and peer groups "toward the formation of a more or less definite, closed view of life and the world, a certain code of behavior as well as often very definite views about things and people and what they are there for" (p. 187). He refers to the adult tendency to respond to the child's incessant questioning with clichés and labels and (elsewhere in his book) he cites Kafka as saying that "probably all education is but two things, first, parrying of the ignorant children's impetuous assault on the truth and, second, gentle, imperceptible, step-by-step initiation of the humiliated children into the lie" (p. 293). Schachtel sees that the parent's efforts to alert the young child to the dangers of the world—everything from the possible threat of strangers to the menace of putting everything in sight into its mouth—may so frighten the child that it will quickly abandon its impulse to explore and strengthen its "tendency to avoid the unknown and remain embedded in the familiar" (p. 187). In particular, the early taboo on touching can lastingly and literally thwart "the person's getting in touch with the world, exploring and trusting it with his hands and entire body." But he also recognizes that parents and teachers, even when transmitting a cultural paradigm to the young, can help to open as well as to close the world for them. The problem is that even when they intend to open it, they inevitably close it as well to a degree, since all adults are embedded to one degree or another in their culture of origin and its language (p. 187). Perhaps even more dangerous than adults to the development of allocentric perception in the young is the pressure of the peer group, whose ridicule and ostracism often make the price of encountering the world "with an open eye and mind" prohibitive, insofar as such encounters involve deviations from the group's shared autocentricity.

The other cultural barrier to allocentric perception, according to Schachtel, is that indispensable cement of human ties and identities, language. As ambivalent in its effects on the young as parents, teachers, and peers, language may provide perspectives that help to open new meanings of the world to us, but its normal usage tends to hinder such perception, creating only the multitudinous cages of secondary embeddedness: "Most of the time, when we listen to the spoken or read the written work, we neither perceive nor imagine the referent of the word but are in contact only with the words (or concepts) . . . in listening or reading we are divorced from any experience of that which the words point to. More often than not, the speaker or writer who uses these words is also in contact only with them and not with the objects which they designate. Used in this way language bars the access to the world, obscures the objects, leads to autocentric perception of familiar clichés rather than to allocentric perception of reality" (p. 189).

Such clichés become organized, Schachtel says, in the discourses ("particular languages") of subgroups, where language loses its potential evocative power. These discourses can be couched in the form of professional jargon, advertising sloganeering, teen slang, and journalese, all of which give to particular circles "a superior feeling of being knowledgeable". Initiates receive from such discourse a sense of belonging, but it is counterproductive in terms of enlarging actual knowledge, or giving a "fresh view" of the matters being referred to. Its main function is to "strengthen . . . the *sociocentric* view of the world shared by the particular group for which [these words are] daily currency," and, Schachtel explains, "sociocentric perception is really a shared autocentricity" (p. 191).

Much to the contrary, an evocative use of language can, according to Schachtel, open the reader or listener to new dimensions of reality. Actually evoking experience is only possible if both speaker and listener are interested in such evocation: on the one hand, if the person speaking or writing is "in contact with the experience about which he speaks and [is] trying to communicate (i.e., evoke in the listener) this experience," and, on the other, if the listener is willing and able to experience what he or she is hearing or reading. Properly evocative language should, Schachtel argues, use words other than those of the conventional clichés, or in any case "[use] them in a way that reveals their original meaning . . . in such combinations, images, positions as will conjure up most concretely the experience about which one is talking or writing."

As an illustration, Schachtel offers the evocative language of "good writers and poets," by which he means in particular the elite intellectuals of modernism: "In our day, they often have to shock the reader out of the state of mind in which he is capable only of taking in clichés and is blind to experience." This need to shock, he believes, explains a good deal of the apparent "obscurity of modern poetry and literature." In a paragraph that makes us think of the use of language of James Joyce or of the scholar Norman O. Brown, or of Simone Weil's essay on the *Iliad* as a poem of force, Schachtel writes: "In its origins language is always evocative. If we take the pains really to fathom a work, even the most worn one will become pregnant with meaning, the word misused in the most banal cliché will again become evocative of experiences. Really listening to the word and all its implications can accomplish such resurrection of its experiential meaning buried under layers of daily use, and very often a tracing of the history of the word, back to its earliest roots, will recover its evocative impact" (p. 191).

This defense of innovative modernism in literature is accompanied by a critique of mass culture that reminds us that Schachtel's book is nearly a half century old: "With the invention of printing and with the constant assault of the modern mass-communication media, language has lost a great deal of its evocative function and the listener or reader merely takes in clichés, which altogether too often is all that the speaker or writer, on his part, was in touch with" (pp. 189–90). Schachtel's critique goes beyond language, implicitly attacking, like many other mandarins of his generation, the hoi polloi. It seems to freeze any kind of popular social identity into a "shared autocentricity" that always and necessarily opposes creative insight. He cites, for example, the "realistic" consensual view in the early modern period that the sun circled around the earth—based on the shared autocentricity of the age—as grounds for the common dismissal of the contrary notions of Galileo and Copernicus as mad.[40]

Here Schachtel's analytic power fails him. Implicitly, the social definition of reality, necessarily framed for Schachtel by the shared autocentricity of blinkered masses, is identified with iniquitous populisms cut off from any truths that go beyond labeled prejudices. As the source of an alternative concept of reality, he can only offer the lonely thinkers and artists who understand that most of the real world is unknown and unknowable, "and that only partial aspects of it ever become visible when man dares to encounter it, that is, when he does not rest content merely with the shared opinions of the many, with the labels and clichés, but experiences for himself the unfathomable and mysterious reality of other beings" (p. 192). In other words, when one experiences the kind of reality perceived by the scientific and literary geniuses whose creations armor the elite culture against sinking into the mass of the hoi polloi. Group identities—shared autocentricity—seem a priori to militate against creative breakthroughs in knowledge, insight, and sensitivity.

Like the utilitarian approach to the world, however, and like language itself, the group identities based on secondary autocentricity cannot be condemned en bloc, since language, culture, and most social activities stem from such identities. Indeed, national identity was in the nineteenth century one of the principal expressions of the Promethean ethos, as was the consciousness of the oppressed during the era of class struggle. E. P. Thompson, in a seminal work of social and cultural history, clearly indicated the merging of these two kinds of identity in the recourse of English radical artisans to the myth of the free-born Englishman during the social conflicts of the early nineteenth century.[41] A comparable argument can be made for French working-class movements and social romanticism during the decades before 1848.[42]

The French case is particularly interesting, since national identity in the romantic period, as the "shared autocentricity" of many in the French middle classes (as well as the popular classes), showed many traits of allocentricity. This allocentric character flowed from the concern of many ordinary Frenchmen, during the thirty-four years of monarchical restoration, with solidifying the achievements of the Enlightenment and the Revolution of 1789–94, a concern that resulted in the intensification in the cultural sphere of some of the open perspectives of the revolution itself. Together with much mythmaking and the construction of historical narratives of national evolution, what we find in the dominant romantic culture of the age is not the exclusion of other identities that later characterized nationalist xenophobia, but precisely an openness to, and an exploration of, all the "others" of middle-class identity which later filled the bourgeoisie with anxiety:[43] the working class (the utopian socialists, Lamennais's *Paroles d'un croyant,* Eugène Sue's *Mystères de Paris,* George Sand's *Compagnon du Tour de France*); the exotic (the canvases of Delacroix); women (the Saint-Simonians—their feminism went to the point of seeking a female pope for their sect—and several novels of George Sand); and children (Victor Hugo's chapters on Cosette in *Les Misérables*).

Contrary, then, to Schachtel's conviction that group identities inevitably express a blinkered autocentricity against which allocentric geniuses had to struggle to achieve creative breakthroughs, certain historical situations have revealed particular manifestations of group identity to be the forges of new collective experience and seedbeds of individual openness to the "other." This is not to say that even in those situations, group stereotypes, discourses, paradigms, and mentalities do not limit the possibilities of individuals to break out of them and obtain original experience. It is merely to distinguish between identities which are exclusively inward-oriented and those which encourage a double perspective: outward, allocentrically, toward other groups and new forms of knowledge and experience, as well as inward, autocentrically, to the preservation of group values and stereotypes. The struggle of reformism in contemporary Iran, for example, reveals that a society can move in the course of a generation or so from a purely autocentric fundamentalism to a partly allocentric view of the world.

In fact, not even the most original and creative of the cultural geniuses cited by Schachtel is humanly conceivable outside of the frameworks of language and group identity from which they emerged. The question, now and in the future, is simply how we can work toward the kind of social organization and identity that will enlarge, rather than punitively limit, the possibilities for creative encounters with otherness, encounters which in our increasingly complex world are probably a condition for human survival. Schachtel's blindness to the social parameters of allocentric perception, while showing the limits of his historical and social awareness, does not undermine the implications of his basic theoretical distinctions between embeddedness and activity affects and between secondary autocentricity and allocentricity as fundamentally different orientations to the human and natural environment.

Dependent as it is on a favorable social context, allocentricity—the Promethean spirit of creative exploration of otherness—has little chance of survival in the existing social order of global capitalism. In this order, the cards are stacked against any but the hermetically closed identities of, on the one hand, the falsely individualistic, utilitarian, market-oriented societies of global capitalism, with their imperatives of growth and consumption and, on the other, the equally autocentric identity cults—xenophobic nationalisms, religious fundamentalisms, insular minority cultures, etc.—that feed on the social anxiety created by the present form of globalization. In the next two chapters I address what now appears to be the central question: How can we move from the closed identities of a completely autocentric social order to a sustainable and just global society which, while protecting local identities and values, will also encourage allocentric openness of individuals and cultures to one another and to the world of nature?

chapter five

The Gathering Global Revolt
against Corporate Capitalism

Preliminary Note

Writing about contemporary history has never been easy, since what seems to be a long-term trend one month can be cast in the rubbish heap the next. Events of the last few years seem to have confirmed that uncertainty principle for all the major ideologies and forces discussed in the three chapters of Part I. World capitalism, which until 2001 had been enjoying the longest and most lucrative boom in its history on the basis of an information technology–led "new economy," a boom for which bull market optimists claimed eternal life, saw its tech bubble burst early in 2001 and slid into an old-style recession. Opposition to laissez-faire capitalism, declared dead after the collapse of both the Soviet Union and the social-democratic welfare state in the 1980s, returned to exuberant life in the protest movements of the late 1990s against corporate globalization, only to be forced off the streets and obliged to metamorphose into an antiwar movement by the militarist response to September 11. And nationalism, which appeared to have been left obsolete by the advance of global capitalism, returned with a rush to the United States after the momentous events of that day, as tens of millions of frightened, angry Americans hung out flags and supported the "war on terrorism" of a president only a quarter of them had voted for.

This book, premised on the long-term perspective of social and ecological menace outlined in the Preface, rejects the notion that the antiterrorist war will obscure the underlying problems addressed by the new social movements for very long. While a response to the criminal attacks of September was justified and inevitable, prolonged war against Central Asian or Middle Eastern states seen as protecting or sponsoring terrorism is hardly a viable option for the United States, since it would lead to abandonment of the United States by its European (and other) allies.[1]

International public opinion will not permit even the most pro-American regimes (like Tony Blair's)[2] to support a wider war for several reasons. One is that the public is aware that the United States has for decades been training terrorists in Fort Benning, Georgia, and is responsible for civilian deaths in Latin America and Asia far in excess of those killed at the World Trade Center. Another is that the

153

number of innocents who would be slaughtered in such a war is chilling, both in itself and for the unifying effect it would have on Muslim sentiment against the West
(and against any regimes that support it, such as those of Pakistan and Saudi Arabia). A third is the awareness that U.S. dependency on Middle Eastern oil, an aspect
of the wastefulness of America's consumer capitalism, is the cause of the U.S. military presence in that region and therefore a major source of the resentment on
which terrorism feeds. Even in the United States, more enlightened spirits like Paul
Krugman and Robert Kennedy Jr. have suggested that dependency on foreign oil
could be lessened or eliminated by intelligent conservation of energy and higher
standards for gasoline engine efficiency in automobiles. Indeed, as I indicated at the
end of Chapter 3, when we consider that Islamic terrorism is a response to the
Western attempt to supply the insatiable energy needs of consumer society by neo-
imperialist control of the oil-producing Middle East, the prospect that defense of
that society will require a decades-long struggle against terrorism is a decisive argument for questioning our way of life.

Since the underlying reality of our time is not the threat of global terrorism but
the menace of ecological disaster and the massive social dislocation inherent in the
present course of the world economy, the following chapter remains, with minor
modifications, substantially as it was drafted before the awful events of September 2001.

§ § §

A central argument of this book is that the Promethean creativity inherent
in the achievements of modernity—democracy, civil liberties, secular aesthetics, and scientific insight into the natural world—has come to a dead
end in nationalism, socialism, and capitalism and is in urgent need of renewal. The likelihood that any new social order will have to build not only
on the existing economic and technological apparatus of global capitalism
but also on contemporary movements against the social injustice and ecological dangers produced by that apparatus, mandates a review of these
movements before broaching the question of a new utopia. First, I sketch
the context and initial results of the renewed opposition to global capitalism. Second, I examine in some detail one crucial instance of it in the heart
of Europe: the origins and manifestations of the new militant Left in France,
from the remarkable events of May 1968 to the socialist government of Lionel Jospin. In a third section I analyze the international activism that has
been accelerating since 1997 and which finally captured the headlines during the anti-WTO "Battle for Seattle" of November–December 1999 and
the Washington protests of April 2000. Finally, I focus briefly on the political prospects, the social-psychological significance, and the relation to the

Promethean ethos of the new kind of radicalism that emerged in the last decades of the twentieth century.

Movements of Resistance to Environmental Destruction and Neoliberal Globalization

In the second half of the twentieth century, consciousness of the dangers to the natural environment of the unbound capitalist Prometheus grew rapidly throughout the developed West, as well as in parts of Asia and Africa. In the United States, ecological awareness dates from the campaigns against atomic testing spearheaded by nuclear physicists and the peace movement in the late 1950s, and from Rachel Carson's *Silent Spring* of 1962, which revealed the danger of synthetic pesticides to human health. Suppressed in the communist world throughout most of the existence of the Soviet Union, this consciousness developed there only after the Chernobyl (Ukraine) nuclear disaster of 1986 and the *glasnost* introduced by Gorbachev.[3] It had long before reached the people of Japan because of their exposure to nuclear attack at the end of World War II and through the fatal irradiation in 1953 of fishermen on the *Lucky Dragon,* some fifty miles from U.S. hydrogen bomb tests in the Pacific. The population of India, sensitized against modern technology by the Gandhian movement that prioritized artisanal village life, became broadly aware of industrial dangers to ecology in 1984 when a leakage of forty tons of lethal gases from a Union Carbide pesticide plant spread over the city of Bhopal, with 900,000 inhabitants, and killed thousands of people in their sleep.[4] Indian peasants are now active in numerous struggles against Monsanto's projects for gen-tech farming and against the large-scale dam projects that have uprooted thirty million people since they were begun under Nehru.[5] And in South America, Brazilian environmental activists have risked their lives in efforts to protect the Amazon rain forest, and its indigenous population, from destruction.

In Europe, ecological consciousness is widespread because of the combination of intense industrialization and demographic density. Nuclear energy is highly developed in some countries, particularly in France, where the country's postwar economic development brought rural electrification based on cheap atomic power, encouraged by both Gaullist and socialist technocrats from 1960 on. Nonetheless, the Chernobyl disaster, which blanketed Western Europe with radiation, dented public confidence in the nuclear lobby, and even in France, where most household electricity and industrial energy is nuclear-fueled, a growing awareness that no system is permanently foolproof and that there is no really safe place on earth to store nuclear waste has created a widespread desire to diminish and if possible eliminate dependence on atomic energy. The social-democratic governments elected shortly before the millennium in France and Germany were committed to responding to this desire, although in both cases they backtracked to avoid direct confrontation with energy companies and unions.[6]

The nuclear problem, because it is related to the possibility of nuclear war, attracted early attention from organizations concerned about world peace, particularly in Japan, which has been mourning the dead of Hiroshima and Nagasaki since 1945. A number of other industrial pollution disasters in postwar Japan sharpened ecological concern there, particularly the mercury poisoning of the fish supply in the Bay of Minamata, long denied by the chemical plant responsible but resulting in permanent injury to the central nervous systems of some three thousand persons.[7]

In addition to the "sudden-death" disasters of nuclear and chemical poisoning, industrialization in the latter half of the twentieth century has had a great many deleterious and perhaps fatal consequences for the global environment: pollution of air, earth, and water by fossil fuels and poisonous chemical wastes; numerous food scares caused by industrial agriculture in the 1990s, from mad cow disease to diseased chickens and pigs to contaminated Coca-Cola; the cutting and burning by commercial interests of huge rain forests in Asia and South America, rain forests essential for the reproduction of the earth's oxygen; and, most menacing of all, the danger that global warming (resulting from the accumulation of industrially emitted greenhouse gases in the atmosphere) will, by melting polar ice, raise sea levels and flood low-lying coastal areas worldwide, as well as dangerously increase average wind velocities in severe storms. (Such a windstorm occurred in central France in the last days of 1999, where half the trees were leveled and ninety people killed by unprecedented hurricanes sweeping across the country—a catastrophe supplemented within two weeks by an oil spill that massacred thousands of seabirds and befouled beaches along France's Atlantic coast.)[8] A much discussed doomsday scenario considers the possibility that the movement southward of near-freezing water caused by ice melting as a result of global warming might cut off the Gulf Stream, thus reversing the temperature increase and creating a new ice age in the northern hemisphere.

Alongside the ongoing environmental damage, the post-Fordist neoliberal form taken by industrial society in the last decades of the twentieth century has created the acute social problems alluded to in the Introduction and Chapter 2. These problems have taken on a different character in the core industrialized countries than in most parts of Asia, Latin America, Africa, and eastern Europe.

In Western and Central Europe, North America, and Japan, partly because of the opening up of so many new sources of cheap labor in Asia, Latin America, and the former communist countries and partly because of the cybernetic revolution in production, services, and communication, every major company has been led to contemplate and in many cases to carry out the downsizing of a large part of its regular work force. The growing legions of the downsized have experienced a general degradation of their social status. Either they have joined the ranks of the unemployed, which for many has meant not just the loss of dignity and self-esteem but actual impoverishment, and forced moves into cheaper quarters. (Sometimes downsizing led to homelessness—a glance at the streets of most major cities reveals the human detritus created by the "new economy.") Or the downsized may have accepted the "flexibility" of the new working conditions. Some shifted eternally from one line of low-paid work to another; others moved to poorly compensated "service" occupations; still others accepted low-paid temporary or part-time positions in their original line of work, frequently with the same companies that fired them. In Europe, where residual unemployment and welfare benefits persist, a large proportion of the unemployed chose the first path, creating a structural unemployment of close to 10 percent in the European Union; in the United States, where welfare has largely been replaced by workfare and where the hype of consumer culture increases the psychological pressure to keep up appearances, most of the unemployed quickly reentered the labor market under demeaning conditions.

In the "peripheral" areas where Western capital has used its newfound mobility to exploit cheap labor supplies, the social problem is different. Noreena Hertz summarizes the situation in these terms:

> Attempts by Third World governments to attract foreign investment, direct or portfolio—ever more urgent because of the dramatic cutback in aid flows over the past few years—often precipitate what has been called a "race to the bottom": they limit or dismantle regulation, lower wages, slash welfare requirements, and tacitly allow corporations to create huge social upheavals. Pension contributions have been scrapped, and health care provision paid for by employers reduced. Potentially disruptive groups such as organised labour, which may jeopardise the quest to attract and use foreign investment and expertise, have been silenced . . ."pollution havens" are created as environmentally unfriendly policies are allowed far below socially desirable levels, human rights abused, a blind eye turned to illegal acts, all in an attempt to attract foreign investment and all in the name of free market capitalism.[9]

In most parts of non-Japanese Asia and in Latin America, the exploitation of ordinary workers by large enterprises—usually Western owned or

Japanese—thus resembles that of England, France, or Germany during the early phases of those countries' first industrial revolution; the rural poverty reminds one of the lot of Russian peasants during the early phases of forced state capitalist industrialization under Stalin. In Mexico, for example, there have been extra pressures on the large, poverty-stricken indigenous (pre-Columbian) farm population because of the industrialization fostered by the Nafta agreement. These pressures were echoed mainly in the anti-globalization Zapatista revolt in Chiapas of the late 1990s, but in the spring of 2000 they seem to have spilled over into Mexico City, where a group of fifteen armed men of the Armed Revolutionary Forces of the People briefly took control of a working-class suburb to protest neoliberal governmental policies.[10] A comparable situation in Ecuador led to an uprising of the indigenous rural population which temporarily took control of the government after it announced it was abandoning the local currency for the American dollar. In Bolivia—also in the spring of 2000—tens of thousands of Indians rioting against major increases in the cost of water, as well as against high fuel prices, unemployment, and pauperization, forced the government to renounce its IMF-inspired water privatization; a London-based consortium, International Water Limited, had to abandon its Bolivian contract.[11]

On the other side of the world, in India, Western capital subsidizes both industrial agriculture of export commodities like sugar, whose needs for water are behind the Narmada Valley Dam project (responsible for the flooding of peasant villages in northern India) and the ongoing industrial growth, concentrated in textiles, chemicals, and computer software. In 1999 a national movement of protest was sparked by the decision of hundreds of villagers to chain themselves to their houses and drown rather than be displaced to urban slums. As mentioned, similar dam projects have resulted over the last forty years in the displacement of tens of millions of Indian peasants into urban shanty towns, where they become available for the industrial reserve army needed by booming industries like the textile trade.[12]

In China, like Vietnam undergoing deregulation and privatization under communist rule, the Three Gorges hydroelectric dam threatens to uproot a million peasants; in February 2000 twenty thousand miners, dismissed (with poor severance pay) because of the expectation that they would be superfluous after China's entry into the World Trade Organization, rioted and fought with police in the provincial city of Yangjiazhangzi.[13] According to Noreena Hertz, "hundreds of [Chinese] trade unionists are in prison or labour camps simply for having tried to form unions in special economic zones for foreigners. . . . China is the country that has benefited most from the greatest amount of FDI [foreign direct investment] over the past few years, and has had astounding year-on-year economic growth for the past twenty-odd years, yet over a fifth of the population lives on less than $1 a day."[14]

Public awareness of this state of affairs produced an increasingly organized international backlash against capitalist globalization. In the United States, a significant wing of American labor began to align itself with environmental and human rights groups in massive protests like the one in November–December 1999 against the World Trade Organization meeting in Seattle, and the April 2000 Washington demonstrations against the IMF and the World Bank. Student organizations (Students Against Sweatshops) and NGOs like Greenpeace have organized effective boycotts of popular (and vulnerable) corporate symbols of the consumer paradise: Nike, Gap, and McDonald's.

In Europe such awareness led to the revitalization of traditional far-left parties (restructured communists, Trotskyists, and anarchists), dissident trade unions, and citizens' groups, which have organized on behalf of the marginalized and powerless: immigrants, the unemployed, the homeless. The same awareness supported the growth of environmental interest and action groups (like Greenpeace, Friends of the Earth, or the Dutch Milieudefensie) and Green parties. The radical fringe of the new movement combined an anarchist political perspective with a keen ecological awareness in militant activist groups such as The Land Is Ours and Reclaim the Streets (in England), the Ruckus Society and the Internet-linked Direct Action Network (in the United States), and Groenfront (in the Netherlands). Actions of such groups ranged from giving a sharper edge to global protests against organizations like the WTO to using nonviolent resistance to block road building or other forms of industrial expansion. Politically conscious young people occupied land or houses, for example, and defended them against projected new roads or rail lines or real estate developers by ingenious forms of civil disobedience. Such activists were the counterparts in the relatively prosperous industrialized West to the Narmada Dam protesters in India.

Left-leaning Green parties, highly sensitive to and critical of neoliberal consumer society's masquerade as Prometheus, are now active in most European countries, where they tend to gather between 5 and 10 percent of the votes nationally and, at the turn of the millennium, were represented in governing left and center-left coalitions in Germany, France, Italy, and Belgium. In most of these countries they held the ministries of environment after the victories of the parliamentary Left in the late 1990s, and in France they were given an additional minister's post for economic solidarity during a reorganization of the cabinet in the spring of 2000. In Germany, their spokesman Joschka Fischer became minister of foreign affairs, and in a number of German Länder (Hesse, for example), they have been junior partners in socialist-led coalition governments.

Yet the political wing of the ecological movement is in an extremely difficult position in such governments. Though the French Verts have seen the gradual implementation of the thirty-five-hour week, which was an important part of their social program, they have had to backtrack on many other issues. Both Les Verts and their German sister party, Die Grünen, have consistently been forced to water down their opposition to nuclear power,[15] and they have on occasion muzzled their pacifist wings, which opposed both the Balkan and the Afghan Wars. In general Green parties in social-democratic governments have been obliged to mute their principled objection to neoliberal globalization, which they well realize is the source of acute ecological and social damage, to fit in with their senior partners' neoliberal policies of privatization and deregulation. Their most serious compromises have been on military questions with a humanitarian echo: the NATO bombing of Serbia and intervention in Kosovo, and, in the fall of 2001, the participation of Germany and France in the U.S.-led "war on terrorism" in Afghanistan. The result has been confusion among their members and constituencies and the shifting of the burden of opposition on both social and ecological matters either to radical political groups to the left of governing coalitions (like the formerly East German communist Partei der Demokratischen Sozialisten (PDS), which garnered nearly half the votes in the 2001 Berlin municipal election, the French Trotskyist parties, and the Dutch GroenLinks and Socialistische Partei) or to the extraparliamentary opposition of the new social movements (the French trade union federation SUD, etc.).

While this new radical periphery of Greens, anarchists, radical unions, and NGOs does not yet represent the kind of threat to the economic and political establishment that the old working-class Left appeared to embody in the first half of the twentieth century, it has, after the collapse of world communism seemingly eliminated the last obstacles to neoliberal globalization, erupted on the world scene with a vigor no one had anticipated. It represents the world's best hope of emerging from industrial Prometheanism and its fetishism of growth to a Shelleyan Prometheanism premised on the reconciliation of humankind and nature.

The renewal of radical purpose has nowhere been more significant than in France, where it brought down a government. To understand that occurrence, a key illustration of the potential power of Promethean radicalism, a digression into recent French history is indispensable. While an exploration of the French case suggests that it is a unique reaction to the global advance of neoliberalism, it also shows us the strength of a universalist revolutionary tradition, active throughout the Western world, which is reformulating libertarian demands for social justice to cope with the ecological and social catastrophes created by corporate industrialism and the centralization of power.

The French Case

THE BACKGROUND OF THE STRIKES OF DECEMBER 1995

To understand the waves of tumultuous opposition that engulfed France in the mid-1990s, one has to take a long historical step backward. This is only reasonable in a country where historical consciousness of the revolution that gave birth to the nation remains so strong that the French Communist Party of the 1930s Popular Front period could be discussed in a monograph titled *The New Jacobins,* and a book on the social-ecological opposition of the nineties could be titled *Les nouveaux sans-culottes.*[16]

In the first part of this book I dealt broadly with the various incarnations of Prometheus in movements and institutions that combined the fervor of radical modernizing elites (in France, symbolized by the Jacobins) with a rebellious, originally preindustrial, common people (the *sans-culottes*). At every point in the French history of the last two centuries, in every step taken by those modernizing elites to unleash the Prometheus of rapid industrial growth, they have been forced to take into account the limiting democratic force of the counter-Prometheus, the collective demand for social justice emanating from those inspired either by republican nationalism or by socialism. This is one of the major structural reasons for the relatively slow economic development of France (compared to Germany, England, and the United States) before the Second World War.

Only under the Gaullist and Socialist dispensations, in the decades after 1960, were modernizing technocrats able to harness the *demos* securely to a long-delayed French industrial revolution which, based on the nuclearization of the energy supply, has led to the present centralized but rather competitive French economy. Those decades, however, were also the period that saw the transition from Fordist to post-Fordist production methods, from the Keynesian welfare state to neoliberal globalization, and from a perspective of rising living standards and secure growth to the present precariousness of the working population and the bleak ecological perspectives mentioned above.

This period was punctuated by two social explosions, one in 1968 and the other beginning in 1995. While much has been written about the student-worker revolt of 1968, the turmoil of the present epoch is less well-known.

The "almost-revolution"[17] of 1968 reflected throughout the prosperous West the profound dissatisfaction of youth, both students and workers, with the Fordist welfare state at its high point. In the first place, young people revolted against the retention of an official morality completely out of synch with the semi-autonomous youth culture that accompanied the unheard-of prosperity and security of the sixties.[18] Second, they rejected the prospect of bureaucratic dullness and alienated labor that awaited both the new student masses being churned out by higher education (in the offices) and the working-class youth (in the factories). Finally they rejected the brutal hypocrisy of an allegedly humanist political ideology that in Vietnam, as earlier in the whole of Indochina and in Algeria, masked capitalist imperialism behind the pretense of democracy and waged war against local movements of national liberation on the pretext that they were pawns of international communism.

These international common denominators concealed major differences between the American and the European versions of the youth revolt, which arose from a divergence in the evolution of the working class. The antiwar student movement in the United States was organized by the New Left, principally the Students for a Democratic Society, whose agenda called for participatory democracy, an end to America's institutionalized racism, and a radical rejection of dog-eat-dog capitalism. Though it was broadly majoritarian on many campuses, and though its antiwar aims had considerable support from the educated middle class, increasingly disgusted by the cruelty and senselessness of the Vietnam War as well as by the mendacity of the government, this militant student movement was violently opposed by most American workers and by their largely conservative, pro-war unions. Proletarian opposition to the peace movement had three sources. One was the employment of a large part of the work force in the military-industrial complex. Another was the absence, with a few notable exceptions, of any socialist or communist influence on the American labor movement. The third was the large presence of workers of East European ethnic origin in many major industries, who identified the Viet Cong, and all radicals opposed to the Vietnam War, with the communist oppressors of their parents' land of origin. Apart from the student movement's support for the black movement for civil rights, then, that movement lacked a link to the American underclass, and to the extent that the students underwent ideological influence in the late sixties, this came in a minor degree from Maoist, anarchist, and Trotzkyist sources, but offered no opening to the workers. Rooted in a generational alienation of middle-class youth, the student antiwar movement fell apart when the war ground to a halt, leaving a small, violent, largely underground group, the Weathermen, in its wake.

It was quite different in Europe, especially in France. Young French workers viewed the occupation of the Sorbonne in May 1968 as a splendid example to follow, a beacon of liberation, particularly since most of the organized French student organizations and especially the so-called *groupuscules* had a strong Marxist, pro-worker slant—usually more Trotskyist or Maoist than Communist, for the deadening Stalinist culture of the French Communist Party was viewed with abhorrence by most students. There were also powerful anarchist and Situationist elements among the students, but even these unorthodox student militants shared the contemporary Marxist valorization of the proletariat as the indispensable standard-bearer of the coming revolution.[19]

The result was that in Paris, the student movement quickly made contact with the red belt of factories to the north and east of the city, mainly fiefs of the pro-communist Confédération Générale du Travail (CGT), where they activated a nerve of antiauthoritarianism among younger workers hostile to assembly-line production and managerial arrogance. The two modes of rebellion fed on each other, since the attitude of the young workers matched the students' own disgust at comparable phenomena in mass higher education. The French student-worker interaction led to a wave of factory occupations, the greatest in French history, exceeding even those accompanying the parliamentary victory of the Popular Front of 1936, and to a serious fear by the Gaullist government of the moment that a popular revolution was in the offing.

In May 1968, fearful of being outflanked by genuine revolutionaries, Communist Party functionaries and their union chiefs initially agreed to assist the chaotic ground swell of student-worker protest and went along with a more or less spontaneous general strike that completely paralyzed the country. Since, however, those "official" leaders of the French Left had long been committed to the parliamentary game, they were actually as aghast at the ongoing revolt as the government and—once the Gaullist government and the employers had agreed to some significant wage concessions—the Communists and the CGT did everything they could to restore order by persuading the workers to abandon their occupations of factories and return to work.[20]

Although the stikes in factories and universities were broken by the summer of 1968, the radicalization of students and workers continued for some years.[21] Repeated attempts to occupy and transform the universities by competing groups of student Trotskyists, Maoists, and anarchists were matched by the simmering rebellion of groups of young workers, their efforts to regain the initiative undermined by the intervention of the major unions in 1968. In 1973, after the owner of the Lip watch factory at Besançon formally liquidated it as unproductive, workers continued production for months without management under the slogan: "It's possible: we manufacture, we sell, we earn!"[22]

Nonetheless, the worldwide recession sparked by the oil crisis of 1974 broke the back of proletarian militancy, particularly since it coincided with the start of the sea change in capitalist production methods known as post-Fordism, a transformation which accelerated in the 1980s and 1990s under the combined impulses of the computerization of production and distribution and the decline and fall of the Soviet imperium.[23] These two factors were the decisive conditions for the main features of post-Fordism: a new global financial market, massive downsizing operations that eliminated much of the traditional factory proletariat, and the new "flexibilization" of what remained of the regular work force and of production.

That the French Socialist Party, in the face of this global offensive of post-Fordist capitalism, was able to come to power in 1981, and retain it for all but four of the following fourteen years of Mitterand's presidency,[24] has to do with the distinguishing characteristics of the French social and political development after the Second World War. There were essentially two political groups of technocratic modernizers in France: a conservative nationalist one that united around the figure of General De Gaulle, and a socialist one. The Socialists, who were entrenched in white-collar unions of government workers and teachers, were until the seventies only a junior partner on the Left. They were divided by feuding factions and party splits, and overshadowed by the Communists (the latter, entrenched in the industrial proletariat, profited more than the Socialists from a record of wartime resistance to the Nazi occupier and, moreover, controlled much of France's postwar intellectual discourse). The result was that a victory of the Left would then have signified, for most middle-class Frenchmen and even many workers and socialists, an unacceptable Communist-led government. From the inception of the Fifth Republic in 1958, this prospect insured two decades of Gaullist governance.

Several political and demographic developments reversed the balance of forces around 1970, both within the Left and between the Left and the Right; they permitted, a decade later, the electoral triumph of a leftist coalition in France for the first time since 1936.

Politically, the increasing evidence of the horrors perpetrated under Stalinism, the rather open break between Mao and Stalin's successors, and the series of national revolts against Communist rule (East Germany, Hungary, Czechoslovakia, Poland) eroded the intellectual support for the Communist Party.

Demographically, the shift of wage labor from proletarian to white-collar employment (a consequence of the factory automation of the 1960s and 1970s) and a major expansion of secondary and higher education increased the socialist constituencies among teachers and white-collar workers and narrowed the Communists' factory base; moreover, increased support for the Socialists was guaranteed by the coming of age of a postwar middle-class youth, a generation open to a leftward turn but immune to the Communists' dogmatism.

Finally, although French Socialists were even more appalled by the events of 1968 than the Communists, many student radicals of 1968 drifted into the orbit of the reorganized Socialist Party during the mid-1970s, because it was less closed to Trotskyists and Maoists than the Communists were and because one of its smaller elements, the "Unified Socialist Party" (PSU) of Pierre Mendes-France and Michel Rocard, had actually supported the student-worker uprising. All this, combined with a decreasing electoral attractiveness of the Right after De Gaulle's departure from politics in 1969, led to the impressive victory of the Left in 1981 under the astute leadership of François Mitterrand.

In the first year of his presidency, Mitterand, who came to power with the Communists as junior partners, actually implemented the radical "common program" worked out with the latter and thereby fulfilled, through a wholesale series of nationalizations, the dreams of many unrepentant leftists. These nationalizations appeared to give new life to a Fordist welfare state, which around this time was being repudiated in England and Germany by the rightward drift of the electorate. As early as 1982, however, when the outflow of hostile capital and foreign investment threatened to wreck the French economy, Mitterand reversed his policies. The Communists left the government, and its economic program turned from nationalization to privatization and budget-cutting. By 1986, disillusion with the Socialists had gone far enough to allow a victory of the Gaullist and liberal parties in parliamentary elections, but they made themselves so unpopular that they could not prevent Mitterand's reelection in the presidential election of 1988, and Mitterrand, using his restored prestige, obtained a new parliamentary majority in the elections to the Assemblée he called that year.

Mitterand's last seven-year term as president was marked by the customary scandals of a long-serving head of state, and these, combined with the total surrender to neoliberal economic pressures for further privatization, deregulation, and curtailing of welfare provisions led again to a massive defection of the Left's electorate and to the election, in 1993, for the last two years of Mitterand's second term, of another right-wing parliament. The Socialists did so poorly in that election (receiving only 17 percent of the vote) that many commentators speculated about an imminent breakup of the Socialist Party. And when Jacques Chirac, the astute Gaullist mayor of Paris, ran for president in 1995 against the relatively unknown socialist, Lionel Jospin, on a populist platform of healing the *fracture sociale,* he returned the Right to power across the board. Nonetheless, Jospin did better than expected in 1995, considering the debacle two years earlier, and in Parisian municipal elections that year, the Left took over half a dozen arrondissements that had for fifteen years had right-wing administrations.[25] It was the first major dent in the Gaullist control of the French capital.

When Chirac appointed the hard-line technocrat Alain Juppé as prime minister, the Gaullist president quickly reneged (much more rapidly than had Mitterrand) on his promise to heal the *fracture sociale.* In response to Juppé's announcement of a wholesale "reform" of France's welfare system— including the retirement benefits for government employees—state and municipal workers launched a protest movement of spontaneous work stoppages and occupations that swelled into a general strike. Because the strikers shut down public transportation, most of French economic life was paralyzed. The strike lasted more than a month and forced Juppé to back down.

The government and the establishment press—and even some intellectual publications (such as the monthly *Esprit*) sympathetic to the Confédération Française Démocratique du Travail (CFDT), a reformist union federation that had supported the Juppé plan—labeled the strikes the rearguard action of an "archaic" and "privileged" labor movement. Two facts make this charge implausible, however: first, the strikes had the support of nonstriking private-sector workers and the sympathy (according to public opinion polls) of a majority in the country as a whole, and second, most city folk endured the breakdown of public transportation and many other services with astonishing humor and solidarity, contributing food and clothing to the strikers. *Le Monde* at one point even called the actions a "strike by delegation," indicating that private-sector workers, poorly organized and without the immediate grievances of the government workers, viewed the strikers as acting on their behalf.

Moreover, most of the oligarchs of organized labor were hostile to the strikes. While the CFDT leadership openly opposed them, neither the communist CGT nor the anticommunist Force Ouvrière supported them. The strikers were led either by local union militants in defiance of their national leadership—mainly CGT or CFDT—or by the new autonomous unions that had been proliferating since the late eighties as a result of purges of leftists from the CFDT—the so-called Group of Ten and the SUD (Solidarité, Unité, Démocratie) group. Indeed, what characterized the strikes was the decentralized, participatory character of their organizations: well-attended local meetings of striking transportation workers, for example, decided every day whether or not to continue and what demands to make, not only in Paris, the heart of the movement, but in Marseilles and other cities as well.

Most important, the strikes occurred in a period of growing resistance at all levels to the results of the neoliberal policies that had been implemented since the eighties and exacerbated by the right-wing Balladur and Juppé administrations. Opposition to unemployment, social exclusion, xenophobia and racism, and environmental perils had grown steadily under governments of the Left as well as the Right for over a decade and had created a panoply of new social movements: against the chauvinistic pseudo-solutions of the far-right Front National and for *les sans* (the "withouts")—those lacking jobs, homes, and (in the case of many immigrants from Africa and Asia) residence permits. Supporting these movements, giving them a broad public resonance, was the reawakened social commitment of French intellectuals, artists, and students.

Pierre Bourdieu, France's best-known theoretical sociologist, was the key figure in this new commitment of the intellectuals. The editor two years earlier of a massive tome documenting global poverty,[26] Bourdieu attained national and international coverage in 1995 when he organized a petition supporting the strikers—signed by hundreds of well-known figures in higher education and the arts—and delivered a sharply militant address to the striking railroad workers in the Gare de Lyon.

In his brief talk to the railwaymen, Bourdieu scourged France's technocratic elites for subordinating French economic policy to the "experts" of the IMF and the World Bank, to "the new Leviathan, 'the financial markets'" and to "the new faith in historical inevitability . . . [of] liberal theorists."[27] The crisis reflected in the strikes was, he argued, a "historic opportunity" for the growing legions of those in France and elsewhere who rejected the alternative of "liberalism or barbarism" to consider alternative, non-technocratic solutions to the problems raised by the strike: problems of the future of public services, of public transportation, education, and health. Intellectuals, writers, artists, and scholars, he said, had an essential role to play in the reinvention of the public services and in the struggle against "the growing precariousness that is affecting the entire personnel of the public services and creating forms of dependency and submissiveness with ruinous consequences for radio, television, or journalism—enterprises of cultural diffusion—and especially for education."

In his closing remarks, Bourdieu apologized for being abstract and theoretical but pointed out that it was important not to fall into a populism that would only play into the technocrats' hands. He had come there, he said, to express his "genuine solidarity with those struggling today to change society" and argued that effective resistance to national and international technocracies would have to occur on their own privileged terrain, that of economic science, "by opposing to their much-vaunted abstract and mutilated knowledge, a knowledge that is more respectful of ordinary people and of the realities they confront."

THE LARGER MEANING OF THE DECEMBER STRIKES

The strikes of French government workers in December 1995 expressed a discontent felt throughout the industrialized world at the neoliberal wave of downsizing, privatization, and tightened work discipline, a discontent that became an important component in the protests against global corporatism that occurred from 1999 on in Europe and America. In *Le tournant de décembre,* two philosophically inclined French sociologists, Jean-Pierre Le Goff and Alain Caillé, published a useful analysis of what those events implied for the increasingly hard-pressed public workers everywhere and for new frameworks of resistance.[28]

The large public sector in France, like similar ones elsewhere, had long been accused of being overly bureaucratic, inefficient, and hierarchical. Government employees, with their unstressed working conditions and generous pensions, had allegedly adopted a "corporatist" mentality and were "pampered." In fact, inefficient bureaucracy is an affliction of every large organization, and, as Le Goff pointed out, the corporatist mentality tied to the employment security of government workers was simply a pejorative description for what could also be viewed as worker sociability, the sense of belonging to a social network that gave workers a sense both of stability and personal identity. It is worth recapitulating Le Goff's analysis, which applies to the situation of government workers wherever they are threatened by neoliberal management techniques borrowed from the private sector.

Le Goff argued that the background of the public-sector strike wave was the imposition (under a Socialist administration!) of a management ideology intended to eliminate bureaucratic and hierarchical inefficiencies—the management ideology that, as we have seen, corresponded to global post-Fordist production conditions in the 1980s and 1990s. The breakup of mass production assembly lines into teams of motivated skilled workers, fully engaged in a specific task, was intended to increase the efficiency of the enterprise as a whole. Applied to government employees, the new system was designed to lead, behind a verbal screen of autonomy and participation, to "an interiorization of constraints and norms";[29] the goal was the creation and exploitation of a guilty conscience in the workers. In a period when enthusiasm for these methods was diminishing in the private sector, Le Goff writes, public-sector administrations and enterprises were increasingly subjected to "campaigns to mobilize personnel, accompanied by the fetishization of the methods and tools of 'human resources administration.' . . . an unprecedented inflation of tools for measuring, evaluating, and controlling the performance of individuals and groups." What was perhaps most painful was that "intrusion of these new discourses and managerial practices went together with budgetary restriction and downsizing."

Worst of all, according to Le Goff, was the government's refusal to acknowledge the specificity of labor relations in the public sector. The prevalent view that public service workers, though modestly paid, were privileged in their secure employment ignored the essential relation between employment security and individual and collective autonomy. Public-sector workers, he argued, had a specific kind of investment in their work that used to allow for a considerable degree of sociability and activities outside the workplace. "By failing to take in to account these constitutive elements of the identity of the public service, the reforms led to disarray and to a long-suppressed revolt."[30]

Le Goff argued that the new managerial methods, insofar as they "dissociated professional existence from its culture, in the sense of the values, social relations, and customs that accompany it," were felt by the workers as "real aggression." Similar to the disruption of labor sociability earlier caused by Taylorism (allegedly done away with in post-Fordist enterprise), the new work rules were imposed by "pseudo-specialists" without any knowledge of the occupations they were supposed to redefine, and they were accompanied by an "unprecedented valuation of the managerial and commercial forces to the detriment of the worker, the technician, or the engineer." Le Goff pointed to the frustration and anger of competent professionals who had come to feel that "the occupations that had structured their individual and social identity had suddenly become obsolete and disreputable." This denigrating attitude of the post-Fordist managerial "modernizers" was reflected in the accusations of the establishment press at the time (supported by the leader of the CFDT) that the government workers' strike was retrograde and that their desire to retain their "privileges" stemmed from an "archaic" and "corporatist" mentality. To the contrary, argued Le Goff, the resistance to the new management techniques arose from "cultures inherent in social classes that it would be futile to want to eliminate."

In the spirit of Durkheimian social thought, Le Goff warned against confusing the concept of corporatism with the narrowly egoistic defense of individual interests. Rather, he wrote, "it [corporatism] implies belonging to a social group structured around a professional culture which helps individuals to forge a social identity, to form relations of solidarity, and to feel part of the collectivity." This sense of belonging to specific occupational groups with their own codes of sociability and solidarity—such a group mentality was particularly strong among the railroad workers, one of the key groups in the strikes of 1995—was a precondition both for a secure identity and for personal dignity: "Recognition of the existence of such groups, of their activity and their characteristic culture, in the heart of civil society, appears . . . to be a constituent element of democracy." More than any specific bread-and-butter issues, it was the prevailing sentiment among government workers that the Juppé reforms were to put the finishing touches to the managerial reformists' ongoing attack on these corporate solidarities that triggered the "first revolt against globalization," as Le Monde's Erik Izraelowicz dubbed the strikes.

While both Le Goff and Caillé were at pains to put the strikes in the broader context of the deteriorating social and political conditions of a globalized economic modernity, Caillé offered some particularly refreshing insights into the context against which the strikers rebelled. Like Le Goff, Caillé addressed an endemic problem of neoliberal capitalism.

Caillé's main point was one that Karl Polanyi had made in The Great Transformation: laissez-faire capitalism's dream—the pursuit of maximum profits free of any kind of social regulation (the utopian ideal of nineteenth-century liberalism)—was impossible. Polanyi pointed out how the brief reign of this utopia in the mid-nineteenth century produced such massive pain and dislocation that it was abandoned in the last quarter of the century. In its place, Polanyi reminds us, came a set of protectionist measures and imperialist policies spurred on by the economic crisis of the 1870s and designed to strengthen the social order built around the nation-state: capitalists were assured protected markets by high tariffs and imperial conquests.[31]

Despite the degeneration of imperialist nationalism into two world wars, the social legislation of the century after 1870 produced a gradual improvement of the workers' lot and a shift of their aspirations from primarily material questions to those of the quality of life. Caillé identifies a qualitative change in workers' expectations that was evident as early as the strike wave that inaugurated the Front Populaire of 1936: in endorsing so enthusiastically the offer of a forty-hour week and paid vacations that settled those strikes, workers showed their concern with "civilizing work through the reinvention of leisure." The comparable strike wave of 1968 "seem[ed] to consummate the liquidation of the old hierarchical world of social orders . . . and open[ed] the way to an unprecedented pluralization of values and ways of life."[32]

As we have seen, however, the passions of 1968 were characteristic of the final phase of the Fordist welfare state. Caillé saw that this earlier development of working-class expectations was colliding throughout the 1980s and 1990s with the neoliberal enthusiasm of post-Fordist global capitalism for downsizing and "flexibility," which meant retaining a smaller number of highly disciplined workers willing to work any hours and periods required for the profitability of their employers. Under the neoliberal dispensation, capitalism thus revived the discredited laissez-faire utopia of the mid-nineteenth century. With it came the old hard-nosed attitude toward labor and the virulent hostility to the regulative role of the state. The new technological base of corporate capitalism permitted the steady attrition not only of industrial and service sector work forces but of the working conditions of the survivors. And as we have seen, the situation of the unemployed also deteriorated. The ability of even left-wing governments (like that elected in France in 1981) to maintain their reforms, let alone cope with the increasing number of those requiring support, was severely limited by the pressure of international regulating bodies (WTO, EU, etc.) and investors; and this same pressure insured steady privatization, deregulation, diminution of corporate taxes, and dismantling of welfare provisions.

In Caillé's analysis, what produced the unprecedented strike wave of December 1995 was the clash between public-sector workers—still imbued with a consciousness derived from the advances of the sixties—and a right-wing government totally dedicated to a program of neoliberal reform. Caillé was aware that the tendency of neoliberal capitalism to leave the impoverished and excluded to their fate could not be counteracted by a restoration of the old Keynesian welfare state, since the numbers of the structurally unemployed and the internationalization of economic life made that impossible. At the same time, he was also aware that the tacit social contract tying citizens to the commonwealth is ruptured under these conditions and that the vehement reaction of the government workers to the Juppé government's "reform" of their status was virtually inevitable. Indeed, the trade unions that had backed the December strikes issued an appeal for a social movement to resist, as a consequence of globalization, the growing precariousness of the workers' condition. The appeal argued that the government and its supporters, "in presenting as privileged groups the last stable islands of salaried personnel, . . . show clearly that they intend to destabilize all of society and that the norm for the greatest number is becoming insecurity and instability."[33]

Caillé, the guiding spirit of the Mouvement Anti-Utilitaire en Sciences Sociales (MAUSS),[34] looks to a European-wide movement against a neoliberal Europe that may soon be no more than "a vast free trade zone." "With no other goal than the free circulation of goods, currency, and information, it would allow no opposing political, social, or cultural principles. Let the peoples and their inherited cultures perish, provided commodities circulate! This risks being the sole regulating principle of a commercial Europe that is politically nonexistent."[35]

In a discussion of economic and social reform in *Le tournant de décembre*,[36] Caillé republished an appeal for a debate on unemployment (then over 10 percent) issued five months before the strike wave.[37] Caillé and his supporters had a three-point program for emerging from the crisis: First, reduction and fair division of the work time available to the total group of workers. In a commentary, Caillé noted that work, having become a rare commodity, had to be redistributed, just like money or wealth, via a nationwide reduction of the legal workweek and the improvement of conditions for part-time work. The choice of whether to work full- or part-time would be left to the worker rather than the employer. Caillé linked the "time thus freed from the mercantile order" by the reduction of the workday to both "a salutary *far niente*," which he considered vital to the preservation of "*un art de vivre européen*" and the establishment of a coherent and powerful third economic sector.

This sector, the second demand in Caillé's appeal, would be "social, convivial, autonomous, solidarist, associationist: the name is unimportant. [It would be] broadly based on the free investment of everyone in activities of common interest, and . . . capable of integrating, according to an infinitely varied set of modalities, with the principles of both the private and the public economy." As a center for socially useful activities, this alternative economy was to be supported by government subsidies and would be based on "new forms of democratic negotiation" that would break the atomizing grip of the state and traditional representative bodies on society. Caillé added in his commentary that the function of this alternative economy is the reestablishment of the social bond. Citing Jürgen Habermas and André Gorz, he wrote: "It is high time to end the colonization of the world of daily life by the system, in other words, by money and by the state." In this context he discussed briefly the local exchange trading systems currently in use.

The third demand in the appeal of the Caillé group was a guaranteed minimum income for all, which would not be conditional on past or present work and would be paid by the state as a right of citizenship. This is an issue still much in vogue among certain groups who despair of a return to full employment and want to avoid the marginalization and exclusion of the unemployed. It has, however, also been criticized for being unrealistic (a universal income allocation would necessarily be too low to live on), for giving employers a basis for very low wages (any remuneration in addition to the minimum income would be cumulative), and for being not altogether consistent with—and possibly substituting for—the redistribution of available work through a reduction of the workday. Indeed, it is remarkable that the guaranteed income idea is supported not only on the Left but by quite a few neoliberal economists of the Right as well, who see in it a cost-saving substitute for the welfare state. In Caillé's appeal, these defects were partly remedied, since he insisted that a guaranteed income had to be coupled with the other two demands: a major redistribution of work by reducing the workweek and the creation of the "third economy."

Caillé's specific proposals have to be understood in the framework of his broader concerns for a reform of democracy and a restoration of civic ethics. He was certainly on the right track in trying to give radical content to the idea of a social and political Europe and in countering the existing commercialization of everything in the neoliberal Europe created by the Maastricht Treaty. One can only agree that a restoration of public morality and a diminution of anomic criminality are contingent on retying the ruptured bonds between citizens and the social order. And I find particularly attractive his idea of rediscovering and relegitimizing direct democracy, as a means of fully engaging people in the *res publica.*

Le tournant de décembre also reprinted the manifestos of rival groups who reacted directly to the strikes. One of them, circulated by a group of intellectuals close to the journal *Esprit* and to the antistrike trade union leader Nicole Notat, supported the Juppé government's "reforms" of the social security system. As mentioned, a second group around Pierre Bourdieu militantly supported the strikers. Denying the charges that the strikes defended the private interests of a privileged group of workers, the "Appeal of Intellectuals in Support of the Strikers" hailed the workers for defending "the most universal acquisitions of the Republic." The strikers were part of a broader movement in defense of social rights, which included the rights of everyone: "women and men, young and old, unemployed and salaried . . . in the public as well as the private sector, immigrants and Frenchmen. . . . All pose the question of what kind of society we want to live in. All pose equally the question of Europe: should it be the liberal Europe that they impose on us, or the social and ecological Europe for citizens that we want?"[38]

The same rejection of the idea that the strikers are defending the privileges of a labor aristocracy, the same insistence on their insertion in a broader social movement, permeates the trade union appeal mentioned above:

> Imposed insecurity, accompanied by bureaucratic control, first attacks the most fragile strata before being extended to the entire social order. The attacks on the rights of foreigners and immigrants and on disadvantaged youth in the slums have been dress rehearsals for the attacks on established rights. Questioning the rights of foreigners to social protection presaged solutions that presupposed inequality. . . . French society is two to three times wealthier than thirty years ago, when unemployment was minimal, social protection assured, and employment stable. The present crisis is really a crisis of distribution and of growing inequality. Setting Frenchmen against foreigners, wage earners against the unemployed and the excluded, is unacceptable, and we reject the way the rich bring about confrontations between the poor and the middle classes. A social movement is meaningful only if it opens perspectives for the entire society.

Caillé, while reprinting the appeals of the Bourdieu group and the trade unionists, remained largely aloof from them. This is not surprising. His "associationist" reference point was a group of intelligent and dedicated academics occupying a middle ground between the more traditional militancy of the social movements supported by Bourdieu and the dissident unionists and the resigned, conformist, center-left intellectuals around *Esprit*.[39] Nonetheless, the perspectives and organizational efforts of both groups are an essential part of the developing movement for a real alternative to neoliberal governance in Europe. The associationist principles and the demand for a redistribution of work-time voiced by Caillé's group are as important as—and are in principle compatible with—the powerful fermentation of ardent commitment and innovative forms of struggle supported by Bourdieu and his group of revitalized militant intellectuals. Indeed, the daily meetings held by the striking public-sector workers were an excellent example of the direct democracy Caillé advocates.

Most significantly for those familiar with the insular character of French cultural life, both groups realize that the solutions to France's acute social problems lie outside its borders, in Europe, and in the global order. Indeed, most of the leading actors in the new social movements—action for ending downsizing and racism, for the regularization of undocumented aliens (mostly Africans), for the rights of the unemployed, homeless, and poorly housed, and for a better life among slum dwellers (usually North Africans) in whom unemployment and rampant crime breed insecurity and anomie— are aware that many of France's acute social problems are intimately linked to neoliberal globalization.

BRINGING DOWN A GOVERNMENT
BUT REMAINING DISSATISFIED

While most of the new militant organizations had been created before the December actions, their activity accelerated in the wake of the popularly supported strikes of government workers, with the result that the right-wing government had to back away from the proposed "reforms." Throughout the winter and spring of 1996, public support for the government waned as militant opponents of racism and social exclusion demonstrated in the streets of Paris and other cities. Numerous empty buildings and churches were occupied by organized groups of homeless people. In August 1996 the government's support fell to a new low after police smashed through the locked door of the St. Bernard Church to end a hunger strike by ten Africans who were seeking regularization of their status. The Africans, accompanied by hundreds of sympathizers (including the film and stage director Ariane Mnouchkine), had taken sanctuary in the church, and the evening TV news presentation of the event was the worst possible advertising for the government. Another popular action in favor of the immigrants was the massive public refusal of more than ten thousand French citizens to comply with the provisions of the so-called Pasqua Law, which required anyone giving shelter to immigrants without proper papers to report them to the police.

Recall that in 1995, the year of the November–December strike wave, the Gaullist president Jacques Chirac had been elected on a platform of healing the *fracture sociale*. Chirac, afraid that the demonstrations against his neoliberal "reform" policies might sweep the Right out of power in the legislative elections of 1998, and hopeful that the Socialists had not yet recovered from the disastrous decline in their fortunes during Mitterand's second seven-year term, called an early election for the spring of 1997. He had apparently not gauged the profound unpopularity of his neoliberal policies. A leftist coalition of Socialists, Greens, and Communists led by Lionel Jospin, the Socialist leader least besmirched by the scandals of the Mitterand years, secured majority support for a program—principally worked out between the Greens and the Socialists—for abrogating the Pasqua Law, gradually dismantling France's nuclear power network (the supplier of 80 percent of the country's energy), and mounting a radical attack on the country's high (12%) unemployment rate, beginning with a reduction of the workweek from thirty-nine to thirty-five hours.

The progressive face of Jospin's new government gave hope to most of the protesters of recent years. It included a Green, the articulate and intelligent Dominique Voynet, as minister of the environment, and several other women in prominent cabinet posts: Elizabeth Guigou, Martine Aubry, and Catherine Trautmann as ministers of justice, labor affairs, and culture. Moreover, it made an outspoken proponent of the Social Europe idea (Pierre Moscovici) its voice on European affairs. Aubry quickly tabled a draft law for a thirty-five-hour week; Voynet was able to close down Superphoenix, one of the country's largest and most controversial nuclear power plants; and Jospin, by putting a halt to the practice of holding multiple government positions—whereby the same person could be simultaneously a parliamentary deputy, a cabinet minister, and a mayor—and by insisting on male-female parity on lists of candidates, made good his reputation for integrity. Nonetheless, the new government quickly revealed itself as no more able than its predecessors to handle the underlying economic and social problems tied to neoliberal globalization.

Part of the responsibility for this failure lay in the division of executive authority between Jospin's Socialist cabinet and the presidential power of Chirac, elected for a seven-year term two years before the 1997 election that installed Jospin.[40] Another was Jospin's unfortunate cabinet choices of Jean-Pierre Chevènement as minister of the interior, a neo-Jacobin politician with a hard line on immigration; of Dominique Strauss-Kahn as minister of finance, who continued the wave of neoliberal privatizations and deregulations begun by his Gaullist predecessor; and of Claude Allegre as minister of education, a physicist whose technocratic tendencies led to a massive strike by teachers and a radicalization of their union.[41] Compounding the difficulties produced by these two problems was the continued pressure exerted on the French government by the European Union's neoliberal policies. In particular a currency stabilization pact, by forbidding budget deficits of more than 3 percent, made impossible the kind of government spending necessary to resolve France's education and social problems. More generally, the conservative interests that dictated social policy frustrated hopes of a Social Europe.

As a result, the social movements that reached their high point in the strikes of 1995 continued to oppose government economic and social policies throughout most of Jospin's term of office, and French public opinion was becoming increasingly aware that the nation's problems could be resolved only through a linking of national and international approaches to the disasters brought about by neoliberal capitalism.[42] In the April 2002 first round of the presidential election, a majority of the Left's electorate voted for six smaller parties critical of the Socialists' embrace of neoliberal economics, and Jospin, with only 16.1 percent of the vote, was edged out of second place (and thereby of participation in the second, deciding round of the elections) by Jean-Marie Le Pen's Front National. While the Left voted against Le Pen in the second round, contributing massively to the 82 percent score of Gaullist Jacques Chirac, the leftist vote against Jospin in the first round had the unintended consequence of ensuring that the French presidency would remain in right-wing hands for the next five years. Legislative elections in June 2002 confirmed the victory of the Right, as many of the leftists who had turned out to vote Le Pen down refused to vote for the Socialists and abstained. Only in Paris, where a strong Green movement (17 percent in the European elections) had already helped to put a Socialist into the City Hall, did the Left successfully resist the conservative trend. It gained three seats from the Right, thus obtaining a majority of twelve of the twenty-one Paris Assembly seats. While the Verts saw their national deputation reduced from seven to three, two of those three seats were gained from the Right in Paris.

Characteristic of the situation during Jospin's premiership was the activity of a peasant federation (Confédération Paysanne) and its leader in the south of France during the summer and fall of 1999. This activity was the first significant social action in France following NATO's military response to Serbian oppression of the Albanian majority in Kosovo in the spring of 1999, which most of Europe's social-democratic governments greeted as a humanitarian crusade. That response, as I argued earlier,[43] served as a fig leaf for the impotence or unwillingness of those governments to contest the stranglehold of neoliberal ideology on their economic policy (the latter had left them with no other recourse for combating unemployment than encouraging capitalist growth). I have also indicated that the war hysteria, apart from giving moral justification to a deluge of bombing that set the Serbian economy back by thirty years, had the incidental effect of pushing news about the extremely important elections to the European Parliament into the back pages or altogether out of the papers. The result was that few people were aware of the stakes in this election, the turnout was extremely low, and, as usually happens with low turnouts, the right-wing parties won a smashing majority of the votes.

One wonders if this disappointing result for the traditional leftist parties was entirely accidental and altogether a cause for mourning among their leaders. The election of a left-dominated parliament would have put two items immediately on the agenda. The first would have been increasing parliamentary power. Since the entire executive of the European Union had recently been forced to resign, after exposure by European Parliament members, in a huge corruption scandal, a leftist majority would certainly have insisted on increasing the parliament's legislative clout, which until then had been virtually nil. This in itself would have constituted a major victory for democracy, since the parliament was, after all, the only directly elected part of the European Union.

The second item would have been the implementation, by this new parliament with its expanded powers, of the Social Europe idea. After all, most of the new social-democratic regimes had been elected on a Social Europe platform—a pledge to counterbalance the neoliberal economic union and the common currency decreed at Maastricht by a continent-wide social protection, and by European Union measures against unemployment, such as a reduction of the workweek and a major expansion and upgrading of Europe's railway infrastructure. Such a program would, however, have meant a break with neoliberal deregulation and a return to some kind of Keynesian economics—a virtual declaration of war on neoliberal corporate capitalism that very few leaders of the Left had any stomach for. One doubts that any of the social-democratic heads of state in Europe shed tears over the results of the elections of June 13, 1999.

In any case, the Kosovo affair and the disaster of the parliamentary elections were signs that the social movement, when it returned, would have to be more independent than ever of the European social-democratic leadership. That movement was quickly able to show what it was capable of. The much-heralded victory of the crusade for a multiethnic society in Kosovo had permitted a return of certain long-simmering trade tensions between Europe and the United States.

Partly in response to Europe's insistence on maintaining preferential treatment for Caribbean banana producers in former European colonies, and partly because of European recalcitrance to allowing genetically modified American grain and hormone-injected beef into the European market, the United States imposed a 100 percent tariff on a wide variety of European goods, including Roquefort cheese. On August 12, 1999, in response to this punitive tariff, the leader of the left-wing French peasant confederation that represented the Roquefort producers of southwest France, José Bové, together with nine other officers of his union, led a few hundred of their followers to a McDonald's under construction in the rural town of Millau (pop. 22,000, about 100 km east of Toulouse), partially demolished it, and obtained instant national popularity.

The act was not gratuitous. José Bové, aged forty-six, was an anarchist-oriented disciple of the French philosopher of modern technology Jacques Ellul. The son of an agronomist who had worked in the United States, he had moved to the Larzac area in 1976. Here, squatting on an abandoned farm, he joined five other farmers in a common livestock enterprise, raising cows and pigs as well as sheep, from whose milk Roquefort cheese is made. He quickly threw himself into the nonviolent struggle against the French military presence in the area and was jailed for three weeks in the same prison he was to enter twenty-three years later. In the summer of 1995, he was the sole French presence on the Greenpeace ship that attempted to halt the French nuclear tests in Polynesia.

After "dismantling" the local McDonald's, Bové, refusing bail, was again jailed for three weeks. His bail was finally paid by a group of sympathizers that included an American farmers' union, a signal that even in the heartland of neoliberal capitalism many were dissatisfied with the prevailing direction.[44] On being released, acknowledging that "agriculture and the food trade will not be saved in the framework of the nation-state against the rest of the world," he called for a "European peasant project."[45] A man with charismatic qualities and a pronounced hostility to neoliberal globalization, Bové galvanized his group into opposing not just the American tariff on Roquefort but also McDonald's as a purveyor of junk food and as a multinational threatening small producers and restaurateurs worldwide. Opinion polls showed that "a large majority of the French identified with him."[46]

To attend their trial on June 30, 2000, José Bové and his nine co-accused chose to enter Millau in a wooden hay cart that markedly resembled the *charettes* that carried victims of the French revolutionary terror—including radical ones like Danton—to the guillotine. It bore a large papier maché cheese with the inscription (in Provençal) "Defend Roquefort, No Excess Import Duties" and a banner with "Trade Unionists in Jail, High Finance in the Box Seats." The streets of Millau were filled with thousands of their supporters, mostly French and to a great extent representing the descendants of the southwestern French rural radicalism that organized the wine-grower's strike and revolt of 1907, made memorable by a mutiny of the army regiment sent to repress it. Also present, however, were representatives of most French parties and NGOs of the Left and the Far Left, from the Socialists and the Greens to the Trotskyist LCR (Ligue Communiste Révolutionnaire), the anarchists, the SUD unionists, the DAL (Droit au Logement, or right to housing), the Droits Devant group, and the ATTAC (Association pour la Taxation des Transactions Financières pour l'Aide aux Citoyens). Pierre Bourdieu was there, as well as the Franco-American economist Susan George and Vandana Shiva, the spokeswoman for peasant protests in India against industrial agriculture; so were observers from Honduras, the United States, Senegal, and the landless peasantry of Brazil. During the trial, some three thousand supporters of the accused standing outside the courthouse periodically cried "Justice is in the streets" (*la justice est dans la rue*). On the evening of the one-day trial, the public prosecutor requested that Bové be given an exemplary one month in prison and, to prevent further militancy, a suspended sentence of nine additional months. For the other nine defendants, whose crime had been indistinguishable from Bové's, the prosecutor asked the court for three-month suspended sentences. The court delayed its verdict until September. The following day, *Le Monde* estimated that fifty thousand people had attended the concerts and lectures organized by supporters of the imprisoned men in Millau. Bové was quoted as saying, "Millau welcomes the entire world," to which *Le Monde* commented wryly: "To each his own globalization."[47]

Roughly midway between the original action against McDonald's and the carnivalesque trial of its perpetrators, Bové addressed a similar crowd assembled to oppose a meeting of the World Trade Organization in Seattle. "We're going to win!" he exclaimed.

Seattle and the Emergence of a New International Opposition

A brief summary: In the late 1990s, despite the weakness of the governmental Left in resisting neoliberalism, a combination of internal schisms within global capitalism and growing popular realization of the dangers inherent in the present expansion of corporate power began to brake the forward progress of the planetary market society. This trend was visible in Europe since December 1995, when strikes by unorganized workers or new trade union groups paralyzed the French economy and government for a month and forced the conservative government of Jacques Chirac to back down on its plans for a wholesale attack on French welfare institutions. In the following years, a number of downsizing efforts by multinational corporations in Europe were opposed by the militant actions of trade unions from two or more countries, most notably those against the 1997 closing of the Renault plant in Vilvorde, Belgium. Throughout the nineties, the proliferation and the increasing activism of environmental and other new social movements signaled that the collapse of international communism and the pusillanimity of Social Democrats had not closed all possibility of opposing neoliberal capitalism. Between 1996 and 1998, voters in England, France, Germany, and Italy, in a quiet electoral revolt against the growing unemployment, insecurity, and sapping of welfare provisions they associated with neoliberalism, ended the conservative stranglehold on their nations' political systems.

The principal beneficiaries of this were the social democrats. Despite their fecklessness, they remained the principal organized political force on the Left, forming governments with groups hostile to the neoliberal dispensation: with the Greens in Germany and Italy, and with the Greens and the Communists in France.[48] Although, as remarked above, the Social Democrats have been either ideologically committed to neoliberal positions or too timid to attack them, the swing to the left, heralded by the French strikes of 1995, reflected the gestation in Europe of a new movement among all those, working- and middle-class alike, whose fears for the future had goaded them into action. The extrapolation of this new militancy to the global arena was evident for the first time in November 1999.

In that month, an important meeting of the World Trade Organization in Seattle, intended to reduce trade barriers and to allow for freer movement of capital, ended in chaos and in failure to agree on anything, even an agenda. Responsibility for this failure was partly because of dissension within the WTO meeting itself but partly also because of the manifest hostility, represented by some fifty thousand demonstrators in the city of Seattle, to the WTO's style of neoliberal globalization.

These protesters had come from the four corners of the earth to demonstrate against the WTO's projects. Although their largest contingent had been organized by the American AFL-CIO, there were in addition tens of thousands of ordinary people, representing some five hundred nongovernmental organizations from North America and other continents, principally in the areas of environmental, social, and human rights.

Although disagreeing on many issues, the protesters had in common an opposition to the present mode of capitalist globalization as a danger to the future of humankind. International proponents of a tax on speculative financial transactions, French and American small farmers against capitalist agriculture, Japanese fisher folk, political ecologists appalled at the environmental consequences of unfettered growth, and intellectuals and students from many countries marched with some thirty thousand U.S. trade unionists fearful of further job loss and declining living standards. A large, carnivalesque demonstration on the first day of the WTO meeting completely paralyzed downtown Seattle and prevented so many of the official delegates from reaching the central meeting place that the opening had to be delayed.

Police efforts to break up the initially peaceful demonstration forcibly were unsuccessful. They only led to nonviolent resistance and, when nonviolent protesters were attacked with rubber bullets and tear gas, a small minority of protesters—mainly an anarchist fringe of fewer than a hundred young people who had come up from Oregon—trashed a number of stores in the downtown area; this provoked the authorities to call in the National Guard, declare a curfew, and go over to mass arrests of demonstrators. Meanwhile, downtown streets in London were paralyzed by demonstrations against global capitalism and automobile culture, organized by a loose coordinating committee called "Reclaim the Streets." Their leaflets consciously echoed favored themes of the French Situationists, and they cited one of the favorite graffiti of Paris in 1968: "Sous les pavés, la plage." These demonstrations too were broken up by massive police violence, as had a demonstration by this group six months earlier that had turned the London stock exchange area into a chaotic carnival.

Many commentators compared the Seattle events to the riots of Chicago in 1968, when student and other demonstrators against the Vietnam War were clubbed and gassed into submission to permit the Democratic Party to nominate the pro-war Hubert Humphrey as its presidential candidate. Unlike the U.S. situation of 1968, however, dissension within the global establishment was so great that, even without demonstrations, it is quite possible that the Seattle WTO meeting would have been a failure anyway.

Internal discord became visible when representatives of a group of some forty African, Caribbean, and Latin American nations in Seattle walked out in protest at the lack of transparency of the leadership's strategy. Lengthy documents prepared long in advance were distributed to delegates only at the plenary session in which they were to be discussed.

Another complaint came from a different source: the capitalist North. President Clinton, realizing that his party's chances in the November 2000 presidential and legislative election depended on the support of labor and environmental groups, heavily represented among the protesters, asked the WTO to prepare measures on minimal labor and environmental standards as preconditions for trade with non-Western countries. These would include prohibitions on the forced labor of children and a semblance of a minimum wage.

This proposal elicited accusations of protectionism from Indian and other representatives. Their claim, that such provisions would throw many Asian workers out of work and leave them to starve, weirdly mirrored neoliberal denunciations of labor or environmental regulation in the "core" countries: jobs would be lost to Asian companies not so regulated.

Another source of discord, the question of agricultural subsidies and food standards, led to confrontation between the United States and Europe.

Heavy European Union subsidies to European agriculture were opposed by the American agro-industrial complex, while European environmental ministers generally opposed the importation of hormone-treated American beef and genetically modified grains.

The establishment press lamented the disunity evident among the 135 nations whose representatives had gathered at Seattle, and deplored the jubilation of the embattled protesters. Martin Wolf of the *Financial Times* condemned them as "cranks, bullies and hypocrites . . . 'consumer activists' who want to prevent people from buying cheap imports; and 'altruists' who want to prevent the exploitation of the poor, particularly when they produce goods for export competitively."[49] Wolf, conveniently forgetting that the Asian and African representatives who opposed as "protectionist" any plea for social control of international trade, including Clinton's proposal for labor and environmental standards, represented the wealthy business elites of their countries, reiterated the neoliberal doctrine that the "spread of the market will do far more to lift hundreds of millions of people from mass destitution than an army of aid workers."

In fact, the complaints of Indian and other Asian and African representatives, which came from precisely the groups responsible for implementing, and profiting from, Western-style capitalism of the rawest nineteenth-century variety in their own countries, were disingenuous. For the condemnation of Clinton's proposal to include minimum social standards in trade agreements—on the grounds that it would block the free economic growth of the less-developed countries and therefore insure the continuation of world poverty—concealed the fact that, as Colin Hines observed, the prosperity of the transnational companies rested on massive and accelerating exploitation of the poorer countries of the world: the ratio of the incomes between the fifth of the world's population living in the richest countries and the fifth living in the poorest, which had been 30:1 in 1960, climbed to 60:1 in 1990 and to 74:1 in 1997.[50]

Indeed, while there is no doubt that Clinton's support for these measures was opportunistic, and would have been unlikely had the WTO meeting occurred six months after the presidential elections of 2000 instead of eleven months before them, the line of reasoning opposing such measures is well grounded in the neoliberal ideology accepted by all wings of the current establishment, from moderate Left to conservative Right: only the growth created by unfettered global market capitalism can, through the well-known trickle-down effect, diminish poverty. Considering the way all previous efforts to halt this neoliberal offensive have been dismissed by the political, economic, and intellectual establishment as "corporatist" and "archaic," the wonder is that the two dominant players in the WTO, the American and European delegates, were both constrained by their domestic constituencies to demand various kinds of regulation. One might say that the dissension within the WTO reflected the increasing power of the opposition of Western electorates to globalization *in its present neoliberal form.*

It is important to bear in mind this qualifier, since the principal organizational medium for bringing together the legions of protesters in Seattle was none other than that summum bonum of global technological change, the Internet. While many of the demonstrators were appalled by the present consequences of globalization—opposed to the growing divide of rich and poor, horrified by the environmental catastrophes it breeds, and eager to retain some sense of locality and rootedness—very few were Luddites seeking to smash modern technology or end global awareness. They did not represent a lunatic fringe, as Wolf suggested, but an increasingly concerned broad stratum of the American and European middle classes. The extent of the popular antagonism to the WTO can be gauged from a poll held in 1999 in the United States, where the population has had less access to dissident views on the subject than in most European countries. The poll revealed that in families earning less than $50,000, a mere 37 percent viewed global free trade positively. Only in the wealthier brackets, families earning above $75,000, was there clear support for it (63 percent), a support that increased with even higher incomes.[51]

Anti-WTO protesters, claiming victory, were of course jubilant that the Seattle meeting ended in failure, and immediately began drafting plans for demonstrations in protest of the next global summit of corporate capitalism's decision makers: the April 2000 Washington meeting of the International Monetary Fund and the World Bank. Since Washington had been a traditional demonstration site of the American Left, gathering hundreds of thousands of demonstrators for civil rights and antiwar protests in the sixties and seventies from the dissent-prone Northeast of the United States, attracting demonstrators should, on the face of things, have been easier than in Seattle. It was not.

The IMF/World Bank protests of April 16–17, preceded by months of recruitment on East Coast campuses and by a week of intensive seminars on the issues and training in nonviolent resistance, did bring together some ten to twenty thousand militants. They produced chaos on the streets of Washington, blocking so much traffic that delegates had difficulty in reaching the IMF and World Bank meetings.[52] On Monday, April 17, most government offices were forced to close because so many streets were shut down by roving bands of demonstrators. Newspaper accounts suggested a ragtag army of anarchists, students, third world sympathizers, environmental militants, and radical artists: a New York group that called itself Art and Revolution prepared giant puppets and colorful posters for large peaceful demonstrations. The latter, however, were overshadowed by nonviolent civil disobedience that provoked police repression.

Nonetheless, the extreme heterogeneity of the participating organizations precluded any joint program more explicit than the demand for "global justice." Moreover, prepared for the scale of disruption by what had happened four months earlier at the WTO meeting, Washington police, backed up by a wide array of military and paramilitary federal forces, were better prepared than their Seattle colleagues; the organizational bases of the protesters were continually being closed down for a variety of (largely spurious) reasons by federal and local authorities. Indeed, a PeaceNet article subsequent to the Washington protests claimed that from the early summer of 1999 on, FBI and other law enforcement agencies had been shifting their principal activities from far-right terrorists (like the one who blew up a federal government building in the Midwest) to the activist Left.[53]

But the relatively weaker showing in Washington of the new international movement against global neoliberalism was not primarily due to more effective police resistance. Washington, D.C., and Seattle are separated by a continent whose two coasts have rather different cultures. The population and cultural setting of the nation's capital made it, despite an east coast reservoir of activists, a considerably less favorable site for protests than Seattle, which was demographically well suited for ecological and social movements against globalization. The city itself, home to Microsoft, Amazon.com, and Boeing as well as a university center, has been described, together with its Pacific Northwest hinterland, as "a haven for the overwhelmingly white and Asian software elite."[54] Many laid-back, middle-class professionals, computer whiz kids, and skilled workers were sympathetic to idealists demonstrating en masse in its streets.

Indeed, though overgrown by a postindustrial high-tech economy, the port of Seattle has a radical tradition of its own: it was the site, eighty years earlier, of one of America's few general strikes and subsequently one of the main organizing bases for Harry Bridges's left-wing West Coast maritime union. Moreover, northern California and the Pacific Northwest have long been hospitable to radical dissenters against the materialism of the American dream. Influenced by the beat generation that made San Francisco its home, the youth rebellion of the sixties had an early start at the University of California at Berkeley.[55] Juliet Schor, noting the frequent appearance of what she called consumer "downshifting" in the region, wrote in 1998: "In Seattle and the Pacific Northwest, a low-spending, alternative, but decidedly middle-class lifestyle is emerging."[56] Coexisting with these elements of a native American radicalism, an ecological cult of nature developed around the abundant forests of the Northwest. Oregon had long had a political mentality to the left of most of the rest of the country, firmly anchored in the faculty and students of the University of Oregon at Eugene. And recall that in the early seventies the Pacific Northwest was host to so many nonconformists that Ernest Callenbach thought it a plausible location for his *Ecotopia,* a novel about a future ecological anarchism strong enough to secede from the union.[57] It was therefore socially and demographically logical that from this area tens of thousands of militant trade unionists, middle-class ecologists, and radical, often anarchist, students would be drawn together to protest the WTO's vision of a commercialized planet based on the neoliberal fetishes of growth and consumption. And it was comprehensible that the local reaction to them would be generally more sympathetic than hostile, and that both the city administration and the local police, hoping to maintain the city's reputation for liberal tolerance, would be slow to crack down on them.

Washington, with all its venerable tradition as a Mecca of demonstrators for every kind of cause, was in many respects the opposite of Seattle. Seat of the world's most powerful government, with little economic activity of any significance, most of its political manipulators, middle-class professionals, and bureaucrats had long lived in outlying suburbs, leaving the city proper, where the protests were to occur, largely to a black underclass of lower-level municipal and federal workers, menials, and janitors burdened by a heavy load of unemployment and misery: idealistic white demonstrators could expect few participants and little sympathy from either suburban commuters or locals. Moreover, the municipal police leadership, generally reflecting the city's ethnic composition, felt none of the middle-class constraints evident in Seattle, where the lack of preparation for anarchist violence against property and the relatively minor amount of police violence led the chief of police to resign after the riots.

On the whole, the demographic resources on which the East Coast protesters could draw were weaker than those of the Seattle group. Lori Wallach of Ralph Nader's Public Citizen, began organizing the Seattle demonstrations a year in advance, using the Internet to substitute for a large staff and expensive facilities.[58] Working together with international organizations like Greenpeace, she could count on a large, committed local base of Northwest environmentalists, trade unionists, and entrenched radical and anarchist contingents in San Francisco and Eugene to bring together not only tens of thousands of outraged Americans but a significant scattering of opponents of the WTO from Europe and the third world. While the Internet organizing was at least as evident before the Washington demonstrations, East Coast radical and environmentalist groups were considerably less experienced and prepared to support a massive demonstration than comparable groups in the Northwest.

From the broad diversity of the groups involved in the Washington protest, one gets the impression that the organizers, perhaps worried that they lacked the numbers and the organizational foundation to bring together a major single-issue protest, avoided formulating specific demands and encouraged everyone to "do their own thing." Because leftists in universities had since the sixties rallied mainly around identitarian causes of radical ethnic and sexual minorities (which meant, postmodernism taught, the abandonment of all "universal" values), it was difficult to bring them together in a national demonstration for "global justice."[59] This identitarian bias was of course changing. On the issue of third world sweatshops and child labor, for example, there had been a spate of organizing efforts by East Coast and Midwest students that provided a minimal base of consciousness for the planners of the anti–IMF/World Bank protests.[60] Nonetheless, it was clear that the new activism was more developed in the Far West of the United States than in the East.[61]

If the numbers in D.C. were lower than those in Seattle, both protests were small compared with the demonstrations of an earlier generation. The number of actual environmental and social movement activists in Seattle had not been great—also between ten and twenty thousand; their force was multiplied by the presence of two to three times as many trade unionists and the symbolically significant presence of a scattering of NGO activists from all over the world. Why so few in a country of more than 250 million people? For one thing, the radical "anti's" had lost most of their army to middle-age respectability since the earlier period. Student rebels had graduated, gotten jobs, become yuppies, and grown older and "wiser." Outside the universities the outraged liberals of the sixties had become complacent shareholders in the eighties and nineties. A new constituency was forming around urgent environmental and social rights questions, but, while profoundly committed, this new constituency was still rather limited, comparable to the peace and civil rights movement of the early sixties rather than to the huge masses of disaffected young people and liberals of the late sixties.

Moreover, the trade unions, which had provided the big battalions for the peaceful side of the Seattle protest, had fewer issues and less reason to participate in the April protests. While many individual unions backed the umbrella organization for the Washington demonstration—Mobilization

for Global Justice—the AFL-CIO and most of its affiliated unions confined
their April activism to lobbying Congress against allowing China into the
WTO, a move which, it was feared, would put many union members out of
work. In the absence of major union participation, the organizers of the
Washington protests (to judge by their websites) gradually shifted their
plans from education, large public demonstrations, and global publicity to
highly visible disruptive actions, which of course produced a great deal of
news coverage.

Another problem in organizing both the Seattle and D.C. protests was
that although the ultimate stakes were heavier than those involved in the
anti–Vietnam War protests and the civil rights movement of the sixties,
they were also less immediate. The drafting of young men, and in particular of college students, to fight in Asian jungles had given an entire generation of young people (already immersed in their own subculture and inclined to mistrust all authority) a deeply personal reason for participating in
strikes, sit-ins, and national protests. Many among that generation's parents
were turned against the war both by television coverage of napalmed villages and by the fear of losing their progeny. And the parallel movement of
black people demanding their civil rights had a more immediate and personal notion of justice than the later protests against the profit-seeking
shenanigans of transnational corporations in faraway continents. By comparison, the sense of immediacy in the new protest movement came from
problems like global warming and downsizing, which might be abstractly,
but not viscerally, related to organizations like the WTO, the IMF, and the
World Bank.

Nonetheless, the contrast between the heterogeneity—even the identitarian specificity—of the organizations involved in the Seattle and Washington protests and the monolithic character of the global capitalist coordinating committees they were attacking was not altogether to the protesters'
disadvantage. The protesters' goals were, to say the least, discrepant—some
of them wanted to reform capitalism, others sought to abolish it while turning its technological accomplishments to human use, still others hoped to
dismantle both the technology and the capitalist system that battened on it
so as to return to a preindustrial existence, and various sexual and ethnic
identitarian groups, convinced that the existing power structure was hostile
to their existence, arrived with their own agendas—but such chaos was a
strength as well as a weakness at this inchoate stage of the new movement,
since it allowed these contrasting groups to meet in a common cause and
seek out their common denominator.

Thus with all their limitations, the demonstrations in Seattle and Washington—and the subsequent, increasingly violent ones in Prague, Quebec, Gothenburg, and Genoa—signaled a major breakthrough for the global movement against capitalist globalization. Coming on the heels of the resistance to neoliberalism in France and other European countries, and paralleling movements of protest by indigenous populations in Latin America and India against the wanton destruction, in the name of "progress" and "reform," of traditional ways of life, the new movement bore immense promise, despite its many inconsistencies. It had at least succeeded in sowing seeds of doubt among the tenants of neoliberal ideology and thus in slowing down, if not reversing, the rapid advance of capitalist globalization.

Then came September 11, and in its wake a tendentious conflation by the media, and by governments in North America and Europe, of opposition to globalization and fundamentalist terrorism.[62] Many in the United States and elsewhere are concerned, at the moment I write (December 2001) that the pervasive anxiety evident in the public reaction to large-scale terrorism on American soil could lead to serious erosion of the civil liberties on which debate about the fundamentals of our society relies. Whether or not this anxiety persists, the long-term problems signaled earlier in this book will not go away.[63] The question then arises: What is the larger historical meaning and potential of the new protest movement?

The Significance of the New Social Movements

In the various collective movements of resistance and liberation that have sometimes furthered and sometimes challenged Promethean change in the modern West, we can distinguish three different sociocultural foundations and configurations of social change.

Preindustrial peasant/artisan strata, rooted in cyclical nature mentalities and motivated by egalitarian resentments against feudal or absolutist hierarchies, were the shock troops of the major revolutions against the old regime in England, France, Russia, and China. Before 1850, modernizing elites from professional, bureaucratic, and mercantile strata, with a linear mentality of progress through work and scientific rationality, harnessed the millennialist aspirations of such preindustrial strata for the revolutionary replacement of old regimes by democratic nation-states.

After 1850, revolutionaries inspired by such ideals of progress and science took up the quest for social justice pursued by their allies in the industrial proletariat and strove for a socialist transformation of the capitalist nation-state. In Western Europe, this effort ended with the Keynesian welfare state—a compromise, compatible with the Fordist stage of capitalist production, that was trashed in the post-Fordist, post–cold war era. In Russia and China, where the economic and social weight of factory workers was far inferior to that of preindustrial peasant masses, revolutionary dictatorships of the Communist Parties were able to offer a secure existence and a rising living standard to the industrial workers, but at a terrible price. With the population controlled by secret police and a brutal bureaucracy, political and cultural freedoms were nonexistent; a state capitalist exploitation of the economy forbade independent unions, dragooned the peasantry into collective farms, and condemned small farmers as counterrevolutionary. By 2000 the economies of both countries, and of most of their satellites, had, under pressure from the West, opened up to private capitalism, though a Communist Party dictatorship clung to power in China.

Since roughly 1960, postindustrial strata of students, women, intellectuals, and technical and scientific professionals have in the West developed a new "modernist" mentality, skeptical of the shibboleths of progress, of scientific rationality, of the work ethic, and of gender stereotypes taken for granted in previous epochs. Many in these strata, as well as increasing numbers of middle- and working-class people, were as dissatisfied with the Left's failed compromise with free enterprise as they are with the cutthroat capitalism that replaced it. Moreover, sensitive to the consequences of corporate neoliberalism—neo-colonialism, the multiple alienations and insecurities of consumer capitalism, and massive environmental pollution—they are aware that the challenge to personal identity and dignity posed by global market society can be confronted only at a planetary level.

This last group, postindustrial and in a sense postmodern, generally seeks a different kind of global society based on a new harmony with nature, a harmony congenial to still-existing preindustrial strata in the Euro-American heartland and especially in the peasant movements of Latin America and India.

On the whole, dissident social movements in the period from the late eighteenth to the mid-twentieth century were rooted in coalitions between social groups or strata with preindustrial and industrial-scientific mentalities, whereas the past half century has seen coalitions between groups with industrial-scientific and postindustrial mentalities. Characteristic, however, of the movement for alternative globalization that came together in 2001 and 2002 in Pôrto Alegre is the convergence of resistance arising from the modernist and postmodernist mentalities with third-world resistance based on peasant movements such as the ones in Brazil, India and Mexico—groups federated with José Bové's Confédération Paysanne in the Via Campesino.[64]

Thus, the preindustrial strata with their millennialist aspirations, so important in the earliest cycle of European revolutions, return to the fore in the recent upsurge of resistance to the commercialization of the world. But whereas before 1850 French revolutionary elites inspired by Enlightenment rationality used the egalitarian impulses of the peasantry to establish a bourgeois republic—in which the preindustrial strata were doomed to extinction—the postindustrial Green movements, driving force of the resistance to globalization, demonstrate in their ideals and goals an elective affinity with agrarian movements of the nonindustrialized world. Such an affinity is particularly clear in José Bové's movement, which seeks not only to protect French peasants from absorption into capitalist agriculture, to preserve the countryside from the ecological destruction caused by it, and to rescue the consumer from the junk food it produces, but also to join with third-world peasant movements to oppose corporate globalization.

This return, at a later historical moment and a higher level of consciousness, of preindustrial movements and mentalities that were condemned as archaic by liberal apostles of modernization theory as well as by the Social Democratic left, mandates a closer look at the broad historical alliances behind the various stages of Promethean "progress."

In the earlier alliances for democratic change between premodern peasant/artisan masses and elite reformers, those two groups pursued fundamentally different goals. The peasant/artisan strata sought collective relief from feudal oppression and bureaucratic modernization and a return to a stable preindustrial existence, while the reformers, imbued with the Enlightenment version of Promethean idealism, usually sought a modernization that would free the economic and intellectual energies of the bourgeois class. The compromise formula, into which each group could read its own aspirations and which permitted their cooperation in toppling the old regime, was revolutionary nationalism. During this period, however, a significant part of the social movement's intellectual leadership ventured into realms of utopian speculation and organization that went beyond existing possibilities for the fulfillment of national revolutionary aspirations. Hegelian dialectical and romantic cyclical theories of social and natural philosophy were partly anchored in premodern mentalities and partly in visions of a postindustrial society.[65] In both cases such theories constituted a radical alternative to the versions of Enlightenment thought that were slowly ossifying into an amoral instrumental rationality.

In the century after 1850, bourgeois reformers, captive to a hard-nosed, nationalist capitalism, turned conservative or reactionary, while the radical vision was for the most part upheld by a small minority of intellectuals from the bourgeois strata who based themselves socially on the industrial proletariat and intellectually on some mixture of Marxist dialectics and scientific rationality. Although many artisans and peasants turned to an authoritarian nationalism, which between the world wars degenerated into fascism, others remained committed to a humanitarian social vision. While some of these supported the Marxist Left, most radicals from a preindustrial background turned to anarchism, revolutionary syndicalism, and agrarian populism.[66]

Movements based on these ideologies were particularly prominent on the margins of the industrialized West, for example, in Spain and Russia. Indeed, the best-known anarchist theorists were Russian: Bakunin and Kropotkin; and the only significant interbellum anarchist movement was the Spanish FAI. But important ideologies of the non-Marxist Left could be found in the most economically advanced countries: in the socialism of William Morris, in the revolutionary thought of Georges Sorel and his circle, and in the anarchism of Gustav Landauer.[67]

In Morris, political significance was linked to a cultural mission. He was part of the pre-Raphaelite brotherhood, a group of mid-nineteenth-century artists who kept the faith, during the generations of Victorian repression, with the romantic imagination and anti-utilitarian outlook of an earlier generation of poets. Morris himself relied heavily in his craft socialism on the traditions of English popular culture. Somewhat later, around the time of the First World War, visionary artists sympathetic to revolutionary social movements—expressionists in Germany and surrealists in France—restored contact, thanks to radical interpretations of Freud, with the depth-psychological complexity and the sensitivity to the popular culture of earlier romantic utopians such as Charles Fourier and Pierre Leroux, as did some of the thinkers of the Frankfurt School (particularly Marcuse, Fromm, and Benjamin). Independent of such overt social radicalism, in the decades before the Second World War creative artists such as James Joyce, D. H. Lawrence, Pablo Picasso, and Igor Stravinsky and aesthetic theorists like Michael Bakhtin represented a linkage between the paradigms of late modernity and the premodern popular culture. Paralleling this linkage in the social movements of the age, minority currents of romantic anarchism and neo-utopianism competed with, at the same time that they partially merged with, Marxism and scientific rationality.[68] But such artists and revolutionaries from the educated classes were a small fragment of the overwhelmingly conservative bourgeois elites in the century between the revolution of 1848 and the Second World War.

After an antifascist war fought in the name of democracy and social progress, bourgeois elites that had earlier been hostile to popular causes saw both the desirability and the possibility of allying themselves with social-democratic forces in the creation of an industrial welfare state. The latter would bind the working class to the cycle of production and consumption necessary for a Fordist production system and create a political-economic bulwark to ward off the new threat of Soviet Communism.

Remarkably, while the Western welfare states were successful in raising living standards and creating an unprecedented level of material security for working and middle classes alike, young people growing to adulthood under them became massively alienated because of their paternalistic, bureaucratic, and authoritarian aspects. In Europe, this was so for workers as well as for middle-class youth. In North America, young workers were much less alienated from the prevailing political mentality, since they were frequently entrenched in ethnic/religious subcultures (like the one in Michael Cimino's film *The Deerhunter*) that largely escaped the middle-class values inculcated under the welfare state. This situation produced the American and European youth revolts of the 1960s and early 1970s, revolts heralding the social movements of recent decades that I have just described.

There were of course earlier youth revolts in the twentieth century, proto-fascist ones that glorified violence as a return to nature and merged it with a celebration of national vitality. But, contrary to conservative arguments that tried to identify the late-twentieth-century youth revolt with the fascist celebration of youth and *Volk,* the later phenomenon was antimilitarist and skeptical of national shibboleths. In the sixties and seventies, it sympathized with third-world movements of national liberation, railed against bourgeois repressiveness, and paved the way for the liberal and social-democratic embrace of multicultural society in the eighties. In the nineties, discontented youth looking for models turned to the radical environmentalism of groups like Greenpeace and to nongovernmental organizations representing the interests of third-world agricultural countries that had been crushed by indebtedness and forced by the IMF to privatize and sacrifice domestic production to make room for the goods of first-world multinationals. In many ways, this anti-globalization militancy of the young revealed affinities not only with third-world agrarian movements like the Zapatistas but also with nonviolent anarchism, as in the Ruckus Society.[69]

Thus, in the various movements that have challenged neoliberal globalization in the last decade, we can find representatives of virtually all the progressive social forces since the middle of the nineteenth century, plus some (certainly in the third world) that clearly represent preindustrial peasant strata. To grasp their meaning and potential, we have to distinguish between the immediate objects of resistance and the long-term problems we are all facing. In general, what has provoked resistance has usually been a specific attempt by neoliberal modernists to extend their control over the social order, either by dismantling elements of the Fordist/Keynesian welfare state or by bringing about the disintegration of ancient village societies to make room for industrial infrastructure (such as dams) and capitalist agriculture: attacks on traditional cultures have provoked peasant movements of resistance in India and Latin America (the Zapatistas of Chiapas are the best-known instance) which are both humanly and politically of great importance.[70]

There are other ties and overlaps between movements in the "core" and the "periphery" in the 1990s than Bové's Confédération Paysanne. One of the principal sources for Washington demonstrators against the IMF and the World Bank in April 2000 was the rapidly spreading Students Against Sweatshops, a pressure group, now present on dozens of campuses, against the use of sweatshop labor in third world countries to manufacture clothing sold to college students. Moreover, resistance in Europe began, as we have seen, in various French movements in defense of African immigrants. The latter, driven from their countries for mixed reasons, were coming into head-on conflict with hard-nosed conservative efforts to play the card of racist xenophobia so as to keep rightist voters from moving to the fascist Far Right—a tactic tempting to many social democrats and communists as well.

The organizations and individuals that have worked in France together with the *"sans-papiers,"* however, supporting them in their demand for regularization of their status, are the same as those who have been active on behalf of many indigenous victims of the *capitalisme sauvage* of the 1990s: the unemployed, the homeless, the downsized, and those threatened with degradation of their social condition like the French public-sector strikers of 1995. Apart from the not inconsiderable organizational efforts of those groups themselves, their supporters can be roughly associated either with the large group of intellectuals, academics, journalists, students, and artists who have since the French Enlightenment sporadically taken the defense of the rights of man as their cause, or with one or another of the political groupings to the left of the Socialist Party: the Greens, the Trotskyists, the (no longer monolithic) Communists, or the new radical unions (SUD, etc.) whose brief extends far beyond the customary bread-and-butter issues.

I have focused considerably on the French situation, but the underlying issues and attitudes in France have much in common with those found in movements against neoliberal globalization elsewhere in Europe and in North America. The most immediate of these concerns in the industrialized West are the global social and economic dangers of an unregulated, frequently overheated investor capitalism and the environmental menace created by the consumer society this every-man-for-himself economy has nurtured. Non-party organizations involved in fighting these issues tend to organize protests as a supplement to political lobbying, journalism, or campaigning—for example, Greenpeace or Friends of the Earth in the environmental area or, in the resistance to uncontrolled corporate capitalism, Ralph Nader's Public Citizen or the Trans National Institute, or ATTAC (the European organization for a Tobin tax to regulate uncontrolled financial speculation).[71]

These organizations frequently base their specific analyses and protests on democratic principles of popular control and ecological ones of a sustainable future. Essentially, these groups are the inheritors of the traditional "modernist" Left that, in its Marxist dispensation, looked to the industrial proletariat for salvation. Their major difference is that their constituency is largely middle class and that their field of action is increasingly international. While they may work together with radical elements of the labor movement, as in the French social unrest since 1995, the Seattle anti-WTO protest, and, to a lesser extent, the anti–IMF/World Bank protests of April 2000, they have a base independent of the trade unions, which on the whole have become conservative and bureaucratic. Particularly when it comes to organizing against such global power centers, they have to build broad coalitions that bring together all those opposed to existing mechanisms of neoliberal globalization. Such coalitions include those who want piecemeal reform within the system, those who would replace it by a system of neo-Keynesian regulation with the limited aims of increasing the degree of democratic control over the market economy and returning to the redistribution ethic of the welfare state, and those whose perspectives are outside of, and opposed to the continuation of, global corporate capitalism, such as the anarchists and the peasant unions affiliated with the Via Campesino.

On the whole, what used to be the Marxist Left goes no further than demanding some kind of return to neo-Keynesian regulation. This is the dominant line in the popular left-wing press: the widely read French monthly *Monde Diplomatique,* the U.S. weekly *The Nation,* the English weekly *Observer* and the daily *Guardian.* Political proponents include leftist socialists like Ken Livingstone, Ken Coates, or Oskar Lafontaine, most remaining Communists, a good many Trotskyists and their sympathizers, and many left-wing Greens. In France, the economist Jean-Paul Fitoussi, in England the economic publicist and journalist Will Hutton, in the United States prominent younger intellectuals and lobbyists like William Greider and Lori Wallach (working for Nader's Public Citizen) are prominent spokespersons for this position, as is the dissident former chief economist of the World Bank, Joseph Stiglitz.

Many in the protest movements that have developed since 1990 hope to go further than simply a regulated, less inequitable, and more ecologically responsible market capitalism. Radical Marxists, most French "associationists," North American and English "communitarians," radical ecologists, and anarchists see the problems of neoliberal globalization as inherent in any kind of market capitalism and believe a basic change of mentality and a deconstruction of the prevailing property system to be indispensable if we are to emerge from the dual dangers of environmental degradation and increasing social injustice.

While most of these more radical groups support, in the name of political realism, peaceful campaigns organized by the proponents of reregulation, often major demonstrations that have been planned for many months by the moderate groups have to contend, as did the Seattle anti-WTO protest, both with anarchists whose urge to smash the state takes the concrete form of pillaging a local McDonald's or Starbuck's, and with police only too eager to use such pillaging as a pretext for massive violence against nonviolent demonstrators.

Indeed, anarchism appears to be a rapidly growing political movement in a number of countries. In England, Reclaim the Streets organized a street carnival in June 1999 in the City (London's stock exchange district) and a flower-planting ceremony in Parliament Square on May Day 2000, both involving tens of thousands of young people and ending in police-provoked violence. In France, anarchists of the Confédération Nationale de Travail are playing a significant role in strikes and demonstrations for the first time since the early twentieth century.[72] In the United States, the radical ecology inspired by Murray Bookchin has for thirty years represented a rebirth of anarchist theory, and the Direct Action Network that helped organized both the Seattle and Washington demonstrations is basically anarchist. And apart from the anarchists, Trotskyists and radical intellectuals like the late Pierre Bourdieu and his followers work closely with the more militant social movements (such as those represented in the French strikes of December 1995) that would go further than simply reform the capitalist system.

With all due respect for the courage and determination of North American reformers and radicals, the most likely arena for radical change is Western Europe rather than the United States. Contrary to the European experi-

ence, where income redistribution in favor of the wealthy meets ongoing resistance, in America the fabulous wealth of the millionaire and billionaire
minority arouses only a feeble opposition from the majority, whose living
standards continue to sink. American capitalism benefits as always from
the imbalance between its continental corporate power and the splintered,
localized forces that oppose it, as well as from its secure ideological dominance. It has used the world's most sophisticated advertising industry to
lure U.S. citizens with declining hourly wages into the purchase of commodities—new cars and appliances, the very latest gadgets of information
technology, expensive soaps and body creams—that supposedly will make
them more powerful, more sophisticated, and more sexually attractive than
ever. The accelerating quest for seemingly indispensable consumer goods,
the accumulation of quickly obsolescent junk, and the consequent mounting consumer debt all come at the increasing expense of family lives and
physical and mental health.[73] Tens of millions of husbands and wives, who
grew up in households where at least one parent was available to bring them
up and focus on the family, must both take jobs under worsening conditions
to maintain the ever higher living standard that omnipresent advertising
and peer pressure convinces them they must have.[74]

Given these overriding values on consumption in the wealthiest and
most powerful nation on earth, the bottom, top, and middle of the American social pyramid react in ways that destroy the social nexus. At the bottom end of the social scale, where the technological revolution has eliminated most regular production jobs, poorly educated adolescents from
impoverished minority backgrounds drift into criminal activity and drugs
to escape slums and hopelessness. At the top end, the 20 percent to whom
an ever larger share of the wealth is being redistributed move into well-
protected, privatized golden ghettos, with steadily decreasing awareness
or concern for those less privileged. Lured by advertisers, the overworked
Americans in the middle imitate the consumption habits of the rich above
them; meanwhile they shun the poor below, fearful either of falling a vic-
tim to criminal elements or of being "downsized" into their ranks. The result is an ever sharper rupture between the middle strata and the underclass, a rupture that paralyzes the potential resistance of the disadvantaged
majority. Everyone is worse off, and most of all the nation's children, who
are systematically deprived of parental nurturance and whose material
future is being pillaged by the waste of resources and poisoning of the
environment.

The American way of life is the most eloquent example of the double wall
presently blocking the human prospect. The extravagant level of waste in

the United States, masked from its citizenry by the continental size of the country but environmentally lethal for the entire planet, is accompanied by the risks of a breathless work-and-spend cycle in which the doped-up hunt for consumer baubles is likely to lead to economic, social, and political collapse. Inhabitants of what Immanuel Wallerstein calls the "core countries" of global capitalism stand to suffer by this impending collapse as much as do the largely victimized citizens of African, Asian, and South American nations.

The European reactions against neoliberal downsizings and privatizations revealed the growing sensitivity of ordinary people, as well as of opinion makers, to these dangers. Nonetheless, the 1990s shift to the political and ecological Left, welcome though it may have been as an echo of the increasingly articulate desperation felt by the hoi polloi, did not move the social-democratic establishment temporarily dominant in most European Union governments to depart significantly from the shibboleths of growth and increased consumption in the framework of market capitalism. Indeed, one crucial component in the new social-democratic European consensus, Blair's New Labour, won the support of many disgusted Tory voters by promising continuation of neoliberal economic policies without scandals and incompetence, and was not going to risk losing that support by abandoning conventional Thatcherite wisdom.

Even the timid Keynesianism being proposed here and there by the more independent-minded social democrats, such as the former German economics minister Oskar Lafontaine and the French economic analyst Jean-Paul Fitoussi,[75] appears to have been too much for the social-democratic establishments of their countries. Lafontaine was pushed to resign in March 1999, and Fitoussi, while highly respected, has had little influence on the Jospin government, which has put neoliberals like Dominique Strauss-Kahn and Laurent Fabius in charge of its economic policies. Given the victory of Christian Democrats and Liberals in the European parliamentary elections of July 1999, and the feebleness of the Dutch and French social-democrats in the elections of 2002, the ideal of a neo-Keynesian Social Europe is further away than ever. Indeed, after the terrorist attacks of September 11 and the war in Afghanistan, the dominant political debate in both Europe and North America turned much more to questions of security and immigration than to the economic and social issues highlighted by the anticorporate Left. And even if, despite these obstacles, a Keynesian program were to be implemented in the European Union, it could at most succeed in preventing a major depression, at the cost of leaving untouched the underlying ecological and social problems.

Yet the only "realistic" program for the coming decade is clearly that of the neo-regulators, around which most serious reformers, even those whose aims are more radical, are currently gathering. France, where opposition to the neoliberal hegemony is most deeply entrenched, is the country whose public opinion and intellectual leadership are most advanced, but the opposition is still rather divided. Whether its spokespersons are more moderate, like Fitoussi and the sociologist Alain Touraine, or more radical, like Susan George, the late Pierre Bourdieu, and Alain Caillé, they are, in the coming decade, going to have to gather their forces and bury their differences if this program is to have a chance.

Indeed, Fitoussi (who opposed the December 1995 public-sector strikes) regularly uses his column in *Le Monde* to beat the drum for a regulated and socially humane European economy as an alternative to American global hegemony; Bourdieu (the principal intellectual supporter of the strikers) set up an organization—Raisons d'Agir—with intellectual and trade union supporters in most European countries to press for the implementation of a Social Europe; on a more modest scale, Caillé, who is not close to Bourdieu and did not sign either of the December 1995 petitions, has with his associates on the Boulevard de Grenelle been campaigning for years for a European citizenship based on reduction of the workweek, government support for civic associations, and a guaranteed wage. And Touraine, long an opponent of Bourdieu both intellectually and politically, supported the anti-WTO demonstrations in Seattle. Perhaps the widespread network established not only in France but throughout Europe by the Keynesian-oriented ATTAC will serve as a rallying point.

Clearly, the renewal of social/political control over capitalism is an urgent next step. If the recession of 2001 is not reversed in 2002, existing differences within the corporate elites and their advisers will no doubt grow, and public opinion everywhere, faced with the decline of the "new economy," will increasingly favor the regulators. Even without such economic pain among the propertied classes, however, growing realization of the injustice, social disintegration, and environmental hazards caused by the present world system was, before September 11, already turning growing numbers of the young against that system and in favor of the regulators.

The military response to the trauma and anxiety aroused by the World Trade Center atrocity brought a momentary patriotic inebriation to the United States in late 2001 and early 2002. Once this mood has passed, one of the first questions that will be raised is the danger of dependency on foreign and unsustainable energy supplies to preserve a pathological overwork-overspend-overconsume existence—all for the sake of maintaining "growth." Just over the horizon, the necessity of ecological reform for a sustainable future will require a great deal of government support and steering: the conversion to renewable energy resources and the rebuilding of transportation infrastructures, indeed of many cities, will become a hugely expensive infrastructural priority of the decades to come, requiring a curtailment of the present consumer mentality and a renewal of the idea of social control over economic life and collective facilities.

What is likely to occur globally then, in the coming decades, is increased social turbulence,[76] in which, optimally, the popular and youth forces currently being unleashed against corporate globalization in Europe and America will push the reformers into a commanding position, from which the social and ecological reform programs I have been discussing can be imposed on a recalcitrant market capitalism. Implementation of the Social Europe proposals of the nineties may yet be a practical first step (though not under the present socialist and Labourite leaderships). Doing so would put U.S. neoliberal ideologists more on the defensive and give the North American Left—in conjunction with the trade unions and the ecological movement—a European reference point for changing the political consensus in the nation.

If, however, the existing diffuse, heterogeneous, and chaotic social movement does manage to create the basis for such reforms, much more will have been changed than the rate of profit or the ease of lucrative global financial transactions. Corporate market capitalism may continue to be dominant, but unlimited consumer appetites will be traded in for a renewal of social ties and environmental security; cities will be rebuilt, and there will be more concern with restoring pure air, water, and food to families and communities than with showing off the newest cellular gadgetry. Under these circumstances basic questions about the means and ends of human existence are bound to be raised and publicly discussed once again.

Prometheus may at that point be broadly understood as having had a sham existence in the "exuberant irrationality" of the 1990s stock market pathology, as well as in all the institutional straitjackets that preceded it, including the welfare state that might then be more or less rationally recreated. The question will be raised of restoring the altruism, inventiveness, and social idealism that earlier guided our species from the poverty and blind authoritarianism of a traditional social order into its current rich but perilous potentialities—a social idealism that ancient myth projected onto a god who suffered torturous punishment for his desire to bestow on humankind the gifts of reason and understanding. The truly utopian question of the social preconditions for restoring and broadening allocentric perception, the basis of Promethean creativity, will then be on the order of the day.

It could turn out that we are closer to this point than we realize. For what is truly anachronistic and archaic today is not the swelling movement against neoliberal "reform" but the perpetuation, in an epoch of unheard-of material abundance, of a society founded on scarcity and of mentalities cultivated by scarcity, a perpetuation that has brought us to the double wall of increasing social injustice and environmental menace. It is a commonplace that most of those in the generations now under thirty face lower living standards and far less material security than their parents. The undermining of both individual character and faith in the future—bequeathed by the combination of neoliberal degradation of labor conditions, corporate indifference to ecological damage, and the antiwelfarist curtailment of state-supported social insurance and pension systems[77]—may first catalyze effective resistance in Europe, but it is being felt everywhere in the industrialized world. Those among the youth now confronting the lifelong sacrifice of their energy and joie de vivre in the service of Mammon, Inc., those of the educated middle class who have exchanged early expectations of a qualitatively better existence for the mess of suburban pottage they are now strangling in, those to whom the multicultural tolerance of the post-Fordist West has permitted the expression of their sexual or ethnic difference while it has rendered them impotent to enjoy those differences in a meaningful and sustainable social order—all these are unlikely to settle for a return to an ecologically manageable and politically regulated form of consumer capitalism.

The postindustrial utopia began with the incredible outburst of energy in 1968, and the Promethean battle cry of *L'imagination au pouvoir!* All power to the imagination! Like the Protestant Reformation, it had an underground history in the preceding century and a half, from the English, French, and German romantics to the expressionists and surrealists of the early twentieth century, all of whom contested the false incarnations of Prometheus in modern institutions and ideologies.[78] Just as did every new vision of social or cultural change, this utopia endured a period of quiescence after its initial appearance in 1968. Its resumption amid the perils of the last decade has been the subject of this chapter. The concluding one will offer a suggestion as to how the Promethean creativity of the postindustrial era may use the breathtaking opportunities now available to it to empower imagination in a democratic and sustainable future.

chapter six

Another World Is Possible

Prometheus or Pandora?

DRIVEN BY THE IDEAL of private ownership of just about everything on Planet Earth, neoliberal capitalism undermines social cohesion and justice for the sake of profits, competition, consumption, and technological growth. I have argued in this book that these values are the last ideological subterfuge of a modernity that has lost its moorings. Their hegemony has resulted in a rule of the marketplace and a commodification of existence that is largely responsible for the double wall of ecological menace and social degradation that blocks the future. In their shadow, the Promethean idealism that created the modern world vanishes. They are compatible neither with the altruistic sacrifice nor with the creative spirit symbolized by the Titan Prometheus. They are light-years away from the Shelleyan Prometheanism we need and are now in a position to implement—the reconciliation, through a liberated humankind, of intelligence, sociability, art, and nature. The contention that global capitalism represents our Promethean potentialities is thus empty. In augmenting material misery and psychological insecurity, the property system underlying global capitalism has endowed us with the gifts of Pandora rather than those of Prometheus.

The Greek culture that first imagined Prometheus as a friend of humankind understood civilization in terms fundamentally different from those inspired by the acquisitive individualism of a capitalist property system: festivals public and private, Dionysian music and dancing, Apollonian art and an intense sociability—all echoed in Shelley's *Prometheus Unbound*—characterized the culture of the Greek city-state. By contrast, the institutionalizing of Prometheus in the economic order of modernity has had two salient features that are diametrically opposed to the values of the ancient Greek cultural order: the repressive "civilizing mission," a crusading moralism that was inherited from Christianity by capitalist individualism in the nineteenth and early twentieth centuries, and, more recently, media "branding" of lifestyles by consumption-oriented corporate capitalism.

The "civilizing mission" was undertaken by enthusiasts of the modern property system among indigenous villagers and tribesmen of a premodern social order who were not yet acquainted with its virtues. Their cultures, condemned by bourgeois and Christian ideologists alike, displayed many of the features of play, sociability, and religious-aesthetic exuberance notable among the Greeks.

A case in point is the nineteenth-century effort of Indian agents of the American government to impose Anglo-Saxon notions of private property in land on American Indians who had hitherto held all land in common.[1] The General Allotment Act of 1879, intended to encourage private farming among the Indians by breaking up their reservations, would have divided their land into properties of 160 acres for heads of families and 80 acres for single persons, with the surplus purchasable by the government. All allotments could be sold by their owners after twenty-five years. The bill was defended by Carl Schurz, secretary of the interior, who said, "The enjoyment and pride of the individual ownership of property is one of the most effective civilizing agencies." The presumed barbarism this civilizing agency was to eradicate is evident in a report from a government Indian agent who supported the bill. Note how closely the archaic customs attributed to the absence of private property approximated those of the original worshippers of Prometheus: "As long as the Indians live in villages, they will retain many of their old and injurious habits. Frequent feasts, heathen ceremonies and dances, constant visiting—these will continue as long as people live together in close neighborhoods and villages. I trust that before another year is ended they will generally be located upon individual land or farms. From that date will begin their real and permanent progress."[2]

Indeed, for the Greeks from whose imagination Prometheus was born, the arts of civilization included everything denounced among the "heathen" Indians. Apologists for neoliberal capitalism contend that only property can guarantee the material and psychological benefits of Promethean modernity. Quite independently, however, of the inversions of those benefits in the double wall created by the modern property system, accumulation of property has resulted in an abrupt decline, wherever it was the guiding principle, of the sociability and rituals that anthropologists understand as central to culture.

In the course of the twentieth century, astute observers of society came to understand that humankind, even in the vast urban spaces of the capitalist metropolises, was to a considerable extent escaping—indeed, fleeing from—the clutch of the civilizing mission and its associated universalist bourgeois and Christian values. Colonizing of heathen mentalities had turned out to be relatively superficial. Between the two world wars, a branch of the escapees, in this case even worse than the civilizers, was able to coerce the latter into a temporary alliance. In Germany and Italy, "blood and earth" fascism, rampant among the unemployed, the young, and the preindustrial strata, forged a strategic alliance with the industrial bourgeoisie under the banner of national autarchy and European conquest.[3] Temporarily, the capitalists were no longer in charge. Since 1945, they have understood they had struck a bad bargain and throughout the industrialized West have put a cordon sanitaire around the Far Right. Nonetheless, quite apart from interbellum fascism, they have had to contend for most of the last hundred years with other large islands of disbelief and resistance: in proletarian slums, among the youth, and among some ethnic and racial minorities.

In the last third of the twentieth century, as consumption-oriented, post-Fordist corporations took over the steering of the capitalist system, they realized that more than simply advertising their wares, they needed to bind major sections of the consuming public to these products by identifying them with the lifestyles of their prospective customers. In the spirit of "if you can't beat them, join them," the values of the civilizing mission were abandoned. Instead, through the commercial colonization of the mass popular culture of middle- and working-class youth, both white and black, corporate advertisers integrated into the nexus of consumer capitalism all those groups that in the sixties and afterward had shown their capacity to develop their own, apparently rebellious subcultures. This occurred through the takeover of major sporting and popular music events by companies like Nike, Gap, Benetton, and Calvin Klein. Naomi Klein defines this phenomenon as the "branding" of lifestyles.[4] World cup games, Olympics, and mass pop concerts as well as electronic or print media are "sponsored" by—and identified with—billionaire corporations. Which leads to a subtle subversion—the French have the word *récupération*—of social phenomena in principle unrelated or even antagonistic to property values, individualism or the work ethic, so as to cultivate identities totally dependent on having the appropriate expensive consumer items. The aim, *pace* the apologists of consumer culture, is not the "carnivalization" of modern culture but, through emulation and conspicuous consumption, the inculcation of all the values necessary for the triumph of consumer capitalism into social strata unreachable by an overt civilizing offensive.

The young and not-so-young who are the object of this selling campaign have begun to reject it. Increasingly, ubiquitous "cool" advertising techniques are parodied and ridiculed by those they are aimed at, countercampaigns are organized by enthusiastic amateurs in organizations like Adbusters, Students Against Sweatshops, and the Direct Action Network. In the black underclass, hip-hop serves a similar function. Using the Internet as an organizational medium, such groups have worked together with more established groups like Public Citizen, Greenpeace, and Friends of the Earth to launch protests like those in Seattle and Washington, D.C., against the World Trade Organization, the IMF, and the World Bank. On May 6, 2000, BBC News publicized a nationwide campaign against the trendy clothing manufacturer Gap in the United States, accused of using sweatshop labor on the U.S.-owned island of Saipan.

If the chosen objects of advertising hype are capable of wielding irony and parody to transgress its message, if the *jeunesse dorée* of the affluent West is capable of militant protest against capitalism's prostitution of intelligence and sensitivity, the information technology base created by modern capitalism as the virtual fortress of its "new economy" can also be turned against it. Indeed, this technology presents humankind with an unprecedented opportunity for a renewal of the Promethean promise, that is, for a better and more secure existence than any previously known and for a return to the autonomous values of art, freedom, and sociability manifested by the culture that invented Prometheus, bearer of fire to humankind. On condition, of course, that we abandon the corporate consumer culture that now governs our lives.

Ernest Schachtel identified the core of the creative geniuses of modernity—Galileo, Spinoza, Voltaire, Diderot, Marx, etc.—as allocentric, or other-oriented, perception,[5] a notion that pinpoints the psychological basis of humankind's Promethean capacities. Schachtel's concept is a psychologically refined version of the emphasis on comprehending otherness found in a broad diversity of epistemologists, anthropologists, and ethical philosophers (among them, Michel Foucault) who for centuries have been concerned with transcending the binary opposition between self and other inherent in Cartesianism. Contrariwise, the possessive individualism, the mania for growth, and the identitarian cocoons that shaped the ideologies that have straight-jacketed Promethean modernity constitute a narcissistic denial of otherness, which Schachtel called secondary autocentricity.

While the credo of possessive individualism, the mainspring of global inequality and social disintegration, is innate to the corporate system that rules the world, the allied concept of growth for its own sake is a tenet of triumphant capitalism that it shares with most of the collective incarnations of Prometheus it has vanquished: nationalism, fascism, socialism, and communism. A rebirth of the Promethean humanism that freed us from subservience to religious and political absolutism thus requires rejecting the ideology of unlimited growth as well as the capitalist property system, both of which have brought us to our present impasse. Such rejection means leaving all the modern incarnations of Prometheus behind us. It does not, however, mean abandoning the founding ideals of Promethean modernity, nor the technological potential created by that modernity, which is indispensable to the future alleviation of human misery and the creation of a just and sustainable world.[6]

In principle, the underlying allocentric values of Promethean modernity—intellectual and affective curiosity (that is, the will to comprehend otherness), the thirst for justice and human solidarity, and the hunger for personal and collective freedom—are utterly incompatible with the possessive individualism currently inspiring the property system of the modern world. Given institutional shape by the most powerful alliance of political power, military force, and corporate wealth the world has ever seen, driven by the ideology of insatiable consumption and the desire for unlimited growth—the twin fetishes of investment capital—this system has already produced an unjust and dangerous global inequality between rich and poor and a growing insecurity for a large majority of the world's population; it will, if unchecked, lead to environmental apocalypse.

The hegemony of a corporate capitalism inspired by those fetishes is thus inherently self-contradictory and unstable. On the one hand, growth fetishism, by endangering the human future through environmental degradation and climatic deregulation, reverses the promise of Promethean emancipation from natural fatality. On the other hand, the ineluctable concentration of property ownership under capitalism, together with the all-absorbing focus on increasing one's individual property, systematically subverts social justice, saps social cohesion, and, by reducing the quality of experience to filthy lucre, mocks the intellectual and emotional curiosity of the allocentric personality. Moreover, the present process of capitalist globalization, entailing as it does massive uprootedness and social degradation, is increasingly incompatible with our existing institutions of democratic control: one national leader after another is elected on the promise to protect his people from it, only to turn around, once in power, to plead the impotence of national governments to resist its powers of economic coercion. And institutionalized democratic control at an international level is nonexistent: neither the giant multinational corporations nor their central committees, the WTO, the IMF, the World Bank, and the EU, are subject to it, which is why opposition to those organizations has taken the form of militant direct action in recent years.

Happily, no system is eternal, and the present corporate governance of the world has begun to manifest its internal contradictions in a manner that bears comparison with the disintegration of the absolutist ancien régime in continental Europe between 1789 and 1848. The twentieth century saw in

1929 a stock market collapse that precipitated a global depression. Its origins have much in common with the cause of the present volatility of world markets: the irresistible lure, for those who desire instant wealth, of new stock market values whose rapid inflation, far beyond any reasonable expectation of a return, is based on the untenable premise that buyers will always be found who will pay even more for them.

The likelihood of a repeat of the thirties in the next few years is particularly great in view of the abandonment of any kind of social regulation of economic activity, the kind of prudent social management that administered the post–World War II economic recovery during the epoch of the Fordist welfare state. A stock market crash devastated the Southeast Asian "tigers" in the late 1990s; a decade-long recession in Japan lingers interminably into the twenty-first century; and the sudden drops in Internet shares in the spring and fall of 2000 presaged the collapse of the telecom sector and a major recession in Europe and the United States. Against this unstable "new economy," a variety of equally new social movements—discussed in previous chapters—raised demands for radical change. At the dawn of the twenty-first century, coalitions of environmental, labor, and anticapitalist groups with little or no connection to the radical movements of the past were attacking major gatherings of global corporate power: the Seattle WTO meeting in November 1999, the Washington IMF and World Bank meetings in April 2000, the Prague meeting of those organizations in September 2000, the Genoa one in 2001. The attacks of September 11 interrupted the rising tide of active dissent, but in Europe it quickly resumed. Peaceful protests at EU summits brought out 100,000 demonstrators in Brussels (December 14, 2001) and 300,000 in Barcelona (March 16, 2002).[7]

While it is impossible to predict either the future of this resistance or its program for an alternative to the present global disequilibrium, the combination of environmental and social demands expressed by the protesters certainly strengthens the plausibility of European movements for a Social Europe. Indeed, if there is a realistic prospect anywhere for an internal transformation of neoliberal capitalism, it is—for reasons discussed above[8]—not in North America but in Europe.

This prospect is implicit and sometimes explicit in the French *gauche de la gauche* and the German PDS as well as in a considerable part of the socialist and Green constituency in France, Germany, Italy, and England, which for years has been frustrated and disgusted by the supine conformism of the social-democratic leadership to neoliberal ideology and the American global model. Sympathetic to prominent left-wing mavericks like Ken Livingstone and Oskar Lafontaine within the social-democratic parties, this radical undercurrent within and to the left of European social democracy has for some time made it clear that it would like to use the institutions of the European Union to create a kind of left-leaning "progressive capitalist" bloc with a renovated, European-wide welfare network. Social thinkers as prominent as Jürgen Habermas and Pierre Bourdieu, pointing out the impotence of national states to protect their people when confronted with the economic power of U.S.-based multinational capitalism, have called on European progressives to support the idea of a European welfare state.[9]

A bloc of this kind, with more internal democracy, better regulation, and better social protection and environmental awareness than either the North American or the East Asian capitalist blocs, could compete with the United States as a global model, offering better trade and lending terms to third world countries willing to comply with certain minimum requirements for social and environmental legislation. As a model, its social legislation, a reflection of the still existing social sense of most ordinary Europeans,[10] would guarantee adequate health, education, and social fallback resources for the ill, the unemployed, and the incapacitated. Its environmental measures would be founded on a rapid conversion to renewable energy resources and would be supported by a material infrastructure of inexpensive, energy-saving public rail transportation to facilitate the transition to a largely automobile-free society. To allow for more leisure, adult education, and political participation, it would also shorten the workweek as productive efficiency increases and as efficient public transportation replaces private.

Furthermore, the increased social cohesion and security would provide a social-psychological base for work time reduction, since the winners/losers mentality, and with it the personal demand now resulting from hyperindividual competition in the acquisition of prestigious but superfluous consumer goods, would be considerably diminished. On the basis of a steady increase in popular participation through the associative life stimulated by it,[11] this program, while permitting (like the welfare states of the sixties) a prominent role for regulated corporate capitalism, could reverse both the downward ecological spiral and the ruinous tendency to the dissolution of the social order into personal acquisitiveness. It could give a decisive stimulus to similarly oriented movements within the American and Japanese blocs that are striving to transform them from within.

Such an evolution might, as I say, reverse the vicious spiral of global inequality, insecurity, and environmental degradation. Nonetheless, a Social Europe with a major corporate capitalist sector—even one subject to reasonable social and ecological limitations—would still be at war with itself, since the basic tendencies of capitalism to resist democratic control, to grow indefinitely, and to cultivate insatiable consumption would persist. There would be no shortage of virulent complaints that capitalism could not survive limits to consumption, and they would not be unfounded.[12] This Social Europe would, however, be no more than a first step, leading, over the course of decades, to a transformation of mentalities and institutions. Given the broader level of debate that such transformed mentalities would support, many would argue that the new Europe was far from a maximum utilization of the potentialities inherent in the extant globalization. Such utilization, which now appears utopian, will be increasingly demanded and defined by the myriad of associations stimulated by a Social Europe.

Certainly, if we grant that the present ecological menace and lack of social justice is inherent neither in economic globalization nor in the technological accomplishments that sustain it, then the key question is how to go beyond the disastrous values and institutions now undermining the human future. Once we see the necessity for a return to social regulation, we can expect a renewal of serious speculative thought about an alternative global order, one which might build on some of the basic principles manifested in the new Social Europe to create a radically different and better world order. This chapter is an exploration of what that order might be based on and what it might look like. My proposals are intended not as a blueprint, but as a contribution to a new utopian vision, necessary if we are to look beyond the double wall blocking the future.

Sustainable Democracies in a Noncapitalist Global Economy

Since the disintegration of the Soviet empire and the collapse of Marxist ideology, debate about utopia, never altogether silenced, has increased.[13] My approach in this chapter, though perhaps idiosyncratic in some respects, is thus part of an ongoing discussion by philosophers, social ecologists, geographers, and sociologists about the good society. A sharply insightful book by Boris Frankel commented on the status of the debate in the mid-1980s, outlining and criticizing books by the French-Austrian economist and philosopher André Gorz, the East German dissident Rudolph Bahro, and others.[14] In adding to this discussion, I am working from multiple points of departure, which, to indicate the line of filiation with the mainstream of critical idealism in the period since the European Enlightenment, I summarize as the other—that is, the Shelleyan—Prometheus. In Chapter 4, I have discussed as a theoretical foundation for this alternative Prometheanism Ernest Schachtel's psychoanalytic notion of allocentric perception. Throughout, in the tradition of many socialist and anarchist thinkers, I have assumed the capacity of humankind, within the framework of material conditions, to transform existing power relations and release itself from the awesome pressures of past and present orthodoxies and tyrannies, a capacity evidenced by all the great political and intellectual revolutions of modernity. The nineteenth-century historian Michelet summed up this transformative potentiality as humanity being its own Prometheus.[15]

My further assumptions in the following pages echo widespread criticisms of the present commercial order of society.

One is that the use of advanced industrial technology within the framework of corporate capitalism is leading to global environmental disasters. Problems like global warming, the destruction of parts of our natural environment, and widespread pollution are sources of international concern and negotiation between existing political entities. Many people now believe that humankind has no future unless social existence is drastically altered so as to reorient energy utilization to sustainable, renewable sources. This means not only the rapid development of solar, wind, and tidal energy technology to replace fossil fuels and nuclear power but also the rebuilding of public transportation networks and the reconstruction of many large cities. Some think this can be accomplished while retaining the existing global market economy. I do not. While such reconstruction may begin under some kind of regulated capitalism, its presuppositions are incompatible with the continuance of our present consumer society.

Another broadly shared criticism is that the subjection of all human relations to the laws of the marketplace has brought about a disintegration of the social and political frameworks necessary for human security and an exacerbation of the extremes of wealth and poverty, both within the industrialized North and between North and South. There are essentially two ways to counteract or reverse this commercialization of existence. A political approach—which generally uses the Keynesian welfare state as its reference point—would restore control over the economy either by the nation-state or by some kind of international political authority, such as the European Union. This is the preferred approach of ATTAC and of many past or present Marxists affiliated with the Trotskyist movement or with the influential *Monde Diplomatique.* A second approach aims at revitalizing social ties and at undermining corporate capitalism by the spread of economic and political citizens' groups based on the ideas of participatory democracy. This "associationist" position, represented by Hilary Wainwright in England and Alain Caillé in France, is preponderant in the European Green movement and inspires many of the local exchange systems in Europe and the Western Hemisphere. As I have indicated, the first of these positions is tactically sensible in the short term, but only the second—closer to the anarchist tradi-tion—has the long-term potentiality for social transformation.

A third point of departure has to do with the nature of work. The burden on the vast majority of humankind of unremitting, exhausting, repetitive, and alienating labor has become potentially obsolete because of technolog-ical advances. Nevertheless, the all-pervasive ideology of the marketplace has prevented us from benefiting from these advances—from transcending our work-earn-spend obsessiveness and making available to all the reasoned and aesthetically sensitive existence that has until now been the preserve of a small minority. Even in the Anglo-American heartland of the capitalist economy, most people are working harder than ever, and their use of scarce leisure time has been largely integrated into an exploitative and expensive commercialism. Moreover, global inequities between North and South keep most Asians, Africans, and South Americans in poverty and force them to work long hours for a pittance, while their governments are crushed by debts. Trade and financial pressures have integrated the third world into global industry, reproducing in it the worst excesses of misery and exploita-tion of early nineteenth-century industrialism.

Two possible utopian alternatives have appeared. One is based on a max-imum use of the new technology to reduce work to a bare minimum: ide-ally, this option would permit machines to do all the necessary labor and al-low humankind to devote itself to purely cultural and social activities. The second alternative would use technology to eliminate not work as such but only the stultifying sort that produces exhaustion, boredom, and alienation, and to loosen the viselike grip of work by bringing it into equilibrium with our cultural and social potentialities. When I started studying these matters a decade ago, I leaned toward the first solution. Gradually I have shifted to the second, for two reasons.

One is that no sharp dividing line separates work that is alienated and un-creative from work that is free, creative cultural activity. Much creative ac-tivity that passes as non-work—because it is often not remunerated—is in-deed work (like the learning of a musical instrument or the writing of a book). Moreover, many of the new kinds of work involving computer pro-gramming, as well as older kinds of artisan work that antedate the indus-trial age and are undergoing a revival, have creative aspects.

The second reason is that in at least one essential area of economic ac-tivity, agriculture, producing in a manner consistent with environmental sustainability and human health requires a sharp break with industrial methods. Subjection of agriculture to the joint principles of large-scale in-dustrialization and market capitalism has produced the ecological menace of soil and water pollution, the health hazard of contaminated food, the social disaster of a near-disappearance of small farms, and the corollary consequence, all over the third world, of urban slums and shantytowns filled with uprooted peasants. The need to return to small-scale organic farming, outlined in 2001 by the Green minister of agriculture in the German government, is a salutary reminder of the limits of technology, which can never take the place of face-to-face human interaction, participation, acculturation, and sociability. Moreover, decentralized organic farming, responsive to the vastly varied climatic conditions and cultural traditions and mentalities on our planet, reminds us of one further given: The future society will not be monocultural but an infinite number of organized sociocultural geographic settings.

On the basis of these points of departure, and from the premise that a European welfare state would be an indispensable first step, I envisage an extrapolation from a radically evolved Social Europe to a world scale: an interdependency of small-scale local cultures, indispensable seedbeds of strong personal identities, with a global, nonmarket economic system fine-tuned to regional tastes, for the satisfaction of all basic needs. The economy would combine the benefits of advanced information technology for large-scale production with artisanal craft production. Provision of essential goods would, wherever possible, be supplied regionally or by local cultures, using every technology from preindustrial crafts and farming to computer programming and automated production. Food would be grown organically according to the desiderata of long-term ecological sustainability, and each region would strive to produce a surplus of grain—perhaps 5–10 percent— to supply other regions hit by drought and potential famine. Should local difficulties arise, an independent planetary economy would insure the maintenance of an adequate standard of living.

In other words, neither a homogenized global society (Benjamin Barber's "McWorld")[16] nor an autarchic utopia based exclusively on premodern artisanal and farming techniques is a viable alternative to the present world order. While imposition of a global totalitarian technocracy would be lethal for the rich diversity of human culture and lobotomizing for human intelligence, it would be suicidal for humankind to turn its back on the global technological achievement that currently holds out the promise of liberation from scarcity and from stultifying work. I shall discuss shortly the various aspects of future local cultures—economic, social, cultural, and political. For the moment, let us consider how our global technology may be used, not with the present-day aim of eternally increasing production to satisfy the needs of competing corporate giants for ever more growth, sales, and profits, but in order to resolve the problems of planetary poverty and exclusion while limiting production to what is necessary for the maintenance of a reasonable, guaranteed standard of living for all human beings.[17]

In effect, there would be a global social contract: a guaranteed living standard that would permit all persons and groups to be maximally free to determine their own ends. In exchange, each individual would accept three civic constraints: participating in the economy at a local, regional, or global economy for a given period of time (as now is the rule with regard to schooling and, in many countries, military service), respecting the rights to self-expression of other groups and individuals, and preserving the integrity and sustainability of the environment.

A decent and secure standard of living for all human beings would include the basic needs for food, drinkable water, housing, clothing, public transportation, renewable energy resources, and labor-saving household appliances, including such amenities as air-conditioning for hot climates and central heating systems for cold ones. The present technology makes such a standard of living, available to all with a fraction of the amount of work required by the prevailing system of consumer capitalism, a realistic target.

Consider that the average workweek in most developed industrial societies is still around forty hours (a level it reached seventy years ago). This means, on the basis of an average period of employment of forty years, about eighty thousand hours during a person's lifetime. But only a minority of those working are actually producing and distributing tangible goods; the rest are in commercial, banking, advertising, and personal services that exist only by virtue of a capitalist economy with extremes of wealth and poverty. If the global production system were limited to satisfying the basic needs I have mentioned, the total amount of necessary work during a lifetime might be limited to thirty thousand hours (fifteen years) or less. Which means that the present work ethic, although not totally abandoned, would be subordinated to a voluntarily chosen deployment of individual and group energies, under the mentioned constraints, in the arts, craft work, sports, philosophical reflection, sensual pleasures, etc.

Shifting the focus of human activity away from work and consumption is not contrary to our nature. History provides many examples of societies whose central values are the intelligent use of leisure rather than the acquisition of material goods; indeed it is difficult to locate a single important ethical philosophy or religion in which acquisitiveness has the importance it has in our world. Today, whatever the burden on humankind of Adam's curse, the necessity to eke out one's days in harsh labor to provide for the material necessities of life has, precisely by the Promethean spirit of humanist inquiry and invention, been ended. The amount of labor necessary for the provision of a reasonable and secure material existence for humankind has, thanks to the technical achievements of the last two centuries, been reduced to the point where, in principle, all men and women (and not just the small minority that have traditionally battened on the surplus that the rest have produced in excess of the minimum needed for their reproduction) should be able to refocus their existence from a life of brute labor to one devoted to reflection, inquiry, play, the creation of beautiful and personally useful things, and care for others—precisely the ideal advanced by Shelley's liberated Prometheus.

This does not mean that productive work in the traditional sense will no longer exist. It signifies, however, that the quantitative presence of this kind of work and its qualitative significance for our lives can be so reduced that, for example, instead of a working life of forty years of forty- to fifty-hour weeks, a working life of perhaps one-third that amount would be sufficient to supply the basic goods mentioned above.

There would, of course, necessarily be a transitional phase of some decades in which a working life closer to our present one than to that of the utopian future would be necessary—perhaps a workweek of thirty hours—during which cities and suburban areas would be rebuilt for public transportation, the conversion to sustainable energy sources would take place, pure water, health care and adequate education would be made available to all, and the earth would be, as far as possible, decontaminated from the pollution it has undergone in the last two centuries. A global charter of the social and environmental rights of man, perhaps under UN auspices, would be a good first step to this transitional phase.

But certainly, by the middle of the present century, a social order based on the vastly reduced work time I am talking about is a realistic goal. In fact, combining automation and computerization has already permitted the massive reduction of industrial work forces. At present, the superabundance the more affluent parts of the world have established as a standard is produced by considerably fewer than those employed thirty years ago and, as indicated, only a minority of those employed are actually involved in producing or distributing it.[18] Apart from the large numbers in unproductive commercial or bureaucratic employment, the reduction or elimination of welfare benefits has forced most of those "downsized" by cost-cutting companies either to take on shoddily paid temporary jobs or to present themselves in the service sector as freelance servants for the affluent, delivering their purchases and taking care of their homes and children for a pittance.

A social system that paid more than lip service to the ideals of democracy and social justice could long ago have started a systematic shortening of the workweek that corresponded to the increased productivity, and by now all

Americans and Europeans might be working a twenty-hour week, with a standard of living higher than that enjoyed in 1970.[19] Instead of this, the tastemakers, state-of-the-art pacesetters, and advertisers have whetted consumer appetites for additional family automobiles, for expensive and ecologically disastrous faraway vacations,[20] and for a large range of electronic gadgetry (home computers, Internet services, video cameras and players, mobile phones, etc.)[21] that make a return to the modest affluence of the seventies unthinkable for many people.

In fact, reduction of work time was incompatible with the personal insecurity and "work-and-spend" values that corporate strategists cultivated to inspire a workaholic consumer society. Exponential increases in productivity were never viewed by those strategists as a means of escaping the curse of Adam, but simply as an opportunity to expand profitability by selling more with a lower wage bill. Furthermore, the wealthy—who would by now also be working a twenty-hour week if work-time reduction had been on the order of the day—might have had to do their own shopping and cleaning, since the pool of inexpensive unemployed labor would then hardly exist. If all this was not sufficient (it usually was) to eliminate work-time reduction as an acceptable way of using productivity increases, prudent liberal economists have constantly reminded the captains of industry that without the large floating industrial reserve army of the downsized, indeed without an unemployment level of 5 percent or more, demands for higher wages might be irresistible.

What keeps the system going then is the near-totalitarian grip on the public mind of a conventional wisdom, which the French call the *pensée unique* and which Margaret Thatcher summarized as There Is No Alternative. Any interference with—even any regulation of—existing property relations is assumed to lead to social collapse into nationalism, communism, and, worst of all, idleness. Given the absence of a known and discussible alternative, the lure of a well-advertised lifestyle—fast cars for all, expensive vacations, luxuriously furnished large houses, and designer clothing—mesmerizes millions into a workaholic existence. That is the carrot. The stick is social fear: wealth is so poorly distributed and the pace of downsizing so unpredictable that most men and women are afraid they will fall into the bottomless pit of an impoverished underclass if they lose their present, rather precarious employment. To hold on to it, and to retain the chimerical possibility of moving into the upper 10 percent of the wealthy, they are willing to neglect their families, their friends, and their souls. This is what keeps them focused on their work and on the rites of insatiable consumption.

Imagine, however, that enough of us in Europe and North America were prepared simply to say, "Basta! Enough of the rat race. Let's cash in our chips *now*, and have a minimum of alienated labor and a maximum of leisure and sociability."[22] We would debate for a long time about what "Basta!" really meant, and, to lessen the social injustice of a North-South divide that presently keeps billions of people in poverty in the third world, we would have to agree to a considerable increase in the extremely low level of economic assistance presently given to undeveloped and developing nations. But in the end we would probably come up with an alternative to the present world economy that would look roughly like what follows.

Clearly a good deal less than half of the current European and American work force is presently engaged in the actual production and distribution of the affluent lifestyle enjoyed by most Europeans and Americans. Moreover, if we had decent rapid public transportation, we could do without most cars, which would curtail the labor cost of constructing, fueling, and repairing them and the environmental impact of driving them. At a rough estimate, between 50 and 75 percent of the present white-collar work time—most of the hours now worked in the banking, advertising, and government administration of public finances—might be superfluous in an economy oriented exclusively to the provision of necessary food, clothing, housing, household appliances, public transportation, and other essential services. Given the rapid increases in productivity of the last decades of the twentieth century and anticipated further increases in the first decades of the twenty-first, a major reduction in our average lifelong labor time is possible, of such a magnitude that a qualitative improvement in the human condition is conceivable.

For example, if in the future all the work to produce a reasonable quantity, quality, and variety of necessary goods were to be fairly divided, our grandchildren might be in a position to decide if they wished, after completing their education, to work a solid stint of ten to fifteen years or to spread out their work obligation through a normal lifetime at two eight-hour days a week. Clearly some skilled work in the engineering or programming or machine tool lines, or in medicine, would require such intensive experience that it would have to be concentrated in the shorter period. And if a particular occupation, immune to the communication possibilities of Internet, required one's presence far away from one's preferred community, that would be another excellent reason for getting the work obligation done in as few years as possible. Many other occupations, however, particularly in the distribution or service sectors, might be sustainable for decades at the more leisurely pace of a couple of days a week. A qualitative improvement in work would be just as important as a quantitative reduction.

Work—whether organic farming, high-tech production of quality goods, craft production, or social services—would be far more likely to engage the personality of the worker than the rote, frequently exhausting routines currently imposed on most of humankind. Moreover, since everyone would be trained to design, administer, and run the systems of production and distribution, the current top-down hierarchies of management could be replaced by a horizontal organization in which all participate cooperatively in basic decisions concerning production methods.

In return for this participation in the partly global, partly regional or local production of food, housing, clothing, medical care, education, and transportation (within the mentioned limits), all of these necessities would be freely available to everyone, from the cradle to the grave. Again, this does not signify regression to the gray, uniform production of collectivist economies in the Fordist era. The clothes, housing, and food need not be any less varied and interesting than our present supply, since they would be created under the same post-Fordist, computer-based flexible production schedules that now provide a rich variety of models for local consumers to choose from. Food, as I have suggested, would be produced under conditions of organic, ecologically sustainable farming, and would be somewhat more labor intensive than manufacturing.[23] Decisions as to increasing the variety and quality of goods would be made in continual consultation and negotiation among the consumer/producers, although tradeoffs would have to be decided at certain points between variety and work time, the only future criterion of cost.

Outside of this limited work experience, however, all activity would be freely chosen at the individual and small group level. While participation in democratic governance would probably receive a high priority everywhere, other local associations might encourage craft activities, local farming, philosophical speculation and the creative arts, sports activities, or even more sophisticated economic activities to supplement, perhaps on a commercial market basis, the goods distributed freely by the global production system—but always with the ecological and social restraints indicated above. Presumably, local systems of exchanging goods or services on a barter or script basis—outgrowths of already existing "local exchange trading systems" (LETS) in Europe and North America[24]—would be widespread.

This speculative model, which we might call a postcapitalist Prometheanism, combines in a loosely unified scheme both the universalist and the particularist achievements of humankind.

On the one hand, the economic system would be universalist in the sense that it would be founded on the global social contract mentioned above and that it would guarantee, on the basis of a modified version of the present global high-tech economy, a basic standard of living to all. In turn, everyone would be trained to participate in this economy to the best of his or her abilities. This global economic structure would provide not only for the production and free distribution of necessary goods; it would also be responsible for guaranteeing both civic welfare (free health care, transportation, and education for all) and ecological equilibrium (diversity and sustainability).

The political system would also have a universalist component to the extent that a democratically elected planetary control would be necessary to insure both world peace (to be premised on the abolition of nuclear and other weapons of mass destruction) and environmental equilibrium (premised on global conversion to sustainable energy supplies).

On the other hand, most aspects of daily life, political as well as economic, would be decided by citizen assemblies or elected bodies at the regional and local levels on the basis, wherever possible, of indigenous custom or choice. The production and distribution of goods would be attuned to the kinds of food, housing, and clothing traditionally used and preferred locally. Except, of course, where particular items (fossil-fuel-powered private cars, for example) were incompatible with ecological sustainability, individuals within each culture should have a range of choice not vastly inferior to what reasonably well-off people now enjoy, in the food, clothing, housing, furniture, and household appliances they acquire. Indeed, the social goal would be a revival of local communities as the optimum source of identity, values, and culture. As a fallback structure in case of major disagreements with the global production and distribution centers, regions should be potentially self-sufficient. Schematically and briefly, the particularist and the universalist social values would be related institutionally as follows.

First of all, the desired social setting, the seedbed for allocentric personalities, would consist of overlapping concentric sociopolitical frameworks for cultural self-definition, within which the collective self-fashioning of identities would be balanced by a cultivated appreciation for other cultures, languages, and mentalities. These overlapping frameworks would exist for everyone at the level of the locality (based on the visual propinquities and personal friendships of village, city, or neighborhood), of the region or nation (based on cultural affinity as well as on native language or dialect), of the continent (North or South American, European, African, Asian) and of global humankind. (In addition, most individuals would be linked to mutual interest groups—popular and classical music, science fiction, gardening, chess, social philosophy, history, etc.—either locally, by face-to-face contact, or globally, via the Internet.) Again, each of these geo-cultural frameworks would have an inward and an outward orientation: inward to provide the necessary sense of local, regional, or continental identity, outward to cultivate the sense of allocentric perception and to create the global sense of one human species, of a basic human equality, despite manifest differences in culture, language, and mentality.

These overlapping identities would simply be an extension and formalization of the ways personalities are presently shaped in complex societies, where, for example, Parisians might feel ties to the friends, shops, and architecture of a specific neighborhood (say the rue Mouffetard), to Paris as a city, to France as a linguistic-cultural unit, to Europe (in which they travel) as a common culture. Moreover each *citoyen* and *citoyenne,* indeed every European, would be sensitive to the achievements and tragedies, the laughter, tears, and common problems of Asians, Africans, and North and South Americans. With an active awareness of other peoples through Internet communication and work experience and a passive understanding gained through press photos, television reports, films, and readings, identification with humanity as a whole would preclude the kinds of murderous wars and genocides that stained the history of the twentieth century.

There is, of course, a bogus, kitsch sense of identification with other peoples, which those in favor of focusing on local, or internal, group identities may justifiably ridicule. The kitsch variety of identification, so often exploited by those with universal-humanist messages and parochial aims, is less an actual comprehension of and empathy with otherness than a projection of narcissistic feelings of self-pity onto certain others whom we believe (only via the media) to be victims, and a projection of rage—a rage that we cannot properly express against abandoning parent figures and tyrannical bosses—onto yet others whom we believe to be their persecutors and oppressors. Such feelings have often been manipulated by propagandists to justify military interventions on behalf of allegedly tyrannized peoples: allied outcries over the German "rape of Belgium" in World War I, the persecution of the Sudeten Germans as the Nazi excuse for invading Czechoslovakia in 1938, the supposed danger of fascist counterrevolution used by Stalinists to justify Russian military action in Hungary in 1956 and (again!) in Czechoslovakia in 1968, the interventions of the United States in Vietnam and, more recently, in Kuwait, Kosovo, and Afghanistan. A real sense of multicultural global solidarity is nonetheless for several reasons possible and even crucial in the world to come.

For one thing, twentieth-century technologies for waging war—nuclear, chemical, and biological—are so dangerous that it is essential to make armed conflict unthinkable. One important way of doing that is to extend to the global limits of all humanity the kind of sympathetic understanding that makes, even today, the use of violence against members of one's own identity group—except under conditions of acute social decomposition—an atavistic remnant of crueler days.

For another, one of the major sources of future conflict, if humankind does not change course, is the geo-cultural divide between a wealthy Euro-American North and an impoverished Latin American, Asian, and African South. Redistributing the world's wealth in such a way as to bring the South close to the level of the North is a feasible and essential goal for the twenty-first century, but it is contingent on three conditions. First, North and South alike (though principally the North) will have to pay the costs of conversion to sustainable energy resources. This conversion will depend both on prioritizing research toward the improvement of wind, solar, and tidal sources of power and on a major reduction of those energy uses which are ecologically and socially destructive and unnecessary, such as the ubiquity of private automobiles. Second, redistribution will have to be accomplished in such a way that it does not lead to a backlash among the populations of the North. Third, there will have to be an expansion, through as much direct experience as possible, of the empathic basis for feelings of global human solidarity.

These matters are linked. An important indirect precondition for the sense of solidarity with global humanity is the elimination of class barriers within each identity group by the redistribution of wealth and by ensuring democratic participation in social, political, and economic decision making. This participation would certainly be made more feasible by reducing the economic and cultural gap—presently enormous even within the industrialized West—between rich and poor. The experience of nineteenth- and twentieth-century Europe shows that where, within the new nation-states, the middle class separated itself as a hegemonic class from the lower orders, it became phobic not only toward the proletariat but toward other nations and races and toward women and children; moreover, it developed pathological fears of nature itself and indeed (in conformity with the hypostatization of its separation from the common people into an exaggerated mind-body split) of its own body.[25] During the transitional phase, redistribution and a better social security net will thus have the benign side-effect of reducing xenophobic tendencies in the Euro-American working and lower middle classes, whose support for the anti-immigrant Right in the last decades of the twentieth century grew in direct proportion to the downsizing and deregulation that undermined their security and identity.

All these social preconditions for the attainment of a globally human allocentric perception depend on a universal satisfaction of basic needs, which, as I have indicated, will include not just material goods but free medical care, transportation, and education for all.

To insure the provision of medical care, there would necessarily be a program of sophisticated medical training, undertaken after the general educational curriculum described below. Those trained as doctors and dentists would be exempted from the requirement to participate in the global production process. If their total work life significantly exceeds that of the rest of the population, they might perhaps be compensated by being given more—or more attractive—living space.

The restructuring of transportation deserves special attention. Although getting around in private vehicles equipped with high-powered engines consumes a great part of the time and the budget of ordinary families and is a notorious source of CO_2 pollution in air as well as land travel, it is an area of contemporary existence which has received relatively little critical discussion.[26] Yet its contemporary form, the privately owned automobile, is simultaneously a crucially profitable area of corporate capitalism, an antisocial ideological trap for the car owners and users, and an environmental hazard more menacing to public health and human survival than tobacco. To drastically reduce the use of fossil fuels, it would be necessary to limit car and air travel and trucking to emergencies and special cases—until and unless nonpolluting forms of transport are devised. Transportation in local areas would be by freely provided bicycles, which have no ecological consequences, and where this is impossible (for reasons of distance, climate, topography, or the infirmity of the traveler), by gratis public transportation, principally in the shape of trams and rapid trains, for which, in the "social capitalist" phase preceding the transformation I envisage, an enlarged infrastructure would everywhere have been created. Improvement and maintenance of this infrastructure and of the vehicles operating within it would be a responsibility shared between the locality, the region, and the global system for production of necessary goods.

Educational goals, after universal schooling in literacy skills, would include curricula in four basic areas: (1) cultural awareness of the history of one's own identity groups and of its relatedness to other such groups in the world—based on a reformulation and integration of present university programs in the humanities and necessarily involving extensive experience of literature and other languages; (2) preparation for participation in democratic decision making, locally, regionally, and globally—an extension of the present study of social sciences; (3) preparation for participation in the global economy, through training in the natural sciences, mathematics, engineering, and computer programming (future doctors would receive a special curriculum weighted toward the biological sciences and chemistry, while everyone would follow a program in environmental studies); (4) training in the mastery of a particular artisanal trade, cultural discipline, or scientific activity, so that everyone will be equipped to contribute creatively to the local and regional culture as well as to participate in the global production of necessities.[27]

The ecological goals, which most people now agree are desirable, are maintenance of biodiversity and sustainability on our planet. Biodiversity will be based on a continual balancing of human needs against those of our natural environment. Clearly, where certain animal predators become a threat to human settlements or livestock, they need to be contained. On the other hand, practices motivated by human cupidity that threaten animal or plant species will be ended. Where humankind requires wood or other biological resources for its basic living standard or for craft economies, it will not remove more of a particular living thing than it can replace. Global agreements on fishing and agriculture will be elaborated from existing international efforts to maintain planetary balance. Sustainable energy supplies—solar, wind, and tidal resources—will become the only permissible ones, unless energy sources can be developed (liquid hydrogen, for example, or nuclear fusion) that do not produce toxic waste.

For the sake of both effective democratic decision making at a global level and the maintenance of a broad allocentric awareness of the infinite variety of human cultures, the educational system would prioritize the learning of languages. Since the nation-state, source of our present language structure, will have few functions in the future, the present tendency of a devolution of authority and education toward regional levels will probably continue, revitalizing ethnic languages and dialects. One would expect that in the future, the educational system will train citizens in the language and culture of their own region (for example, Breton, Provençal, Basque, Catalonian, Frisian, Welsh, Bayrisch), in the language and culture of the larger national group to which they are historically or linguistically affiliated (French, Spanish, German, English, Dutch), in another of the major languages spoken on their continent, and in one of the world languages understood by a minimum of, say, 300 million people (English, Spanish, Russian, and Chinese are the most obvious candidates).

Problems: Unequal Endowment, Corruption, and Criminality

I am aware that many of my proposals will seem impossibly idealistic to those aware of the potential for evil in the human animal. While—I repeat—the viewpoint outlined above is to be construed not as a blueprint but as a broad vision of a possible future, a number of practical questions are evident, and a preliminary answer to them is in order.

To start with the last point discussed, the system of education, it will no doubt appear to many that in positing the acquisition of multiple linguistic skills by everyone, as well as equality of training for economic and political decision making, I am setting impossibly high standards. Only a minority, they will say, can become fluent in three languages or more. And obviously there are differences in intelligence and temperament that equip some people to participate in the management of the global economy at a much more sophisticated level than others. Why not, then, reserve technical education (for the management and maintenance of the high-tech industrial and distribution centers) to the 10 to 20 percent of the population with the appropriate talents and IQs? This limitation, one might argue, would certainly permit a more efficient educational system and a better technology.

There are multiple problems with this "meritocratic" solution. For one thing, the same argument could be—and has been—used to oppose universal suffrage. Why indeed allow those of inferior intelligence to participate at all in political or social decision making? Of course, past arguments for a restricted suffrage have not been based openly on differences in intelligence, but rather on one's belonging to an economic or social (or gender!) elite that was held (by its publicists) to possess a civic intelligence absent in the less fortunate. The old liberal argument went that wealth gave one a stake in the commonwealth, which legitimized active participation in it. Although it may have been masked by the assumption that elite schooling and culture provided one with the wisdom to run the commonwealth, the criterion for participation in a restricted suffrage was usually little more than an income significantly greater than that of one's fellows.

Those who opposed this elitist suffrage did so for two reasons. The denial of an equal voice was culturally demeaning to the excluded. Moreover, the elite that arrogated decision-making power to itself may have claimed to be acting in the interest of all, but in fact its decisions usually benefited only its own class interest: most of the social and cultural policies adopted under such governments aimed at the perpetuation of class rule and the continued subservience of the lower orders. Normally the motives for schooling the children of the poor under such elitist regimes were providing some minimal skills for a low-level participation in the new industrial society and training workers to obey their class superiors. Proponents of political equality believed that only under universal suffrage would there be a realistic chance of using the educational system to raise the cultural and living standards of the poor, and they were right. Those masses who had been looked down upon for centuries as incapable of reasoning and governing themselves proved, when given the opportunity, quite capable of both.

Behind the meritocratic argument, then, is the old elitism of those who have "made it" and do not consider the mass of their compatriots as capable of doing so. In the United States it was not only the rich who used this argument, against the poor, but also the older WASP settlers, against every ethnic immigrant or racial minority in the country. All over the earth, it has long been used by wealthy and aristocratic elites against the peasantry, against the working poor, and, when the poor could no longer be excluded from full citizenship, against women. In European countries with a large population from Africa or the Middle East, it is now directed by the indigenous white population against immigrant outsiders, frequently Muslims.

In the twentieth century this elitism has often relied on biological theories of hereditary intelligence to justify class or racial oppression. In fact, however, intelligence and many other traits are powerfully subject to environmental conditions.[28] Stigmatized cultures of poverty, usually characterized by hopelessness, cynicism, and brutality, are terrible environments for learning. Poor family learning situations tend to be self-perpetuating, but the generational sequence can be broken. In most countries, simply an adequate knowledge of the national language by the children of immigrants has accelerated both integration and social ascent. Eliminating the sense of social exclusion that comes with impoverished backgrounds also improves the learning possibilities of the children of the poor. Certainly, there are a number of ethnic subcultures in the United States where a large part of the group has risen in two or three generations from the poor and illiterate status of non-English-speaking immigrants to the college-educated middle class. Giving children from culturally deprived backgrounds a good education may not in one generation produce a population as well equipped to handle the supervision of a high-tech economy and to participate actively in human affairs as young people from educated middle-class homes now seem to be, but there is no reason to think that this cannot be accomplished in two or three generations—at least if we prioritize it as a goal.

A second question is that of equal distribution of necessary goods, which is in principle a difficult but not an impossible matter. How could one ensure something close to the present variety of food, clothing, and housing? Distribution of entitlement tickets guaranteeing everyone a certain amount of food per month, clothing per year, and housing and appliances per lifetime would certainly be better than the "Comes the revolution, you'll eat strawberries and cream and like it" approach. What this amount would be, and how wide the variety, could be determined by public debate and referenda. One might expect that most goods would be produced either locally or in the larger economic region (Europe or North America or East Asia, for example), with global networks for the production and distribution of a limited number of desirable products that many regions may want but cannot themselves produce (coffee, tea, rice, bananas, wool, cotton, and rubber, for example).

Housing would be particularly difficult to distribute, since much of it would have to be redistributed from the existing urban supply. If we consider that living in central city areas is likely to be more attractive than in outlying areas, then there would have to be some kind of trade-off between size and location: those wishing more space than average would, except perhaps for doctors, generally live further out. Those who wanted the amenities of central locations would accept smaller quarters. A crucial criterion for the distribution of housing would be that all growing children have space of their own—perhaps minimally eight to ten square meters—in which to live, play, and do homework, much of which would require a home computer.

Decisions about town planning would also be primarily local. New housing might be planned (as often is the case, at least in Europe) by elected regional or local councils, but with an eye to demographic and social needs rather than commercial considerations. In contrast to the modernist separation of work and living that prevailed in most twentieth-century planning, neighborhood integration of homes, work space, schooling, associational life, cultural institutions, and health services would be on the order of the day, with abundant parkland and recreational facilities for young people nearby. In many local cultures (as in the more advanced ones today) municipal authorities would make space for cooperative or collective living as well as for single-sex couples or groups. While the future of the nuclear family is impossible to predict, the guaranteed living standard would obviate a part of its reason for being, and one might expect a significant increase in communal and sexual experimentation.

A third problem area is the political one: what will take the place of the democratically elected governments of nation-states, and how would one avoid the current problems of corrupt political machines and mafias? This subdivides into the questions of democratic decision making at the global, regional, and local levels, of enforcement powers and control of criminality, and of how to control the enforcers—balance of powers or direct democracy?

To begin with, while the direct democracy of assembled citizens may be able to settle many questions locally, and referenda resolve other matters regionally or globally, there would have to be a stratification of legislative, executive, and judicial organs at all three levels. Maintaining existing principles of checks and balances between different branches of government would no doubt help to curtail tendencies toward autocratic or inquisitorial tyranny, but equally important for preventing both machine politics and bureaucratic autonomy would be the principle of rotation. With a better-schooled population trained in self-governance from childhood on, a population in which social equality prevailed, participation in governance at any level could be as much a civic obligation as jury duty now is in those nations with a jury system. Perhaps a combination of democratically elected members of a global parliament—some elected directly, some appointed by lesser legislative bodies—with those chosen by rotation from the general population would insure against ossification and machine politics. Similarly, bureaucratic positions might be filled on a two-year basis by rotation from the large pool of the population with minimal administrative skills.

The level of governance at which particular kinds of legislative and executive decisions might be taken—global, regional, or local—would be debated and decided in much the same way as in Europe today jurisdictions are determined between the European Union level, the national level, and the provincial or the municipal level; or in the United States, between federal, state, county, and local ones.

Much of the economic, political, and cultural decision making could be done locally by direct participation of those concerned in town meetings or, indirectly, by elected city councils. Take the question of food production and consumption. Most of the food consumed would be grown and prepared locally—grain and bread, for example, or milk products, fruits, vegetables, and meats—and the quantities and varieties to be produced would be decided democratically, after considerable local debate, either by consensus or in referenda. Areas whose locally grown food was insufficient for a minimum health standard (one comparable to the European one, with an average of fifty grams of meat or fish per person per day)[29] would automatically receive the necessary supplement from the regional or global level. A particular kind of food from outside the area would be obtained if a certain (low) percentage of local people petitioned for it—perhaps a half of one percent in an area numbering at least a hundred thousand people.

For decisions concerning regional or global production and distribution—both of food and of all other consumption goods—citizens' debates and referenda could be effectively maintained through an expansion of the current global infrastructure of Internet communication. Considering that everyone would be schooled in at least one, and hopefully more than one, of the world languages, there would be a broad linguistic base for these debates, and computers might come equipped with a translation program that would render contributions from an unmastered world language comprehensible to all. At a certain point, of course, debates would have to be closed and referenda held: what that point might be would be one of the first subjects of Internet and local assembly discussions.

The same procedures would apply to the allocation of scarce resources for necessary scientific research or production based on it, for example, in the area of pharmaceuticals. Weighing the desirability and feasibility of democratic control against the decision-making control and expertise of the researchers themselves is something that will have to be worked out in practice. Certainly the basic directions of research cannot be left to the specialists alone, and one can foresee considerable public debate over the guidelines given to medical researchers regarding the focus of their research and their freedom to initiate, within the framework of such guidelines, their own programs. The result of such debates, decided either through referenda or through a global legislature, will probably never be satisfying to everyone engaging in it. Yet, consensus on most issues involving a sizable group of people is always difficult; at a certain point, debate will have to be followed by Internet voting for competing proposals.

Skeptical readers will no doubt wonder how this intricate global system will cope with those whose dissent from established norms and rules takes the form of criminal transgression, even to the extent of mafia formations, or of communities inspired by fundamentalist convictions to subjugate their neighbors. Answers to this will have to cover several problem areas: one is the global limitation of and control over the means of violence: weaponry. Another is the specific policing agencies for tracking and apprehending criminals, and the limitations on such agencies. A third is a judicial system for judging suspects and meting out punishment. Before entering any of these questions, one general comment on the problem of criminal transgression: the provision of a humane and generous living standard to all will remove the major source of crime today: cultures of poverty. But it will not end the criminality that arises from personalities twisted by early trauma into antisocial revenge scenarios. Nor will it eliminate the possibility of fundamentalist cults immune to an allocentric ethic. For the reduced but persisting criminal activity related to these latter two sources, some system of coercive reform will remain necessary.

Disarmament, both at the national and the individual level, will of course be one of the first general protocols to be accepted by the coming global social order. Guns, apart from a limited quantity of individually licensed hunting guns, which would be kept in local communal depots when not in use, would not be available to private persons, to say nothing of armaments above the level of handguns and rifles; the latter would be restricted to regional or global police forces. Chemical and biological laboratories would be under strict global supervision to prevent their covert use for manufacturing weaponry.

Police forces, considerably reduced by comparison with present numbers, would exist at regional and global levels, for the enforcement of laws promulgated at these levels. To prevent their becoming collecting points for authoritarian and sadistic personalities, they would be staffed by draftees chosen by a lottery from the local population for a limited period—perhaps eighteen or twenty-four months. Their members would require, as now, judicial warrants for any transgression of privacy, and their behavior would be closely monitored by citizens' groups delegated by global and regional authorities to prevent unnecessary violence.

Justice would be swift and humane. The death penalty would be uniformly outlawed as barbaric, but so would our present system of incarceration, a breeding ground of sexual torment and hardened criminality. The aim of justice would not be punishment, but the prevention of recidivism. This might be accomplished by the subjection of criminal personalities or groups to reeducation programs in farms and workshops, to training in sensitivity to others, and, wherever necessary, to extensive therapy. But, as now, suspects will be presumed innocent until proven guilty. Judges will be elected for a nonrenewable term of no more than four years. Before they can announce their candidacies, however, they will have to pass examinations certifying to their knowledge of the law and their equanimity. Juries will be chosen, as they now are in many systems, from the general population.

The Historical Foundations of Social Justice

There are, of course, more fundamental political objections that will be raised to my ideas. What I am proposing in this chapter amounts to a radical abolition of the existing property and market systems, which many will view as either utterly unrealistic or as a potentially disastrous return to "command economy" thinking associated with the worst abuses of Soviet Communism. It is neither. To the contrary, it is historically realistic, in two senses.

In the first place, it is simply a recognition and a humanization of the process of rationalization which Max Weber believed, at the beginning of the twentieth century, to be the metahistorical red thread of human, and especially, Western historical development. Weber saw this rationalization as permeating all areas of human activity—political, economic, religious, intellectual-scientific, cultural—in a double sense. There was an increasing tendency toward instrumental rationality in all these areas, and an increasing centralization of activity. Both rationalization and centralization were indispensable to the development of democracy and social justice.

The process of centralization was visible, for example, in the gradual curtailment, within the developing state systems, of the feudal aristocracy's military and political autonomy, and in the gradual subordination of religious to secular authority. Most historians are aware that for roughly a thousand years before A.D. 1500, armies were in principle private affairs, hired out occasionally by more or less powerful feudal aristocrats to monarchs with sufficient funds to buy their services, and that it was a long and hard struggle by centralizing princes to disarm the barons and dukes of their realms. One might also argue that the slow rise of democracy—rule by the majority, judged to know its own interests—represents a rationalization of political power, premised on the assumption of fundamental human equality and on the relatively recent argument that it is irrational to permit birth to be a criterion for political and economic power.

My proposal merely extends these historical trends to the economic sphere. If private—feudal—ownership of the means of coercion could be abolished in the modern state system under the principle that social peace could only be assured if the state monopolized the legitimate use of force, then private ownership of the means of production and distribution of essential goods can be abolished for comparable reasons of social justice and ecological equilibrium. Just as the basic challenge of modern political thought—and the motor of many national revolutions—has been the democratization and rationalization of the state apparatus, the motor of contemporary and future revolutions will be the democratization and rationalization of the means of production.

Comparison to the command economies of the defunct Soviet empire is in this context an impermissible red herring. The command economy developed by Stalinism was developed not to humanize abundance but to build a power base for Communist Party elites that would enable them to defend themselves against and compete economically with Western capitalism. The Stalinist system hid its ruthless exploitation of a forcibly collectivized peasantry and of slave labor in extraction industries behind a facade of Promethean work values (Stakhanovism) and cradle-to-grave welfare provisions for the urban working class it claimed to represent, but the function of its command economy was simply the most rapid possible accumulation of capital in order to create the infrastructure of the single party that ran state and economy alike. Repressing protest as counterrevolutionary, and as indifferent to the environmental impact of rapid industrialization as Western market capitalism, it produced one ecological disaster after another. Designed to transform a peripheral, premodern economy into a major competitor of the capitalist West, that system is best characterized as totalitarian state capitalism. Its point of departure was one of the most brutal and backward political economies in Europe, one that had ruled by the cossack's knout until 1917 and had abolished serfdom only two generations earlier.

By contrast, my proposal for domesticating and humanizing an out-of-control economic apparatus is projected at the highest level of an already existing information technology and is based on the goal of ecological restoration and the democratic values of social justice and equality. Both the political and the economic transcendence of capitalism will depend on the democratic utilization of the new Internet communications as well as of the computerized and automated high-tech production processes that are eliminating most of the stupefying, brute labor of past millennia.

Change never occurs in a vacuum, and it cannot occur in monolithic civilizations supported by fanatic conviction. Until, of course, the system begins to crack and the conviction to fragment. That disintegration is a matter of internal dynamics, which, sooner or later, has afflicted all civilizations, from ancient Egypt to the Chinese empires that persisted until this century. As in the case of the Roman empire, it may be followed by prolonged cultural and social decline. One cannot exclude the possibility that the present social and ecological wall before the future may prove permanent, that we have gone too far down the road of reckless squandering of the planet's resources and that the future, if there is one, will be grim indeed. But there is reason to think that this degradation of the human condition is not the only possibility.

Human solidarity and creativity, symbolized by the altruistic genius of the Greek god Prometheus, have in the past eliminated many seemingly eternal sources of human misery, overcome absolutist old regimes, feudal tyranny, and, at least in a part of the world, much of the disease, fear, and hunger that earlier made our lives brutish and short; it has led us, with many zigzags, to our present dangers and possibilities. This progress has depended on the conjunction of three active forces: human reason, the social passion to change inhuman circumstance, and, often forgotten, the radical use of new technologies.

It is arguable that the development of information technology will offer the same opportunities for an improvement of the human condition that the invention of printing did in the premodern and modern eras, and on the same scale. Printing was probably the key to the permanent breakup of a corrupt and hierarchical western Christianity in the sixteenth century and of absolutism in the seventeenth through nineteenth centuries. Numerous reform movements to purify the church and clergy had emerged in medieval Christianity from the tenth century on, but they had all been either co-opted, crushed, or completely marginalized until the Lutheran Reformation, whose plea for a priesthood of all believers could be supported by the circulation to Luther's followers both of the translated Bible and of a flood of anti-Roman pamphlets in the new print medium.[30]

The zigzags I have referred to are obvious in the uses to which print—as well as most other modernist technologies—have been put in the past five centuries. Certainly, they confirmed as well as undermined dogmatic belief. The printing of the word of God showed everyone the only true path, at the same time that it undermined the unquestioned authority of the church hierarchy. From the standpoint of mentalities, print culture was both an important tool for the civilizing mission in the struggle of bourgeois and Christian elites to suppress orally transmitted popular cultures and, in the nineteenth century, a means for historians and ethnologists to preserve the vanishing oral lore. Moreover, the printing press, before it significantly undermined traditional authority, provided the infrastructure of absolutism, enabling absolute princes to codify and circulate administrative decrees. Yet, in the same way that in the sixteenth century religious transcendence of a corrupt Christianity developed through the new medium of the printed word, the philosophical transcendence of feudal absolutism in the high Enlightenment depended on the illegal flow of bootlegged books and pamphlets across the borders of pre-revolutionary France.[31] The part of the new print technology used for transgressive literature grew in the nineteenth century to include treatises, essays, novels, and poetry that undermined not only the economic principles but the social morality and sexual repressions of the new middle-class holders of power. Every revolution from the proto-bourgeois English one of the seventeenth century to the antibourgeois "almost revolution" of 1968 has been prepared, sustained, and debated through a flood of pamphlets, manifestos, and petitions in a medium that did not exist before 1450.

Information technology has until now been used primarily to cut wage costs in the production and distribution sectors of market capitalism by making large numbers of workers superfluous. It has also been used to achieve instant transmission of information by businesses and governments.

But the same technology is being used by groups and individuals exchanging—or making freely available—information and ideas that have nothing to do with commodity transactions: information and ideas that can augment knowledge, sensitivity, and power among those completely opposed to the present commodification of everything.

The use of the Internet to organize global movements and demonstrations, supplemented though it may be by a great deal of face-to-face organizing, is simply the prelude to the future use of this instrument to organize global democratic debate and political participation. Even at the level of production, the information technology that now provides the infrastructure for neoliberal globalization can be used in a future, more reasonable, world to assure us all a secure supply of life's necessities, without the nagging fear that we are making the planet uninhabitable for future generations. So that we can get on with the important thing: lives based on reflection, personal creativity of all sorts, and human compassion.

Against Despair

We need a European constitution to give a voice to European citizens. The construction of Europe lends itself to the social forces opposed to liberal globalization just as the construction of a welfare state was used by earlier progressive forces against the omnipotence of the market. We can only be truly social and ecological today if we are truly European. To make Europe loved, we must define a Europe worthy of being loved.

ALAIN LIPIETZ, member of the European
Parliament for Les Verts

THIS BOOK STEMS FROM the perception that a double crisis, fueled by the corporate economy now dominating the world, enshadows the future of humankind. Looming ecological disasters, engendered by consumer capitalism's fetishizing of growth and power, menace the continuance of our species. And massive inequalities, exacerbated by the post-Fordist system of production that underlies consumer capitalism—unprecedented wealth for a few, based on the increasing precariousness and declining income of the many—shatter hopes for a more just existence. Moreover, revolutions thought to demolish inhuman tyrannies have so often led to new enslavements of spirit and body that today, as in the early nineteenth century, most of those who once believed in radical transformation are pessimistic.

My intent in writing has been to break through this pessimism by means of an examination of what has gone wrong, and, by drawing on the history of ideas and culture, to explore the overt resistance to neoliberal corporatism and the hidden potentialities for change in contemporary society. More specifically, my purpose has been to work out a possible link between past, present, and future—a sketch for a new utopia—through an exploration of the sense of human potentiality suggested in the psychoanalytic theory of Ernest Schachtel. Unhappily, most of the modernist ideologies that end in the worship of power and technology, source of our present impasse, lay claim to the mantle of Prometheus, perverting or obliterating the implications of the Titan's self-sacrifice and resistance to divine tyranny. Schachtel's work, in my analysis, provides a theoretical basis for an alternative, nontechnological main current of modernity that I define as "the other Prometheus"— the liberated Prometheus of the poet Shelley.

Shelley was one of the small tribe of those who, defying the Reaction that triumphed over the French Revolution, continued to maintain their faith in the potential liberation of our species. His was a difficult time for those who believed in revolutionary transformation. Two centuries later, such belief is even more problematic. Yet, echoes of this hope for liberation recur in much of the critical social thought and in many of the social movements that have confronted the bleak ruins of progressive modernity in the past hundred years. Schachtel's critical psychoanalysis provides a theoretical framework both for a disenchanted analysis of our world of institutionalized egoism and for reasoned hope in a potential *ricorso* to that "other Prometheus." Like those of the Frankfurt School with which Schachtel was connected, his theories are powerful evidence that the rationality that broke through in the European Enlightenment did not necessarily have to degenerate either into the instrumental rationality of liberal capitalism or into the willed irrationality of much modern philosophy.

The problem that has plagued those who expected radical social movements to rid humankind of its despots and propertied parasites is that, where victorious, such movements invariably have fallen into ideological and institutional straightjackets that have crushed their creativity and soured the hope of those who had sacrificed for them. This has been true of the Protestant Reformation, the source of the Weberian metaphor of the iron cage. It has also been true of the French revolutionary republicanism of 1793, a seedbed of both nationalism and socialism. And it applies to those noxious blends of Marxism and Asiatic despotism, the Russian and Chinese revolutions, which led their adherents into totalitarian nightmares. The consumerist ideology that is all-powerful today—the latest incarnation of liberal capitalist modernity and, for its proponents, a new realm of Promethean freedom—cultivates pure acquisitiveness, dogmatic mistrust of social control, and indifference to any future beyond tomorrow's stock quotations. Survivor of the hecatomb of modernist ideologies of the last century, its success in circulating the commandment of work-own-consume-and-invest beyond the confines of interested capitalists has made it the immediate source of the ecological and social catastrophes that undermine our future.

That ideals degrade once they are transformed into ideology, and that victorious movements ossify once institutionalized, are common perceptions today, as is the notion that most of the important movements, ideologies, and institutions of modernity suffered from a major discrepancy between their exalted ends and the feeble social and material means available to realize them. All this is spectacularly evident in the movements emanating from the French Revolution. Democratic nationalism, for example, assumed, on the one hand, a political equality of citizens that the social *in*equalities of the class societies supporting such nationalisms contradicted, and, on the other, an equality and mutual respect between nations that was out of touch with the geopolitical realities of the age. Choked off by the febrility of the "springtime of nations"—the failed democratic nationalist uprisings of 1848—this idealism terminated in imperialist nationalism, which in turn produced the jingoism, obsessive racism, and mutual slaughter of two world wars.

In attempting to oppose such massacres and end exploitation, socialism and communism both ascribed Promethean qualities to serflike proletarians. But the working classes of Central Europe and Russia which, in the apocalypse of war and total misery, empowered revolutionary parties promising bread and freedom, were quickly lashed to the new elites' drive for industrial power, a condition hardly better than that which they had left behind. Marx's idea of the proletariat as agent of revolutionary change turned out to be wishful thinking: only a stratum that came from outside the dominant socioeconomic order (a stratum like the bourgeoisie in relation to feudalism, but not one that, like the working class, was a subordinate part of capitalism) might be capable of establishing a fundamentally different society. In any case, Marx's view of history—which was that socialism could take the place of capitalism only when capitalism itself had fully developed—was continually being gutted of its utopian potential by the Marxist parties themselves: the socialists ended up with a complete acceptance of the growth imperative of consumerist capitalism, the communists with nothing more than a state capitalism designed to compete with the private variety.

Thus has capitalism devoured its antagonists. Even the revolutionary aesthetics of modernist culture, from romanticism to expressionism, surrealism, and their various inheritors of the 1960s and 1970s, have been instrumentalized into vehicles of kitsch, useful for selling everything from soap to computers and designer clothing.

I am aware that this book has, until its last chapter, been more concerned with the historical journey than with the future destination, and that in my summary suggestion of what that destination might be I have emphasized the material frameworks—economic and political—rather than their cultural and spiritual contents. This is paradoxical, since I am aware that these contents inevitably will develop on the basis of existing and past cultures, to the study of which I have devoted my life. Yet those material frameworks—and the ideological obstacles to their development in a humane and rational direction—appear to be too important, too formative to ignore.

The various obstacles to any development toward an ecologically sound and socially just world have been made abundantly evident in the important events of the past two years.

In 2000, the reactions of the peoples of the industrialized world to a sharp rise in oil prices, the renewal of fanatical ethnic and religious hatreds between Israelis and Palestinians, the revolution that toppled the Serbian despot Slobodan Milosevic, and the installation in the United States of the most conservative government since Ronald Reagan—all these events showed the entrenched character of obsolete mentalities as well as the hopelessness of the ideological solutions offered by the power-oriented modernity that has evolved since the French Revolution.

In 2001, terrorist attacks on the United States threw its people into a patriotic panic and assured overwhelming support to what the government billed as a war on terrorism and what more sober spirits understood to be a war to secure U.S. access to Middle Eastern and Caspian Sea oil reserves.

The shortage of oil, which is chronic and which now and in the future will push up the cost of heating homes and operating motor vehicles, is actually a blessing in disguise for the human species. Those concerned with posterity are fully aware that unless there is a fairly rapid and radical turn away from fossil fuels, the greenhouse effect caused by their use will lead to ever greater climatological disasters: a heightening of global wind velocities and temperatures and a larger number of violent storms will lead to ever greater damage to crops, people, and wooded areas (like the French storms at the end of 1999, which, apart from killing about a hundred people, eliminated half the forests in central France), to flooding of low-lying coastal areas as a result of melting polar ice, and to the endangering of arctic animal species.

In this context, oil shortages, whatever difficulties they may cause in the short term, are our long-term salvation, inasmuch as the higher price of oil will make alternative energy sources competitive and desirable. A few decades ago, this would have meant nuclear energy, but Chernobyl, successive scandals about leakage of radiation from "safe" reactors in the West, and a growing awareness of the dangers of storing radioactive waste anywhere on the planet have led to fierce resistance to any spread of nuclear energy.[1] Greens in a number of European governments have obtained commitments for the eventual termination of dependence on nuclear power.

The real alternative to fossil fuels today is renewable energy from the sun, the winds, and the tides. The opinion makers and governments are fully aware of this situation. Indeed, ecologically conscious governments in Europe have for some years been imposing ecological taxes on fuel both to pressure manufacturers into producing more efficient cars and heating systems and to persuade their citizens to use public transportation. If the peoples— and the major parties—of Europe and North America had not been brainwashed by multibillion-dollar automobile advertising, supported by consumerist ideologies of brainless acquisitiveness, the oil price rise of 2000 would have been the moment for the European Union to announce and implement a rapid expansion of collective public transportation, based on a sober evaluation of the price we pay for our current enslavement to the internal combustion engine.

Any accountancy survey calculating the probable ecological and social cost of continuing in our present path over the next generation would show the long-term wisdom of such a shift, whatever the bill. But the prevailing neoliberal ideology, given muscle by pressures from banks and investors, has tabooed this sort of measure as Keynesian, indeed socialist, interference with the market economy. So instead, social-democratic governments fearful for their popularity quickly caved into the fall 2000 Poujadist uprising of indignant, road-blocking auto and truck drivers, and cut the eco-taxes on transportation fuel drastically.

Fear for a further rise in oil prices was also behind the European and American frenzy to prevent a new Middle Eastern war in October 2000. Not particularly sensitive to the suffering of ten million Palestinians and Jews in a new war that might result from the unleashing of fundamentalist and nationalist extremism on both sides, a war that might destroy all hope of a peaceful future for a generation, global capitalism realized that Arab unity behind the Palestinians could be disastrous for the world economy if it took the form of the kind of oil embargo that accompanied the Yom Kippur War of 1973, or even if it resulted in the temporary sharp increase of oil prices that occurred during the Gulf War of 1991. After five years of unprecedented economic expansion and a bull market on their exchanges, the corporations that work closely with the governments of the industrialized world were witnessing a decline in profits and expansion which, partly manipulated by central bank interest rate increases, had led to a volatile downward trend in world markets. Many feared this downward trend could expand into a major crash if a steep rise in oil prices—the principal economic weapon of the major Arab nations—should fuel a rapid inflation, since the latter would necessitate further interest hikes in a period of economic slowdown.[2]

Joint examination of, on the one hand, the industrial nations' dependency on oil, which underlay their frantic efforts to prevent a new war between Israel and its neighbors, and, on the other, the nationalist hatreds behind the explosive violence in the Middle East and in the Balkans reveals the obsolescence of all the ideologies of modernity. The nationalist hatred and religious fanaticism both in Israel/Palestine and in the former Yugoslavia represented the continuation of the nationalist wave that crested in Europe in the nineteenth and early twentieth centuries, now extending into a period in which Western elites, for their own self-preservation, have abjured the messianic nationalism that produced two world wars, and in which the nation-state itself is succumbing to the pressures of global capitalism.[3]

In Serbia we witnessed under Milosevic the unacknowledged transformation of one bankrupt ideology—the Titoist variant on Stalinism—into an equally obsolete (if admittedly more popular) one: ethnic nationalism. After the Kosovo War, the Serbs, partly in the name of resistance to political despotism and partly because of the material hardship that resulted from their leadership's defiance of the world in its treatment of its Albanian minority, deserted Milosevic and his hybrid ideology, but without renouncing ethnic nationalism. Their democratic revolution, spurred by Milosevic's refusal to recognize the election of the opposition's candidate, was genuine, and deserves the respect owing to all nations which, delegitimizing despotic regimes, rise against army and secret police. Nonetheless, their prospects—like those of every people emerging from Soviet totalitarianism in the last decade—remain grim, since awaiting them, after the democratic nationalist euphoria has subsided, is nothing better than the carrot of consumer society and the stick of global capitalism, with its downsizing, deregulation, privatization, and dismantling of welfare provisions. If they are reluctant to implement this program, they will soon be informed by their elites that the aid packages they receive to rebuild the infrastructure shattered by the bombs of 1999 are contingent on it.

The turn of events in the United States since the elections of November 2000 similarly confirm the main theses of this book. As usual, about half of the electorate, unable to distinguish clearly between the Democratic and Republican Parties on the issues that affected their daily lives, did not vote. The two and a half million votes cast for a Green Party candidate (Ralph Nader), who did represent a serious alternative, were held responsible for the installation of Bush the Second and the advent of his neo-Reaganism, although most of those votes came from people who would have refused to vote anyway, and the only really enfranchised voters, in the face of Gore's popular majority and the shenanigans of George W's brother in Florida, turned out to be nine members of the Supreme Court.

In any case, there was little practical difference between the predictable policies of both candidates on the gut social, economic, and ecological issues. Both men supported neoliberal free-trade policies that have accentuated the existing inequalities between poor and rich both globally and within the United States. And despite Gore's rhetoric on ecological matters, he would, after putting the country to sleep with a long speech about how sad it was that the Senate was unanimously opposed to the Kyoto treaty on greenhouse gas reductions, have acquiesced in principle to the same anti-environmental policies now so "energetically" pursued by George the Second. Public opinion polls, which have showed massive public support for "all the environmentally friendly stuff [Vice President] Cheney derides— more conservation, investment in wind and solar power and fuel cells,"[4] would have been no more effective under Gore in swaying the votes of senators dependent for their election funds on oil producers and oil-hungry heavy industry than it is today under Bush.

To sum up: In all five of these cases—the oil scare, the related crisis in the Middle East, the latest turn of Balkan nationalism, the power grab, in both senses, of the conservative Right in the United States, and the post–cold war "war on terrorism"—the bankruptcy of the now hegemonic ideologies and institutions is evident. They all require new approaches from the powers controlling the industrialized heartlands, approaches which can unblock the future. I have indicated in the last two chapters why I believe such new approaches to be a practical possibility (if not a short-term likelihood) only in the framework of a Social Europe, a concept which has been discussed for nearly a decade. By this framework, I understand a Europe more united than it now is, united on the basis of a democratically elected executive and a parliament with legislative power to control the European economy. And as the foundation of such a Europe I understand a charter not simply of human but of *social, political, and ecological* rights, so as to provide its citizens with a realistic perspective of social justice, growing equality and participation in state and economy, and a sustainable environment.[5]

Only from within such a framework can realistic policies for the protection of Europe's working people and for conversion to sustainable energy sources be implemented. Only from within such a framework can realistic alternatives to neoliberal globalization on the American model be developed, can major programs of assistance to developing countries be drafted, including those in the Middle East, with the serious goal of saving lives and cultures rather than immolating both on the altar of multinational corporations. A Europe thus conscious of its social identity and willing to play an independent role in international affairs can, moreover, exert pressure on the United States itself, at the very least to accept the responsibility of a country that is more culpable than any other for creating the double wall before the future, to break down that wall, to rebuild its automobile- and growth-obsessed culture in such a way as to give future generations the chance to breath without oxygen masks. Finally, perhaps, within the broader concept of human solidarity symbolized by such a Social Europe we can begin to focus in practical terms on the full transcendence of technological growth-fetishism by the "other Prometheus," a Shelleyan Prometheus of human communities made sufficiently secure by the rational use of global technology to devote themselves to the integration of nature, human sociability, and the creative arts.

Notes from a Hijacked Planet

With all due respect to President Bush, the people of the world do not have to choose between the Taliban and the US government. All the beauty of human civilisation—our art, our music, our literature—lies beyond these two fundamentalist poles.

ARUNDHATI ROY, "War Is Peace"

For some time I had had the feeling of being on a hijacked plane. It was called Earth, and the pilots were the elites and opinion makers who rule and brainwash the peoples of the world. While imagining they were taking us with them to a paradise of ever increasing productivity and power—the economically correct version of Promethean prosperity—they were actually flying us all to destruction, ecologically, socially, and humanly. My only hope lay in the fact that increasing numbers of my fellow hostages seemed to be contesting this apocalyptic course.

Since September 11, 2001, the world has had a second set of mad hijackers to worry about, the kind that could seize passenger airliners, symbols of a mass tourism many of us saw as problematic, and, with a hundred tons of aviation fuel in the tanks, slam them into other symbols, huge structures where tens of thousands of human beings were working. Presumably, these latter were deemed to bear responsibility for Western domination and the exploitation of non-Western peoples. That most of those incinerated bore no responsibility for the suffering, that a good many were as victimized socially as the Islamic masses in whose name this atrocity was committed, that indeed a considerable fraction of the victims were themselves Muslims, seems to have been irrelevant to the perpetrators. The symbolism of destroying presumed nerve centers of "Satanic" U.S. commerce and military power appeared to be the only issue they, and those driven by misery, ignorance, and hatred to support them, were concerned with.

My initial reaction to the disasters of September 11 was thus a mixture of horror at the immolation of thousands of innocent human beings and profound pessimism for the future of humankind. If my sentiment was correct that the planet had long been hijacked by those now presenting themselves as aggrieved defenders of freedom and democracy, the net effect of the new tragedy had been, after several years of a swelling mutiny by unwilling passengers, to reinstate in all their awful glory the captains of the doomed airliner Earth. And to the extent that those captains catered to xenophobic cries for vengeance against the Islamic world, we were in greater jeopardy than ever.

The escalating protests against capitalist globalization before September 11 were undertaken by groups opposed to the infliction of neoliberal hegemony on the third world. They were often motivated by compassion for the fate of non-Western "others" whose suffering, the protesters felt, was beyond the ken of a corporate ideology concerned only with the expansion of trade and productivity. But the terrorists, who also claimed to act on behalf of the victims of Western hegemony, had no compassion for their own "others." They confronted their enemies in a no-man's-land of absolute evil where the reality of other human beings disappeared no less categorically than it did in the mental world of the powers their terror was directed against. Presumably acting in the name of oppressed Islam, the suicide bombers displayed an inability to see or feel anything beyond their own identities and interests. In this sense, the attacks demonstrated the common denominator of the attacker and the system attacked. In other words, third-world fundamentalists, originating in an earlier phase of the historical juggernaut of modernity, claimed to oppose the U.S. hegemony they held responsible for the world's misery, but in fact they shared with that power a bone-chilling indifference to human suffering.[1]

Outside of the strange world of publicity for the hijackers' local constituencies—a world of images and sound bites that the hijackers shared with some of their victims—the inhuman transformation of jetliners into artisanal weapons of mass destruction seemed at first glance to have been spectacularly counterproductive. It created an unprecedented sheen of martyrdom for the country attacked and its destroyed symbols, and it gave a sudden, unquestioned authority to those who had been systematically misleading and manipulating the victims of the attack.[2] It led directly to a war against the Taliban leaders of Afghanistan, resulting in thousands of further deaths of innocent civilians. From the terrorists' standpoint, however, the aggressiveness of the American response may have been exactly what they sought to provoke, since nothing brought the supporters of Bin Laden closer to power in nuclear-armed Pakistan than the stream of photos of martyred Afghan children.

So the terrorists were successful in their aim of polarizing the world. Coming at the cost of death and destruction for the American and the Afghan peoples, such polarization not only produced a surge of popularity in the Muslim world for the Al Qaeda network, but it benefited the attacked American power as well. For the murderous assault on U.S. symbols and people was a great boon to George Bush's beleaguered right-wing administration. Just before September 11, nearly every major aspect of Bush's program had been in trouble. The Democrats had taken control of the Senate and were threatening to block the missile shield, the energy proposals, the privatization of social security, and many other measures. Anti-globalization protesters, after making the headlines in Seattle, Washington, Prague, Quebec, Gothenburg, and Genoa, were gearing up for the largest radical demonstration since the 1970s in Washington at the end of September (against a meeting of the IMF and World Bank).

After September 11, however, the U.S. anti-globalization movement went into a state of suspended animation. Even before the World Bank and the IMF announced the cancellation of the September 2001 Washington meeting, the main protest organization called off its demonstrations. On the very morning of the attack, the first of an announced series of full-page articles on the new anticapitalism had appeared in the *Financial Times*. It was reflective and generally favorable to the protesters. The remainder of the series was scrapped in favor of page-long articles on the "Assault on America."[3] Recapitulating the movement's abrupt disappearance, a single piece in the *Financial Times* some ten days later had the character of an obituary.

In American politics, the rally-round-the-president mood and flag-waving created a situation in which even the relatively mild resistance to Bush's policies from liberal Democrats became temporarily unthinkable. Despite a Democratic majority in the Senate, the most right-wing administration since Ronald Reagan could count on bipartisan support for a $1.3 trillion tax cut favoring wealthy corporations and for an anti-ecological, anti–civil liberties, and anti–public regulation program that had been little more than a reactionary utopia on September 10. Moreover, less than two months after the attacks, "nobody noticed" (in the words of the *Guardian*'s Simon Tisdall)[4] that the United States, Russia, and China were on the point of reaching agreement on Bush's Star Wars plan (contested by Democrats before those attacks)—this despite the certainty that it could do nothing against the kind of terrorism just suffered by the American people and that its abrogation of the ABM treaty was certain to create a new nuclear arms race. Anticorporate demonstrators in Europe and America, realizing the danger to world peace, indeed to all the peoples of the world, of the Bush government's tendency to manipulate public fear into a war psychosis and a police state, quickly metamorphosed into an antiwar movement that attempted to restrain the demand for revenge of the American government and a considerable majority of the American people. Demonstrations of tens of thousands of worried Europeans were echoed by similar ones in the United States, culminating in a combined antiwar, anti-globalization, and pro-Palestinian demonstration in April 2002 that attracted 75,000 participants to Washington, D.C. Moreover, at the meeting of the World Social Forum in Pôrto Alegre in February 2002, more than 50,000 individuals and representatives of social movements and NGOs—roughly three times as many as the preceding year—gathered to discuss alternatives to the plans of global corporate elites, who were meeting at that moment in the World Economic Forum in New York City.[5]

In Europe, opposition to free-market capitalism recovered from the shock of September 11 more quickly than in the United States. Demonstrators were particularly active against European implementation of neoliberal ideology. In December 2001, 100,000 trade unionists and about 25,000 adherents of radical groups hostile to corporate globalization demonstrated in Brussels against neoliberal projects of the European Union. On March 16, 2002, Catalonian militants against neoliberalism assembled 300,000–500,000 Europeans, mostly Spanish, to protest at a European Union top in Barcelona. In April, plans by the right-wing Berlusconi government to privatize much of Italy's public sector provoked a one-day general strike that brought a million and a half trade unionists to a monster demonstration in Rome.

I write this in June 2002. It is not yet clear if the "war against terrorism" will be a short-term stratagem or a long-term strategy, expandable to Iraq and other miscreant states. There is questioning of its means as well as its purposes, in halls of parliaments as well as in the general public throughout the world. The direction of public opinion, particularly in the United States, will, of course, depend on whether the present anxiety about new forms of terrorism, encouraged by constant warnings from the Bush administration, deepens in coming months or subsides, if and when the warnings prove baseless.

The longer-term implications of the attack are in any case beginning to emerge, clarifying many of the basic issues its immediate impact obscured, strengthening the antithesis many of those in the anticorporate movement had felt between "their" vision and "ours." For one thing, the attack has given the corporate-political Right a new lease on life, at a moment when the confident neoliberal ideology of the 1990s—privatization and deregulation on a global scale, the recession-proof "new economy," permanent expansion—was collapsing into bear market pessimism. Exchanging overnight the post–cold war triumphalism of Fukuyama's "end of history" for Samuel Huntington's "clash of civilizations," the ideologues of American conservatism, from Henry Kissinger to Donald Rumsfeld, are now preaching a more or less permanent war on terrorism, which translates the old idea of an ever expanding economy into the notion of an ever spreading state of war, terror, and insecurity.

No doubt, the overt justification for this hawkishness lies in the traditional concern of Western foreign policy in the Middle East: securing oil supplies for a Euro-American corporate culture hooked on automobiles, tourism, and ever-improved gadgetry, and in danger of going into shock if deprived of its daily dose of consumption.[6] The permanent military engagement necessary to this security has, of course, terrible implications for the future of civil liberties in the West, bringing into focus the conditions of fear and totalitarian control prophesied by Orwell in 1984. But it also may resolve, in the manner familiar to those who noticed the about-face from deregulation to bailout whenever a part of the banking system threatened to go under, the problem of deepening recession. A war Keynesianism underlies the return of the military-industrial complex: $15 billion to near-bankrupt airlines, $30 billion for a new fighter aircraft awarded to Lockheed, a huge handout to the aerospace industry for Star Wars, and an even greater one, in the form of tax cuts, to corporate America are only the beginning. According to the *New York Times* of March 5, 2002, the Bush administration is "planning to spend close to a trillion dollars on new weapons systems over the next decade."[7]

There are, however, aspects of the abrupt policy shift since September 11 that can be exploited by the anticorporate movement. Like the total bankruptcy of aviation security on September 11, war Keynesianism shows the opportunistic hollowness of the neoliberal rejection of political and social controls on capitalism, of the triumphalism of the "end of history." And exposing the real motives for the attack on Afghanistan allows the anticorporate movement a more solid platform than before to oppose both the consumer capitalism that is premised on expanding energy resources and the war it necessitates.[8]

In addition, the present situation lays bare the universal anxiety, the gangrene, at the heart of America. In a country where the disintegration of the social bond has resulted in a pervasive fear of street crime and serial killers, to say nothing of the danger of being downsized by one's employer, public alarm about terrorism—airline, bio, and nuclear—gave an exponential increase and an officially sanctioned outlet to all the other anxieties. The government's response to public concern for security was twofold: a proxy war that seems to have been more successful than past British and Russian efforts to subjugate Afghan tribal warriors, and a domestic antiterrorist

Patriot Act that seriously jeopardized the constitutional freedoms it purported to protect.

But if the watchword of the coming age is to be "security," then we need to ask some hard questions about the privatization and deregulation of the American economy. Everyone knows that deregulation of the airlines played into the terrorists' hands. In the name of cost-reducing competitiveness, security provisions to protect planes and passengers had been hollowed out by hiring only temporary (often non-English speaking) security guards at the minimum wage and grossly neglecting to protect pilots and cockpits from terrorists. (In the hijacked planes, there was virtually no separation between cockpit and passenger cabin.) An expert on CNN estimated the cost of such protection would have been no more than three thousand dollars per plane—the cost of two transatlantic economy tickets—but it was never done. Antiterrorist air marshals, such as those on all El Al flights, were dropped by most airlines shortly after the last wave of hijackings a generation ago.

Another security matter: Where has the security been for the millions downsized from a secure middle-class existence into poverty by the drive for cost-cutting, profitability, and investor favor? Moreover, where has the security been for the peoples of the third world, in the best of cases rushed from villages into urban slums where they could manufacture clothing for us at thirty cents an hour, and, in the worst, left to starve, like the peoples of Afghanistan and many other countries, when no longer useful as pawns in the cold war against communism? Bin Laden, or whoever authored the September massacres, may be a cruel fanatic, but without the soil of human misery fertilized by Western indifference and exploitation, he would be an isolated, powerless madman.

A program for those who believe in democracy and respect global humanity emerges from these questions. Apart from the obvious measures necessary to restore security in air travel, and to limit the damage terrorists can inflict on Western cities, security needs to be redefined politically to include the real, everyday security of all humankind.

First, economic security. Those in the West as well as in the third world thrown out of their jobs by the present global recession, as well as the armies of those previously downsized by neoliberal "reform," must be considered to be as needful of assistance as corporations threatened with bankruptcy. The workweek should be reduced to create employment and until that takes effect, they must be directly and massively assisted with restored government unemployment insurance.

Another aspect of security: ecological and biological. In our thirst for growth and increased productivity, we have been creating numerous ecological and public health time bombs, whose effects in coming generations will vastly exceed the ravages of September 11. Paul Krugman, in a *New York Times* column, has pointed out that derelictions of public regulation for the sake of profits, comparable to the ones that ruined airline security, could lead to public health disasters that would dwarf the Twin Towers massacre.[9] Those concerned with ecological security can call for new social and economic interventions to really create a more secure world for future generations. To lessen ecologically ruinous dependence on private automobiles and air travel, governments could put the unemployed to work on vast public works projects to rebuild the public transportation and energy infrastructures of Western economies.

And above all, a drastic reform of Western aid to developing countries is in order. We in the (still) relatively affluent West must provide increased security—in the form of direct aid and debt relief—for the impoverished, starving millions of the third world, without whose misery and ignorance terrorism would be powerless. The sources of our present physical insecurity lie not only in fundamentalist fanaticism but in decades of IMF- and World Bank–imposed "reforms" of the third world's economies and military support for its dictators. Instead of bringing about the promised "modernization" and "democratization" of the third world, the neoliberal program has created new poverty and a hatred of the West so profound that millions of the Islamic poor hailed the kamikaze butchers of September 11 as heroes, and Bin Laden as a messiah.

Nonetheless, implementation of this entire program, more a rallying cry than a feasible option at the moment, would do no more than restore the sense of public responsibility that prevailed in most European welfare states before neoliberal globalization undermined them a generation ago. Any serious effort to improve the human prospect will require fundamental debate about the failures and creative potentialities of modern society. *Prometheus Revisited* was written to stimulate that debate.

Notes

1. Cf. "A Rising Tide of Defense Dollars," *New York Times,* May 5, 2002: "With Washington planning to spend close to a trillion dollars over the next decade, stock prices are soaring at companies like Lockheed Martin, Raytheon, Northrop Grumman and General Electric." The economist Richard Du Boff (personal communication, May 11 2002) estimates the military budget at two trillion dollars over the next five years. Sources cited by Du Boff are the Center for Defense Information, Washington, D.C., *The Defense Monitor,* February 2002; Jennifer Love, "House Nears Major Boost in Defense Dollars, *Philadelphia Inquirer,* May 10, 2002: R. W. Stevenson and Elisabeth Baumiller, "President to Seek $48 Billion More for the Military," *New York Times,* January 24, 2002; A. M. Squeo, "The Ripple Effect," *Wall Street Journal,* March 28, 2002. Gabriel Kolko, author of *Another Century of War* (New York: New Press, 2002), refers to the Bush administration's economic policy as "military Keynesianism" (p. 128).

Preface

1. Robert Owen and Charles Fourier were respectively English and French representatives of the pre-Marxist socialism of the first half of the nineteenth century, which was characterized by visionary ("utopian") descriptions of a future society without exploitation. Cf. Robert Owen, *A New View of Society and Other Writings* (London: J. M. Dent, 1949); Charles Fourier, *Le nouveau monde amoureux* (Geneva: Slatkine Reprints, 1978). *A Clockwork Orange* was a film of 1971 by Stanley Kubrick (based on Anthony Burgess's novel of 1961) that depicted a future world with extremes of wealth and poverty, in which conscienceless delinquent youth terrorized the citizenry and were in turn repressed by a totalitarian police apparatus. *Soylent Green* was a science fiction movie of the seventies about a totally polluted and hellishly overpopulated twenty-first-century New York, where a cheap protein wafer distributed by the Soylent Corporation turns out to be made of involuntarily "euthanized" human remains. See Noreena Hertz, *The Silent Takeover: Global Capitalism and the Death of Democracy* (London: Heinemann, 2001), pp. 185–86.

2. Ulrich Beck, *Risk Society: Towards a New Modernity* (London: Sage, 1992).

3. Ulrich Beck, "Globalisation's Chernobyl," *Financial Times,* November 6, 2001.

4. Paul Krugman "Another Useful Crisis," *New York Times,* November 11, 2001.

5. Adam Clymer, "With Sagging Economy as Ally, Democrats in Congress Go on the Attack," *New York Times,* November 11, 2001. On December 2 the *New York Times* reported: "The latest survey by Public Opinion Strategies, a prominent Republican polling company, found that for the first time [since 9–11] concern about 'the slowdown of the economy' eclipsed that about 'the threat of terrorism

on U.S. soil.' And the survey found the public to be far less concerned about the drive to eradicate terrorism overseas" (Richard L. Berke and Thom Shanker, "As Guns Still Blaze, Bush Aides Debate Shifting Focus to Butter").

6. "El Niño is estimated to have displaced nearly 5 million people, injured 118 million and caused almost 22,000 deaths. The worldwide costs were estimated to be as high as $33 billion. Many scientists believe that the ferocity of the El Niño storms was due to global warming. The storms ruined harvests and fueled forest fires from Indonesia to Brazil." *Human Development Report 1999* (Oxford: Oxford University Press, 1999).

7. *New York Times,* August 19, 2000, as quoted in *Le Monde,* August 22.

8. *Financial Times,* August 21, 2000.

9. "Hard rains in Nicaragua herald El Niño's menace," *Financial Times,* May 30, 2002; Bob Herbert, "How Hot is Hot," *New York Times,* June 24, 2002.

10. "The rise in grain prices has encouraged the feeding of less expensive materials to cattle, especially substances with a high protein value that accelerate growth. About 75% of the cattle in the United States were routinely fed livestock wastes— the rendered remains of dead sheep and dead cattle—until August of 1997. They were also fed millions of dead cats and dead dogs every year, purchased from animal shelters. . . . But cattle blood is still put into the feed given to American cattle. Steven P. Bjerklie, a former editor of the trade journal *Meat & Poultry,* is appalled by what goes into cattle feed these days. 'Goddamn it, these cattle are ruminants,' Bjerklie says. 'They're designed to eat grass and, maybe, grain. . . . They are not designed to eat other animals.'" Eric Schlosser, *Fast Food Nation: The Dark Side of the All-American Meal* (Boston: Houghton Mifflin, 2001).

11. A Dutch investment bank news bulletin on Asian bond markets in August 2000 (Effectenbank Stroeve *Research Obligatie Visie Azië Special,* August 22, 2000) gave positive ratings only to Singapore, Taiwan, and Hong Kong, advising against investment in eight other countries.

12. George Soros, in *Le Monde,* December 10, 1998.

13. I discuss this European swing to the left in Chapter 5.

14. The French socialists alone have attempted to control neoliberal capitalism. See Chapter 5.

15. Naomi Klein acknowledges this double wall: "The unsustainable search for profits that, for example, leads to the clear-cutting of old-growth forests is the same philosophy that devastates logging towns by moving the mills to Indonesia. John Jordan, a British anarchist environmentalist, puts it this way: 'Transnationals are affecting democracy, work, communities, culture and the biosphere. Inadvertently, they have helped us see the whole problem as one system, to connect every issue to every other issue, to not look at one problem in isolation.'" Klein, *No Logo* (London: Flamingo, 2000), p. 266.

16. Available at www.panda.org.

17. Kenneth S. Deffeyes, *Hibbert's Peak: The Impending World Oil Shortage* (Princeton, N.J.: Princeton University Press, 2001).

18. Michael T. Klare, *Resource Wars: The New Landscape of Global Conflict* (New York: Metropolitan Books, 2001), p. 43.

19. John Thornhill, in a discussion of a new book on consumer culture, expresses a growing consensus that "shopping is not merely the acquisition of things but the buying of identity. For some people, consumption—in its widest sense—has even replaced religion as their main source of solace and comfort." *Financial Times,* August 21, 2000.

20. Jeremy Rifkin, *The End of Work: The Decline of the Global Labor Force and the Dawn of the Post-Market Era* (New York: Putnam, 1995); Richard Sennett, *The Corrosion of Character: The Personal Consequences of Work in the New Capitalism* (New York: Norton, 1998); Christophe Desjours, *Souffrance en France: La banalisation de l'injustice sociale* (Paris: Seuil, 1998).

21. According to the French economist Jean-Paul Fitoussi, the lack of forethought in the design of our computers, which created a problem for the year 2000, was the result of a more general inability to conceptualize the future: "Are we so caught up in the short term that the day after tomorrow seems too distant to take into account, while tomorrow seems already fixed: without control over tomorrow, without a project for the day after tomorrow, is it any wonder that our society is gripped by a diffuse feeling of insecurity?" (*Le Monde,* December 23, 1998). See also the comprehensive study by the political scientist Pierre-André Taguieff, *L'éffacement de l'avenir* (Paris: Galilée, 2000). Of course the anxiety aroused by fears of terrorism in the fall of 2001 also fostered frenetic consumption. See Shawn Hubler, "Americans Fend Off Sorrow with Laden Fork and Spoon," *Los Angeles Times,* October 2, 2001.

Introduction: The Other Prometheus

1. The similarity between Prometheus and Christ was acknowledged as early as the third century by the Church father Tertullian (Louis Séchan, *Le mythe de Prométhée* [Paris: Presses Universitaires de France, 1951], p. 16).

2. Kate Soper's highly intelligent *What Is Nature?* (Oxford: Blackwell, 1995), which broadly reflects feminist and ecological concerns, refers to Prometheanism seven times, more or less incidentally, in these terms.

3. Don Slater, *Consumer Culture and Modernity* (London: Polity Press, 1997), p. 16.

4. Terry Eagleton's summary (in "Self-Realization, Ethics and Socialism," *New Left Review,* no. 237 [1999]) of Sean Sayer's argument in *Marxism and Human Nature* (London: Routledge, 1998).

5. *The Complete Poetical Works of Percy Bysshe Shelley* [henceforth *Poetical Works of Shelley*], edited by Thomas Hutchinson (London: Oxford University Press, 1947), p. 574. On the Peterloo massacre of 1819 and its context: E. P. Thompson, *The Making of the English Working Class* (New York: Vintage, 1963), pp. 602–710. Joyce Malow, *The Peterloo Massacre* (London: Readers Union, 1970).

6. *Poetical Works of Shelley,* pp. 338–44; Gerald McNiece, *Shelley and the Revolutionary Idea* (Cambridge: Harvard University Press, 1969), pp. 62–65.

7. Karl Heinrich Marx, *Differenz der demokritischen und epikureischen Naturphilosophie.* In *Gesammelte Schriften von Karl Marx und Friedrich Engels 1841 bis 1850,* edited by Franz Mehring, 2d ed. (Stuttgart: Dietz Verlag, 1913), 1:68 ("Prometheus ist der vornehmste Heilige und Märtyrer im philosophischen Kalender"). In English in Stanley Edgar Hyman, *The Tangled Bank: Darwin, Marx, Frazer and Freud as Imaginative Writers* (New York: Atheneum, 1962), p. 86. Cf. Dominique Lecourt, *Prométhée, Faust, Frankenstein* (Paris: Livre de Poche, 1996), pp. 71–72.

8. Richard Holmes, *Shelley: The Pursuit* (London: Penguin, 1974), pp. xii, 208–9.

9. Karl Marx, and Friedrich Engels, *Der Briefwechsel* (Munich: Deutsche Taschenbuch Verlag, 1983), 1:14 (Engels to Marx, February 22 1845).

10. Hans Achterhuis, *Natuur tussen mythe en techniek* (Baarn, Netherlands: Ambo, 1995), p. 228.

11. Cf. M. H. Abrams, *Natural Supernaturalism: Tradition and Revolution in Romantic Literature* (New York: Norton, 1973), p. 300.

12. An early reference to Prometheus in the notes to *Queen Mab,* relying on Hesiod's account, sees his torment on the rock as an allegory of man's self-punishment for eating meat, the consequence of his discovery of fire. Six years later, there is no trace of this notion in *Prometheus Unbound.* Apparently, Shelley read Aeschylus's version of the myth of Prometheus only after finishing *Queen Mab.*

13. Holmes, *Shelley,* p. 208.

14. This and the previous quote are from *Poetical Works of Shelley,* pp. 805–6.

15. Kenneth Neill Cameron, *The Young Shelley: Genesis of a Radical* (London: Gollancz, 1951), p. 243.

16. Ibid.

17. Holmes, *Shelley,* p. 401. *Queen Mab*'s title, recalling the fairy queen evoked by Mercutio in *Romeo and Juliet* to explain how dreams are put in our sleeping brains, is thus misleading. Holmes sees Spenser's *Faerie Queen* as the "literary model, in so far as it has one" of *The Revolt of Islam,* but the topicality and political thrust of Spenser's poem could be seen as inspiring both this work and *Queen Mab.* Walter Edwin Peck (*Shelley: His Life and Work* [London: Ernest Benn, 1927], 1:285) writes that "the composition of *Queen Mab* went forward in the intervals of Shelley's excursions into the poetry of Spenser, Sir William Jones, Southey, Wordsworth, and Coleridge; the novels of Godwin; and Thomas Trotter's essay on the Nervous Temperament."

18. For an explication of "The Cave of Mammon" in terms of Renaissance neo-Platonism, see Frank Kermode, *Shakespeare, Spenser, Donne: Renaissance Essays* (London: Routledge & Kegan Paul, 1971), pp. 60–83.

19. John Cameron Bryce, "Edmund Spenser," in *Encyclopaedia Britannica,* 14th ed.

20. See Shelley's preface to *Prometheus Unbound,* in *Poetical Works of Shelley,* p. 205: "The only imaginary being resembling in any degree Prometheus, is Satan; and Prometheus is, in my judgment, a more poetical character . . . because . . . he is . . . exempt from the taints of ambition, envy, revenge, and a desire for personal aggrandisement, which, in the Hero of *Paradise Lost,* interfere with the interest."

21. Christopher Hill brings up extensive evidence of Milton's ties to the revolutionary Puritanism of his day in *Milton and the English Revolution* (London: Faber and Faber, 1979).

22. Cf. Michael Löwy et Robert Sayre, *Révolte et mélancholie: Le romantisme à contre-courant de la modernité* (Paris: Payot, 1992), pp. 46–64, 104–14, 160–200. Löwy and Sayre's definition of Romanticism lacks historical specificity, but there are many fine insights in this work, particularly on the nineteenth-century aesthetic opposition to capitalist modernity.

23. Abrams, *Natural Supernaturalism.*

24. *The Revolt of Islam,* canto 5, stanzas 38–58 (*Poetical Works of Shelley,* pp. 87–94). According to McNiece (*Shelley and the Revolutionary Idea,* pp. 117–18), "Shelley had available to him a good many specific descriptions of the fêtes," specifically works by Helen Maria Williams, Mary Wollstonecraft, Godwin, John Adolphus, and Rabaut St. Étienne. The last two were apparently the sources for "the two revolutionary spectacles which apparently influenced Shelley most particularly, the first great fête of the federation . . . and Robespierre's fête of the Supreme Being" (p. 119). The concluding stanza of canto 5, which begins with "And joyous was our feast" and ends with "The multitudes went homeward to their rest, / Which that delightful day with its own shadow blessed," bears comparison with the "Ainsi finit le meilleur jour de notre vie," a quote from a participant's report that Michelet subsequently cited at the close of his description of the rural festivals of federation (Jules Michelet, *Histoire de la Révolution française* (Paris: Pléiade, 1952), 1:412.

25. Shelley was forced by his printer, who feared prosecution for immorality, to eliminate the incestuous relationship in the original version of *The Revolt of Islam,* called *Laon and Cythna.* Holmes views this imposed revision as "a major blow to the ideology of the poem," which was "revolutionary and socially iconoclastic" (Holmes, *Shelley,* pp. 390–91, 402).

26. Raymond Trousson, *Le thème de Prométhée dans la littérature européenne,* 2d ed. (Geneva: Droz, 1976), p. 323.

27. Holmes, *Shelley,* p. 38. Jones's *Palace of Fortune* is claimed as a model for *Queen Mab* by Cameron, *Young Shelley,* p. 244. E. Wasserman ("Mythmaking in *Prometheus Unbound,*" *Modern Language Notes* 70 [March 1955], p. 182), confirming Mary Shelley's opinion, points out that in *Prometheus Unbound,* act 1, lines 826–33, "we are told that because of Asia's 'transforming presence' the once desolate Indian vale is now rich with flowers and herbs. In one of her symbolic meanings, then, Asia is the creative Venus, the generative spirit in Nature."

28. *Poetical Works of Shelley,* p. 272.

29. Abrams, *Natural Supernaturalism,* p. 344.

30. Ibid., pp. 343–44.

31. Quotes from Soper, *What Is Nature?* pp. 5, 24, 30.

32. Ibid., p. 94.

33. Bakhtin, quoted in ibid., p. 95.

34. Soper, *What Is Nature?* p. 97.

35. Ibid.

36. One can discern the Promethean ethos mixed with Christian imagery in the poetry of militant Puritanism (Milton), then, more abstractly presented, as the driving force behind the English political economy and social philosophy of Locke and his successors, behind French encyclopedism, and subsequently behind nineteenth-century liberalism and socialism in most countries.

37. Norbert Elias, *Über den Prozess der Zivilisation,* 2d ed. (Bern: Francke Verlag, 1969); Robert Muchembled, *Popular Culture and Elite Culture in France, 1400–1750* (Baton Rouge: Louisiana Sate University Press, 1985).

38. Jeffrey Herf, *Reactionary Modernism: Technology, Culture, and Politics in Weimar and the Third Reich* (New York: Cambridge University Press, 1984).

39. Muchembled, *Popular Culture and Elite Culture,* pp. 47–49; Emmanuel Le Roy Ladurie, *Montaillou, village occitan de 1294 à 1324* Paris: Gallimard, 1975), pp. 419–501, esp. pp. 493–94.

40. Cf. Karl Polanyi, *The Great Transformation: The Political and Economic Origins of Our Time* (Boston: Beacon, 1960), p. 45: "According to the historians, the forms of industrial life in agricultural Europe were, until recently, not much different from what they had been several thousand years earlier. Ever since the introduction of the plow—essentially a large hoe drawn by animals—the methods of agriculture remained substantially unaltered over the major part of Western and Central Europe until the beginning of the modern age." Concerning local food and handicraft markets, Polanyi writes (p. 62): "Gatherings of this kind are not only fairly general in primitive societies, but remain almost unchanged right up to the middle of the eighteenth century in the most advanced countries of Western Europe. They are an adjunct of local existence and differ but little whether they form part of Central African tribal life, or a *cité* of Merovingian France, or a Scottish Village of Adam Smith's time."

41. The elimination from the hexagon of the Norman feudal power, which claimed most of northern and western France for the English successors of William the Conqueror, required a hundred years of struggle in the fourteenth and fifteenth centuries. Brittany was annexed to the French monarchy only in 1532, Burgundy in 1482, though it retained a large measure of local autonomy until the eighteenth century. In the case of southern France, centralized political control went hand in hand with the religious centralization of the area, since the prevalent Albigensian culture, with its Cathar religion, was viewed as heretical by the Roman church: the early thirteenth-century military conquest of the area by Simon de Montfort, which occurred under clerical as well as royal auspices, was known as the Albigensian Crusade.

42. Muchembled, *Popular Culture and Elite Culture.* This "civilizing process" is alluded to above and discussed more broadly in the next section.

43. Edward Whiting Fox, *The Other France: History in Geographical Perspective* (New York: Norton, 1971). Fox views the geopolitical dichotomy of coastal centers of commercial capitalism and centralized continental bureaucratic monarchy (based on an agrarian-feudal military ruling caste) as characteristic of European history before the French Revolution. He establishes the symbiotic nature of this rela-

tionship between the French cities that financed the monarchy and the royal power that protected their trade. The separateness of the urban economic order from the emerging national monarchies they financed is emphasized by Polanyi (*Great Transformation,* p. 63): "Right up to the time of the Commercial Revolution what may appear to us as national trade was not national, but municipal. The Hanse were not German merchants; they were a corporation of trading oligarchs, hailing from a number of North Sea and Baltic towns. Far from 'nationalizing' German economic life, the Hanse deliberately cut off the hinterland from trade. The trade of Antwerp or Hamburg, Venice or Lyons, was in no way Dutch or German, Italian or French. London was no exception: it was as little 'English' as Luebeck was 'German.'"

44. Maurice Dobb, *Studies in the Development of Capitalism* (New York: International Publishers, 1947), pp. 42–50.

45. Père Maldonnat, cited in George Snyders, *La pédagogie en France aux XVIIe et XVIIIe siècles* (Paris: Presses Universitaires de France, 1965), p. 264.

46. William Sewell Jr., *Work and Revolution in France: The Language of Labor from the Old Regime to 1848* (Cambridge: Cambridge University Press, 1980); Robert Darnton, *The Great Cat Massacre and Other Episodes in French Cultural History* (London: Allen Lane, 1984), pp. 107–43.

47. It was the merit of Henri Pirenne to have pointed out the novel geopolitical significance of the European Middle Ages, in which, from the time of the Carolingian kingdom onward, a new civilization evolved that was not, as had the Roman and Merovingian empires before it, given unity by a body of water or, as with earlier existing Middle Eastern or Asian empires, been centered around a single river basin. It is arguable that this lack of a unifying aquatic feature insured continued political instability into the modern era and, with that, a degree of economic and social volatility unknown in other civilizations. See Pirenne, *Mohammed et Charlemagne* (Paris: Félix Alcan: 1937).

48. See Georges de Lagarde, *La naissance de l'esprit laïque au déclin du moyen age,* 2 vols. (Louvain: E. Nauwelaerts, 1956–58). Early examples of an implicitly subversive rationalism in the medieval church were the ideas of Abelard, William of Occam, and Marsilio of Padua. Later, John Calvin and other successful reformers can be considered as subversive rationalists who condemned church doctrine from within as rationally inconsistent. Heretical creeds of poverty were advanced in the later Middle Ages by the Waldensians and the third order of the Franciscans, then by the Hussites and the followers of Thomas Münzer. Communist sects of the English Civil War, such as Gerald Winstanley's "Diggers," were another example of the Christian heresy of poverty.

49. A subtle exploration of the social-psychological part of this undermining in eighteenth-century France can be found in Fred Weinstein and Gerald Platt, *The Wish to Be Free: Society, Psyche and Value Change,* Berkeley: University of California Press, 1969.

50. *Nations and Nationalism* (London: Blackwell, 1992), pp. 18–38.

51. On the antithesis of *Kultur* and *Zivilisation* in Germany, see Elias, *Über den Prozess der Zivilisation,* 1:1–64.

52. Priscilla P. Clark (*The Battle of the Bourgeois: The Novel in France, 1789–1848* [Paris: Didier, 1973], pp. 169–95) draws on Bourdieu's concept of cultural field in her analysis of the tension between writer, market, and bourgeoisie. For a subsequent, broader sociology of French literature by the same scholar, see Priscilla Parkhurst Ferguson: *Literary France: The Making of a Culture* (Berkeley: University of California Press, 1987). An earlier study is César Graña, *Bohemian vs. Bourgeois: French Society and the French Man of Letters in the Nineteenth Century,* New York: Harper-Torchbooks, 1964). Balzac's *Les illusions perdues* (1837–39) exemplifies the Romantic artist coping with the world of journalism and publishing.

53. In *Past and Present* (1844).

54. Paul Bénichou, *Le temps des prophètes* (Paris: Gallimard, 1979), dissects carefully the differences between the more authoritarian utopian creeds, such as that of the Saint-Simonians and the Fourierists, and the more humanitarian thinkers who approached socialism either from a libertarian dissidence within those creeds (like Pierre Leroux) or from social Romanticism.

55. Jules Michelet, *Le peuple* (1846; reprint, Paris: Flammarion, 1974).

56. By the reforms of the Napoleonic epoch, the scope of the government-controlled *"université"* extended to primary and secondary as well as higher education. This definition persists today.

57. Sophie Leterrier, *L'institution des sciences morales* (Paris: L'Harmattan, 1995); Patrice Vermeren, *Victor Cousin, le jeu de la philosophie et de l'état* (Paris: L'Harmattan, 1995).

58. The post-Seattle judicial repression of dissent includes a twenty-two-year sentence handed down on June 11, 2001, in Eugene Oregon to punish an ecological "terrorist" for two arson incidents. The more serious of the two, to which the young man (himself twenty-two years old) confessed, was setting fire to a Chevrolet dealership to protest the environmental damage caused by automobile culture. Total damage was the destruction of three pickup trucks, worth $40,000. Twenty-two years! (L. A. Kauffman, "Hard Time," *Free Radical, Chronicle of the New Unrest,* no. 17 [2001], www.free-radical.org).

59. What has recently been called "postmodernism" is little more than an exaggerated and rather confused modernist attack on the last ideological "paradigm" of modernism, that of structuralism. As such, postmodernism has itself become an ideology, congruent with and, as far as its skepticism regarding objective social forces is concerned, partly derivative of the individualist neoliberalism that dominates the world economy.

60. It is useful to recall that the first measures for securing the welfare of the new working classes were implemented by Prussian conservatism under Bismarck, in the 1880s, as a means of diminishing socialist fervor among badly exploited industrial workers, and had been preceded ideologically by English "Tory socialism," the conservative riposte to militant chartism. See Benjamin Disraeli, *Sybil or the Two Nations* (1845; reprint, London: Oxford University Press, 1965).

61. Krishan Kumar, *From Post-Industrial to Post-Modern Society* (Oxford: Blackwell, 1995).

62. In January 2000, for example, the future acting head of the IMF, Stanley Fischer, rejected an appeal by the U.S. Treasury secretary to limit its support activities to

financial crises. According to the *Financial Times* of January 7, 2000, Fischer "described the IMF as 'the most important way that the international community promotes good macroeconomic policies throughout the world.'" The meaning of such promotion—the iron hand in the velvet glove—appeared in further remarks of Mr. Fischer in which he suggested that the IMF's "loan programmes with countries when crises did not loom" were dependent on "economic surveillance and . . . technical assistance."

63. Schor, *The Overspent American* (New York: Basic Books, 1998).

64. See "Anatomy of Defeat," in Chapter 2.

65. Cf. Susan Strange, *Mad Money* (Manchester: Manchester University Press, 1997) and *Casino Capitalism* (Oxford: Blackwell, 1986).

One. The Nationalist Face of Prometheus

1. "Bush's New Rules to Fight Terror Transform the Legal Landscape," *New York Times,* November 25, 2001. The presidential order to try terrorism suspects in military courts was described by Anthony Lewis as "the broadest move in American history to sweep aside constitutional protections" ("Wake Up America," *New York Times,* November 30, 2001). While the Bush order applied "only" to some twenty million noncitizens, Lewis pointed out that it "could easily be extended to citizens, under the administration's legal theory. Since the Sixth Amendment makes no distinction between citizens and aliens, the claim of war exigency could sweep its protections aside for anyone in this country who might fit the vague definitions of aiding terrorism."

2. Alexander Stille, "Suddenly, Americans Trust Uncle Sam," *New York Times,* November 3, 2001, Web edition.

3. Kevin Phillips, "The Political Clock Is Ticking," *Los Angeles Times,* November 11 2001, Web edition.

4. Caroline Lucas, "Doha spells disaster for development," *Observer,* November 18, 2001; Jeff Faux, "A Deal Built on Sand," *American Prospect* 13, no. 1 (January 1–14, 2002).

5. Schor, *Overspent American.*

6. A decade after the disappearance of the Soviet Union and after the gutting of most welfare programs for the poor, the welfare state for corporate America's military-industrial complex is still going strong. After a modest decline in the 1980s and 1990s, the second Bush administration, in the wake of the terror attacks of September 11, obtained congressional approval for massive military expenditures. (See "Post Script: Notes from a Hijacked Planet" below.) Many of these were, of course, planned before those attacks ("Acquisition Panel Approves $60 Billion Fighter Program," *New York Times,* August 16, 2001). It was because George Orwell early intuited the basic similarities between the states on either side of the cold war divide—in particular their manipulation of the opposite side's alleged menace to survival to create a permanent state of terror—that he situated the future totalitarian state of *1984* in the former Anglo-European heartland of capitalism and the welfare state.

7. One sees the turn from social revolutionary zeal with a nationalist tinge to xenophobic nationalism in the rise of Italian fascism from a wing of pre–World War I revolutionary syndicalism, which used the Sorelian ideal of violence as a means of restoring nationalist idealism in the wake of the war, and in the Communard roots of two important figures of fin-de-siècle French anti-Semitic nationalism, Edouard Drumont and Henri Rochefort, who attached the Blanquist revolutionary ideal of *la patrie en danger* to the cause of *revanche* against the German victors of 1870 and their presumed Semitic accomplices. (It is only fair to add that most Italian revolutionaries and most Communards remained faithful to the ideals of working-class internationalism.)

8. Adolphe Thiers was the principal July Monarchy liberal in favor of this policy, which was opposed by the more conservative Guizot and by Louis-Philippe. One might view Thiers's failed effort to transmute domestic dissent into support for a vaguely revolutionary (or Bonapartist) national expansionism as the last chance of longevity for the Orleanist regime, which, turning to the rigid conservatism of Molé and Guizot in its final decade, lacked any alternative method for channeling popular discontent and thereby evading the oncoming alliance of reformists and democrats that triumphed in 1848.

9. Geoff Eley, *Reshaping the German Right: Radical Nationalism and Political Change after Bismarck* (New Haven: Yale University Press, 1980); David Blackbourn, *Class, Religion and Local Politics in Wilhelmine Germany* (New Haven: Yale University Press, 1980).

10. This is made evident not only by the Schreber case studied by Freud but also by a study of posture pedagogy: David Yosifon and Peter N. Stearns, "The Rise and Fall of American Posture," *American Historical Review* 103, no. 4 (October 1998), pp. 1057–95. Fear of decadence was of course quite compatible with fascination for it, as has been shown by Bram Dijkstra, *Idols of Perversity* (New York: Oxford University Press, 1986); Peter Gay, *The Bourgeois Experience: Victoria to Freud,* vol. 2, *The Tender Passion* (New York: Norton, 1986); and George Mosse, *Nationalism and Sexuality* (New York: Howard Fertig, 1985).

11. Denis Bertholet, *Le bourgeois dans tous ses états: Le roman familial de la Belle Époque* (Paris: Olivier Orban, 1987).

12. In the first round of the French presidential elections of 2002—primarily because of the dispersal of the Left vote among eight parties, most of them critical of Jospin's neoliberal policies—Le Pen edged Socialist Lionel Jospin out of the second round runoffs. Between the two rounds occurred the French May 1 demonstrations: an unprecedented million and a half French citizens took to the streets in demonstrations against Le Pen. Le Pen lost the second round to conservative Jacques Chirac, massively supported by the Left, by 82 percent to 18 percent.

13. "The largest zone economy is China, where by conservative estimates there are 18 million people in 124 export processing zones. In total, the International Labor Organization says that there are at least 850 EPZ's in the world, but that number is likely much closer to 1,000, spread through seventy countries and employing roughly 27 million workers" (Klein, *No Logo,* p. 205).

14. Abandonment of the welfare state by social-democratic parties did not go unnoticed in the French and Dutch elections of the spring of 2002, when many of their core voters deserted them—in France, for parties to their left; in the Netherlands, for the Christian Democrats and the right-populist "List Pim Fortuyn."

15. Even the left-wing critics published by *Le Monde Diplomatique,* which has for years been attacking social democracy as a movement enserfed to neoliberal capitalism, rarely are able to go beyond Keynesianism. An article of January 1999, for example, denounces the deflationary monetarism of the new European central bank for accentuating "the risks of a serious recession by drying up internal demand, while consumption and internal investment represent the essential dynamic . . . the Central Bank [should be] an instrument in the service of growth and job creation" (Laurent Carroué, "L'euro, verrous de l'orthodoxie," *Le Monde Diplomatique,* January 1999, p. 5). As for the social democrats currently in power in Europe, even the former German finance minister Oscar Lafontaine, whose program was quite Keynesian, felt constrained to separate himself from Keynesianism in a public statement issued shortly before his abrupt resignation in March.

16. Russell Jacoby, *The Last Intellectuals: American Culture in the Age of Academe* (New York: Basic Books, 1987).

17. Michel Schooyans, *La dérive totalitaire du libéralisme* (Paris: Éditions Universitaires, 1991).

18. Cf. Ernest Gellner, *Nations and Nationalism* (London: Blackwell, 1992), p. 18: "What happens when a social order is accidentally brought about in which the clerisy does become, at long last, universal, when literacy is not a specialism but a pre-condition of all other specialisms? . . . A high culture pervades the whole of society, defines it, and needs to be sustained by the polity. *That* is the secret of nationalism." See also Benedict Anderson, *Imagined Communities* (London: Verso, 1993).

19. Theda Skocpol, *States and Social Revolutions* (Cambridge: Cambridge University Press, 1979), sees the trauma of military defeat or economic collapse as the active catalyst of the French, Russian, and Chinese Revolutions, but her analysis applies equally to the new national consciousness that arose in the course of those revolutions. Mutatis mutandis, it can be applied to the sources of virtually all nationalisms.

20. The prolonged civil and tribal warfare characterizing many of the Central African states is evidence of the difficulty of this integration.

21. I refer to the imposition on Louis XVI by a revolutionary Third Estate of a constitutional, parliamentary regime, with only limited veto rights preserved by the (previously absolute) monarch. Edmund Burke denounced all such limitations as contrary to the legitimacy given by history, in his *Considerations on the Revolution in France.*

22. Anderson, *Imagined Communities;* Gellner, *Nations and Nationalism;* Eric Hobsbawm, *Nations and Nationalism since 1780* (Cambridge: Canto, 1994).

23. In the Netherlands, Frisian is the official language in Friesland and there is a strong

movement to make Limburgs, spoken by most local people, the language of schooling and administration in the southeastern province of Limburg.

24. Ethnic separatism in Galicia, one of Spain's poorer areas, also has a strong left-wing stance. *Financial Times,* March 1, 2000.

25. "A sign on the wall said this room was 'A gift of the Kingdom of Saudi Arabia.'" Thomas Friedman, "In Pakistan, It's Jihad 101," *New York Times,* November 13, 2001, Web edition. According to Friedman, 39,000 such madrasas have come in the place of Pakistan's public school system in the last twenty years.

26. Klare, *Resource Wars,* p. 17.

27. "China is seriously interested in Caspian Sea hydrocarbon resources, and has even reported an interest in a pipeline to the Arabian sea, with a view to importing gas and oil by supertanker." Richard Tanter, "Pipeline Politics: Oil, Gas and the US interest in Afghanistan," ZNET, November 2001. Tanter also points out that in connection with high costs and the vulnerability of an overland pipeline to separatist movements in western China, China National Petroleum recently jettisoned an agreement with Kazakhstan to build such a west-east conduit.

28. Jules Michelet, *Histoire de la Révolution française* (Paris: Bibliothèque de la Pléiade, 1952), 2:623.

29. Copy in the Musée d'Orsay, Paris. See also the reproductions "Garibaldi sous les traits du rédempteur" and "Jésus le montagnard," in *Le printemps des peuples* [Paris: French National Assembly, 1998), pp. 81, 140, the catalogue of the 1998 exposition at the French National Assembly titled "Les révolutions de 1848: L'Europe des images." Flaubert parodied this conflation of Jesus Christ with republican socialism in his description of a Second Republic painting that "represented the Republic, or Progress, or Civilization, in the guise of Jesus Christ driving a locomotive through a virgin forest" (*The Sentimental Education* [New York: New American Library, 1972], p. 293).

30. As in the Fourierist Alphonse Toussenel's *Les juifs, rois de l'époque: Histoire de la féodalité financière* (Paris: L'École Sociétaire, 1845); or in Daumier's caricature of Louis-Philippe, notorious for his link to high finance, as "Prince Juif."

31. Ironically, but in line with the general tendency of bourgeois progressivism to harden into reaction after the mid-nineteenth century, French doctrines of a multiplicity of human races had initially been endorsed in the 1840s by anticlerical liberals and republicans as a scientific refutation of the biblical account of the creation.

32. *Archiv für Sozialwissenschaft und Sozialpolitik.*

33. *Socialismus und sociale Bewegung im neunzehnten Jahrhundert* (Bern: Gesellschaft für ethische Kultur, 1897). This paragraph is based on part 2 of my *Sociology and Estrangement: Three Sociologists of Imperial Germany* (New York: Knopf, 1973).

34. Interesting examples in nineteenth-century France are to be found in Jules Valles, *L'enfant,* in *Oeuvres II, 1871–1885* (Paris: Bibliothèque de la Pléiade, 1990); and Louis Pergaud, *La guerre des boutons* (1912; reprint, Paris: Mercure de France, 1944).

35. Natalie Zemon Davis, "The Reasons of Misrule: Youth Groups and Charivaris in Sixteenth Century France," in *Society and Culture in Early Modern France* (Stanford: Stanford University Press, 1971), pp. 97–123. Jacques Le Goff and Jean-Claude

Schmitt, *Le Charivari: Actes de la table ronde organisée à Paris (25–27 avril 1977) par l'E.H.E.S.S. et le C.N.R.S.* (Paris: École des Hautes Études en Sciences Sociales, 1981).

36. Yves-Marie Bercé, *Fête et révolte: Des mentalités populaires du XVIe au XVIIIe siècle* (Paris: Hachette, 1971); Muchembled, *Popular Culture and Elite Culture*, pp. 49–61, 168.

37. George Sand's *Le compagnon du tour de France* (1841) is a good novelistic version of this.

38. Darnton, *Great Cat Massacre.*

39. The persistent problem of gang aggression, theft and random vandalism, aggravated by ghettoization, poverty, loss of identity in immigrant subcultures, and high youth unemployment (among ghetto youth as much as four times the unemployment level for those over twenty five), creates dangerous anxieties in middle classes all over the world. It is a problem that many cities in the United States cope with only by massive repression and the flight of the affluent to privately guarded suburbs and exclusive shopping malls. In Europe, where middle classes cling to traditional inner cities, ghettoization occurs largely in suburbs, but problems comparable to those of American cities are growing, largely among non-European immigrant groups. Insofar as a considerable part of the middle-class electorate is fair game for the xenophobic nationalism of the Far Right, youth crime and vandalism was the source of great concern for the social-democratic governments that in 2001 were in power in thirteen of fifteen European Union nations. I will return to this question in Part II.

40. Anthony Esler, ed., *The Youth Revolution* (Lexington, Mass.: Heath, 1974). Lewis S. Feuer, *The Conflict of Generations* (London: Heinemann, 1969); Walter Laquer, *Young Germany* (London: Routledge and Kegan Paul, 1962); Helmut Kreuzer, *Die Boheme* (Stuttgart: Metzler, 1971); Jean Claude Caron, *Générations romantiques: Les étudiants de Paris et le quartier latin (1814–1851)* (Paris: Armand Colin, 1991); Roger-Henri Guerrand, *Lycéens révoltés: Étudiants révolutionnaires au XIX siècle* (Paris: Éditions du temps, 1969). John G. Gallaher, *The Students of Paris in the Revolution of 1848* (Carbondale: Southern Illinois University Press, 1980). On Flaubert: Jean-Paul Sartre, *L'idiot de la famille* (Paris: Gallimard, 1971), 2:1331–467.

41. The relationship of naturism to German nationalism has frequently been analyzed, but nowhere more sensitively than in George Mosse, *Nationalism and Sexuality* (New York: Howard Fertig, 1985).

42. Franz Neumann, *Behemoth: The Structure and Practice of National Socialism, 1933–1944,* rev. ed. (London: Cass, 1967); Robert G. L. Waite, *Vanguard of Nazism: The Free Corps Movement in Post-war Germany, 1918–1923* (Cambridge: Harvard University Press, 1952).

43. "True artists do not make good political disciples, for they are incapable of taking their opponent's death lightly. They are on the side of life, not of death. They are the witnesses of the flesh, not the law. They are condemned by their vocation to understand the very one who is their enemy. That does not mean that they are incapable of judging good and evil. On the contrary. But their aptitude for living the lives of others enables them to recognize, even among the most criminal, the

constant justification of men, namely suffering. That is what will always keep us from pronouncing absolute judgment and, consequently from endorsing absolute punishment. In the world of condemnation to death which is ours, artists bear witness to that in man which refuses to die. No one's enemy, unless it be the hangman's!" Albert Camus, "The Artist as Witness of Freedom," trans. Bernard Frechtmen. *Journal for the Protection of All Beings* (San Francisco, City Lights Books), no. 1 (1961): 36.

Two. Socialism, the Welfare State, and the Heritage of the Left

1. A study of the Far Left in contemporary France by Jean-Christope Brochier and Hervé Delouche, *Les nouveaux sans-culottes: Enquête sur l'extrême gauche* (Paris: Grasset, 2000), suggests in its title the origins of contemporary French radicalism in the original revolutionary moment. The Zapatistas, based on the solidarism of Mexican indigenous peasant communities resisting capitalist agriculture, but inspired by the Mexican revolution of the early twentieth century, are another example of preindustrial rootedness.

2. Christopher Hill, *Puritanism and Revolution* (London: Heinemann, 1958).

3. Thompson, *Making of the English Working Class;* Sewell, *Work and Revolution.*

4. Peter N. Stearns, *European Society in Upheaval: Social History since 1800* (New York: Macmillan, 1967), pp. 138–58.

5. Leszek Kolakowski, *Main Currents of Marxism* (Oxford: Oxford University Press, 1981), 1:412–13. In the interesting conflation of Marxism and postmodernism by Michael Hardt and Antonio Negri, *Empire* (Cambridge: Harvard University Press, 2000), we see the same Promethean definition of liberated human nature in terms of productivity: "the desire to exist and the desire to produce are one and the same thing" (p. 349); and "we . . . speak . . . from the perspective of a humanity that is constructed productively, that is constituted through the "common name" of freedom" (p. 350).

6. The function of orally transmitted popular myth as a continuing catalyst of social action, though generally underestimated, has been understood by the more subtle social thinkers of the modern era. Michelet was quite aware of the social importance of the myth of the French Revolution of 1789 (in his lectures in the months preceding the revolution of 1848 he urged his students to speak to the old men in their *quartier* to make contact with the revolutionary spirit of the nation, and his *History of the French Revolution* begins with an exploration of the popular legend of the revolution's meaning). Georges Sorel based his *Réflexions sur la violence* on a myth of the proletarian general strike that probably reflected the revival of the French revolutionary myth in the Paris Commune. On the whole, one has to distinguish between the active life of a collective myth, which is no longer than the life of the oldest people who experienced the social convulsion on which the myth was based (they serve as a bardic point of reference, a living *lieu de mémoire,* for the young), and the passive afterlife of such a myth. In the case of the French Revolution of 1789, the terminus of its effectiveness as myth was probably the Commune of 1871, eighty-two years later. In the case of the German national revolution of 1848, its

end point seems to have been the Nazi seizure of power of 1933, eighty-five years later. The subject of revolutionary myth was treated (though not in these terms) during the 1988 annual meeting of the Centre de Recherche sur l'Imaginaire at the University of Grenoble: Yves Chalas, ed., *Mythes et révolutions* (Grenoble: Presses Universitaires de Grenoble, 1990).

7. Most socialist parties were split between an avowedly revisionist wing, like that of Bernstein, which advocated a parliamentary path to socialism, and an "orthodox" group, like that around Karl Kautsky in Germany, who continued to argue theoretically for revolution, while in practice accepting the revisionist position. The Bolsheviks, the Luxemburg group in Germany, and the Gorter–Roland Holst group in the Netherlands became, in their total rejection of parliamentary socialism, the core of the post-1918 communist movement. On the German case, see Carl E. Schorske, *German Social Democracy, 1905–1917: The Development of the Great Schism* (New York: John Wiley and Sons, 1965), and Peter Gay, *The Dilemma of Democratic Socialism: Eduard Bernstein's Challenge to Marx* (New York: Columbia University Press, 1954).

8. Rosa Luxemburg, founder of the German Communist Party, sharply criticized the antidemocratic authoritarianism of Lenin immediately after the 1917 revolution in *The Russian Revolution* (Ann Arbor: University of Michigan Press, 1961).

9. This last phase is analyzed minutely for the case of Communist Vietnam in Gabriel Kolko, *Vietnam: Anatomy of a Peace* (London: Routledge, 1997). *Le Monde* of January 15, 1999, contains an account of the social effects of the introduction of market capitalism in northwest China: one could as well be reading a description of unemployed workers in the European and American depression of the 1930s. More recently, the situation of workers in Chinese toy factories producing primarily for Wal-Mart was elucidated in a 58-page report by the National Labor Committee, "Toys of Misery." According to a summary of the report by Jim Hightower ("How Wal-Mart Is Remaking Our World," *Hightower Lowdown,* April 26, 2002, Web version), production workers in Guangdong province, "mostly young women and teenage girls," received 13 cents an hour—less than half of the Chinese minimum wage—during working days that normally lasted 13–16 hours, but with 20-hour shifts in peak seasons. Workers lived in 7 × 7 ft. squatters shacks, or were crammed twelve to a cubicle in dormitories that cost them $1.95 per week. Without medical insurance and subject to dismissal if they were too sick to work, workers complained, according to Hightower's summary, of "constant headaches and nausea from paint-dust hanging in the air; the indoor temperature tops 100 degrees; protective clothing is a joke; repetitive stress disorders are rampant; and there's no training on the health hazards of handling the plastics, glue, paint thinners, and other solvents." Wal-Mart, according to Hightower, imports "$10 billion worth of merchandise from several thousand Chinese factories." The recent accession of China to the World Trade Organization will no doubt increase its exports to the United States. See also "Les Vietnamiens saisis par le capitalisme," *Le Monde,* September 5, 2001: "With residential suburbs, golf, industrial zoning, and even a stock exchange, Communist Vietnam, following China, is trying its hand at the market economy. Prudently and unostentatiously, local entrepreneurs are getting

rich, especially in the South near the old city of Saigon, which has become the business capital."

10. Robert B. Reich, *The Work of Nations: Preparing Ourselves for 21st Century Capitalism* (New York: Vintage, 1992); *The Downsizing of America* [a special report of the *New York Times*] (New York: Random House, 1996); Rifkin, *End of Work;* Sennett, *Corrosion of Character;* William Julius Wilson, *When Work Disappears: The World of the New Urban Poor* (New York: Vintage, 1996); Bernard Perret, *L'avenir du travail: Les démocraties face au chômage* (Paris: Seuil, 1995); Robert Castel, *Les métamorphoses de la question sociale: Une chronique du salariat* (Paris: Fayard, 1995); Dominique Méda, *Le travail, une valeur en voie de disparition* (Paris: Aubier, 1995): Christophe Desjours, *Souffrance en France: La banalisation de l'injustice sociale* (Paris: Seuil, 1998); Viviane Forrester, *L'horreur économique* (Paris: Fayard, 1996); idem, *Une étrange dictature* (Paris: Fayard, 2000); André Gorz, *Métamorphoses du travail: Quête du sens* (Paris: Galilée, 1988); idem, *Misères du présent, richesse du possible* (Paris: Galilée, 1997).

11. In the Netherlands, both kinds of jobs were on the point of disappearing in 2001.

12. Two examples from Naomi Klein's *No Logo* (p. 248): "In 1993 American Airlines outsourced the ticket counters at twenty-eight U.S. airports to outside agencies. Around 550 ticketing-agent jobs went temp and, in some cases, workers who earned $40,000 were offered their same jobs back for $16,000. A similar reshuffling took place when UPS decided to turn over its customer-service centers to outside contractors—5,000 employees earning $10 to $12 an hour were replaced with temps earning between $6.50 and $8."

13. I borrow these terms from Immanuel Wallerstein's books on the capitalist world system.

14. The United States contains 9,363,000 km², while the fifteen nations now loosely associated in the European Union have together about 3,250,000 km²: roughly one-third as much. The largest of these states are France, with 543,000 km², and Spain, with 505,000 km², each of them only about 6 percent as large as the United States. The United Kingdom, Germany, and Italy, with respectively 245,000 km², 357,000 km², and 301,000 km², are individually between 2 and 3 percent the size of the United States. The Benelux countries—Belgium, the Netherlands, and Luxemburg—have together considerably less than 1 percent of the territory of the United States.

15. Between 1947 and 1979, according to a study by the Economic Policy Institute, income for the bottom 20 percent of Americans grew by 120 percent, and for the top 20 percent by 94 percent. Between 1979 and 1998, contrariwise, income for the bottom 20 percent *fell* by 5 percent, while it grew by 38 percent for the top 20 percent. Cited in "Questions from the Floor," *Nation,* October 16, 2000.

16. For statistics on the decline of U.S. hegemony: Richard du Boff, "Hegemony Ain't What It Was," a paper presented to the conference Reflections on the Social Import of American Multinational Corporations, held in Grenoble, France, on January 11–12, 2002.

17. Annual European mergers and acquisitions increased, between 1995 and 1999,

from about $300 billion to over $1,200 billion. About half of this increase occurred after the introduction of the euro on January 1, 1999 (*Financial Times,* January 1, 2000, p. 26). The acceleration in mergers and acquisitions continued from the first half of 1999 ($485 billion, according to the *Financial Times* of July 5, 1999) to the second half (apparently over $700 billion).

18. I wrote this paragraph shortly before reading an article about the "Macho takeovers" of the late nineties in the pro-business Dutch *NRC Handelsblad* of December 11, 1999. The author of the article, Menno Tamminga, fully supports my view. Tamminga refers to the present era as "the years of rough-and-tumble capitalism *{klits-klets-klander kapitalisme},* in which top managers behave openly as predators: it is eat or be eaten. If managers cannot realize their ambitions for increasing scale and cutting costs with the agreement of their desired partner for merger or takeover, they hesitate less then ever to try a hostile takeover."

19. For instance, discussing the possibility that investors may shift in the coming years from equities to bonds because of weakened consumer demand, which would depress the stock market, John Plender writes, "Many assume that globalization will solve the problem. People in mature economies with poor profit opportunities will invest in youthful emerging markets, where returns are higher" ("A Bumpy Ride to the Market," *Financial Times,* January 3, 2000).

20. Despite imitation of the Japanese model by American auto makers, Japanese superiority continued until the end of the twentieth century, when Toyota's factory in Ontario was declared still more efficient in terms of labor costs than any of its North American competitors ("Japanese Car Plants Keep Productivity Lead in US," *Financial Times,* June 6, 1999).

21. A multinational corporation, the combination of more than one nationally based capitalist enterprise, is usually dominated by its largest national component. A transnational corporation is a corporation in which the national base has been cut off to allow for more "flexible" investment policies.

22. "Of the $10,000 paid to GM [for a Pontiac Le Mans], about $3,000 goes to South Korea for routine labor and assembly operations, $1,750 to Japan for advanced components (engines, transaxles and electronics), $750 to West Germany for styling and design engineering, $400 to Taiwan, Singapore, and Japan for small components, $250 to Britain for advertising and marketing services, and about $50 to Ireland and Barbados for data processing. The rest—less than $4,000—goes to strategists in Detroit, lawyers and bankers in New York, [lobbyists] in Washington, insurance and health-care workers all over the country, and General Motors shareholders—most of whom live in the United States, but an increasing number of whom are foreign nationals." Robert Reich, *Work of Nations,* p. 113. Reich also informs us that "by 1990, Chrysler Corporation directly produced only about 30 percent of the value of its cars; Ford, about 50 percent. General Motors bought half its engineering and design services from 800 different companies" (p. 94).

23. Now that the erstwhile Philips production center in Eindhoven, Netherlands, has been scattered to the winds of (cheap) global production, the grounds are being turned into a large research center.

24. One of the many statements of this dilemma is Philip Stephens, "Markets March across Europe" (*Financial Times,* January 7, 2000), which underlines the responsibility of the Maastricht Treaty in the undermining of national sovereignty by "stateless European corporations": "The market-driven integration of European businesses promises to bypass elected governments while leaving them to deal with the consequences. Shareholders may decide whether long-established businesses are lost to merger and acquisition, but national politicians will be unable to escape the impact—social, economic and electoral—of the new phase of integration." Stephens adds ominously: "And we will all discover soon enough that the new religion of shareholder value is far from infallible."

25. This was written before the sharp rise in U.S. unemployment in the recession of 2001. In any case, American unemployment figures would be higher if they included the two million citizens, mostly from minority groups, in prison.

26. Tom Nairn cited this sentence in "Ukania under Blair," a brilliant critique of the "corporate populism" and the "over-adaptation to the economics of Thatcherism and deregulated liberalism" of the present Labour government (*New Left Review,* n.s., no. 1 [January/February 2000]: 73, 94).

27. Indulging an unusual taste for fantasy, the editorialist imagined the Lisbon summit as the board meeting of Europe Inc. and spelled out the condemnation by a Lady Thatcher-like CEO of welfare state remnants—persisting unemployment insurance and the abhorrent thirty-five-hour week in France—and her praise for New Labour: "Mr Blair, I like the way your government has looked after Britain's finances and I admire the tough line with idlers in the workforce. You will run France." Possibly as a riposte to this neoliberal fairy tale, Will Hutton, in *The Observer* of April 2, 2000, pointed out that the United Kingdom, with more workers in a forty-eight-hour week than anywhere else in Europe and with an economic establishment continually decrying the inflexible and insufficient hours of continental workers, had 20 percent less productivity per worker than its member nations of the European Union. Two years later, a columnist in the *International Herald Tribune* cited Peter Mandelson, Blair's principle adviser as saying, "We are all Thatcherites now" (Joseph Fitchett, "The Global Class," *International Herald Tribune,* June 13, 2002).

28. Exceptionally, the Socialist government of Lionel Jospin condemned the planned firing of thousands of Michelin workers in October 1999. This may have been for tactical reasons, since the French Communist, Trotskyist, and Green parties, all to the left of the Socialists, had just won over 21 percent of the votes in the European parliamentary elections.

29. In the Netherlands, the PVDA (Labor Party) was in coalition not merely with the centrist D66 (liberal democrats), but also with the economically and socially conservative and neoliberal VVD.

30. "Ethnic Albanians bent on revenge set fire to the Serb-populated village of Belo Polje despite the presence of Italian peace-keepers, and an elderly Serb woman watched over the body of a daughter she said had been raped and stabbed by men in rebel uniform. Two more bodies were found in the provincial capital Pristina after at least 14 murders late last week" ("Kfor [Nato forces in Kosovo] Struggles in

Kosovo as UN Police Force Delayed," *Financial Times,* June 28, 1999); see also "Refugee Influx Brings Looting and Murders," *Financial Times,* June 26–27, 1999; and "Church Warns over Attacks on Serbs," June 29, 1999. Six months after these reports on the return of Kosovo's Albanian population, an Independent Television (ITV) documentary in January 2000 made the point that "the 'ethnic cleansing' of Albanians by Serbs has been halted, only to be replaced by the ethnic cleansing of Serbs by Albanians . . . 75 per cent of the original Serb population [has been] driven out" (*Financial Times,* January 16, 2000). Far from abating, Albanian hatred of the Serb minority required the permanent presence of NATO "peace-keepers" to protect the remaining fifty thousand Serbs.

31. "Europe's Apathetic Voters Stay Away from the Polls," *Financial Times,* June 14, 1999. Apathy was greatest, particularly among normally leftist voters, in Great Britain (only 23 percent voted) and the Netherlands (30 percent), the two countries where social-democratic parties most blatantly represent neoliberal capitalist interests.

32. Regionalism, albeit de facto rather than de jure, also appears to be far advanced in North America, where "'patriotism' will become increasingly regional as people in Alberta and Montana discover that they have far more in common with each other than they do with Ottawa or Washington, and Spanish-speakers in the Southwest discover a greater commonality with Mexico City" (Robert Kaplan, *The Coming Anarchy* [New York: Vintage, 2001]).

33. C. B. Macpherson, *The Political Theory of Possessive Individualism: Hobbes to Locke* (Oxford: Clarendon Press, 1962), p. 275.

34. Michel Albert, *Capitalisme contre capitalisme* (Paris: Seuil, 1991).

35. Comparable to the undermining of the German Rhineland model has been the subversion of the Dutch *poldermodel* by Americanization of its management. This has gone so far that Aegon (an insurance firm), a flagship of the Dutch economy, now has an American CEO, Don Shepard, and holds its board meetings in English. According to Menno Tamminga (*NRC Handelsblad,* November 10, 2001), the same Americanization is well advanced in other large Dutch corporations: ABN Amro, Ahold, ING, Philips, VNU, Numico, and Wolters Kluwer.

36. Paul Krugman, "The 55-cent Solution," *New York Times,* November 21, 2001.

37. One of the causes for concern about the state of the American economy has been that for years American consumers were borrowing more heavily than ever to finance their purchases: in 1999, they spent about $1.06 for every dollar earned.

Three. Consumer Paradise

1. Martin Wolf, "Individualism Shows the Way," *Financial Times,* March 3, 2000, p. 11. In this review of Deepak Lal's *Unintended Consequences,* Wolf reveals Lal's interesting argument that individualism was advanced unintentionally by medieval popes who merely wanted the wealthy to be able to bequeath their lands to the church and who did not realize that the resultant rise of economic freedom would create a market economy and jeopardize the traditional values the church was based on. In the latter part of his article, Wolf discusses Lal's contention "that any

non-western society able to adopt [the west's] material beliefs in science and the market economy should be able to rival its prosperity . . . without adopting the west's faith in the primacy of personal liberty over social obligations."

2. The aggregate wealth of the world's richest two hundred billionaires comes, according to a news report of the spring of 1999, to a trillion dollars, to which the president of Microsoft alone contributes nearly 10 percent (92 billion dollars).

3. The advertising world fully recognizes this situation. In the spring of 1997, BBC news reported action by the British medical profession against a radio commercial for a pharmaceutical company's latest painkiller, one that exploited the pervasive anxiety about downsizing. The commercial evoked sympathetically the painful accompaniments of a flu and asked, "Who would go to work in a state like this?" and answered categorically: "The person who wants your job, that's who. Take ——— for instant relief."

4. Gellner, *Nations and Nationalism,* p. 22. Henry Adams said something similar: "We have a single system . . . in that system the only question is the price at which the proletariat is to be bought and sold, the bread and circuses" (quoted in Gore Vidal, *Armageddon* [London: André Deutsch, 1987], p. 122).

5. Gellner, *Nations and Nationalism,* p. 22.

6. James B. Twitchell, *Adcult USA: The Triumph of Advertising in American Culture* (New York: Columbia University Press, 1996), p. 11.

7. Slater, *Consumer Culture and Modernity,* p. 185.

8. Michelet, *Le peuple,* p. 97.

9. Slater, *Consumer Culture and Modernity,* pp. 183–86.

10. David Harvey, *The Condition of Postmodernity* (Oxford: Blackwell, 1990), p. 126.

11. The classic muckraking essay on advertising is Vance Packard, *The Hidden Persuaders* (New York: David McKay, 1957). Since then, Stephen Fox's more positive monograph, *The Mirror Makers: A History of American Advertising and Its Creators* (New York: William Morrow, 1984), has been countered by critical essays by Herbert Schiller (*Culture, Inc.: The Corporate Takeover of Public Expression* [New York: Oxford University Press, 1989]), C. Edwin Baker (*Advertising and a Democratic Press* [Princeton, N.J.: Princeton University Press, 1994]), Robert Goldman (*Reading Ads Socially* [London: Routledge, 1992]), and Sylvan Leslie (*The Sponsored Life: Ads, TV and American Culture* [Philadelphia: Temple University Press, 1994]). An erudite and well-written historical treatment that puts American advertising in a framework of literature and social thought is Jackson Lears, *Fables of Abundance: A Cultural History of Advertising in America* (New York: Basic Books, 1994). James Twitchell's *Adcult USA* is cynical but lively and well informed. His bibliography lists some two hundred books and articles, about 80 percent of them written since 1975.

12. "How to Spend It" is the literal title of a thick, glossy supplement to the weekend *Financial Times,* in which the managerial elite is instructed in the art of conspicuous consumption.

13. For an excellent critique of "consumption as freedom," see Conrad Lodziak, *The Myth of Consumerism* (London: Pluto Press, 2002), pp. 68–86. Two months after the

leveling of the World Trade Center, a *New Yorker* (November 12, 2001) cartoon parodied the connection of patriotic hype and hedonistic consumer capitalism in a depiction of a bleary-eyed but well-dressed man in a bar saying to his companion, "I figure if I don't have that third Martini, then the terrorists win."

14. Slater, *Consumer Culture and Modernity*, p. 33 (see also pp. 38, 42, 54). The presumed autonomy of this "rational" male consumer links him to the mysogynist assumptions of liberal Prometheanism (hence Slater's insertion of *sic*). The more cynical perspective of the advertising executive banks on "the supposedly feminine character of the irrational, manipulated and domestic consumer," a point of view cogently presented in Émile Zola's novel of the department store world, *Au bonheur des dames*.

15. Aleksei Stakhanov was a Soviet miner whose near-miraculous feats of productivity—he was alleged to have mined 102 tons of coal in a single shift—were widely propagandized by the regime as a model for his peers. In 1951, the Stakhanovite movement was renamed "The Movement of Shock Workers and Innovators."

16. Thorstein Veblen's argument, that the conspicuous consumption of aristocracies served as a magnet for the ambitions of the classes below them, inspired much of the literature on consumption in the twentieth century, but has been deprecated as an explanation of English middle-class consumption in the Victorian era by Lori Ann Loeb in *Consuming Angels: Advertising and Victorian Women* (New York: Oxford University Press, 1994), pp. 159–61. Loeb writes that "Neither paternalism, dandyism or the cavalier tradition with their emphasis on restraint . . . could provide any meaningful impetus for mass consumption," and views the retail revolution of the standardized department store as a displacement of popular fairs and markets. Colin Campbell, after a more nuanced critique of aspects of Veblen's theory in *The Romantic Ethic and the Spirit of Consumerism* (Oxford: Blackwell, 1987), pp. 49–57, still finds strong links between the aristocratic models of the cavalier and the dandy and bourgeois consumerism; and Rosalind Williams, in *Dream Worlds, Mass Consumption in Late Nineteenth-Century France* (Berkeley: University of California Press, 1982), also applies the Veblenite thesis of the importance of aristocratic models to France in a chapter on "Dandies and Elitist Consumption." No doubt both popular and aristocratic models were viable alternatives to bourgeois restraint.

17. Slater, *Consumer Culture and Modernity*, pp. 40–50, 77–81.

18. These social thinkers were, in France, the *nouveaux philosophes* of the 1970s and 1980s, such as Bernard-Henri Lévy and André Glucksman.

19. A dichotomous view of modern society similar to that of Zola's, but based on the romantic celebration of individual genius rather than on the revolutionary tradition, appeared on the other side of the Rhine in the work of the economist Werner Sombart. Two decades after Zola's apotheosis of the modern capitalist in *Au bonheur des dames* and *L'Argent*, Sombart was celebrating the modern capitalist entrepreneur as culture hero (in *Der Bourgeois*) at roughly the same time that he was condemning modern consumer society as decadent in the avant-garde review *Morgen*. (See A. Mitzman, *Sociology and Estrangement: Three Sociologists of Imperial Germany* [New Brunswick, N.J.: Transaction, 1986].)

20. Martin Jay, *The Dialectical Imagination: A History of the Frankfurt School and the Institute of Social Research, 1923–1950* (Boston: Little, Brown, 1973); Rolf Wiggershaus, *The Frankfurt School: Its History, Theories and Political Significance* (Cambridge: MIT Press, 1994).

21. Herbert Marcuse, *One Dimensional Man: Studies in the Ideology of Advanced Industrial Society* (Boston: Beacon, 1964), p. 32.

22. Ibid., p. 74.

23. Ibid., p. 75.

24. Quoted in Slater, *Consumer Culture and Modernity,* p. 124.

25. See Holly Yeager, "The Rise of Consumption Man," *Financial Times,* April 26, 2000 (a review of David Brooks, *Bobos in Paradise: The New Upper Class and How They Got There* [New York: Simon and Schuster, 2000]). A similar point is made by Bruce J. Schulman in "Eco-Kapitalisten komen zich zelf tegen," *NRC Handelsblad,* May 13, 2000. Schulman cites the cases of prominent yippies of the sixties who became yuppie models in the eighties.

26. Klein, *No Logo,* p. 291. Europe is no different. In France, obtaining consumer goods is the goal of much of the organized social aggression of the lower orders, which shows the ideological power of consumer society on those unable to participate in it by normal means. When Parisian secondary school students demonstrated in the fall of 1998 for better schooling, unemployed immigrant youngsters from the slums on the edge of the city preempted the demonstration by massive plundering of the shops at the assembly point. A French sociologist, Didier Lapeyronnie, has said, "I am always struck by the extraordinary psychological power of the world of consumption in the *cités* [suburban working-class housing]. In the secondary schools, boys can be beaten up for not wearing clothes with the right label. We're not dealing with the excluded. When you talk calmly with youth who have been violent, they know where they're at, they have well-defined moral values. They are informed people, who participate directly in our society, if only through consumption, through their cultural reference points" (*Le Monde,* January 12, 1999, p. 10). Another French sociologist, Laurent Mucchielli, attributes youth violence in the impoverished suburbs (*banlieues*) to, among other things, "increasingly individualist societies, ever more focused on consumption, where major collective beliefs and political leadership have both been discredited" (interview, *Le Monde,* November 13, 2001).

27. Gellner, *Nations and Nationalism,* p. 18. Don Slater, like Gellner, refers to consumer culture as a "'bribe' in that workers . . . are offered freedom and relative plenty in the sphere of consumption in exchange for . . . rationalization, alienation and utter lack of control over their work life, and for politically accepting a 'democratic' system that manages but does not fundamentally challenge capitalism" (*Consumer Culture and Modernity,* p. 188).

28. Thorstein Veblen, *Theory of the Leisure Class* (1899; reprint, New York: Modern Library, 1934).

29. Ernest van den Haag, "Of Happiness and Despair We Have No Measure," in *Man*

Alone, Alienation in Modern Society, edited by Eric Josephson and Mary Josephson (New York: Dell, 1962), p. 181.

30. Ibid., p. 184.

31. David Riesman, *The Lonely Crowd* (New Haven: Yale University Press, 1961), p. 147.

32. Max Horkheimer did recognize affinities between Riesman's approach and the Frankfurt School's, particularly on the question of anti-Semitism. Commenting on a manuscript on that subject by Riesman, Horkheimer wrote Marcuse: "Who is this Mr Riesman? His ideas coincide strangely with our own. . . . He seems either to be a very intelligent man or to have studied successfully our publications" (Wiggershaus, *Frankfurt School,* p. 424).

33. For the concept of cultural distinction, see Pierre Bourdieu, *Distinction: A Social Critique of the Judgement of Taste* (London: Routledge and Kegan Paul, 1984).

34. Mike Featherstone, *Consumer Culture and Postmodernism* (London: Sage, 1991), p. 22.

35. Ibid.

36. Kaplan, *Coming Anarchy,* p. 91. According to a CNN documentary cited by Kaplan, the spectators themselves (who often brought young children to these massacres) talked about wanting to see blood.

37. Only in a dystopia like Kubrick's *Clockwork Orange* is gang violence revealed as the other side of consumer society.

38. Geov Parrish, "Bush's Sickening Super Bowl Propaganda," Feb. 4, 2002 (www. alternet.org). Parrish pillories the linking, in $1.6 million U.S. government Super Bowl advertising, of the "War on terrorism" to the "War on Drugs." He reminds us that it was the "terrorist" Talibans who *eliminated* the poppy/heroine cultivation (and been financially remunerated by the U.S. for doing so only months before 9/11) while it was the Northern War Lords the U.S. armed to oust the Taliban who *restored* it. Parrish also points out that much of the money paid by car-addicted American consumers to fuel their expensive and polluting gas buggies ends up in terrorist hands through the Saudi oil sheiks that U.S. companies buy their oil from. See the last part of this chapter.

39. Twitchell, op. cit., p. 138.

40. "Dot Com Advertising Invades the Super Bowl," *Financial Times,* January 28, 2000.

41. Mikhail Bakhtin, *Rabelais and His World* (Cambridge: MIT Press, 1968); Peter Stallybrass and Allon White, *The Politics and Poetics of Transgression* (Ithaca, N.Y.: Cornell University Press, 1986).

42. Featherstone, *Consumer Culture and Postmodernism,* p. 22.

43. Ibid. Featherstone's precise terminology is that "these enclaved liminal moments of ordered disorder were not completely integrated by the state or the emerging consumer culture industries and 'civilizing processes,'" which is putting it very mildly indeed.

44. Ibid., p. 23. I have omitted Featherstone's source citations.

45. Ibid., pp. 23–24. For an erudite critique of the "aestheticization of everyday life" thesis in contemporary theorizing about consumer culture, with special attention to Featherstone, see Lodziak, *Myth of Consumerism,* pp. 38–45.

46. In Ensor's painting of 1888, a sad-eyed savior on a donkey is welcomed to the Belgian capital by fat-cheeked burghers in carnival dress and a garish brass band.

47. Alain Faure, *Paris carême-prenant: Du carnaval à Paris au XIXe siècle* (Paris: Hachette, 1979).

48. The centuries of persecution of the popular culture (though not the decades of rejuvenation after the French Revolution) are analyzed in Muchembled, *Popular Culture and Elite Culture.*

49. Faure, *Paris carême-prenant.*

50. On the privatization of public space in the American shopping mall, see Lizabeth Cohen, "From Town Center to Shopping Center: The Reconfiguration of Community Marketing Places in America," *American Historical Review* 101, no. 4 (October 1996). Naomi Klein has a brief discussion of this ("Privatizing the Town Square") in *No Logo,* pp. 182–90. For earlier phases of the privatization and compartmentalization of public space, see Richard Sennett, *The Fall of Public Man* (New York: Alfred A. Knopf, 1977), and Jane Jacobs, *The Death and Life of Great American Cities* (New York: Random House, 1981).

51. Klein (*No Logo,* p. 130) writes: "we live in a double world: carnival on the surface, consolidation underneath, where it counts. Everyone has, in one form or another, witnessed the odd double vision of vast consumer choice coupled with Orwellian new restrictions on cultural production and public space."

52. See Twitchell's documentation of advertisers' control of media (under the heading "Adcult rule number one: Speech is never free") in *Adcult USA,* pp. 116–20.

53. Schlosser, *Fast Food Nation.*

54. Robert H. Frank, *Luxury Fever: Money and Happiness in an Era of Excess* (Princeton, N.J.: Princeton University Press, 1999), p. 19.

55. My point is comparable to that made by the French American economist Susan George in *The Lugano Report* (London: Pluto, 1999), in which a fictional group of economic advisers make recommendations (plausible in terms of present-day neoliberal strategy) for drastic world population reduction through covert stimulation of famine, war, and disease in the third world. More concise than Susan George's black satire is the remark made by Vandana Shiva on June 13, 2002 (on Amy Goodman's *Democracy Now* radio show) that "the war against terror is being converted into a war against Terra."

56. Deffeyes, *Hubbert's Peak.* See also: Johnny Angel, "Its the Oil," *L.A. Weekly,* September 21–27, 2001, Web edition; Rich Duncan, "Running on EMPTY. The Oil Crash and You," *OnEmpty2,* August 30, 2001, Web edition.

57. Gabriel Kolko, *Another Century of War* (New York: New Press, 2002), pp. 22–24.

58. When the United States wanted to punish Iraq in 1998 for refusal of UN inspection teams, it was able quickly to station an armada of two aircraft carriers (with seventy-five aircraft each), a cruiser (armed with Tomahawk and Harpoon missiles),

four destroyers (ditto), three guided missile frigates, an attack submarine, and two minesweepers in the Persian Gulf. (Klare, *Resource Wars,* p. 63).

59. Iraq's invasion of Kuwait, tacitly encouraged by the U.S. ambassadress when she did not include Kuwait in a list of areas worthy of U.S. strategic interest, was motivated by a long-standing quarrel with the emirate over a large oil reserve that ran under both countries. Annexing the Kuwaiti oil reserves would have put fields nearly as great as those of Saudi Arabia under the direct control of a formerly pro-Soviet military power that might next have threatened the Saudi reserves themselves. George Bush Sr. justified military intervention in these words: "Our country now imports nearly half the oil it consumes and could face a major threat to its economic independence . . . the sovereign independence of Saudi Arabia is of vital interest to the United States" (ibid., p 34).

60. The Saudi-funded Koran schools became necessary when the World Bank, in line with neoliberal ideology, threatened to cut loans to Pakistan unless its government cut spending to the bone and transferred vital public services to the private sector. The school system was virtually wiped out, and the private schools that replaced it were the Saudi-supported madrasas. Another kind of blowback.

61. Chalmers Johnson, *Blowback: The Costs and Consequences of American Empire* (New York: Henry Holt, 2001), pp. 10–11.

62. Bernard Lewis, "The Revolt of Islam," *The New Yorker,* November 19, 2001, p. 62.

63. The Israeli connection may not be as important (in U.S. eyes) as the oil issue or (in Al Qaeda's eyes) as the question of American hegemony, but the apparent refusal of the Israelis to end West Bank settler expansionism is a persistent thorn in the side of Muslim dignity and the suicide tactics of the Islamic irreconcilables in Hamas and Hezbollah were the model for those used by Mohammed Atah and his companions.

64. In a polemic against the claim of radical fundamentalists that Islam's "humiliation" by the West was responsible for the attacks of September 11, the psychoanalyst Fethi Benslama ("Islam: Quelle humiliation?" *Le Monde,* November 28, 2001) sees a combination of petro dollars and indigenous corruption, particularly in the Saudi elites, as supporting an archaic domination that crushes enlightenment and political opposition. Writing of the Saudi elites, Benslama says, "The theme of [Arab] humiliation by the United States or the West allows them to escape their primary responsibility." While agreeing that these elites only retain power thanks to the complicity of the West and that the United States, uninterested in the people supposedly represented by the Saudi state, "is hated for its arrogant power," he attributes the world's "detestable image of the Arabs" to the Saudi elites' "indecency of . . . displays of wealth and the ugliness of their manners, which they pretend is a cultural patrimony." Benslama recognizes the peculiar symbiosis I have signaled between the power of archaic but oil-rich sheiks and neoliberal capitalism:

> Monopolization of wealth and subordination of the state to the private interests of families and super-rich clans has propelled them, in their very archaism, into the avant-garde of the neoliberalism of the world market. . . .

That's what explains their powerful alliance with the American neoliberal camp. . . . Profiting from the Cold War, . . . the [petrol-owning] families finance the emergence of radical Islamic movements to destroy the forces of liberation, stop the interpretation of ancient texts and spread their own values. They succeed beyond their hopes. With the left destroyed, political action has no other possibility than to take the form of an emotionally armored religious ideology mixed with nostalgia for a golden age. It converts the exclusion of the masses into a powerful resentment against modernity.

Four: Theoretical Interlude

1. See Chapter 2, notes 26, 27.

2. In contemporary political philosophy, individualism is attacked by communitarians such as Michael Walzer, Amitai Etzioni, and Charles Taylor. Perhaps the decisive (if implicit) refutation of possessive individualism is the ethical philosophy of Immanuel Kant. Kant postulated a categorical imperative that imposed social restraint through the imaginary extrapolation of individually useful acts: lying or stealing may serve individual interests, but are excluded from legitimation precisely because their collective elaboration makes any kind of communication or orderly relations between individuals impossible. In the history of European social theory, possessive individualism has been directly attacked or relativized in the nineteenth century by French thinkers as diverse as Félicité de Lamennais, Charles Fourier, Jules Michelet, and Émile Durkheim; by Germans as varied as Friedrich Karl von Savigny, Karl Marx, and Ferdinand Tönnies; by the anthropologist Marcel Mauss, the economist Karl Polanyi, and the critical theorists of the Frankfurt School in the early twentieth century. The more recent versions of this attack come from critics such as André Gorz, David Harvey, Hilary Wainwright, Alain Caillé, Dominique Méda, and Don Slater; from the social and cultural historians E. P. Thompson and Raymond Williams; and from the followers of Lucien Febvre and Marc Bloch.

3. Cf. Weinstein and Platt, *Wish to Be Free.*

4. David Landes, *Prometheus Unbound: Technological Change and Industrial Development in Western Europe from 1750 to the Present* (Cambridge: Cambridge University Press, 1969).

5. On the symbiotic relationship between French capitalists of the early modern period and the old regime Bourbon monarchy, see Fox, *History in Geographic Perspective.*

6. "The assumptions of possessive individualism have been retained in modern liberal theory, to an extent not always realized" (Macpherson, *Political Theory of Possessive Individualism,* pp. 270–71).

7. Freud discusses narcissism in "On Narcissism: An Introduction," in *Collected Papers,* vol. 4 (New York: Basic Books, 1959), and in *The Ego and the Id* (New York: Norton, 1960), p. 36. I discuss Schachtel's "secondary autocentricity" in the latter part of this chapter.

8. Slater, *Consumer Culture and Modernity,* p. 124. Slater also remarks: "It is generally

accepted by most parties that a commercial society is systemically dependent on the insatiability of needs: put crudely, commodity production requires the sale of ever-increasing quantities of ever-changing goods; market society is therefore perpetually haunted by the possibility that needs might be either satisfied or underfinanced" (p. 29). Boris Frankel, criticizing Alvin Toffler's ideal of combining reduced consumption, social equality, and ecological production with the maintenance of transnational corporate capitalism, makes a similar point: "Given the crisis in profitability of many existing enterprises, it is pure fantasy on Toffler's part to believe that such a massive drop in overall consumption would not result in the possible collapse of capitalist economies." Frankel, *The Post-Industrial Utopians* (London: Polity Press, 1987), p. 38.

9. Slater, *Consumer Culture and Modernity,* p. 10.

10. Ibid., p. 152.

11. Schachtel argues that the unique linguistic and, by implication, social attributes of humankind are tightly linked to this biological singularity:

> Biologically, the singular position of man . . . is largely brought about by the degree of his cerebralization and by the fact that, in comparison with those mammals which are most closely related to him in the evolutionary scale, he is born a year too early. This means that processes of maturation which in the highest mammals take place in the uniform environment of the maternal womb, in man take place outside of the womb in an infinitely richer . . . environment. . . . In this interaction with the environment the infant develops the distinctly human capacity of upright posture, and of language and insightful action, whereas the higher mammals are already born as more or less complete, small reproductions of the adult animal. . . . The infant's large cortex, especially the large association areas of its brain, make for a less direct control of behavior by environmental stimuli. (*Metamorphosis: On the Development of Affect, Perception, Attention, and Memory* [New York: Basic Books, 1959], pp. 200–201)

On the biological uniqueness of the human infant Schachtel cites Adolf Portmann, *Biologische Fragmente zu einer Lehre vom Menschen* (Basel: Schwabe, 1951).

12. Even capitalist management experts, like John Kay, director of London Economics, acknowledge this today: "Grassland hunting was more productive when groups of hunters pooled their knowledge of animal spoors and shared their catch. . . . So genetics favour co-operative man over rational economic man. Man is a social animal. This is an observation by biologists who have compared human behaviour with that of other species." John Kay, "Social Route to Economic Success," *Financial Times,* March 15, 2000.

13. Sigmund Freud discussed the "oceanic feeling" of union with the cosmos (in *Civilization and Its Discontents*) in the framework of his correspondence with the celebrated French novelist Romain Rolland. Cf. William B. Parsons, *The Enigma of the Oceanic Feeling: Revisioning the Psychoanalytic Theory of Mysticism* (Oxford: Oxford University Press, 1999), pp. 19–52.

14. There is an overlap here between Riesman's typology and the "civilisatory process" of affect control discussed by Norbert Elias, who, like Riesman, locates the domination of this process in the early modern age.

15. Examples of such legitimation are the French and Dutch laws of the 1990s giving the same status to same-sex partnerships and marriages as to heterosexual marriage, the controversial efforts in the U.S. armed forces to end discrimination against homosexuals, and the attempt in February 2000 in the United Kingdom to repeal the law that prohibits discussion of homosexuality in schools as a reasonable sexual orientation.

16. Ernest Schachtel discusses the development of play from infant autocentric pleasure in *Metamorphosis,* pp. 136–37.

17. Juliet Schor, *The Overworked American: The Unexpected Decline of Leisure* (New York: Basic Books, 1991).

18. The World Water Forum held in the Hague in March 2000 pointed to the imminent inaccessibility to pure water of half of the world's six billion people—the poorer half, of course.

19. Nancy Chodorow, in an excellent study that argues for the mutual interdependence of psychoanalysis and feminism, grants that "Freud was indeed sexist. He wrote basically from a male norm and ignored women. He repeated cultural ideology in a context where it can be mistaken for scientific findings" (*Feminism and Psychoanalytic Theory* [New Haven: Yale University Press, 1989], p. 172).

20. In *Freud and His Followers* (New York: Alfred A. Knopf, 1975) Paul Roazen provides a running psychobiographical commentary on Freud's difficulties with women, as well as a survey of the dissenting views on female sexuality of his early followers Jung, Adler, and Rank (pp. 44, 54, 91, 190, 216, 251, 267, 398, 428, 430, 472–73, 478). On Otto Gross, see A. Mitzman, "Anarchism, Expressionism and Psychoanalysis," *New German Critique* 10 (1977): 77–105.

21. See the excellent chapter on "The British Schools" in J. A. C. Brown's *Freud and the Post-Freudians* (Harmondsworth, England: Penguin Books, 1967).

22. Erich Fromm, *Love, Sexuality and Matriarchy: About Gender* (New York: Fromm International, 1997). For Fromm's critique of Freud see his *Greatness and Limitations of Freud's Thought* (New York: Harper, 1980).

23. Schachtel's *Metamorphosis,* which contains references to Marcuse's *Eros and Civilization,* includes his "On Memory and Childhood Amnesia" of 1947, an essay that Marcuse uses importantly in his own book.

24. "The most important factor in the early environment, the mother, plays a crucial role in the conflicts around the relation of the potentialities of the infant to the actualities he will realize" (Schachtel, *Metamorphosis,* p. 15).

25. Page references in the text are to Schachtel, *Metamorphosis.*

26. Sigmund Freud, "Thoughts for the Times on War and Death" [1916]; *Beyond the Pleasure Principle* [1922] (New York: Bantam Books, 1959); *Civilization and Its Discontents* [1930] (New York: Norton, 1962).

27. "The fact that certain sensory stimuli are attractive and pleasurable for the newborn infant is the complement, in the perceptual sphere, to what I have called

activity-affect in the emotional sphere" (ibid.). This idea of the neonate's active quest for contact with the world has been confirmed by Jean Decety in a lecture at the University of Paris in October 2001 ("Le sens des autres," *Le Monde,* November 2, 2001), which posits a notion similar to Schachtel's and underlines its implications for a concept of human nature. Arguing that psychological research since 1980 had overturned earlier theories that portrayed the neonate as socially isolated, Decety wrote: "We know now that from birth on babies are attracted by social stimuli (particularly the face, odor, and voice of the mother). This important orientation to others permits them to engage, from birth onward, in social interactions in the rhythm of their characteristic cycles of waking and sleeping. . . . Thus, starting at birth, the neonate interacts with culture. . . . There is no reason to oppose nature and culture; rather we should investigate their respective contributions." There is no indication in Decety's text that he was aware of Schachtel's earlier work.

28. See note 11 above.

29. Schachtel cites comparable passages by Paul Valery, Paul Cezanne, and Henri Matisse on the aesthetic blindness created by the object-of-use perspective (p. 177 n).

30. Dominique Méda, *Qu'est-ce que la richesse?* (Paris: Aubier, 1999), pp. 24–30.

31. See the powerful indictment of India's Narmada River dam program in Arundhati Roy, *The Cost of Living* (New York: Random House, 1999), pp. 1–90.

32. Cf. C. Wright Mills, *White Collar: The American Middle Classes* (New York: Oxford University Press, 1956), pp. 161–82,

33. "The views of preadolescents and adolescents tend to be, if anything, even more rigorously limiting and 'closed' than that of many parents. To have interests, perceptions, thoughts which deviate from those of the peer group carries with it the danger of scorn, ridicule, and ostracism, of social isolation" (Schachtel, *Metamorphosis,* p. 188).

34. This impulse Schachtel describes as "a closed pattern of life, by which man seeks to re-establish something akin to the security of the womb *after* the object world has emerged . . . in the exploratory play and learning of childhood" (ibid., p. 176).

35. Cf. the critical presentation of the Cartesian tradition in Fritjof Capra, *The Turning Point: Science, Society and the Rising Culture* (London: Fontana, 1988), pp. 41–281. One need not be convinced by the author's New Age mysticism to see the value of his extensive history of scientific ideas.

36. Cf. Snyders, *La pédagogie en France,* p. 265.

37. See the chapters on "The Circuitous Journey" in Abrams, *Natural Supernaturalism,* pp. 141–325.

38. In this respect, Schachtel's distinction between secondary autocentricity and allocentric perception parallels dichotomies in the sociology of Max Weber and Ferdinand Tönnies. For Tönnies, *Gemeinschaft* as an ideal form is undergirded by the perceptual mode of *Wesenwille* in which relationships are entered for their own sake, whereas *Gesellschaft* is in principle the realm of utilitarian perceptions and relations, based on a perceptual mode Tönnies called *Kürwille.* The analogous categories in the sociology of Weber are those of asceticism—closely related to the

utilitarian means-ends separation—and mysticism, characterized by "acosmic love," as two opposed paths of salvation. See my *The Iron Cage: An Historical Interpretation of Max Weber,* 2d ed. (New Brunswick, N.J.: Transaction, 1985), and *Sociology and Estrangement.*

39. Sam Mendes's film *American Beauty* reveals this transformation in the life of a white-collar worker, as did E. M. Forster in the character of Leonard Bast *(Howard's End).*

40. Schachtel's distance from the shared autocentricity of his colleagues is evident: "If there had been psychiatrists in Copernicus's time and he had told them of his idea . . . they would at best have dismissed it as an *idée fixe* and at worst would have considered him completely insane because of his 'obvious' distortion of reality" (*Metamorphosis,* p. 192).

41. Thompson, *Making of the English Working Class.*

42. Sewell, *Work and Revolution;* Arthur Mitzman, *Michelet, Historian: Rebirth and Romanticism in 19th-Century France* (New Haven: Yale University Press, 1990).

43. For a sensitive exploration of these anxieties via an analysis of family magazines at the end of the nineteenth century, see Bertholet, *Le bourgeois dans tous ses états.*

Five. The Gathering Global Revolt against Corporate Capitalism

1. The *New York Times* of December 2, 2001, was categorical on the attitude of official Arab opinion about widening the war to Iraq: "Every major Arab ally has told the White House that a long military campaign that takes the anti-terror war to Iraq would inflame the region, splinter the coalition and undermine the peace process. The Egyptian Foreign Minister, Ahmed Maher, visiting Washington, told one audience that a broader war will look like a Western assault on Islamic countries and 'will have a negative impact all over.'"

2. The weekly *Observer* of December 2, 2001, carried a front page article detailing U.S. plans to carry the war to Iraq in the face of Blair's refusal to cooperate.

3. But not in Belorusskaya, only a few miles north of Chernobyl: "Les enfants de Tchernobyl face á la 'mort invisible,'" *Le Monde,* May 20, 2000.

4. According to the Trade and Environment Database (TED), case study 233, estimates of those killed directly in Bhopal are as high as 4,000, and of the injured, 400,000 (www.american.edu/mandala/TED/BHOPAL.HTM). Most of the dead occurred among impoverished people in shanty towns adjacent to the factory. Fifteen years after the Union Carbide disaster, ground and groundwater samples at the factory site showed levels of toxic mercury contamination to be between 20,000 and 6,000,000 times the normal background level, according to a Greenpeace press release of November 29, 1999 ("Former Union Carbide Site Still Heavily Contaminated 15 Years On"). Greenpeace believes 16,000 died in all because of the accident. An estimate from the time of the disaster (in Paul Shrivastava, *Bhopal: Anatomy of a Crisis* [Cambridge, Mass.: Ballinger, 1987], p. 13) gives 2,500 dead and "180,000 other casualties."

5. For an Internet description of the Karnataka State Farmers Association (KRRS), which claims ten million members: www.dsl.nl/icc/ICC-en/KRRS-en.htm. On

the dams, their effects, and the resistance to them: Arundhati Roy, "The Greater Common Good," in *The Cost of Living* (New York: Modern Library Paperback, 2000), pp. 1–90. In the state of Maharashtra (pop. 75,000,000) the nonviolent anti-dam movement Narmada Bachao Andolan works together with Greenpeace and more than a dozen trade unions and civic and tribal organizations in the National Alliance of People's Movements (NAPM), which deals with issues of land, water, and forest rights, local self-government, displacement, labor and poverty in town and country, and women's rights. In April some two thousand representatives of the affiliated organizations of the NAPM assembled for "songs, dances and street theatre" and to attend discussion panels (article of April 11, 2000, on the website of the Mobilization for Global Justice: "Two Thousand Participate in Public Hearing in India," <www.a16.org/feature.cfm?ID=1>).

6. In Germany, where the *Grünen* had expected a withdrawal from nuclear power within a decade, a government proposal in April 2000 to close Germany's atomic power stations in thirty years met with irreconcilable opposition from power companies ("Talks Stall over Closure of German Atomic Plants," *Financial Times,* April 18, 2000).

7. Trade and Environment (TED), case 245, www.american.edu/mandala/TED/BHOPAL.HTM.

8. "Le catastrophe: The Bill for the Gales That Uprooted Forests and the Oil Spill That Is Killing Thousands of Sea Birds Could Top £7 Billion," *Guardian,* January 9, 2000.

9. Hertz, *Silent Takeover,* p. 42.

10. *Le Monde,* April 12, 2000.

11. *NRC Handelsblad,* April 11, 2000. The government gave in after a declaration of martial law and the arrest of twenty trade unionists failed to end the protests. In Achacachi, Aymara Indians armed with machetes stormed a hospital to lynch an army officer after two peasants were killed in riots. The city of Cochabamba remained for several days in the hands of rebels, and police in La Paz and Santa Cruz occupied their own headquarters and prisons to demand a 50 percent salary increase, using tear gas against besieging army units. The government charged that the cocaine mafia had organized the protests, an accusation which, considering the character and extent of the riots, lacks plausibility. (For an excellent analysis of the Bolivian revolt against water privatization and the role of the I.M.F. and World Bank, see William Finnegan, "Letter from Bolivia: Leasing the Rain," *New Yorker,* April 8, 2002, pp. 43–53; the April 9, 2000, report by Jim Schulz, "A Crisis Continues in Bolivia," on the Mobilization for Global Justice website <www.a16.org>, offers a detailed presentation of the uprising in Cochamba.) In a brief survey of Indian protest movements in the Andean republics (Bolivia, Peru, Ecuador, Venezuela, and Colombia), Richard Lapper ("Anger in the Andes," *Financial Times,* April 26, 2000) indicates the general tendency of "indigenous groups who have historically been marginalised socially and economically" to flee the dominant social-democratic and centrist parties that are "narrowly based on the white elites" and have embraced IMF-sponsored neoliberal "modernization." Instead, such

marginalized groups support outsiders with "strongly Indian features" like Peru's Alejandro Toledo (paradoxically, a former World Bank economist) and Venezuela's Hugo Chavez, who condemns "the scourge of neoliberalism" and admires Fidel Castro. Two years after Lapper's report, Peruvian popular support for Toledo seemed to be declining rapidly, as his government's sale of state-owned electricity companies to the French Suez Lyonnaise des Eaux sparked widespread riots in Peru's second-largest city. "The protesters, worried that the . . . sale . . . would mean higher utility prices and layoffs, spilled into the center of Arequipa, a city of one million people. The police used tear gas . . . to disperse crowds; one canister killed a twenty-five-year-old university student. . . . Mr. Toledo's government . . . has been buffeted by protests from people frustrated with the administration's inability to relieve poverty. . . . The crisis in Arequipa . . . underscores the deep frustration across Latin America with government efforts to privatize state industry. . . . 'The response from Latin America, the grass-roots response, has been growing rage over the privatization thrust,' said Larry Birns, director of the Council on Hemispheric Affairs in Washington, which has studied privatizations" (Juan Forero, "Peruvians Riot over Planned Sale of 2 Regional Power Plants," *New York Times,* June 18, 2002, Web edition.)

12. Roy, "Greater Common Good."

13. "Social Combustion in China," *New York Times,* April 7, 2000. On capitalism in China and Vietnam, see Chapter 2, note 9.

14. Hertz, *Silent Takeover,* p. 42. In June 2002, low wages in China were attracting U.S. textile and automobile-parts factories that had earlier moved to Mexico because of the cheap labor there. Since the end of 2000, according to the *Washington Post,* 250,000 factory workers along the U.S.-Mexican border have lost their jobs and 500 foreign-owned assembly-line factories out of 3,700—*maquiladores*—have closed because of the lure of cheaper labor in Asia. Instead of a Mexican starting wage of $1.50 to $2 an hour, for example, hungry proletarians in the People's Republic of China are willing to work for 25 cents an hour (Mary Jordan, "Mexican Workers Pay for Their Success," *Washington Post,* June 21, 2002, posted on *International Herald Tribune,* www.iht.com). A week later, the *Financial Times* reported a three-day riot against security guards in the Nanxuan wool textile factory in South China (15,000 workers) in which dozens were injured. The industrial area near Hong Kong where the factory is located "is rapidly becoming the workshop of the world as foreign manufacturers invest in droves to take advantage of a seemingly limitless supply of cheap and diligent labour." Some 30 million workers in the area are part of a 170 million-strong group of surplus Chinese farm laborers, whose earnings often are no more than $2 a day: "Many have to work 90 hours a week, some are forced to complete 30-hour shifts, and bullying by ill-trained security guards as in Nanxuan is relatively common. . . . when patience snaps, a riot can quickly ensue" (James Kynge, "Working Conditions Fuel Unrest in China." *Financial Times,* June 29, 2002).

15. The *Financial Times,* April 18, 2000, reported that the German Greens were "increasingly frustrated at the failure to make progress on [this] fundamental part of their party programme."

16. Daniel R. Brower, *The New Jacobins: The French Communist Party and the Popular Front* (Ithaca, N.Y.: Cornell University Press, 1968); Brochier et Delouche, *Les nouveaux sans-culottes.*

17. Allan Priaulx and Sanford J. Ungar, *The Almost Revolution: France, 1968* (New York: Dell, 1969).

18. At three of the main university centers of the international youth revolt, Nanterre (a new campus of the University of Paris), Columbia, and Berkeley, archaic prohibitions on visits of the opposite sex in dorms were a main source of contention.

19. The Situationists, like the Surrealists of the interwar era, fused a playful, modernist aesthetic with Marxist revolutionary perspectives. They were influential in Strasbourg, where they took over the student union from the Communists, and in Nanterre, where they were close to Daniel Cohn-Bendit's "March 22nd" anarchists. See Guy Debord, *The Society of the Spectacle* (New York: Zone Books, 1994); Debord and Gianfranco Sanguinetti, *The Veritable Split in the International: Public Circular of the Situationist International* (London: Chronos Publications, 1990); Ken Knabb, ed. and trans., *The Situationist International Anthology* (Berkeley: Bureau of Public Secrets, 1981). On the relationship between the Situationists and the dissident Marxist Socialisme ou Barbarie group in Paris, see Daniel Blanchard, "Debord in the Resounding Cataract of Time," in *Revolutionary Romanticism: A Drunken Boat Anthology,* ed. Max Blechman, pp. 223–36 (Berkeley: City Lights, 1999).

20. History was repeating itself. When faced with a previous situation fraught with revolution—the mass factory occupations and general strike of 1936—Maurice Thorez, then head of the Communist Party, told the workers, "Il faut savoir finir une grève" (you have to know how to end a strike) and quickly tried to engineer an anti-Nazi "French Front" that included every non-Hitlerian party to the right, including the semi-fascist *Croix de feu.*

21. Hervé Hamon and Patrick Rotman, *Génération 2: Les années de poudre* (Paris: Seuil, 1988).

22. "C'est possible, on fabrique, on vend, on se paie!" Henri Weber, *Vingt ans après: Que reste-t-il de 68?* (Paris: Seuil, 1988), p. 41. According to Weber, from the mid-sixties to the mid-seventies the high point of Fordist production saw both an elevated level of worker consciousness, particularly among young workers stimulated by their contact with student Marxists, and a shortage of labor that put wind in the sails of proletarian militancy. Weber was a Trotskyist student leader in 1968, a political scientist when he wrote *Vingt ans après,* and in the 1990s a principal adviser to a moderate Socialist, Laurent Fabius, who became minister of finance under Lionel Jospin in April 2000.

23. The long British miners' strike of 1984 was both the conclusive proof of the impotence of traditional proletarian militancy when faced with the new (neoliberal) capitalism represented by the Conservative Party and the first real evidence of the popular discontent with Mrs. Thatcher's policies that would lead to the Labour victory of 1997. In England, however, in contrast to France, the new

radical opposition was totally opposed by the social-democratic party's leadership which, under Tony Blair, openly implemented neoliberal principles.

24. In 1986–88 and 1993–95, the last two years of each of Mitterand's seven-year terms, the Right won the legislative elections.

25. The Parisian trend continued in 2001, when Socialists and Greens, winning a majority of the arrondissements, took over the City Hall and installed Paris's first left-wing municipal government since the Paris Commune of 1871.

26. Pierre Bourdieu, ed., *La misère du monde* (Paris: Seuil, 1993). The sale in 1996 of tens of thousands of copies of this heavy tome encouraged Bourdieu and his friends to launch a highly successful series of small, inexpensive books under the label "Liber Raisons d'Agir."

27. Pierre Bourdieu, "Contre la destruction d'une civilisation," in *Contre-feux* (Paris: Liber Raisons d'Agir, 1998).

28. Jean-Pierre Le Goff and Alain Caillé, *Le tournant de décembre* (Paris: La Découverte, 1996). Le Goff is the author of *Le mythe de l'entreprise: Critique de l'idéologie managériale* (Paris: La Découverte, 1992). Caillé is the editor of the twice-yearly *La Revue de M.A.U.S.S.* (Mouvement Anti-Utilitaire en Sciences Sociales) and the author of several books and articles. With ideas that build on the rich French tradition of social theory (in particular, Marcel Mauss's notion of *le don,* or gift exchange, as an alternative to commodity exchange), Caillé contributed importantly to the renewal of radical social criticism in the 1990s.

29. Le Goff and Caillé, *Le tournant de décembre,* p. 40.

30. Ibid., p. 41.

31. Continuing Polanyi's thought into the area of imperialist nationalism, which he did not discuss, we might add that the same imperialism provided workers with a jingoistic identification with the nation that further reduced class consciousness. Where jingoism was insufficient, industrial and preindustrial workers alike were weaned from revolutionary movements of the Left or the Right through social legislation protecting them from immiserization or (in the case of the preindustrial peasants and artisans) from extinction.

32. Le Goff and Caillé, *Le tournant de décembre,* pp. 85–86.

33. Ibid., p. 164.

34. A play on the anti-utilitarian thought of the French sociologist Marcel Mauss, who analyzed *le don* as an anthropologically widespread alternative to market exchange.

35. Le Goff and Caillé, *Le tournant de décembre,* p. 120.

36. Ibid., pp. 128–36.

37. First published in *Le Monde,* June 28, 1995. The thirty-four cosigners included the social theorists and philosophers André Gorz, Antonio Negri, and Serge Latouche; economists of labor time such as René Passet, Bernard Perret, and Alain Lipietz (the last a spokesman for the French Green Party and currently a member of the European Parliament); and prominent figures in the associationist movement: Jacques Robin, Valérie Peugeot, and Patrick Viveret.

38. Ibid., pp. 161–62. Among the hundreds of signatories were luminaries such as Jacques Derrida, Regis Debray, Etienne Balibar and Pierre Vidal-Naquet

39. Caillé has close ties to the "associationist" center on Paris's Boulevard de Grenelle, where the lively monthly *Transversales* is published by Patrick Viveret and a number of other activities are supported, mainly by volunteers.

40. Within weeks of the Left's return to power, a clash occurred between Jospin and Chirac on the crucial issue of Europe. At a meeting of the European heads of state in Amsterdam in June 1997, intended to implement the Maastricht Treaty for monetary union, Jospin and Moscovici threatened to block French approval of the final plans for a financially unified European Union until and unless there were concrete steps made toward a European-wide plan (social network and public works) for alleviation of the widespread problem of unemployment and exclusion: that is, toward the long-promised goal of a Social Europe. Chirac, opposed to this, insisted that only he could speak for France, and to avoid a potentially disastrous rupture with the still popular president, Jospin and Moscovici backed down, obtaining only a vague promise to discuss Europe's social problems at an October meeting of EU leaders in Florence.

41. By 2000, all three men had been replaced.

42. Nonetheless, during the cabinet reshuffle that followed the resignation of Allegre in the spring of 2000, Jospin did make a significant concession to the "associationist" Left, appointing Guy Hascoët, a Green member of parliament, to a new ministerial post for *économie solidaire*. It remains to be seen whether this is more than a gesture.

43. See "The Twilight of the European Left" in Chapter 2.

44. "Des syndicalistes américains de l'agriculture proposent de payer la caution de José Bové," *Le Monde,* September 4, 1999.

45. "José Bové calls . . . for a European alliance between farmers and consumers. He wants to struggle against 'economic, social, and environmental dumping' and pressure the WTO. 'There is a national consensus against junk food,' he asserts" ("Les nouvelles frontières des paysans," *Le Monde,* September 9, 1999).

46. "La véridique histoire de José Bové," *Le Monde,* June 29, 2000.

47. Articles in *Le Monde,* June 27–July 1, 2000. Nearly two years later, on June 19, 2002, Bové began his prison term, leisurely driving to prison on a tractor over a sixty-mile route through the southern French countryside, accompanied by several other tractors driven by militants of his peasants union, all of them bearing large signs reading *Farine animale = poison, Lutte syndicale = prison* (Cattle feed made from animal carcasses = poison, Union struggle = prison) (*Le Monde,* June 20, 2002).

48. Actually, the biggest governmental role of a European Green Party resulted from a large ecological vote in the June 1999 elections in Belgium, where corruption scandals involving the major parties as well as food scandals worked in the Greens' favor, but their partners, the Socialists, with too few votes to form a leftist coalition, were obliged to form a government with the liberals, which insured inaction on the social front.

49. Martin Wolf, "In Defence of Global Capitalism," *Financial Times,* December 8, 1999. A subsequent article by Jagdish Bhagwati ("An Unjustified Sense of Victory," *Financial Times,* December 21, 1999), which depicted the Seattle protesters as hostile to poor nations, was answered by Ralph Sato in the *Financial Times* of January 3, 2000. Sato argued that many of the demonstrators were *from* poor nations, demonstrating against "the disruptive effects of opening markets to trade in food products, [which] could have a devastating effect on small farmers in poor nations, since 80 per cent of agricultural trade is dominated by a handful of large corporations. Sato also pointed out that anti-WTO protesters supported the protests of delegates of poor nations against the domination of the WTO by the rich ones.

50. Letter to the editor, *Financial Times,* December 13, 1999.

51. Timothy Egan, "Free Speech vs. Free Trade," *New York Times,* December 5, 1999. The poll was conducted by the Pew Research Center.

52. Only one important government representative was unable to get through the protesters: the French finance minister Laurent Fabius, whose staff ignored police warnings to get to the meeting place before 6 A.M.

53. "JUSTICE: Police State Targets the Left," PeaceNet website, May 8, 2000.

54. Robert D. Kaplan, *An Empire Wilderness: Travels into America's Future* (New York: Random House, 1998), p. 326.

55. James Miller, *Democracy Is in the Streets: From Port Huron to the Siege of Chicago* (Cambridge: Harvard University Press, 1994), pp. 45–47, 223.

56. Schor, *Overspent American,* p. 139.

57. Ernest Callenbach, *Ecotopia: The Notebooks and Reports of William Weston* (Berkeley: Banyan Tree Books, 1975).

58. Lori Wallach, "Lori's War" (interview), *Foreign Policy,* spring 2000. On the use of the Internet as a vehicle of global resistance, see Klein, *No Logo,* pp. 357, 393–95.

59. I follow Russell Jacoby's intelligent dissection of left-wing multiculturalism in *The End of Utopia: Politics and Culture in an Age of Apathy* (New York: Basic Books, 1999). In her book about the commercialization of world society and the resistance to it, Naomi Klein is caustic about the Left's focus during the eighties and nineties on the politics of multiculturalism: "In this new globalized context, the victories of identity politics have amounted to a rearranging of the furniture while the house burned down" (*No Logo,* p. 123).

60. Liza Featherstone, "The New Student Movement," *Nation,* May 15, 2000.

61. William Finnegan shows that the small band of militants preparing East Coast college students for the D.C. demonstrations contained a large proportion of organizers from the San Francisco area (Finnegan, "After Seattle: Why Anarchism Is Making a Comeback," *New Yorker,* April 17, 2000, pp. 40–51).

62. "Peace Terrorists" (*Vredesterroristen*) was the headline of the lead article in the Saturday supplement of the Dutch *NRC Handelsblad* of September 29, 2001, citing a *Washington Post* column that linked anti-globalization protesters to the mentality of Al Qaeda terrorists. It is widely feared that U.S. antiterrorist legislation will be

used against peace and anti-globalization demonstrators. In Europe, proposed legislation in the European Parliament would penalize as terrorist even nonviolent civil disobedience against capitalist globalization. See Alima Boumediene-Thiery, Alain Krivine, and Giuseppe Di Lello Finuoli, "Europe: Vers l'état d'exception," *Le Monde,* November 29, 2001. (The authors are deputies in the European Parliament, members of its Commission on the Freedoms and Rights of Citizens.)

63. The Mexican minister of foreign affairs, Jorge Castenada, interviewed in *Le Monde* (December 2–3, 2001) argued that the September 11 attacks on America constituted a tragic episode rather than a rupture in the course of international affairs: "the other themes, development, poverty, are more long-term." Castenada said that whether the attacks led to isolationism or multilateralism in the United States, they did not signify a turning point in world history: "It's not the fall of the Berlin Wall. If the United States is unaccustomed to terrorism, Europeans are. Unfortunately, Israel too. Like many Latin American countries. For the first time, the United States finds itself in a situation comparable to other countries." Castenada expressed agreement with the view of Latin American circles who view terrorism as "a result of neoliberalism in the Islamic world." And he continued, "This effect is not so different from that provoked in the heart of the Latin-American world, whether among the indigenous peoples of Chiapas or in the shanty towns around the great Latin-American agglomerations."

64. José Bové, and Gilles Luneau, *Paysan du monde* (Paris: Fayard, 2002); Bové, "A Farmer's International," *New Left Review,* n.s., no. 12 (November–December 2001): 89–101.

65. In thus suggesting a link between Marxist Hegelianism and the romantic utopians Marx despised, I am making a liaison that may shock theorists of Marxism, romanticism, and the history of ideas in general. But in establishing affinities of this sort, it is better to ignore antipathies and look at implicit similarities, in the same way that one can now discern links between fascist and Stalinist mentalities of the thirties, or between postwar Fordist productivism in the West and Soviet planning. On the link of Marx with social romanticism, see Löwy and Sayre, *Révolte et mélancholie.*

66. The anarchist movement was particularly strong in Spain (in the Federación Anarquista Ibérica) as well as in the Ukraine and Bulgaria. Anarcho-syndicalist unionists controlled the powerful Confederación Nacional del Trabajo in Spain, but were marginalized elsewhere in Europe. On Spanish anarchism, see Murray Bookchin, *The Spanish Anarchists: The Heroic Years 1868–1936* (New York: Free Life Editions, 1977). On anarchism in France, see Jean Maîtron, *Le mouvement anarchiste en France* (Paris: Maspero, 1975). On anarchism in Russia, see Paul Avrich, *The Russian Anarchists* (Princeton, N.J.: Princeton University Press, 1967). The agrarian populists of the Social Revolutionary Party were the largest party in Russia at the time of the October Revolution, but the Constituent Assembly, in which they won a majority of seats, was dispersed by the Bolsheviks before it could meet (O. H. Radkey, *The Sickle under the Hammer: The Russian Socialist Revolutionaries in the Early Months of Soviet Rule* [New York: Columbia University Press, 1963]). On anarchist ideas in general, see David Miller, *Anarchism* (London: J. M. Dent, 1984).

67. On Morris's fusion of aesthetics and social radicalism, see Jack Lindsay, *William Morris* (New York: Taplinger, 1975), pp. 218–386; E. P. Thompson, *William Morris: Romantic to Revolutionary* (London: Merlin, 1977). On Sorel, see J. R. Jennings, *Georges Sorel: The Character and Development of His Thought* (Oxford: Macmillan, 1985); Richard Vernon, *Commitment and Change: Georges Sorel and the Idea of Revolution* (Toronto: University of Toronto Press, 1978); Jacques Julliard, *Georges Sorel en son temps* (Paris: Seuil, 1985); Michel Charzat, *Georges Sorel et la révolution au XXe siècle* (Paris: Hachette, 1977). On Landauer, see Eugene Lunn, *Prophet of Community: The Romantic Socialism of Gustave Landauer* (Berkeley and Los Angeles: University of California Press, 1973).

68. In France, the Situationists (see note 19 above) represented a combination of Marxism, the surrealist tradition, and anarchism. For an original restatement of anarchist theory in ecological terms see Murray Bookchin, *Post-Scarcity Anarchism* (London: Wildwood House, 1974).

69. John Sellers, "The Ruckus Society," *New Left Review,* n.s., no. 10 (July/August 2001): 71–85; Naomi Klein, "Reclaiming the Commons," *New Left Review,* n.s., no. 9 (May/June 2001): 81–89; Esther Kaplan, "Keepers of the Flame: As Moderate Groups Turn Down the Heat, Anarchists Light a New Way for Dissent," *Village Voice,* January 30, 2002, Web edition from ZNET <www.zmag.org>; Barbara Epstein, "Anarchism and the Anti-Globalization Movement," *Monthly Review* 53, no. 4 (September 2001), Web edition from <www.monthlyreview.org/0901epstein.htm>.

70. On India, see Roy, *Cost of Living;* Bové and Luneau, *Paysan du monde,* pp. 365–99. On Chiapas, see Neil Harvey, *The Chiapas Rebellion: The Struggle for Land and Democracy* (Durham, N.C.: Duke University Press, 1999); Bové and Luneau, *Paysan du monde,* pp. 143–75; Roger Burbach, *Globalization and Postmodern Politics: From Zapatistas to High-Tech Robber Barons* (London: Pluto, 2001), pp. 105–44.

71. In 2000–2001, ATTAC, which began in France, claimed to have branches in Belgium, the Netherlands, Finland, Greece, Ireland, Italy, Luxemburg, Portugal, Spain, and Sweden as well as in nine non-European countries. ATTAC was initiated by Bernard Cassen, editor of *Le Monde Diplomatique.* See Bernard Cassen, Liêm Hoang-Ngoc, and Pierre-André Imbert, eds., *Attac: Contre la dictature des marchés* (Paris: La Dispute/Syllepse/VO Éditions, 1999).

72. See Brochier and Delouche, *Les nouveaux sans-culottes,* pp. 79–82.

73. Schor, *Overworked American.* According to a Reuters dispatch of September 21, 2001 ("Shift Work Said to Have Health, Societal Costs," posted on the Yahoo news website of the same day), an article in the *Lancet* of September 22 detailed the health costs of night work that arise from a disruption of the body's biological rhythms: "chronic sleep disturbances, gastrointestinal problems and even heart disease." In *The Overspent American,* Schor reports that many new upper-middle-class homes are sold with an extra storage room to take on retired appliances.

74. Schor, *Overspent American.*

75. See Jean-Paul Fitoussi, "Peut-on être Keynesien aujourd'hui?" *Le Monde,* November 3, 1998.

76. Wallerstein also sees unrest coming in *Utopistics,* where he uses the term "particularly explosive" (p. 58).

77. See Sennett, *Corrosion of Character;* Desjours, *Souffrance en France;* Taguieff, *L'efface-ment de l'avenir;* and Gorz, *Métamorphoses du travail.*

78. The particular influence on the German expressionists Ernst Toller and Georg Kaiser of Shelley's *Revolt of Islam,* prototype of his *Prometheus Unbound,* has been re-marked by Holmes (*Shelley,* p. 402 n).

Six. Another World Is Possible

1. Edmund Wilson, *Apologies to the Iroquois* (London: W. H. Allen, 1960), pp. 276–78.

2. Ibid., p. 276. A senator from Colorado opposed the bill, claiming it showed a com-plete ignorance of Indian character, laws, morals, and religion. "The real aim of this bill," he said, "is to get at the Indian lands and open them up to settlement. The provisions for the apparent benefit of the Indian are but the pretext to get at his lands and occupy them. . . . If this were done in the name of greed, it would be bad enough; but to do it in the name of humanity, and under the cloak of an ardent de-sire to promote the Indian's welfare by making him like ourselves, whether he will or not, is infinitely worse" (p. 277). There is a distant anticipation here of Arund-hati Roy's denunciation (in *The Cost of Living*) of the leveling of villages for dam construction in contemporary India.

3. Perhaps a similar fascist alliance of autarchic capitalism and preindustrial resis-tance to cosmopolitan modernity is at the base of the terrifyingly effective inter-national network of Al Qaeda, financed by dissident Saudi capital hostile to the Saudi oil elite's cozy relationship with the West.

4. Klein, *No Logo.*

5. See Chapter 4.

6. On this point, as on others, one cannot help but agree with Viviane Forrester who, in her impassioned *Une étrange dictature,* warns against the equation of the new technologies of globalization with neoliberalism:

> These technological advances are inseparable from globalization, but not from the ideology that claims to be identical to them. While these technologies may have permitted liberalism to triumph, they are completely distinct from it. . . . They neither depend on it nor originate in it, and could easily be dis-sociated from it without changing at all. To the contrary . . . they would then finally have the capacity of becoming beneficial, instead of ruinous, to the greatest number. Neoliberalism and globalization are not synonymous. . . . We have come to confuse the prodigies of the new technologies, their irre-versibility, with the political regime that utilizes them. As if it went without saying that the immense potentiality of freedom and social dynamism offered to the human species by research, inventions and recent discoveries should have been transformed into a disaster and into the incarceration of humanity in the pit of this disaster. (pp. 17–18)

7. Ramón Fernández Durán, "The Barcelona Breakthrough: Lessons from the Largest Ever Demonstration against Corporate Globalisation in Europe," interview, *Cor-porate Europe Observer,* May 11, 2002, www.corporateeurope.org. Durán, a Spanish ecologist, makes clear the important role of radical Catalonian organizations and of

the left-wing Barcelona city government in organizing this huge protest, thus demonstrating the interaction between leftist opponents of neoliberalism and the Catalonian regionalist movement.

8. See Chapter 5, pages 196–200.

9. Pierre Bourdieu, "Le mythe de la 'mondialisation' et l'État social européen" and "Pour un nouvel internationalism," in Contre-feux, pp. 34–50, 66–75; Jürgen Habermas, "There Are Alternatives," New Left Review, no. 231 (1998): 3–12; "Europe and Globalization," New Left Review, no. 235 (1999): 46–59; and "Why Europe Needs a Constitution," New Left Review, n.s., no. 11 (2001): 5–26. In a manifesto issued at the end of April 2000, Bourdieu and his Raisons d'Agir group appealed for an estates general of European social movements to draft a common program: "Pour des Etats généraux du mouvement social européen," Le Monde, April 28, 2000.

10. Emmanuel Todd, L'illusion économique: Essai sur la stagnation des sociétés développées (Paris: Gallimard, 1998).

11. Social ecologists and libertarian social thinkers such as Murray Bookchin, André Gorz, Alain Caillé, and Patrick Viveret (editor of the French monthly Transversales) have pioneered in discussing the details of the associative networks that would be essential to prevent a Social Europe from lapsing into bureaucratically controlled capitalism. See, for example, Gorz, "Sortir de la société salariale," in Misères du présent, Richesse du possible (Paris: Galilée, 1997), pp. 123–78.

12. See Chapter 4, note 8 .

13. André Gorz, writing shortly before the end of the Soviet system, announced the demise of the capitalist industrial utopia of the last two centuries and demanded a new utopian vision to enable us "to perceive the potential of liberation that the current transformation contains" (Métamorphoses du travail, p. 22). At roughly the same time, Seyla Benhabib published a brilliant study of the Frankfurt School that pointed out the utopian implications of Habermas's ideas (Benhabib, Critique, Norm, and Utopia: A Study of the Foundations of Critical Theory [New York: Columbia University Press, 1986]). Immanuel Wallerstein, director of the Fernand Braudel Center at Binghamton University, has coined the term "utopistics" to describe this renewed discourse (Wallerstein, Utopistics: Or Historical Choices of the Twenty-first Century [New York: New Press, 1998]). Daniel Singer gave the title "Realistic Utopia" to the concluding chapter of his Whose Millennium? Theirs or Ours? (New York: Monthly Review Press, 1999). See also David Harvey, "The Utopian Moment," in Spaces of Hope (Berkeley: University of California Press, 2000), pp. 133–96; Miguel Abensour, L'utopie de Thomas More à Walter Benjamin (Paris: Sens & Tonka, 2000), and Le procès de rêveurs (Paris: Sulliver, 2000); the survey by Raymond Trousson, D'utopie et d'utopistes (Paris: L'Harmattan, 1998); Yona Friedman, Utopies réalisables, 2d ed. (Perreux: L'Éclat, 2000).

14. Frankel, Post-Industrial Utopians.

15. Against fatalistic ideas of natural determinism, Michelet wrote: "It is the powerful work of self on self [travail de soi sur soi] in which France, by its own progress, transforms all its basic elements. . . . In human progress, the essential comes from the

living force, which is called humanity. *Humanity is its own Prometheus."* "I had only Vico as my master. His principle of the living force, of *humanity which created itself,* made both my book and my teaching." Jules Michelet, "Préface de 1869 à *L'histoire de France,"* in *Introduction à l'histoire universelle. Tableau de la France. Préface à "L'histoire de France"* (Paris: Bibliothèque de Cluny, 1962), pp. 168, 170, italics in original. A similar notion, but more individuated, is represented today by Martha Nussbaum, a philosopher who takes seriously the question of human nature: "The core idea is that of the human being as a dignified free being who shapes his or her own life in cooperation and reciprocity with others, rather than being passively shaped or pushed around by the world in the manner of a 'flock' or 'herd' animal. A life that is really human is one that is shaped throughout by these human powers of practical reason and sociability." Nussbaum, *Women and Human Development: The Capabilities Approach* (Cambridge: Cambridge University Press, 2000), p. 72.

16. Benjamin R. Barber, *Jihad vs. McWorld: How Globalism and Tribalism Are Reshaping the World* (New York: Ballantine Books, 1996).

17. Those familiar with the literature on this subject will note that I am in basic agreement with Boris Frankel's critique (*Post-Industrial Utopias,* pp. 65–102) of Rudolf Bahro, the principle advocate of a utopia of autarchic artisan-based communes, as well as of Alvin Toffler and Barry Jones, whose goals, while comparable to mine, would be attained while leaving intact the basic framework of corporate capitalism. My own views are close to the two-tiered economy advocated by André Gorz, the criticism of whom by Frankel appears to me overly severe.

18. Some statistics culled at random from Rifkin, *End of Work* (pp. 134–38): The United States Steel Corporation employed 120,000 workers in 1980. In 1990, U.S. Steel produced the same output with 20,000 employees. Using a computerized manufacturing process, the number of production workers needed to make a ton of steel fell to one-twelfth of what it was in "a giant integrated steel mill." In OECD (Organization for Economic Cooperation and Development) countries, employment in the steel industry fell by more than 50 percent between 1974 and 1989, while production dipped only 6 percent. The International Association of Machinists, which claimed to represent a million workers in the mid-sixties, saw "the number of machinists in the country [dwindle] to less than 600,000" three decades later. "Between 1973 and 1991, output in the household appliance industry increased at an annual rate of 0.5%." That means an overall increase of around 10 percent for the period. During the same period, thanks to an average annual increase in output per employee-hour of 2.7 percent, "employment declined sharply from 196,300 to 117,100, and the Bureau of Labor Statistics expects . . . [that] by the year 2005, a mere 93,500 workers—fewer than half the number employed in 1973—will be producing the nation's total output of home appliances." The overall growth in population means that the employment situation for industrial workers is even worse than these figures suggest.

19. It is remarkable that the normal workweek in the industrialized West, which dropped precipitously in the advanced industrial countries from about sixty hours at the end of the nineteenth century to about forty hours half a century later, has, in the midst of productivity increases comparable to those of the earlier period,

hardly been lowered in the last fifty years. Indeed, in the United States, the average workweek has actually increased (see Schor, *Overworked American*).

20. See note 26 below.

21. No doubt, not all of this equipment is superfluous: the Internet, surfed by means of personal computers, has a powerful democratic potential for circulating news and ideas, for organizing dissent, and, in a future global democracy, for disseminating debates and referenda essential to widespread global participation in decision making (see below). This positive potential is, at the moment, overshadowed by the negative, commercial functions of information technology: serving as a surrogate for white-collar personnel, thus permitting massive downsizing and fostering social exclusion, and as a global marketplace for the selling of just about everything. But most of the other electronic gadgets—mobile telephones, video cameras etc.—lack any positive potential. The phones may prove damaging to health; the cameras may be used for Big Brother-type security surveillance.

22. Many have already taken this step. In *The Overspent American* Juliet Schor refers to those who have said "enough" as "downshifters." Interestingly, she notes a marked concentration of those Americans questioning the values of consumption in the Pacific Northwest, and particularly in Seattle, site of massive demonstrations against the World Trade Organization meeting of November 30, 1999. Theoretical arguments for such limitation are to be found in Dominique Méda, *Qu'est-ce que la richesse?* and Alan Durning, *How Much is Enough: The Consumer Society and the Future of the Earth,* (New York: Worldwatch-Norton, 1992).

23. Organic food production need not be much less efficient than large-scale capitalist agriculture. A field experiment, conducted in Switzerland from 1978 to 1999, systematically compared two organic farming methods with two conventional ones in the same area. Crop yields in organically run small farms proved to be approximately 20 percent lower than in industrial farms. But organic farming caused virtually no soil erosion, produced no nitrogen fertilizer pollution (soil fertility was maintained through crop rotation), and used 50 percent less energy, 97 percent less pesticide, and 51 percent less fertilizer. Potato crops in organic farms were only 58–66 percent of conventional farming yields (crop pests were a greater problem), but wheat crops were about 90 percent of conventional yields. Paul Mäder et al., "Soil Fertility and Biodiversity in Organic Farming," *Science* 296 (May 31, 2002): 1694–97; Emily Green, "Organic Farms Viable despite Lower Yields, Study Finds," *Los Angeles Times,* May 31, 2002, www.latimes.com.

24. In 1995, more than a thousand such networks were found in Great Britain, and they were spreading rapidly in the Ariège region of southwestern France. See Alain Caillé, "Vers un nouveau contrat social," in *Le tournant de décembre,* p. 132; also Gorz, *Misère du présent,* pp. 165–74.

25. These phobias are intelligently analyzed in the case of the French bourgeoisie at the end of the nineteenth century in Bertholet, *Le bourgeois dans tous ses états.*

26. For statistics on, and costs of, U.S. gasoline consumption, from someone who broke out of the automobile trap, see Ryan Singel, "Addicted to Oil: Confronting America's Worst Habit," *LiP Magazine,* June 17, 2002, www.alternet.org. According to the U.S. Bureau of Labor Statistics, transportation, which had consumed 1–2 per-

cent of average family budgets around 1900, now absorbs 20 percent of such budgets ("What We Work for Now," *New York Times,* September 3, 2001). The environmental impact of this increase is considerable, as much from air travel as from ground. On May 1, 2000, Friends of the Earth, the Aviation Environment Federation, the National Society for Clear Air, and the Heathrow Association for the Control of Aircraft Noise issued a report, "Aviation and Global Climate Change," in which they contended that a return flight from London to Miami produced 2,415 kg of CO^2 *per passenger,* more than an average British motorist produced in a year ("Pollution Warning on Holiday Flights," *BBC News Online,* May 1, 2000). The magnitude of the problem is suggested by the general increase in international tourism over the course of the past half century. International tourist visits grew from 25 million in 1950 to 700 million in 2002, and the travel industry anticipated that there would be about 1.6 billion per year in 2002 (David Nicholson-Lord, "Green Tragedy: The Blight of Eco-Tourism," *Resurgence,* June 13, 2002, www.alternet.org.). Major reductions in air travel both before September 11 (because of recession) and after were expected to prove ephemeral: in November 2001 London's Heathrow Airport announced plans for a fifth terminal. George Monbiot wrote in the *Guardian* ("Terminal Disease," November 23, 2001), "Heathrow produces 10% of all organic pollutants in Britain: if the poisoning costs now carried by the NHS [National Health Service] were charged to the airlines, they would be paying some £1.3 billion a year. Terminal 5 mocks the promises on climate change the government made a few days ago in Marrakesh. Aeroplanes are the world's fastest growing source of carbon dioxide, and their impact on world temperatures may be doubled or even quadrupled by the nitrogen oxides and vapour trails they produce."

27. How many years of education this program would necessitate, and whether these goals could best be attained by maintaining or eliminating the existing separation between secondary and higher education, would be the subject of public and professional debate. The structures and curricula of education would no doubt vary according to local cultures. I doubt, however, if an education that did not cover the four areas mentioned would be adequate to the social transformations I have proposed.

28. For example, monozygotic twins separated at birth and raised in different families are known to show widely different intelligence quotients.

29. Lower meat consumption obviates much of the economic argument for industrial agriculture, since most of the grain so cheaply raised in North America feeds cattle, not people. This is why it was feasible in 2001 for Renate Künast, a Green Party member and Germany's minister for agriculture, to obtain broad public support for a proposal to return to small-scale farming as a remedy for the health problems created by industrial agriculture.

30. Elizabeth L. Eisenstein, *The Printing Press as an Agent of Change,* 2 vols. (Cambridge: Cambridge University Press, 1979); Eisenstein, Anthony Grafton, and Adrian Johns, "AHR Forum: How Revolutionary Was the Print Revolution?" *American Historical Review* 107, no. 1 (February 2002): 84–128.

31. Robert Darnton, *The Literary Underground of the Old Regime* (Cambridge: Harvard

University Press, 1982); Darnton, *The Forbidden Best-Sellers of Pre-Revolutionary France* (New York: Norton, 1995).

Conclusion: Against Despair

1. Even in benighted Austria, boycotted by the rest of the European Union for having voted a far-right party into office, masses of anti-nuclear demonstrators blockaded roads from the Czech Republic in the fall of 2000 in protest against a new Czech nuclear central on the other side of the border. In December, the Czech government gave in to these protests.

2. Alan Friedman, "Middle-East Weighs on World's Economies," *International Herald Tribune,* October 16, 2000.

3. This is not to deny either the legitimacy of Palestinian resistance to the deprivation of civil rights and exploitation to which they have been subjected by the Israelis, or the right of self-defense of Israelis confronted by Palestinian suicide bombers. It is nonetheless difficult, in today's secular, globally interdependent world, to find merit in the religiously tinted nationalist fanaticism that motivates some Israelis to deny Palestinian desires for statehood and advocate ethnic cleansing of the Palestinian territories, and some Palestinians to cling to their dream of driving the "Zionists" into the sea and replacing them by refugees who fled Israel in 1948.

4. Gerard Baker, "A Test for the 'Eat Your Spinach' Presidency," *Financial Times,* May 17, 2001.

5. In an important statement of May 28, 2001, on the future of the European Union, Lionel Jospin, then France's Socialist prime minister, indicated that the Social Europe concept would be a central issue in the 2002 French presidential elections. According to the *Financial Times* of May 28, 2001, "In Mr. Jospin's eyes, Europe must build its identity around defence of its model of social development, with an emphasis on the role of public services. In a globalised economy . . . Europe must balance the forces of the free market with proper regulation and a continuing spirit of solidarity with the underprivileged. He sees Europe as a crucial moderator in the anti-globalisation debate." Jospin's retention of a left-wing position on Europe was no doubt a response to the continued militancy of the new French social movements (see Chapter 5) as well as to the electoral menace of parties to the left of his Parti Socialiste. Nonetheless, in the first round of the presidential elections of 2002 (April 25), six parties opposing Jospin from the Left totaled 24.5 percent, dwarfing the 16.2 percent for the Socialists, and permitting Jean-Marie Le Pen's Front National (16.8 percent) to edge the Socialists out of participation in the deciding round on May 5, 2002.

Postscript: Notes from a Hijacked Planet

1. This argument has been made by others, but nowhere more eloquently than in Arundhati Roy, "War Is Peace," *Outlook,* October 29, 2001, Web edition.

2. "Within weeks, the number of people who said they trusted the government to

do what is right most of the time hit its highest levels in 30 years, rising to 55% in a recent New York Times/CBS poll . . . suddenly a majority of Americans felt that the country was moving in the right direction, even though the stock market was falling precipitously and hundreds of thousands of workers were losing their jobs." Alexander Stille, "Suddenly, Americans Trust Uncle Sam," *New York Times,* November 3, 2001. Polls showed the number of Americans who supported Bush's air war against the Taliban to be at 88 percent. This support was, of course, within a few months, relativized by concerns about the failing economy (see note 5 in the Preface).

3. It was, however, placed on the *Financial Times* website in mid-October.

4. Simon Tisdall, "How the Future was Shanghaied," *Guardian,* October 26, 2001.

5. Marc Cooper, "From Protest to Politics," *Nation,* March 11, 2002.

6. Rob Nixon, "A Dangerous Appetite for Oil," *New York Times,* October 29, 2001; John Pilger, "Hidden Agenda behind War on Terror," *ZNET,* October 30, 2001; Roy ("War Is Peace") makes the same point. The Bush administration's concerns for securing the oil supplies of the Middle East and the Caspian Sea for the American economy are set out in *National Energy Policy,* the May 2001 "Report of the National Energy Policy Development Group" submitted to George W. Bush by his vice president and most of the members of his cabinet (U.S. Government Printing Office, www.bookstore.gpo.gov). It is useful to recall that Bush and Cheney are both oil millionaires, and that Cheney said in 1998, "I can't think of a time when we've had a region emerge as suddenly to become as strategically significant as the Caspian. It's almost as if the opportunities have arisen overnight" (quoted in Roy, "War Is Peace"). The new pipeline mentioned in *National Energy Policy* as of strategic value runs from Baku through Azerbaijan, Georgia, and Turkey to the Gulf port of Ceyhan, but clearly a route through the first two named states, as parts of the ex-USSR in chronic turmoil and subject to Russian pressure, ought not, in the eyes of an energy-hungry United States, to be the only way for the rich Caspian Sea oil to come to open seas. As Pilger says, "Only if the pipeline runs through Afghanistan can the Americans hope to control it."

7. "A Rising Tide of Defense Dollars, "*New York Times,* May 5, 2002.

8. The premise of expanding energy resources is the point of departure for the Bush cabinet's *National Energy Policy,* which forecasts an increased need of energy for the U.S. economy in the next twenty years on the order of 32 percent (chap. 1, p. 1, Web edition).

9. Paul Krugman, "Paying the Price," *New York Times,* September 16, 2001, citing Laurie Garrett, *Betrayal of Trust: The Collapse of Global Public Health.* Even after the Lockerbie disaster a decade earlier, concern for the security of airline passengers was nil. An article in the *Los Angeles Times* of September 23, 2001, pointed out that while Lockerbie cost the airline concerned $3 billion, they thought the cost of having a Lockerbie once in ten years was preferable to the cost of taking proper precautions to prevent it. In fact, all the techniques—both information technology and interviewing—for screening out potential terrorists from groups of passengers have been known for over a decade, but have rarely been used by airlines, apart from El Al, precisely because the costs would interfere with profits.

Bibliography

Abensour, Miguel. *Le procès des maîtres rêveurs suivi de Pierre Leroux et l'utopie.* Arles: Sulliver, 2000.

——. *L'utopie de Thomas More à Walter Benjamin.* Paris: Sens & Tonka, 2000.

Abrams, M. H. *Natural Supernaturalism: Tradition and Revolution in Romantic Literature.* New York: Norton, 1973.

Achterhuis, Hans. *Natuur tussen mythe en techniek.* Baarn, Netherlands: Ambo, 1995.

Albert, Michel. *Capitalisme contre capitalisme.* Paris: Seuil, 1991.

Amin, Samir. *L'empire du chaos: La nouvelle mondialisation capitaliste.* Paris: L'Harmattan, 1991.

Anderson, Benedict. *Imagined Communities.* London: Verso, 1993.

Angel, Johnny. "It's the Oil." *L.A. Weekly,* September 21–27, 2001, Web edition.

Avrich, Paul. *The Russian Anarchists.* Princeton, N.J.: Princeton University Press, 1967.

Baker, C. Edwin. *Advertising and a Democratic Press.* Princeton, N.J.: Princeton University Press, 1994.

Balzac, Honoré de. *Les illusions perdues.* 1837–39. Reprint, Paris: Louis Conard, 1949.

Barber, Benjamin R. *Jihad vs. McWorld: How Globalism and Tribalism Are Reshaping the World.* New York: Ballantine Books, 1996.

Beck, Ulrich. "Globalisations's Chernobyl." *Financial Times,* November 6, 2001.

——. *Risk Society: Towards a New Modernity.* London: Sage, 1992.

Bell, Daniel. *The Cultural Contradictions of Capitalism.* London: Heinemann, 1976.

Benhabib, Seyla. *Critique, Norm, and Utopia: A Study of the Foundations of Critical Theory.* New York: Columbia University Press, 1986.

Bénichou, Paul. *Le temps des prophètes.* Paris: Gallimard, 1979.

Benslama, Fethi. "Islam: Quelle humiliation?" *Le Monde,* November 28, 2001.

Bercé, Yves-Marie. *Fête et révolte: Des mentalités populaires du XVIe au XVIIIe siècle.* Paris: Hachette, 1976.

Berke, Richard L., and Thom Shanker, "As Guns Still Blaze, Bush Aides Debate Shifting Focus to Butter." *New York Times,* December 2, 2001.

Bertholet, Denis. *Le bourgeois dans tous ses états: Le roman familial de la Belle Époque.* Paris: Olivier Orban, 1987.

Bhagwati, Jagdish. "An Unjustified Sense of Victory." *Financial Times,* December 21, 1999.

Blackbourn, David. *Class, Religion and Local Politics in Wilhelmine Germany.* New Haven: Yale University Press, 1980.

Blechman, Max, ed. *Revolutionary Romanticism.* San Francisco: City Lights, 1999.

Bookchin, Murray. *The Ecology of Freedom: The Emergence and Dissolution of Hierarchy.* Rev. ed. Montreal: Black Rose Books, 1991.

——. *The Spanish Anarchists: The Heroic Years 1868–1936.* New York: Free Life Editions, 1977.

Boumediene-Thiery, Alima, Alain Krivine, and Giuseppe Di Lello Finuoli. "Europe: Vers l'état d'exception." *Le Monde,* November 29, 2001.

Bourdieu, Pierre. *Contre-feux.* Paris: Liber Raisons d'Agir, 1998.

——. *Distinction: A Social Critique of the Judgement of Taste.* London: Routledge and Kegan Paul, 1984.

——. "Pour des Etats généraux du mouvement social européen." *Le Monde,* April 28, 2000.

——, ed. *La misère du monde.* Paris: Seuil, 1993.

Bové, José. "A Farmer's International." *New Left Review,* n.s., 12 (November–December 2001): 89–101.

Bové, José, and François Dufour. *The World Is Not for Sale: Farmers against Junk Food.* London: Verso, 2001.

Bové, José, and Gilles Luneau. *Paysan du monde.* Paris: Fayard, 2002.

Brochier, Jean-Christophe, and Hervé Delouche. *Les nouveaux sans-culottes: Enquête sur l'extrême gauche.* Paris: Grasset, 2000.

Brower, Daniel R. *The New Jacobins: The French Communist Party and the Popular Front.* Ithaca, N.Y.: Cornell University Press, 1968.

Brown, J. A. C. *Freud and the Post-Freudians.* Harmondsworth, England: Penguin Books, 1967.

Bruggen, Carrie Van. *Prometheus: Een bijdrage tot het begrip der ontwikkeling van het individualisme in de litteratuur.* 2d ed. Introduction by H. A. Gomperts. Amsterdam: Van Oorschot, 1946.

Burbach, Roger. *Globalization and Postmodern Politics: From Zapatistas to High-Tech Robber Barons.* London: Pluto, 2001.

Burke, Edmund. *Reflections on the Revolution in France.* 1790. Reprint, Indianapolis: Library of Liberal Arts, 1955.

Caillé, Alain, ed. *L'autre socialisme: Entre utilitarisme et totalitarisme. La revue du M.A.U.S.S. semestrielle,* no. 16 (2000).

——. *Comment peut-on être anticapitaliste? La revue du M.A.U.S.S. semestrielle,* no. 9 (1997).

——. *Qu'est-ce que l'utilitarisme? Une énigme dans l'histoire des idées. La revue du M.A.U.S.S. semestrielle,* no. 6 (1995).

——. *Une seule solution, l'association? Socio-économie du fait associatif. La revue du M.A.U.S.S. semestrielle,* no. 11 (1998).

Callenbach, Ernest. *Ecotopia: The Notebooks and Reports of William Weston.* Berkeley: Banyan Tree Books, 1975.

Cameron, Kenneth Neill. *The Young Shelley: Genesis of a Radical.* London: Gollancz, 1951.

Campbell, Colin. *The Romantic Ethic and the Spirit of Consumerism.* Oxford: Blackwell, 1987.

Camus, Albert. "The Artist as Witness of Freedom." Translated by Bernard Frechtmen. *Journal for the Protection of All Beings* (San Francisco, City Lights Books), no. 1 (1961): 30–37.

Capra, Fritjof. *The Turning Point: Science, Society and the Rising Culture.* London: Fontana, 1988.

Carlyle, Thomas. *Past and Present.* 1843. Reprint, London: Oxford University Press, 1960.

Caron, Jean Claude. *Générations romantiques: Les étudiants de Paris et le quartier latin (1814–1851).* Paris: Armand Colin, 1991.

Carroué, Laurent. "L'euro, verrou de l'orthodoxie." *Monde Diplomatique,* January 1999.

Cassen, Bernard, Liêm Hoang-Ngoc, and Pierre-André Imbert, eds., *Attac: Contre la dicature des marchés.* Paris: La Dispute/Syllepse/VO Éditions, 1999.

Castel, Robert. *Les métamorphoses de la question sociale: Une chronique du salariat.* Paris: Fayard, 1995.

Castenada, Jorge. Interview. *Le Monde,* December 2/3 2001.

Chalas, Yves, ed. *Mythes et révolutions.* Grenoble: Presses Universitaires de Grenoble, 1990.

Charzat, Michel. *Georges Sorel et la révolution au XXe siècle.* Paris: Hachette, 1977.

Chodorow, Nancy. *Feminism and Psychoanalytic Theory.* New Haven: Yale University Press, 1989.

Clymer, Adam. "With Sagging Economy as Ally, Democrats in Congress Go on the Attack." *New York Times,* November 11, 2001.

Cohen, Lizabeth. "From Town Center to Shopping Center: The Reconfiguration of Community Marketing Places in America." *American Historical Review* 101, no. 4 (1996): 1050–81.

Comeliau, Christian. *Les impasses de la modernité: Critique de la marchandisation du monde.* Paris: Seuil, 2000.

Darnton, Robert. *The Forbidden Best-Sellers of Pre-Revolutionary France.* New York: Norton, 1995.

———. *The Great Cat Massacre and Other Episodes in French Cultural History.* London: Allen Lane, 1984.

———. *The Literary Underground of the Old Regime.* Cambridge: Harvard University Press, 1982.

Davis, Natalie Zemon. "The Reasons of Misrule: Youth Groups and Charivaris in Sixteenth Century France." In *Society and Culture in Early Modern France,* pp. 97–123. Stanford: Stanford University Press, 1971.

Debord, Guy. *The Society of the Spectacle.* New York: Zone Books, 1994.

Debord, Guy, and Gianfranco Sanguinetti. *The Veritable Split in the International: Public Circular of the Situationist International.* London: Chronos, 1990.

Decety, Jean. "Le sens des autres." *Le Monde,* November 2, 2001.

Deffeyes, Kenneth S. *Hibbert's Peak: The Impending World Oil Shortage.* Princeton, N.J.: Princeton University Press, 2001.

Deléage, Jean-Paul, Jean-Claude Debeir, and Daniel Hémery. *In the Servitude of Power: Energy and Civilization through the Ages.* London: Zed Books, 1991.

Desjours, Christophe. *Souffrance en France: La banalisation de l'injustice sociale.* Paris: Seuil, 1998.

Dijkstra Bram. *The Idols of Perversity: Fantasies of Feminine Evil in Fin-de-siècle Culture.* New York: Oxford University Press, 1986.

Disraeli, Benjamin (Lord Beaconsfield). *Sybil, or the Two Nations.* 1845. Reprint, London: Oxford University Press, 1965.

Dobb, Maurice. *Studies in the Development of Capitalism.* New York: International Publishers, 1947.

Donkin, Richard. *Blood, Sweat and Tears: The Evolution of Work.* New York: Texere, 2001.

The Downsizing of America. New York: Random House, 1996.

Durning, Alan. *How Much Is Enough? The Consumer Society and the Future of the Earth.* New York: Worldwatch-Norton, 1992.

Eagleton, Terry. *The Illusions of Postmodernism.* Oxford: Blackwell, 1996.

———. "Self-Realization, Ethics and Socialism." *New Left Review,* no. 237 (1999): 150–161.

Eisenstein, Elizabeth L. *The Printing Press as an Agent of Change,* 2 vols. Cambridge: Cambridge University Press, 1979.

Eisenstein, Elizabeth L., with Anthony Grafton and Adrian Johns. "AHR Forum: How Revolutionary Was the Print Revolution?" *American Historical Review* 107, no. 1 (February 2002): 84–128.

Eley, Geoff. *Reshaping the German Right: Radical Nationalism and Political Change after Bismarck.* New Haven: Yale University Press, 1980.

Elias, Norbert. *Über den Prozess der Zivilisation.* 2d ed. Bern: Francke Verlag, 1969.

Ellul, Jacques. *The Technological Society.* New York: Vintage, 1964.

Epstein, Barbara. "Anarchism and the Anti-Globalization Movement." *Monthly Review* 53, no. 4 (September 2001), www.monthlyreview.org/0901epstein.htm.

Esler, Anthony, ed. *The Youth Revolution.* Lexington, Mass.: Heath, 1974.

Faure, Alain. *Paris carême-prenant: Du carnaval à Paris au XIXe siècle.* Paris: Hachette, 1979.

Featherstone, Liza. "The New Student Movement." *Nation,* May 15, 2000.

Featherstone, Mike. *Consumer Culture and Postmodernism.* London: Sage, 1991.

Ferguson, Priscilla Parkhurst. *Literary France: The Making of a Culture.* Berkeley: University of California Press, 1987.

—— [Priscilla P. Clark]. *The Battle of the Bourgeois: The Novel in France, 1789–1848.* Paris: Didier, 1973.

Feuer, Lewis S. *The Conflict of Generations: The Character and Significance of Student Movements.* London: Heinemann, 1969.

Finnegan, William. "After Seattle: Why Anarchism Is Making a Comeback." *New Yorker,* April 17, 2000, pp. 40–51.

Fitoussi, Jean-Paul. *Le débat interdit: Monnaie, Europe, pauvreté.* Evreux: Arléa, 1995.

——. "Peut-on être Keynesien aujourd'hui?" *Le Monde,* November 3, 1998.

Flaubert, Gustave. *The Sentimental Education.* New York: New American Library, 1972.

Forrester, Viviane. *L'horreur économique.* Paris: Fayard, 1996.

——. *Une étrange dictature.* Paris: Fayard, 2000.

Forster, E. M. *Howard's End.* 1910. Reprint, New York: Alfred Knopf, 1921.

Fox, Edward Whiting. *The Other France: History in Geographical Perspective.* New York: Norton, 1971.

Fox, Stephen. *The Mirror Makers: A History of American Advertising and Its Creators.* New York: William Morrow, 1984.

Frank, Robert H. *Luxury Fever: Money and Happiness in an Era of Excess.* Princeton, N.J.: Princeton University Press, 1999.

Frank, Thomas. *One Market under God: Extreme Capitalism, Market Populism, and the End of Economic Democracy.* New York: Doubleday, 2000.

Frankel, Boris. *The Post-Industrial Utopians.* London: Polity, 1987.

Freud, Sigmund. *Beyond the Pleasure Principle.* New York: Bantam Books, 1959.

——. *Civilization and Its Discontents.* New York: Norton, 1962.

——. *The Ego and the Id.* New York: Norton, 1960.

——. "On Narcissism: An Introduction." In *Collected Papers.* Vol. 4. New York: Basic Books, 1959.

——. "Thoughts for the Times on War and Death." In *Collected Papers.* Vol. 4. New York: Basic Books, 1959.

Friedman, Yona. *Utopies réalisables.* 2d ed. Perreux, France: L'Éclat, 2000.

Fromm, Erich. *Greatness and Limitations of Freud's Thought.* New York: Harper, 1980.

——. *Love, Sexuality and Matriarchy: About Gender.* New York: Fromm International, 1997.

Gallaher, John G. *The Students of Paris in the Revolution of 1848.* Carbondale: Southern Illinois University Press, 1980.

Gay, Peter. *The Bourgeois Experience: Victoria to Freud.* 5 vols. New York: Norton, 1985–1996.

——. *The Dilemma of Democratic Socialism: Eduard Bernstein's Challenge to Marx.* New York: Columbia University Press, 1954.

Gellner, Ernest. *Nations and Nationalism.* London: Blackwell, 1992.

Goldman, Robert. *Reading Ads Socially.* London: Routledge, 1992.

Gorz, André. *Métamorphoses du travail: Quête du sens.* Paris: Galilée, 1988.

——. *Misères du présent: Richesse du possible.* Paris: Galilée, 1997.

——. "Sortir de la société salariale." In *Misères du présent, richesse du possible.* Paris: Galilée, 1997.

Graña, César. *Bohemian vs. Bourgeois: French Society and the French Man of Letters in the Nineteenth Century.* New York: HarperTorchbooks, 1964.

Greider, William. *One World Ready or Not: The Manic Logic of Global Capitalism.* Harmondsworth, England: Penguin, 1997.

Guerrand, Roger-Henri. *Lycéens révoltés: Étudiants révolutionnaires au XIX siècle.* Paris: Édition du temps, 1969.

Haag, Ernest van den. "Of Happiness and Despair We Have No Measure." In *Man Alone,* edited by Eric Josephson and Mary Josephson. New York: Dell, 1957.

Habermas, Jürgen. "Europe and Globalization." *New Left Review,* no. 235 (1999): 46–59.

——. "There Are Alternatives." *New Left Review,* no. 231 (1998): 3–12.

——. "Why Europe Needs a Constitution." *New Left Review,* n.s., no. 11 (2001): 5–26.

Hamon, Hervé, and Patrick Rotman. *Génération 2: Les années de poudre.* Paris: Seuil, 1988.

Hardt, Michael, and Antonio Negri. *Empire.* Cambridge: Harvard University Press, 2000.

Harvey, David. *The Condition of Postmodernity.* Cambridge: Blackwell, 1990.

——. *Spaces of Hope.* Berkeley: University of California Press, 2000.

Harvey, Niel. *The Chiapas Rebellion: The Struggle for Land and Democracy.* Durham, N.C.: Duke University Press, 1999.

Herf, Jeffrey. *Reactionary Modernism: Technology, Culture, and Politics in Weimar and the Third Reich.* New York: Cambridge University Press, 1984.

Hertz, Noreena. *The Silent Takeover: Global Capitalism and the Death of Democracy.* London: Heinemann, 2001.

Hill, Christopher. *Milton and the English Revolution.* London: Faber and Faber, 1979.

——. *Puritanism and Revolution: Studies in the Interpretation of the English Revolution of the 17th Century.* London: Heinemann, 1958.

Hobsbawm, Eric. *Nations and Nationalism since 1780.* Cambridge: Canto, 1994.

Holmes, Richard. *Shelley: The Pursuit.* London: Penguin, 1974.

Hubler, Shawn. "Americans Fend Off Sorrow with Laden Fork and Spoon." *Los Angeles Times,* October 2, 2001.

Human Development Report 1999. Oxford: Oxford University Press, 1999.

Hyman, Stanley Edgar. *The Tangled Bank: Darwin, Marx, Frazer and Freud as Imaginative Writers.* New York: Atheneum, 1962.

Jacobs, Jane. *The Death and Life of Great American Cities.* New York: Random House, 1981.

Jacoby, Russell. *The End of Utopia: Politics and Culture in an Age of Apathy.* New York: Basic Books, 1999.

——. *The Last Intellectuals: American Culture in the Age of Academe.* New York: Basic Books, 1987.

Jay, Martin. *The Dialectical Imagination: A History of the Frankfurt School and the Institute of Social Research, 1923–1950.* Boston: Little, Brown, 1973.

Jennings, J. R. *Georges Sorel: The Character and Development of His Thought.* Oxford: Macmillan, 1985.

Johnson, Chalmers. *Blowback: The Costs and Consequences of American Empire.* New York: Henry Holt, 2001.

Julliard, Jacques, *Georges Sorel en son temps.* Paris: Seuil, 1985.

Kaplan, Esther. "Keepers of the Flame: As Moderate Groups Turn Down the Heat, Anarchists Light a New Way for Dissent." *Village Voice,* January 30, 2002, Web version from ZNET <www.zmag.org>.

Kaplan, Robert D. *The Coming Anarchy.* New York: Vintage, 2001

——. *An Empire Wilderness: Travels into America's Future.* New York: Random House, 1998.

Kay, John. "Social Route to Economic Success." *Financial Times,* March 15, 2000.

Kermode, Frank. *Shakespeare, Spenser, Donne: Renaissance Essays.* London: Routledge and Kegan Paul, 1971.

Klare, Michael T. *Resource Wars: The New Landscape of Global Conflict.* New York: Metropolitan Books, 2001.

Klein, Naomi. *No Logo.* London: Flamingo, 2000.

——. "Reclaiming the Commons." *New Left Review,* n.s., no. 9 (May/June 2001): 81–89.

Knabb, Ken, ed. and trans. *The Situationist International Anthology.* Berkeley: Bureau of Public Secrets, 1981.

Kolakowski, Leszek. *Main Currents of Marxism.* 3 vols. Oxford: Oxford University Press, 1981.

Kolko, Gabriel. Another *Century of War.* New York: New Press, 2002.

——. *Vietnam: Anatomy of a Peace.* London: Routledge, 1997.

Kreuzer, Helmut. *Die Boheme.* Stuttgart: Metzler, 1971.

Krugman, Paul. "Another Useful Crisis." *New York Times,* November 11, 2001.

——. "The 55-cent Solution." *New York Times,* November 21, 2001.

Kumar, Krishan. *From Post-Industrial to Post-Modern Society.* Oxford: Blackwell, 1995.

Lagarde, Georges de. *La naissance de l'esprit laïque au déclin du moyen age.* 2 vols. 2d ed. Louvain: E. Nauwelaerts, 1956–58.

Landes, David, *The Unbound Prometheus: Technological Change and Industrial Development in Western Europe from 1750 to the Present.* Cambridge: Cambridge University Press, 1969.

Lapper, Richard. "Anger in the Andes." *Financial Times,* April 26, 2000.

Laquer, Walter. *Young Germany: A History of the German Youth Movement.* London: Routledge and Kegan Paul, 1962.

Latouche, Serge. La mégamachine: Raison technoscientifique, raison économique et mythe du progrès. Paris: La Découverte/M.A.U.S.S., 1995.

Le Goff, Jacques, and Jean-Claude Schmitt. *Le charivari: Actes de la table ronde organisée à Paris (25–27 avril 1977) par l'E.H.E.S.S. et le C.N.R.S.* Paris: École des Hautes Études en Sciences Sociales, 1981.

Le Goff, Jean-Pierre, and Alain Caillé. *Le tournant de décembre.* Paris: La Découverte, 1996.

Lears, Jackson. *Fables of Abundance: A Cultural History of Advertising in America.* New York: Basic Books, 1994.

Lecourt, Dominique. *Prométhée, Faust, Frankenstein.* Paris: Livre de Poche, 1996.

Le Roy Ladurie, Emmanuel. *Montaillou, village occitan de 1294 à 1324.* Paris: Gallimard, 1975.

Leslie, Sylvan. *The Sponsored Life: Ads, TV and American Culture.* Philadelphia: Temple University Press, 1994.

Leterrier, Sophie. *L'institution des sciences morales.* Paris: L'Harmattan, 1995.

Lewis, Bernard. "The Revolt of Islam." *New Yorker,* November 19, 2001, pp. 50–63.

Leys, Colin, *Market-Driven Politics.* London: Verso, 2002.

Lindsay, Jack. *William Morris.* New York: Taplinger, 1975.

Lipietz, Alain. *La société en sablier: Le partage du travail contre la déchirure sociale.* Paris: La Découverte, 1996.

Lodziak, Conrad. *The Myth of Consumerism.* London: Pluto Press, 2002.

Loeb, Lori Ann. *Consuming Angels: Advertising and Victorian Women.* New York: Oxford University Press, 1994.

Löwy, Michael, et Robert Sayre. *Révolte et mélancholie: Le romantisme à contre-courant de la modernité.* Paris: Payot, 1992.

Lunn, Eugene. *Prophet of Community: The Romantic Socialism of Gustave Landauer.* Berkeley and Los Angeles: University of California Press, 1973.

Luxemburg, Rosa. *The Russian Revolution.* Ann Arbor: University of Michigan Press, 1961.

Macpherson, C. B. *The Political Theory of Possessive Individualism: Hobbes to Locke.* Oxford: Clarendon Press, 1962.

Maîtron, Jean. *Le mouvement anarchiste en France.* Paris: Maspero, 1975.

Malow, Joyce. *The Peterloo Massacre.* London: Readers Union, 1970.

Marcuse, Herbert. *Eros and Civilization: A Philosophical Inquiry into Freud.* Boston: Beacon, 1955.

———. *One Dimensional Man: Studies in the Ideology of Advanced Industrial Society.* Boston: Beacon, 1964.

Markovits, Andrei S., and Philip S. Gorski. *The German Left: Red, Green and Beyond.* New York: Oxford University Press, 1993.

Martin, Hans-Peter, and Harald Schumann. *Le piège de la mondialisation.* Mayenne, France: Solin Actes Sud, 1997.

Marx, Karl. *Differenz der demokritischen und epikureischen Naturphilosophie.* In *Gesammelte Schriften von Karl Marx und Friedrich Engels 1841 bis 1850,* edited by Franz Mehring. Stuttgart: Dietz Verlag, 1913.

Marx, Karl, and Friedrich Engels. *Der Briefwechsel.* Munich: Deutsche Taschenbuch Verlag, 1983.

McNiece, Gerald. *Shelley and the Revolutionary Idea.* Cambridge: Harvard University Press, 1969.

Méda, Dominique. *Le travail, une valeur en voie de disparition.* Paris: Aubier, 1995.

———. *Qu'est-ce que la richesse?* Paris: Aubier, 1999.

Michelet, Jules. *Histoire de la Révolution française.* 1847–53. Reprint, Paris: Bibliothèque de la Pléiade, 1952.

——— *Introduction à l'histoire universelle. Tableau de la France. Préface à l'Histoire de France.* Paris: Bibliothèque de Cluny, 1962.

———. *Le peuple.* 1846. Reprint, Paris: Flammarion, 1974.

Miller, David. *Anarchism.* London: J. M. Dent & Sons, 1984.

Miller, James. *Democracy Is in the Streets: From Port Huron to the Siege of Chicago.* Cambridge: Harvard University Press, 1994.

Mills, C. Wright. *White Collar: The American Middle Classes.* New York: Oxford University Press, 1956.

Mitzman, Arthur. "Anarchism, Expressionism and Psychoanalysis." *New German Critique,* no. 10 (1977): 77–105.

———. *The Iron Cage: An Historical Interpretation of Max Weber.* 2d ed. New Brunswick, N.J.: Transaction, 1985.

———. *Michelet, Historian: Rebirth and Romanticism in 19th-Century France.* New Haven: Yale University Press, 1990.

———. *Sociology and Estrangement: Three Sociologists of Imperial Germany.* New York: Knopf, 1973.

Monbiot, George. "Terminal Disease." *Guardian,* November 23, 2001.

Mosse, George. *Nationalism and Sexuality.* New York: Howard Fertig, 1985.

Mucchielli, Laurent. Interview. *Le Monde,* November 13, 2001.

Muchembled, Robert. *Popular Culture and Elite Culture in France, 1400–1750.* Baton Rouge: Louisiana Sate University Press, 1985.

Nairn, Tom. "Ukania under Blair." *New Left Review,* n.s. no. 1 (January/February 2000): 69–103.

Nestle, Marion, *Food Politics: How the Food Industry Influences Nutrition and Health.* Berkeley: University of California Press, 2002.

Neumann, Franz. Behemoth: *The Structure* and *Practice of National Socialism, 1933–1944.* Rev. ed. London: Cass, 1967.

Nicholson-Lord, David. "Green Tragedy: The Blight of Eco-Tourism." *Resurgence,* June 13, 2002.

Nussbaum, Martha. *Women and Human Development: The Capabilities Approach.* Cambridge: Cambridge University Press, 2000.

Orwell, George. *1984.* London: Victor Gollancz, 1948.

Packard, Vance. *The Hidden Persuaders.* New York: David McKay, 1957.

Peck, Walter Edwin. *Shelley: His Life and Work.* London: Ernest Benn, 1927.

Pergaud, Louis. *La guerre des boutons, roman de ma douzième année.* 1912. Reprint, Paris: Mercure de France, 1944.

Perret, Bernard. *L'avenir du travail: Les démocraties face au chômage.* Paris: Seuil, 1995.

Phillips, Kevin. "The Political Clock Is Ticking." *Los Angeles Times,* November 11, 2001, Web edition.

Pirenne, Henri. *Mohammed et Charlemagne.* Paris: Alcan, 1936.

Polanyi, Karl. *The Great Transformation: The Political and Economic Origins of Our Time.* Boston: Beacon, 1960.

Portmann, Adolf. *Biologische Fragmente zu einer Lehre vom Menschen.* Basel: Schwabe, 1951.

Priaulx, Allan, and Sanford J. Ungar. *The Almost Revolution: France, 1968.* New York: Dell, 1969.

Printemps des peuples. Paris: French National Assembly, 1998. Catalogue of an exhibition.

Radkey, O. H. *The Sickle under the Hammer: The Russian Socialist Revolutionaries in the Early Months of Soviet Rule.* New York: Columbia University Press, 1963.

Reich, Robert B. *The Work of Nations: Preparing Ourselves for 21st Century Capitalism.* New York: Vintage, 1992.

Riesman, David. *The Lonely Crowd.* New Haven: Yale University Press, 1961.

Rifkin, Jeremy. *The End of Work: The Decline of the Global Labor Force and the Dawn of the Post-Market Era*. New York: Tarcher/Putnam, 1995.

Roazen, Paul. *Freud and His Followers*. New York: Alfred A. Knopf, 1975.

Robbins, John, *The Food Revolution: How Your Diet Can Help Save Your Life and Our World*. Berkeley, Calif.: Conari, 2001.

Roy, Arundhati. *The Cost of Living*. New York: Random House, 1999.

Sand, George. *Le compagnon du tour de France*. 1841. Reprint, Paris: Éditions Aujourd'hui, 1979.

Sartre, Jean-Paul. *L'idiot de la famille*. Paris: Gallimard, 1971.

Schachtel, Ernest. *Metamorphosis: On the Development of Affect, Perception, Attention, and Memory*. New York: Basic Books, 1959.

Schiller, Herbert I. *Culture, Inc.: The Corporate Takeover of Public Expression*. New York: Oxford University Press, 1989.

Schlosser, Eric. *Fast Food Nation: The Dark Side of the All-American Meal*. Boston: Houghton Mifflin, 2001.

Schooyans, Michel. *La dérive totalitaire du libéralisme*. Paris: Éditions Universitaires, 1991.

Schor, Juliet. *The Overspent American*. New York: Basic Books, 1998.

———. *The Overworked American: The Unexpected Decline of Leisure*. New York: Basic Books, 1991.

Schorske, Carl E. *German Social Democracy, 1905–1917: The Development of the Great Schism*. New York: John Wiley and Sons, 1965.

Schulman, Bruce J. "Eco-Kapitalisten komen zich zelf tegen." *NRC Handelsblad*, May 13, 2000.

Séchan, Louis. *Le mythe de Prométhée*. Paris: Presses Universitaires de France, 1951.

Sellers, John. "The Ruckus Society." *New Left Review*, n.s., no. 10 (July/August 2001): 71–85.

Sennett, Richard. *The Fall of Public Man*. New York: Alfred A. Knopf, 1977.

———. *The Corrosion of Character: The Personal Consequences of Work in the New Capitalism*. New York: Norton, 1998.

Sewell, William, Jr. *Work and Revolution in France: The Language of Labor from the Old Regime to 1848*. Cambridge: Cambridge University Press, 1980.

Shelley, P. B. *The Complete Poetical Works of Percy Bysshe Shelley*. Edited by Thomas Hutchinson. London: Oxford University Press, 1947.

Shrivastava, Paul. *Bhopal: Anatomy of a Crisis*. Cambridge, Mass.: Ballinger, 1987.

Singer, Daniel. *Whose Millennium? Theirs or Ours?* New York: Monthly Review Press, 1999.

Skocpol, Theda. *States and Social Revolutions*. Cambridge: Cambridge University Press, 1979.

Slater, Don. *Consumer Culture and Modernity*. London: Polity, 1997.

Snyders, George. *La pédagogie en France aux XVIIe et XVIIIe siècles*. Paris: Presses Universitaires de France, 1965.

Sombart, Werner. *Der Bourgeois: Zur Geistesgeschichte de modernen Wirtschaftsmenschen*. Munich: Duncker & Humblot, 1913.

———. *Socialismus und sociale Bewegung im neunzehnten Jahrhundert*. Bern: Gesellschaft für ethische Kultur, 1897.

Soper, Kate. *What Is Nature? Culture, Politics, and the Non-human*. Oxford: Blackwell, 1995.

Sorel, Georges. *Réflexions sur la violence*. Paris: Rivière, 1908.

Soros, George. *The Crisis of Global Capitalism {Open Society Endangered}.* London: Little, Brown, 1998.

Stearns, Peter N. *European Society in Upheaval: Social History since 1800.* New York: Macmillan, 1967.

Stephens Philip. "Markets March across Europe." *Financial Times,* January 7, 2000.

Stille, Alexander. "Suddenly, Americans Trust Uncle Sam." *New York Times,* Nov. 3, 2001, Web edition.

Strange, Susan. *Casino Capitalism.* Oxford: Blackwell, 1986.

———. *Mad Money.* Manchester: Manchester University Press, 1997.

Taguieff, Pierre-André. *L'éffacement de l'avenir.* Paris: Galilée, 2000.

Tanter, Richard. "Pipeline Politics: Oil, Gas and the US Interest in Afghanistan." ZNET, November 2001.

Tartakowsky, Danielle. *Le pouvoir est dans la rue: Crises politiques et manifestations en France.* Paris: Aubier, 1998.

Thompson, E. P. *Making of the English Working Class.* New York: Pantheon Books, 1964.

———. *William Morris: Romantic to Revolutionary.* London: Merlin, 1977.

Todd, Emmanuel. *L'illusion économique: Essai sur la stagnation des sociétés développées.* Paris: Gallimard, 1998.

Tönnies, Ferdinand. *Community and Society.* New York: HarperTorchbooks, 1963.

Touraine, Alain. *Critique de la modernité.* Paris: Fayard, 1992.

Toussenel, Alphonse. *Les juifs, rois de l'époque: Histoire de la féodalité financière.* Paris: L'École Sociétaire, 1845.

Trousson, Raymond. *D'Utopie et d'utopistes.* Paris: L'Harmattan, 1998.

———. *Le thème de Prométhée dans la littérature européenne.* Genève: Droz, 1976.

Twitchell, James B. *Adcult USA: The Triumph of Advertising in American Culture.* New York: Columbia University Press, 1996.

Valles, Jules. *L'enfant.* In *Oeuvres II, 1871–1885.* Paris: Bibliothèque de la Pléiade, 1990.

Veblen, Thorstein. *The Theory of the Leisure Class.* 1899. Reprint, New York: Modern Library, 1934.

Vermeren, Patrice. *Victor Cousin, le jeu de la philosophie et de l'état.* Paris: L'Harmattan, 1995.

Vernon, Richard. *Commitment and Change: Georges Sorel and the Idea of Revolution.* Toronto: University of Toronto Press, 1978.

Vidal, Gore. *Armageddon.* London: André Deutsch, 1987.

Wainwright, Hilary. *Arguments for a New Left: Answering the Free Market Right.* Oxford: Blackwell, 1994.

———. *Notes Towards a New Politics: New Strategies for People Power.* Amsterdam: Transnational Institute Briefing Series (Porto Alegre Special), 2002/3.

Waite, Robert G. L. *Vanguard of Nazism: The Free Corps Movement in Post-war Germany, 1918–1923.* Cambridge: Harvard University Press, 1952.

Wallerstein, Immanuel. *Utopistics: On Historical Choices of the Twenty-first Century.* New York: New Press, 1998.

Wasserman, E. "Mythmaking in *Prometheus Unbound.*" *Modern Language Notes* 70 (March 1955): 182.

Weber, Henri. *Vingt ans après: Que reste-t-il de 68?* Paris: Seuil, 1988.

Weinstein, Fred, and Gerald Platt. *The Wish to Be Free: Society, Psyche and Value Change.* Berkeley: University of California Press, 1969.

Wiggershaus, Rolf. *The Frankfurt School: Its History, Theories and Political Significance.* Cambridge: MIT Press, 1994.

Williams, Rosalind. *Dream Worlds, Mass Consumption in Late Nineteenth-Century France.* Berkeley: University of California Press, 1982.

Wilson, Edmund. *Apologies to the Iroquois.* London: W. H. Allen, 1960.

Wilson, William Julius. *When Work Disappears: The World of the New Urban Poor.* New York: Vintage, 1996.

Wolf, Martin. "In Defence of Global Capitalism." *Financial Times,* December 8, 1999.

———. "Individualism Shows the Way." *Financial Times,* March 3, 2000.

Yeager, Holly. "The Rise of Consumption Man." *Financial Times,* April 26, 2000.

Yosifon, David, and Peter N. Stearns. "The Rise and Fall of American Posture." *American Historical Review,* 103, no. 4 (1998): 1057–95.

Zola, Émile. *Au bonheur des dames.* In *Les Rougon-Macquart: Histoire naturelle et sociale d'une famille sous le second Empire.* Vol. 3. Paris: Gallimard, 1964.

———. *L'Argent.* In *Les Rougon-Macquart: Histoire naturelle et sociale d'une famille sous le second Empire.* Vol. 5. Paris: Gallimard, 1967.

Index